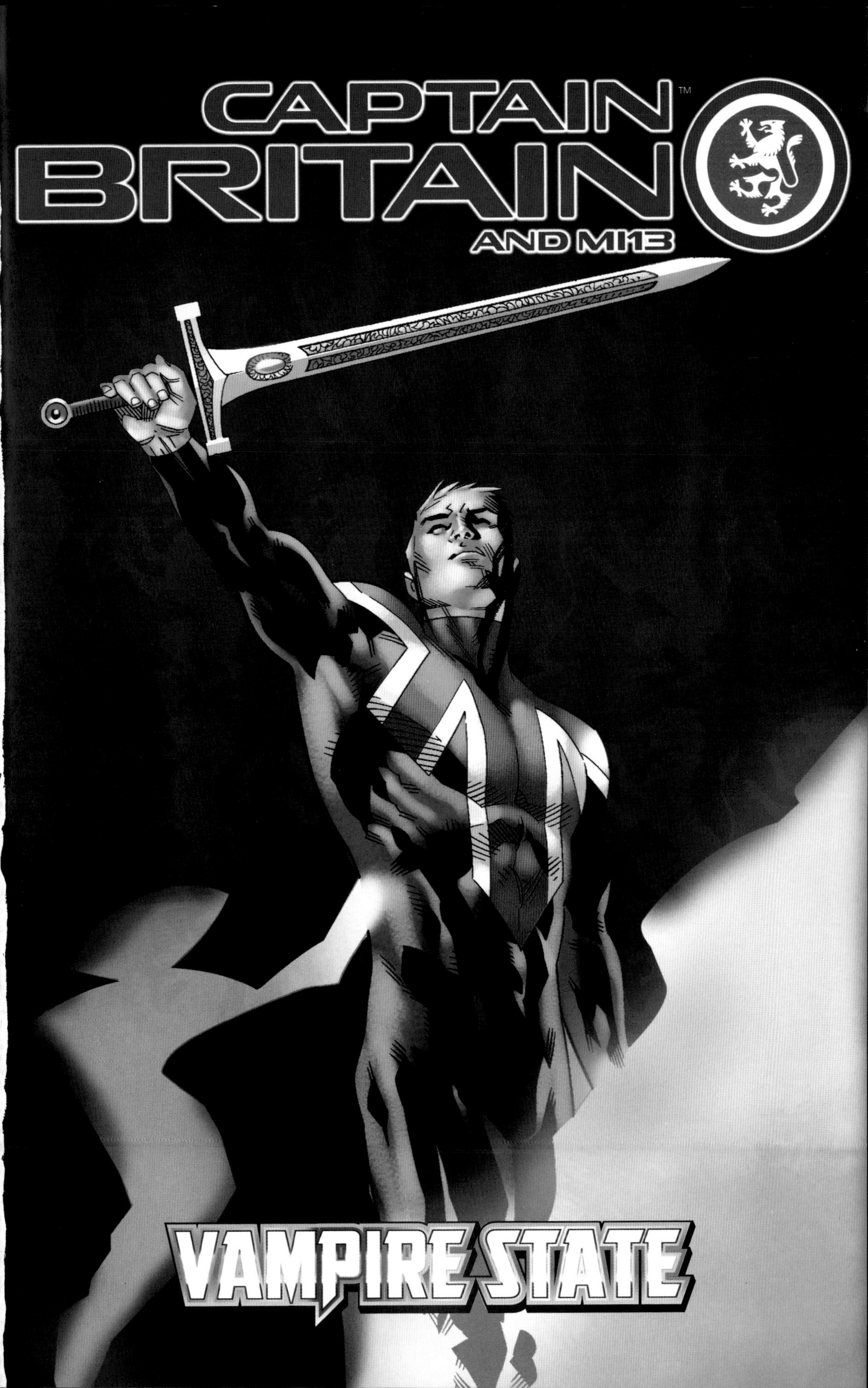
CAPTAIN BRITAIN™
AND MI13
VAMPIRE STATE

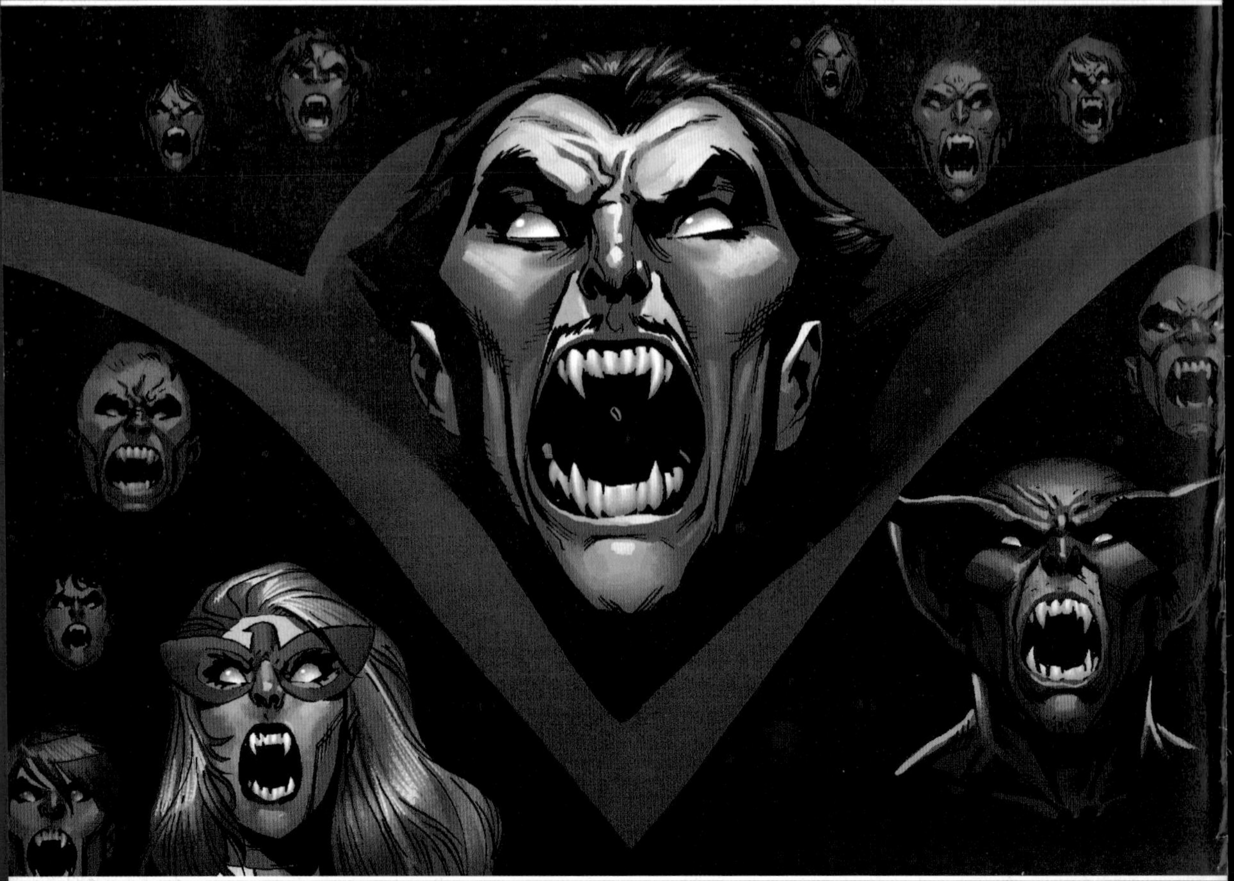

Reader Services

CUSTOMER SERVICE IN THE UK AND REPUBLIC OF IRELAND

How to continue your collection:
Customers can either place an order with their newsagent or receive issues on subscription.
Back issues: Either order through your newsagent or write to: Marvel Collection, Jacklin Enterprises UK, PO Box 77, Jarrow, NE32 3YH, enclosing payment of the cover price plus £1.00 p&p per copy. (Republic of Ireland: cover price plus €1.75).
Subscriptions: You can have your issues sent directly to your home. For details, see insert in issue 1 or phone our Customer Service Hotline on 0871 472 4240 (Monday to Friday, 9am-5pm, calls cost 10p per minute from UK landline). Alternatively you can write to Marvel Collection, Jacklin Enterprises UK, PO Box 77, Jarrow, NE32 3YH, or fax your enquiries to 0871 472 4241, or e-mail: marvelcollection@jacklinservice.com or visit www.graphicnovelcollection.com

CUSTOMER SERVICE IN OVERSEAS MARKETS

Australia: Back issues can be ordered from your newsagent. Alternatively telephone (03) 9872 4000 or write to:
Back Issues Department, Bissett Magazine Services, PO Box 3460, Nunawading Vic 3131. Please enclose payment of the cover price, plus A$2.49 (inc. GST) per issue postage and handling. Back issues are subject to availability.
Subscriptions: You can have your issues sent directly to your home. For details, see insert in issue 1 or phone our Customer Service Hotline on (03) 9872 4000. Alternatively you can write to Hachette subs offer, Bissett Magazine Services, PO Box 3460, Nunawading Vic 3131, or fax your enquiries to (03) 9873 4988, or order online at www.bissettmags.com.au

New Zealand: For back issues, ask your local magazine retailer or write to: Netlink, PO Box 47906, Ponsonby, Auckland.
South Africa: Back issues are available through your local CNA store or other newsagent.
Subscriptions: call (011) 265 4309, fax (011) 314 2984, or write to: Marvel Collection, Private Bag 10, Centurion 0046 or e-mail: service@jacklin.co.za
Malta: Back issues are only available through your local newsagent.
Malaysia: Call (03) 8023 3260, or e-mail: sales@allscript.com
Singapore: Call (65) 287 7090, or e-mail: sales@allscript.com

Published by Hachette Partworks Ltd, Jordan House,
47 Brunswick Place, London, N1 6EB
www.hachettepartworks.co.uk

Distributed in the UK and Republic of Ireland by Marketforce

This special edition published in 2013 by Hachette Partworks Ltd. forming part of The Ultimate Marvel Graphic Novel Collection.

Printed in China.
ISBN: 978-1-908648-24-2

MARVEL
marvel.com
hachette PARTWORKS LTD

CAPTAIN BRITAIN AND MI13

PAUL CORNELL
WRITER

LEONARD KIRK, MIKE COLLINS,
ARDIAN SYAF & ADRIAN ALPHONA
ARTISTS

BRIAN REBER, RAIN BEREDO,
JAY DAVID RAMOS & CHRISTINA STRAIN
COLOURS

JAY LEISTEN, ROBIN RIGGS,
CRAIG YEUNG WITH LIVESAY
INKS

VIRTUAL CALLIGRAPHY'S
JOE CARAMAGNA
LETTERS

STUART IMMONEN, MICO SUAYAN,
MORRY HOLLOWELL, GREG LAND & JUSTIN PONSOR
COVER ARTISTS

WILL PANZO & DANIEL KETCHUM
ASSISTANT EDITORS

NICK LOWE
EDITOR

JOE QUESADA
EDITOR IN CHIEF

CAPTAIN BRITAIN AND MI13:
VAMPIRE STATE

Marco M. Lupoi
*Panini Publishing Director
(Europe)*

Though many of Marvel's stories seem to use New York as a touchstone, the Mighty World of Marvel is just that — a whole planet filled with super powered adventure. From Germany to Japan, super heroes are a global presence. No matter what nationality you are, there's a hero for you.

Mainly thanks to the now-defunct, but never forgotten, Marvel U.K. (a satellite office that Marvel had in London from the 70s through to the early 90s, which yours truly has very fond memories of), along with the influence of countless English, Welsh, Scottish and Irish creators, the U.K. seems to have more than its fair share of national heroes. The most famous, of course, is Brian Braddock AKA Captain Britain.

There is a tendency with Captain Britain for people to dismiss the character as merely an anglicised Captain America clone. As you have already seem from Alan Moore and Alan Davis' work in *A Crooked World*, this couldn't be further from the truth. Since his inception in 1973, Cap B has had an incredibly varied career. Though his earliest adventures were traditional super hero fare, he has gone on to feature in much more avant-garde tales, thanks mainly to his responsibilities as a member of the multi-verse spanning Captain Britain Corps.

Launched during the *Secret Invasion* crossover event, *Captain Britain and MI13* saw the return of Captain Britain leading a team of U.K. heroes. With seasoned Brit writer Paul Cornell (best known for his work on both the *Doctor Who* comic strip and television series) at the helm, the series struck a chord with hordes of U.K. Marvel fans, overjoyed to have their most famous hero back in action again.

Sadly, despite its popularity in the U.K., U.S. audiences weren't as enthusiastic. Overseas sales weren't enough to sustain it and the series came to an end after only 18 issues and one annual. But… even though *Vampire State* represents the team's final arc, it is most definitely a lesson in how to go out with a bang!

So make yourself a pot of tea, spread some Marmite on your toast and get ready to discover one of the most quintessentially British comics Marvel has ever created.

ntains material originally published in magazine form as Captain Britain and MI13 #10-15 and Annual #1. Senior Editor (Hachette Partworks Ltd.). Sarah Gale. Packaged by Panini Publishing. a division Panini UK Limited. Mike Riddell, Managing Director. Alan O'Keefe, Managing Editor. Simon Frith, Senior Editor. Ed Hammond, Editor. Sam Taylor, Editorial Assistant. Marco M. Lupoi, Publishing Director rope. Tim Warran-Smith, Designer. Additional content: Mike Conroy. Office of publication: Brockbourne House, 77 Mount Ephraim, Tunbridge Wells, Kent TN4 8BS. No similarity between any of the name racters, persons and/or institutions in this edition with those of any living or dead person or institution is intended, and any such similarity which may exist is purely coincidental. This publication may not except by authorised dealers, and is sold subject to the condition that it shall not be sold or distributed with any part of its cover or markings removed.

THE STORY SO FAR...

Events leading up to Captain Britain & MI13: Vampire State

Brian Braddock was part of a cutting edge team of physicists working at Darkmoor Nuclear Research Centre, when an incredibly powerful villain known as the **Reaver** attempted to harness the power of Darkmoor's reactors. Brian managed to escape on his motorbike but lost control of the vehicle and was thrown from a steep cliff to the valley below.

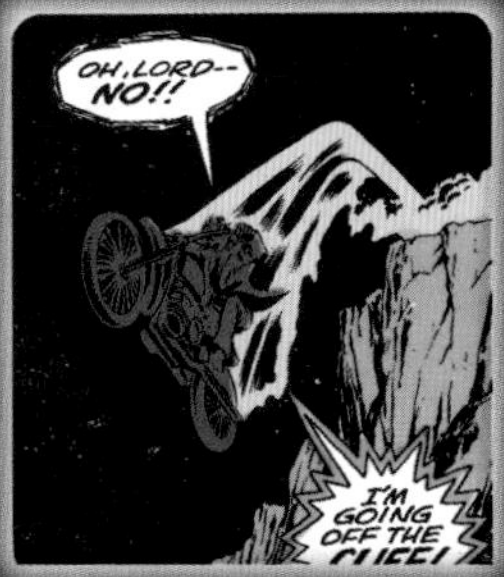
OH, LORD-- NO!!
I'M GOING OFF THE

Fatally wounded, the young scientist landed within an ancient ring of menhirs, where apparitions of the legendary magician **Merlin** and his daughter, the **Omniversal Guardian Roma** appeared before him. The mystical pair offered Brian a choice, between the **Amulet of Right** or the **Sword of Might**. Knowing himself to be no warrior, Brian chose the Amulet. Miraculously healed, he was transformed into Captain Britain, becoming the country's sworn protector.

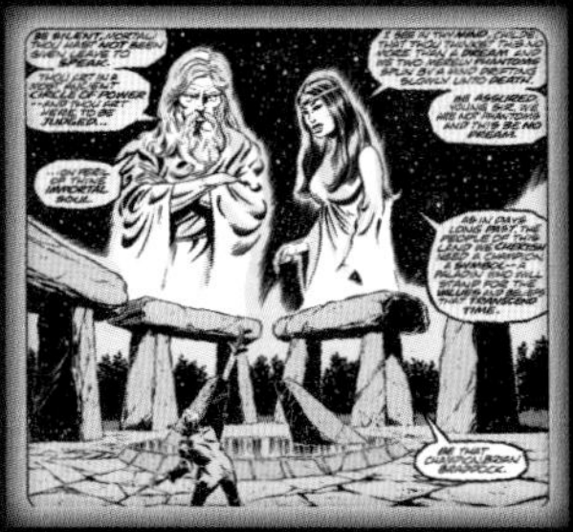

In the following years, Brian went on incredible adventures, travelling to many dimensions and times. Aware of his responsibility as the vanguard of British safety, he established **Excalibur**, a collective formed of members of the mutant team, the **X-Men. Nightcrawler**, **Shadowcat**, **Rachel Summers** and eventually **Juggernaut** all answered his call to arms. They were joined by the empathic shape-shifter, **Meggan Puceanu**, whom Brian fell in love with, and eventually married.

Brian then discovered a hologram of his deceased father, **James Braddock.** He explained that Brian was to be the rightful heir of an alternate dimension known as the **Otherworld.** Brian took Meggan to the Otherworld and the two became rulers of the realm.

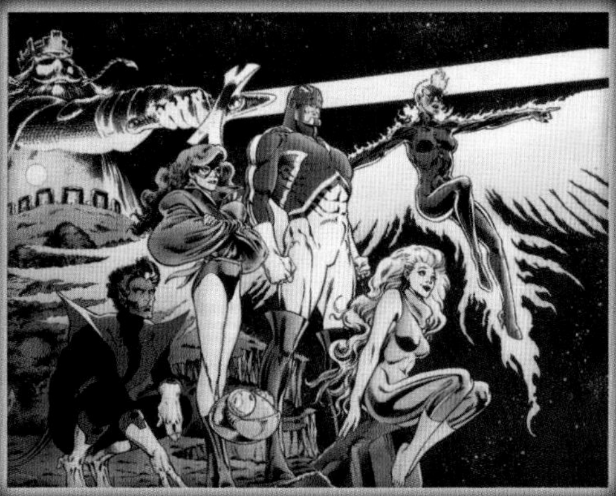

Soon after, the couple were summoned to a parallel version of Earth to help stop the **House of M** reality shift from destroying the rest of the Marvel **Multiverse.** Meggan sacrificed herself to close a tear between dimensions. In a cruel twist of fate, Brian lost all recollection of these events and the knowledge of his wife's selfless act.

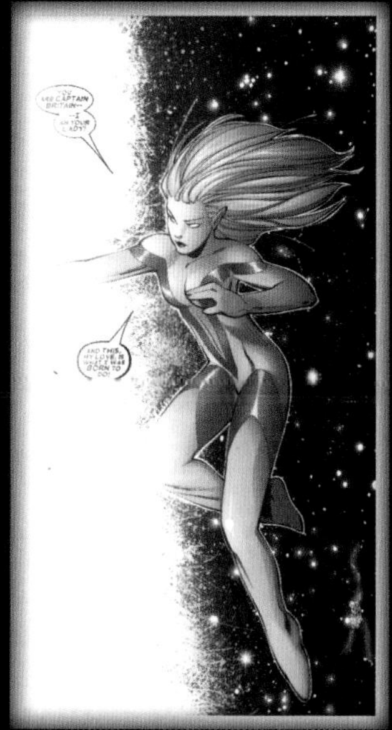

The hero was soon summoned to join **MI13**, a sector of the British government dealing exclusively with supernatural anomalies and threats. His new team mates included **Pete Wisdom**, **Spitfire**, the **Black Knight** and his new 'squire', **Faiza Hussain**. Together, the team fought relentlessly against the invading **Skrull** army during the alien race's **Secret Invasion.** Eventually, Brian was forced to sacrifice himself to rid the United Kingdom of the invading aliens, but was resurrected by Merlin. Incredibly powerful, his abilities are now dependant on his confidence — theoretically infinite, but nonexistent in times of doubt.

Following the Skrull invasion, MI13 dealt with **Plokta**, a lord of Hell who had chosen to conquer the world, starting from a tower block in Birmingham. Able to twist an individual's perception to display their utmost wants and desires, the team was briefly enslaved by Plokta's mind control. They managed to break free of the archdemon's grasp and defeat him, but not before Plokta teased that he possessed something Brian desired more than anything else — Meggan.

Captain Britain and MI13 #10
COVER ARTWORK

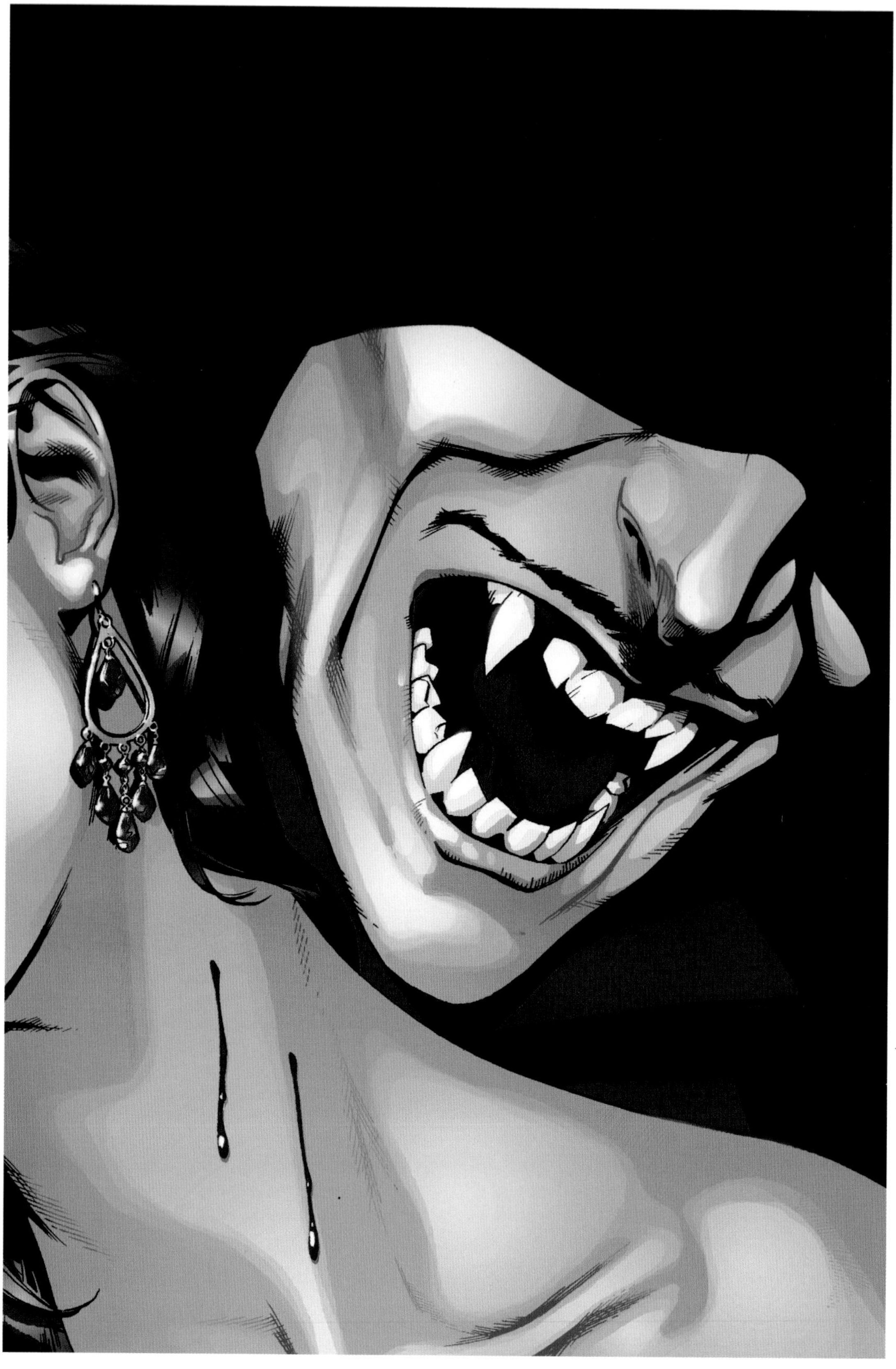

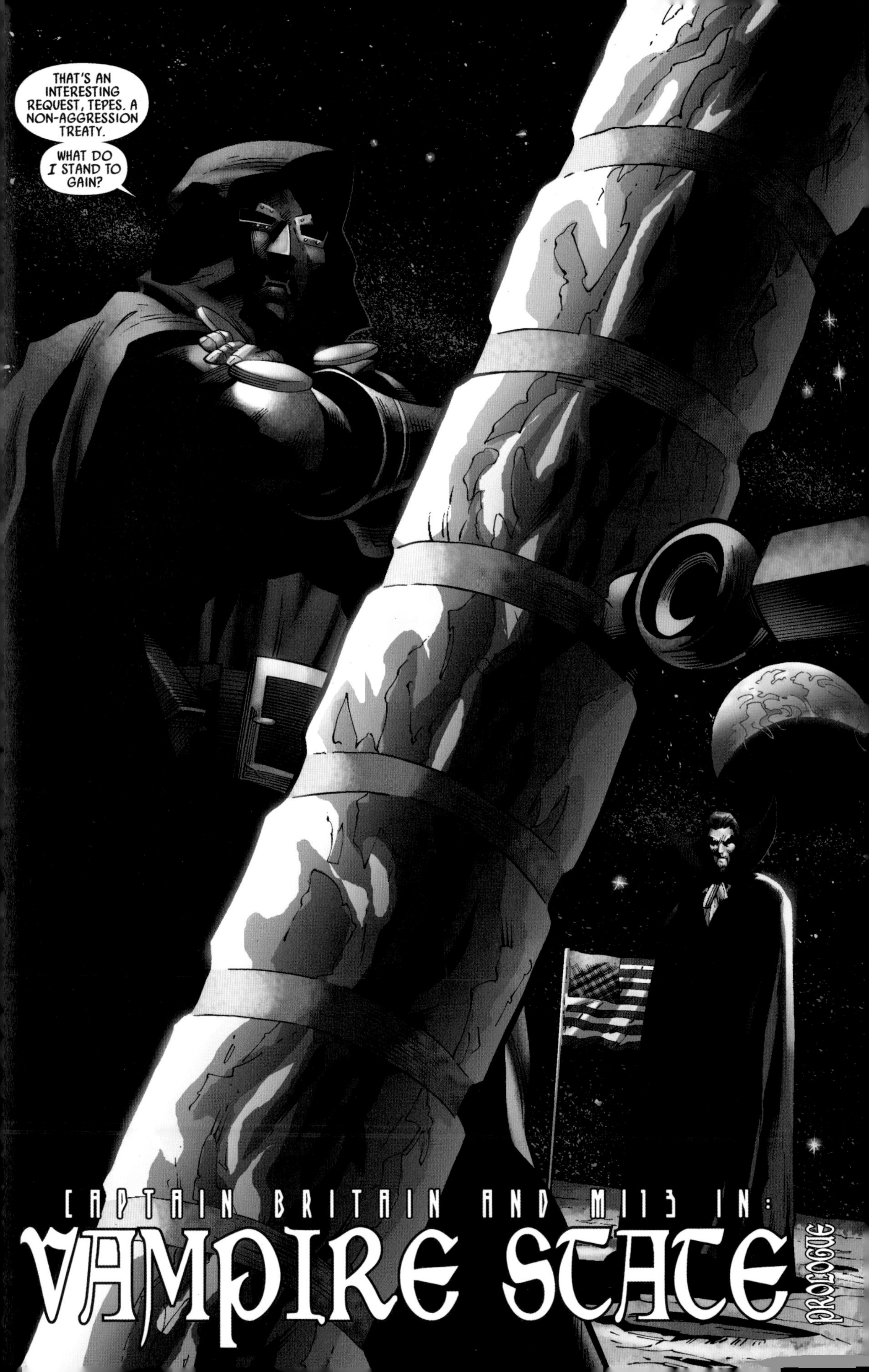
THAT'S AN INTERESTING REQUEST, TEPES. A NON-AGGRESSION TREATY.
WHAT DO *I* STAND TO GAIN?
CAPTAIN BRITAIN AND MI13 IN:
VAMPIRE STATE
PROLOGUE

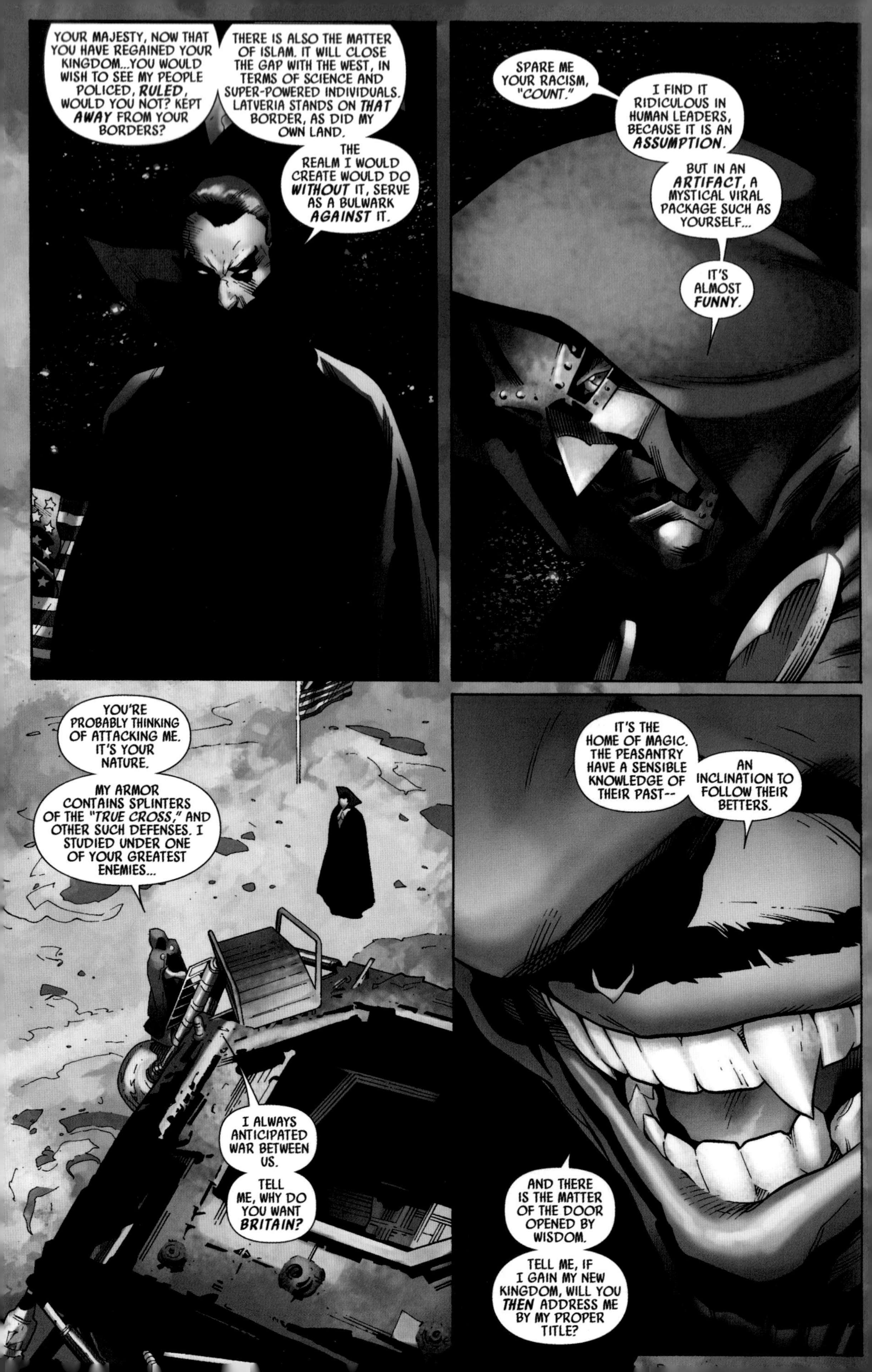
YOUR MAJESTY, NOW THAT YOU HAVE REGAINED YOUR KINGDOM...YOU WOULD WISH TO SEE MY PEOPLE POLICED, RULED, WOULD YOU NOT? KEPT AWAY FROM YOUR BORDERS?
THERE IS ALSO THE MATTER OF ISLAM. IT WILL CLOSE THE GAP WITH THE WEST, IN TERMS OF SCIENCE AND SUPER-POWERED INDIVIDUALS. LATVERIA STANDS ON THAT BORDER, AS DID MY OWN LAND.
THE REALM I WOULD CREATE WOULD DO WITHOUT IT, SERVE AS A BULWARK AGAINST IT.
SPARE ME YOUR RACISM, "COUNT."
I FIND IT RIDICULOUS IN HUMAN LEADERS, BECAUSE IT IS AN ASSUMPTION.
BUT IN AN ARTIFACT, A MYSTICAL VIRAL PACKAGE SUCH AS YOURSELF...
IT'S ALMOST FUNNY.
YOU'RE PROBABLY THINKING OF ATTACKING ME. IT'S YOUR NATURE.
MY ARMOR CONTAINS SPLINTERS OF THE "TRUE CROSS," AND OTHER SUCH DEFENSES. I STUDIED UNDER ONE OF YOUR GREATEST ENEMIES...
I ALWAYS ANTICIPATED WAR BETWEEN US.
TELL ME, WHY DO YOU WANT BRITAIN?
IT'S THE HOME OF MAGIC. THE PEASANTRY HAVE A SENSIBLE KNOWLEDGE OF THEIR PAST--
AN INCLINATION TO FOLLOW THEIR BETTERS.
AND THERE IS THE MATTER OF THE DOOR OPENED BY WISDOM.
TELL ME, IF I GAIN MY NEW KINGDOM, WILL YOU THEN ADDRESS ME BY MY PROPER TITLE?

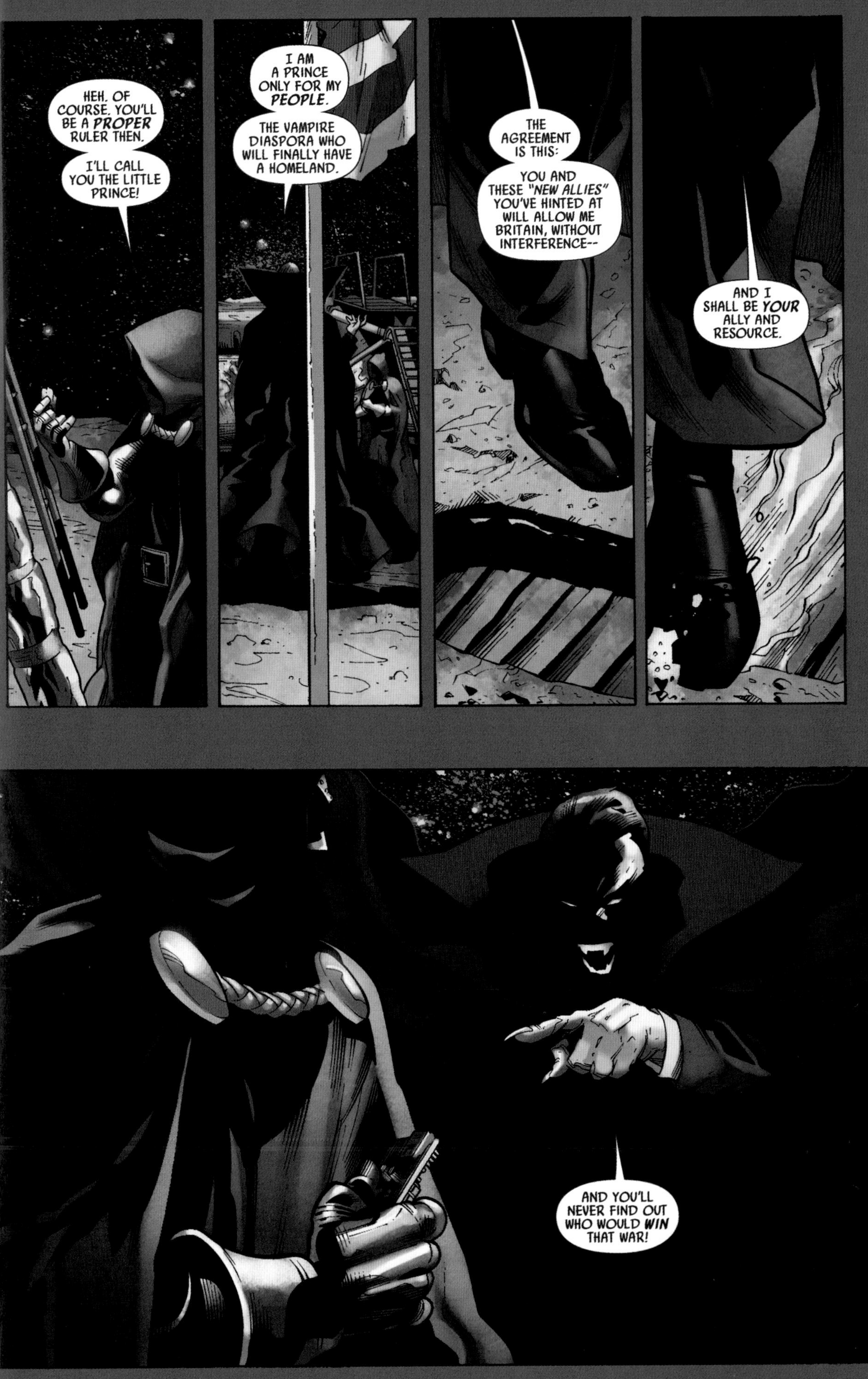

HEH. OF COURSE. YOU'LL BE A *PROPER* RULER THEN.
I'LL CALL YOU THE LITTLE PRINCE!
I AM A PRINCE ONLY FOR MY *PEOPLE*.
THE VAMPIRE DIASPORA WHO WILL FINALLY HAVE A HOMELAND.
THE AGREEMENT IS THIS:
YOU AND THESE "*NEW ALLIES*" YOU'VE HINTED AT WILL ALLOW ME BRITAIN, WITHOUT INTERFERENCE--
AND I SHALL BE *YOUR* ALLY AND RESOURCE.
AND YOU'LL NEVER FIND OUT WHO WOULD *WIN* THAT WAR!

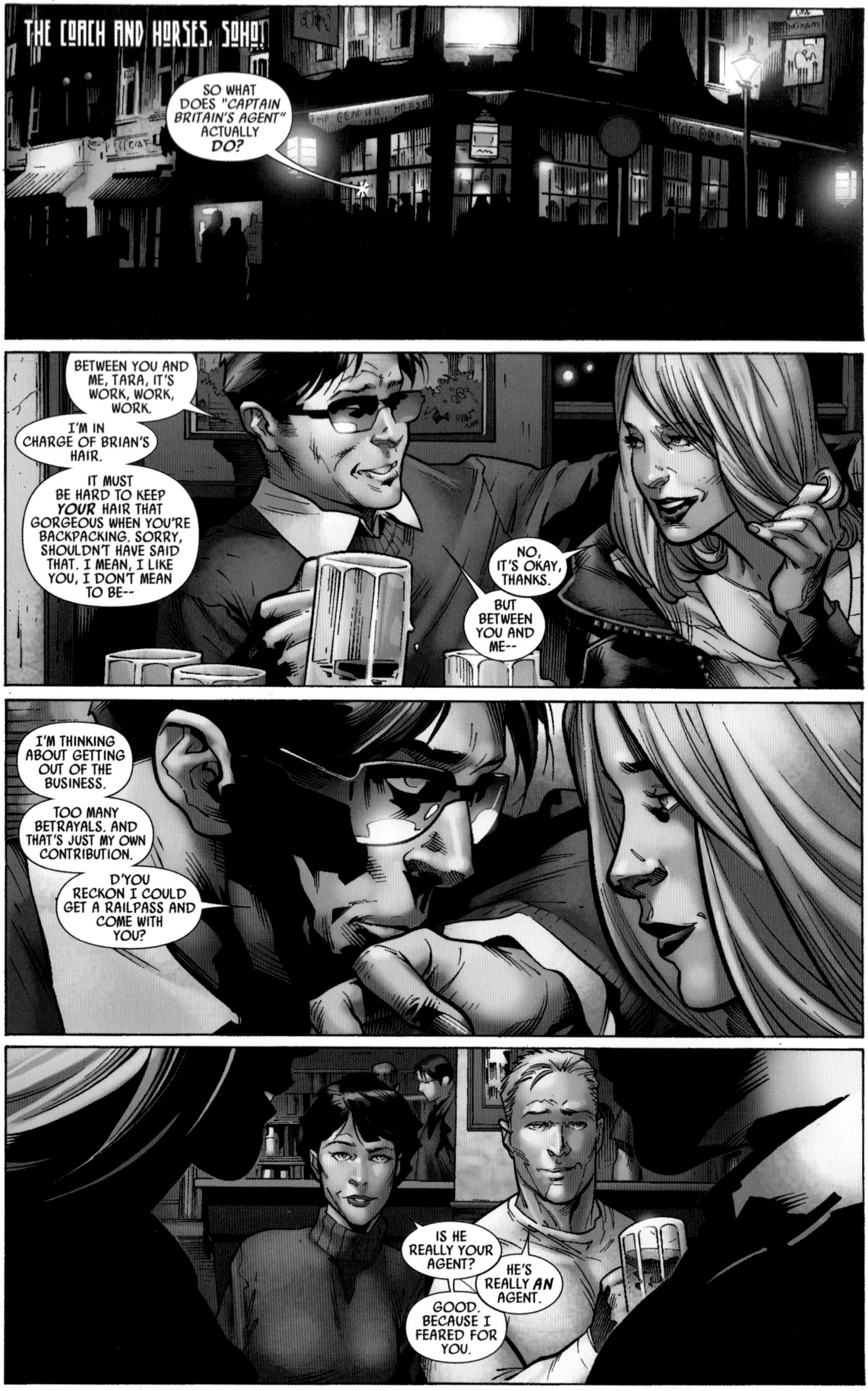
THE COACH AND HORSES, SOHO.
SO WHAT DOES "CAPTAIN BRITAIN'S AGENT" ACTUALLY DO?
BETWEEN YOU AND ME, TARA, IT'S WORK, WORK, WORK.
I'M IN CHARGE OF BRIAN'S HAIR.
IT MUST BE HARD TO KEEP YOUR HAIR THAT GORGEOUS WHEN YOU'RE BACKPACKING. SORRY, SHOULDN'T HAVE SAID THAT. I MEAN, I LIKE YOU, I DON'T MEAN TO BE--
NO, IT'S OKAY, THANKS.
BUT BETWEEN YOU AND ME--
I'M THINKING ABOUT GETTING OUT OF THE BUSINESS.
TOO MANY BETRAYALS. AND THAT'S JUST MY OWN CONTRIBUTION.
D'YOU RECKON I COULD GET A RAILPASS AND COME WITH YOU?
IS HE REALLY YOUR AGENT?
HE'S REALLY AN AGENT.
GOOD. BECAUSE I FEARED FOR YOU.

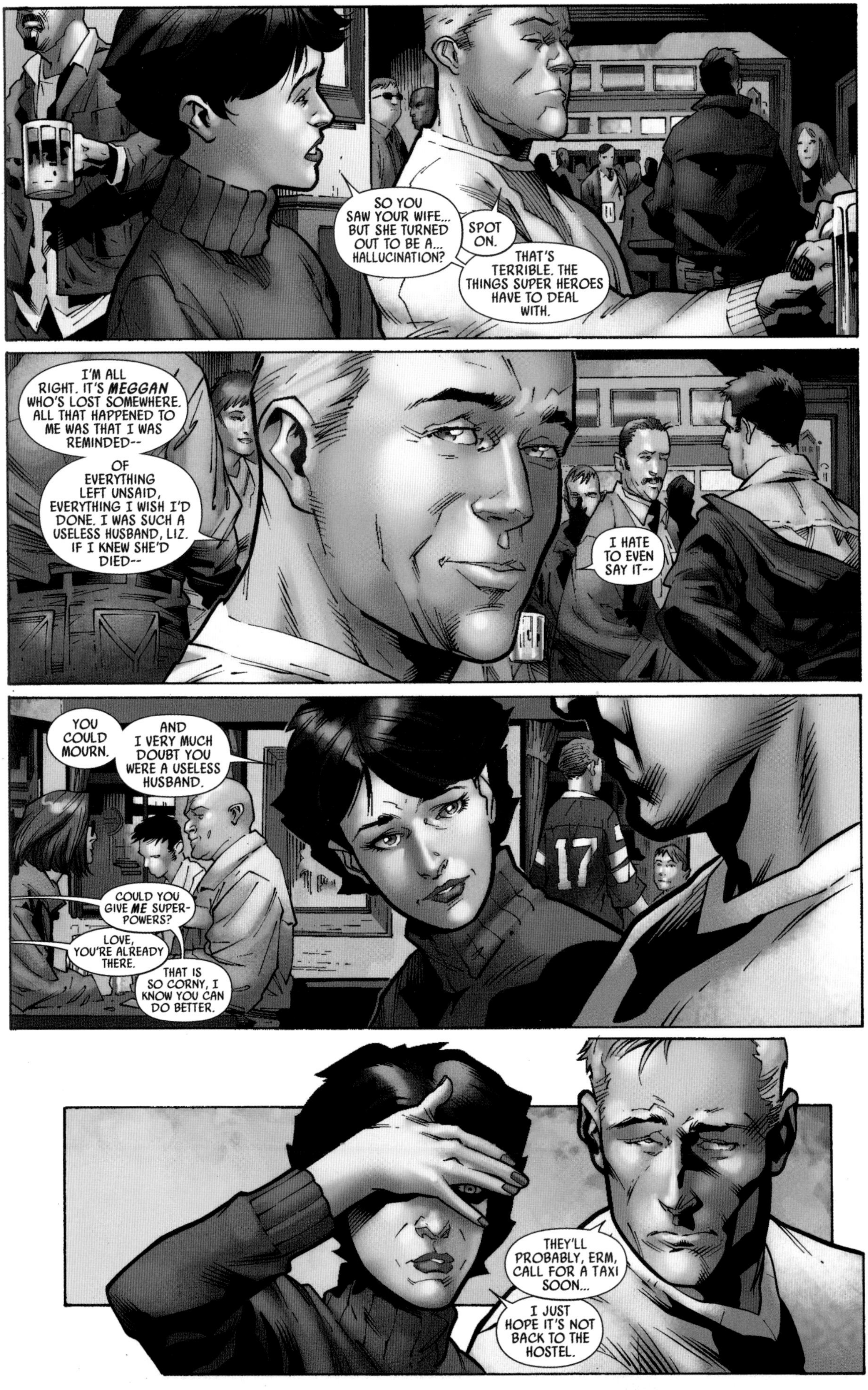
SO YOU SAW YOUR WIFE... BUT SHE TURNED OUT TO BE A... HALLUCINATION?
SPOT ON.
THAT'S TERRIBLE. THE THINGS SUPER HEROES HAVE TO DEAL WITH.
I'M ALL RIGHT. IT'S MEGGAN WHO'S LOST SOMEWHERE. ALL THAT HAPPENED TO ME WAS THAT I WAS REMINDED--
OF EVERYTHING LEFT UNSAID, EVERYTHING I WISH I'D DONE. I WAS SUCH A USELESS HUSBAND, LIZ. IF I KNEW SHE'D DIED--
I HATE TO EVEN SAY IT--
YOU COULD MOURN.
AND I VERY MUCH DOUBT YOU WERE A USELESS HUSBAND.
COULD YOU GIVE ME SUPER-POWERS?
LOVE, YOU'RE ALREADY THERE.
THAT IS SO CORNY, I KNOW YOU CAN DO BETTER.
THEY'LL PROBABLY, ERM, CALL FOR A TAXI SOON...
I JUST HOPE IT'S NOT BACK TO THE HOSTEL.

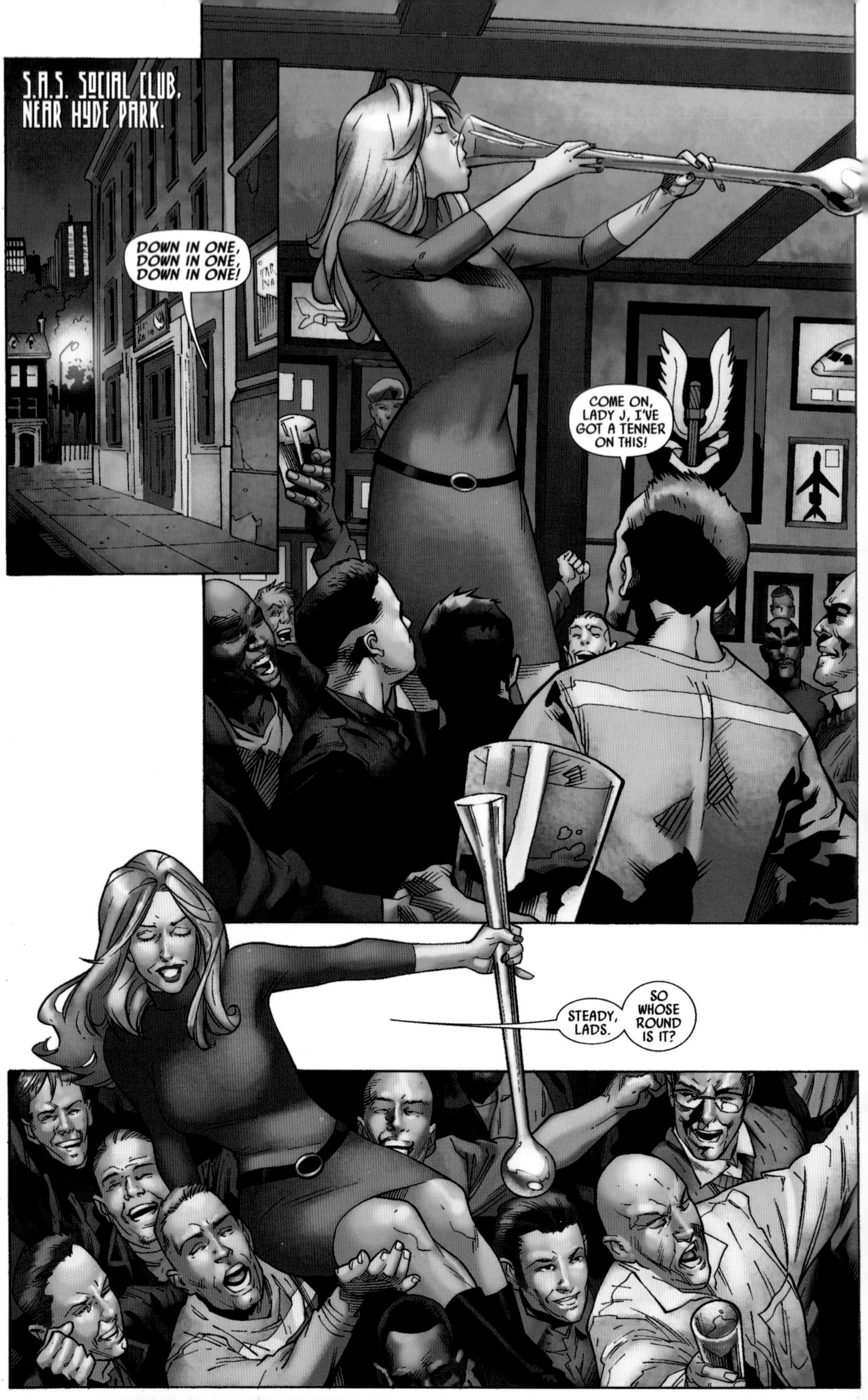
S.A.S. SOCIAL CLUB, NEAR HYDE PARK.
DOWN IN ONE, DOWN IN ONE, DOWN IN ONE!
COME ON, LADY J, I'VE GOT A TENNER ON THIS!
STEADY, LADS.
SO WHOSE ROUND IS IT?

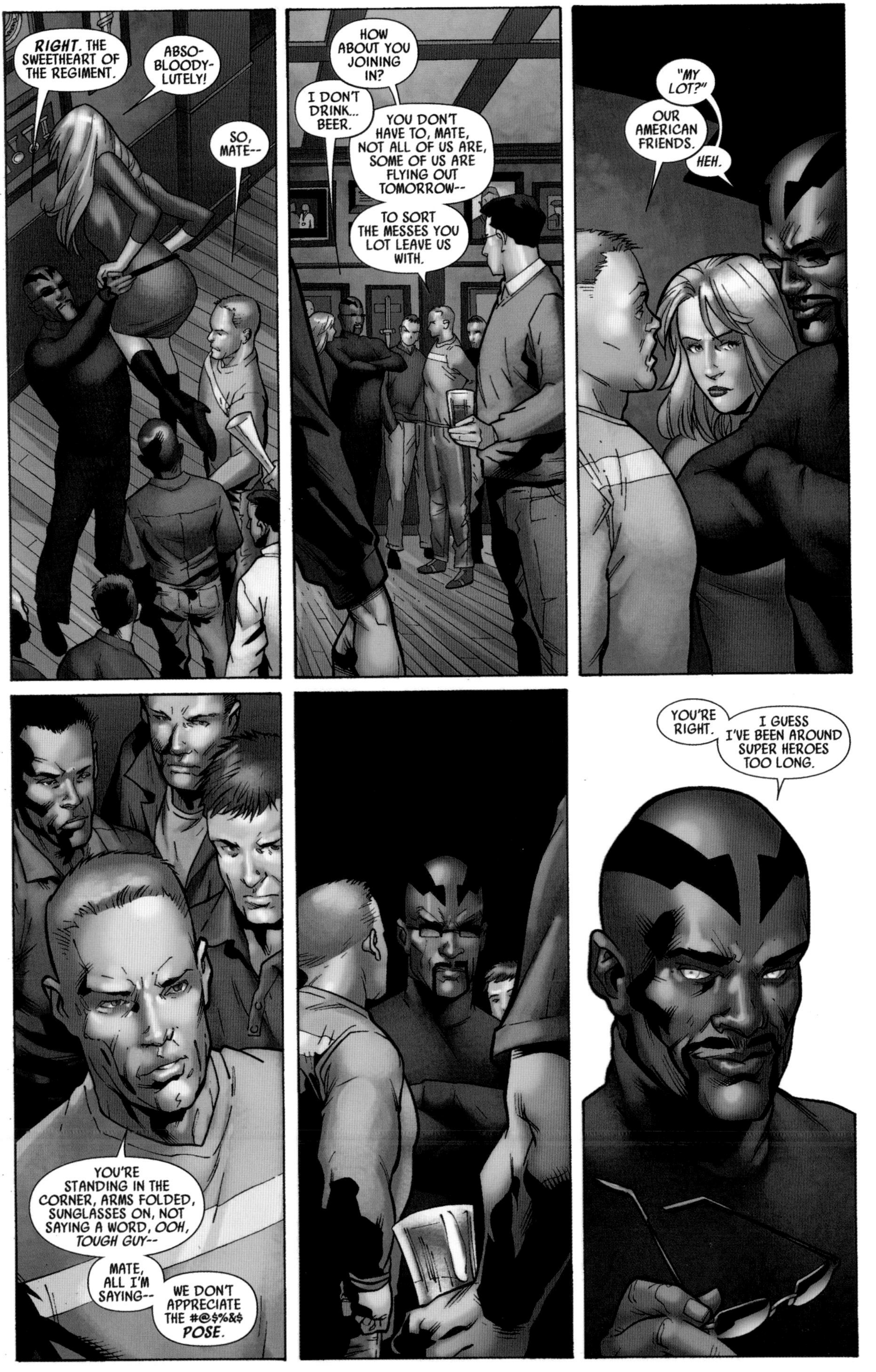
RIGHT. THE SWEETHEART OF THE REGIMENT.
ABSO-BLOODY-LUTELY!
SO, MATE--
HOW ABOUT YOU JOINING IN?
I DON'T DRINK... BEER.
YOU DON'T HAVE TO, MATE, NOT ALL OF US ARE, SOME OF US ARE FLYING OUT TOMORROW--
TO SORT THE MESSES YOU LOT LEAVE US WITH.
"MY LOT?"
OUR AMERICAN FRIENDS.
HEH.
YOU'RE STANDING IN THE CORNER, ARMS FOLDED, SUNGLASSES ON, NOT SAYING A WORD, OOH, TOUGH GUY--
MATE, ALL I'M SAYING--
WE DON'T APPRECIATE THE #@$%&$ POSE.
YOU'RE RIGHT.
I GUESS I'VE BEEN AROUND SUPER HEROES TOO LONG.

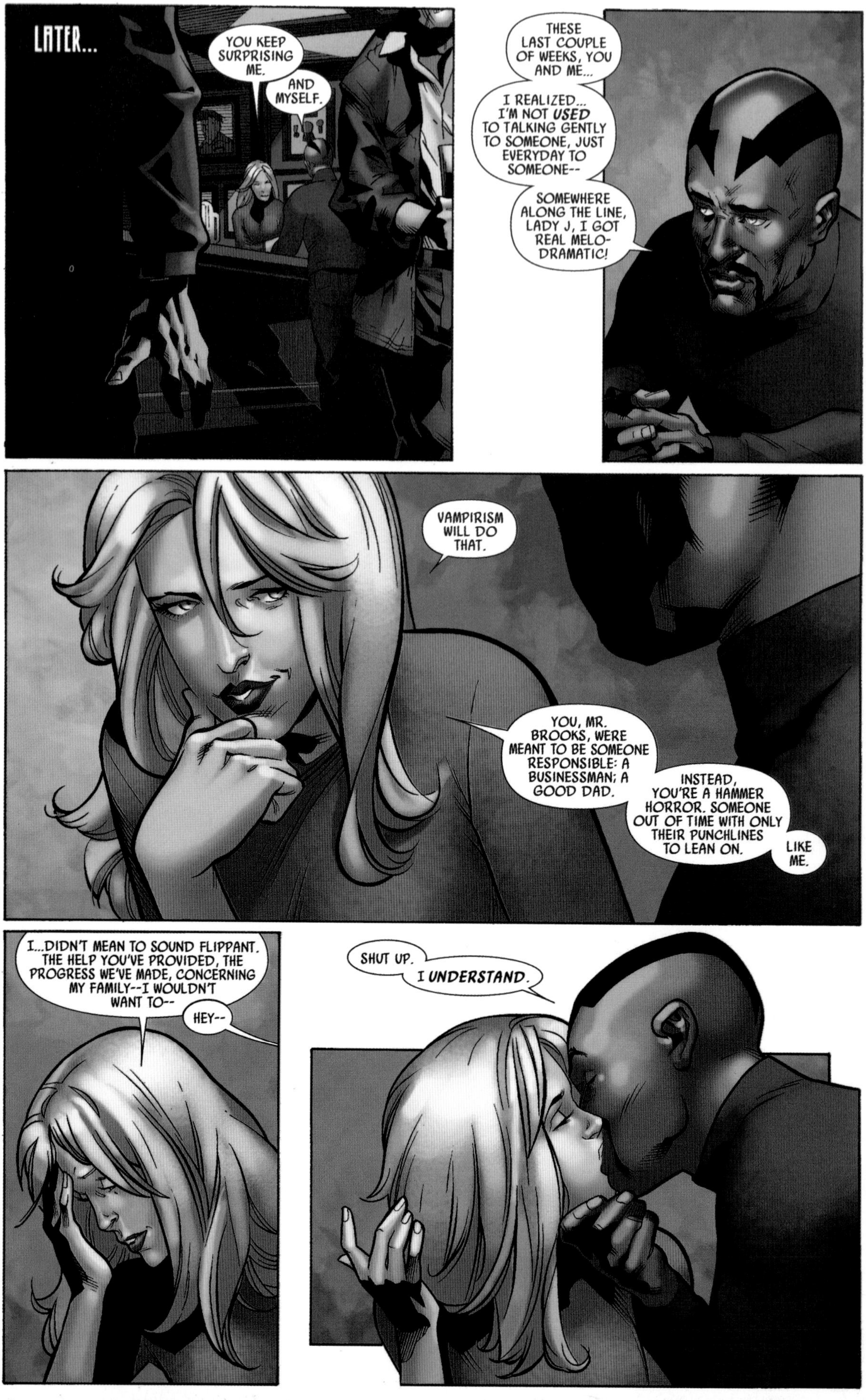
LATER...
YOU KEEP SURPRISING ME.
AND MYSELF.
THESE LAST COUPLE OF WEEKS, YOU AND ME...
I REALIZED... I'M NOT USED TO TALKING GENTLY TO SOMEONE, JUST EVERYDAY TO SOMEONE--
SOMEWHERE ALONG THE LINE, LADY J, I GOT REAL MELO-DRAMATIC!
VAMPIRISM WILL DO THAT.
YOU, MR. BROOKS, WERE MEANT TO BE SOMEONE RESPONSIBLE: A BUSINESSMAN; A GOOD DAD.
INSTEAD, YOU'RE A HAMMER HORROR. SOMEONE OUT OF TIME WITH ONLY THEIR PUNCHLINES TO LEAN ON.
LIKE ME.
I...DIDN'T MEAN TO SOUND FLIPPANT. THE HELP YOU'VE PROVIDED, THE PROGRESS WE'VE MADE, CONCERNING MY FAMILY--I WOULDN'T WANT TO--
HEY--
SHUT UP.
I UNDERSTAND.

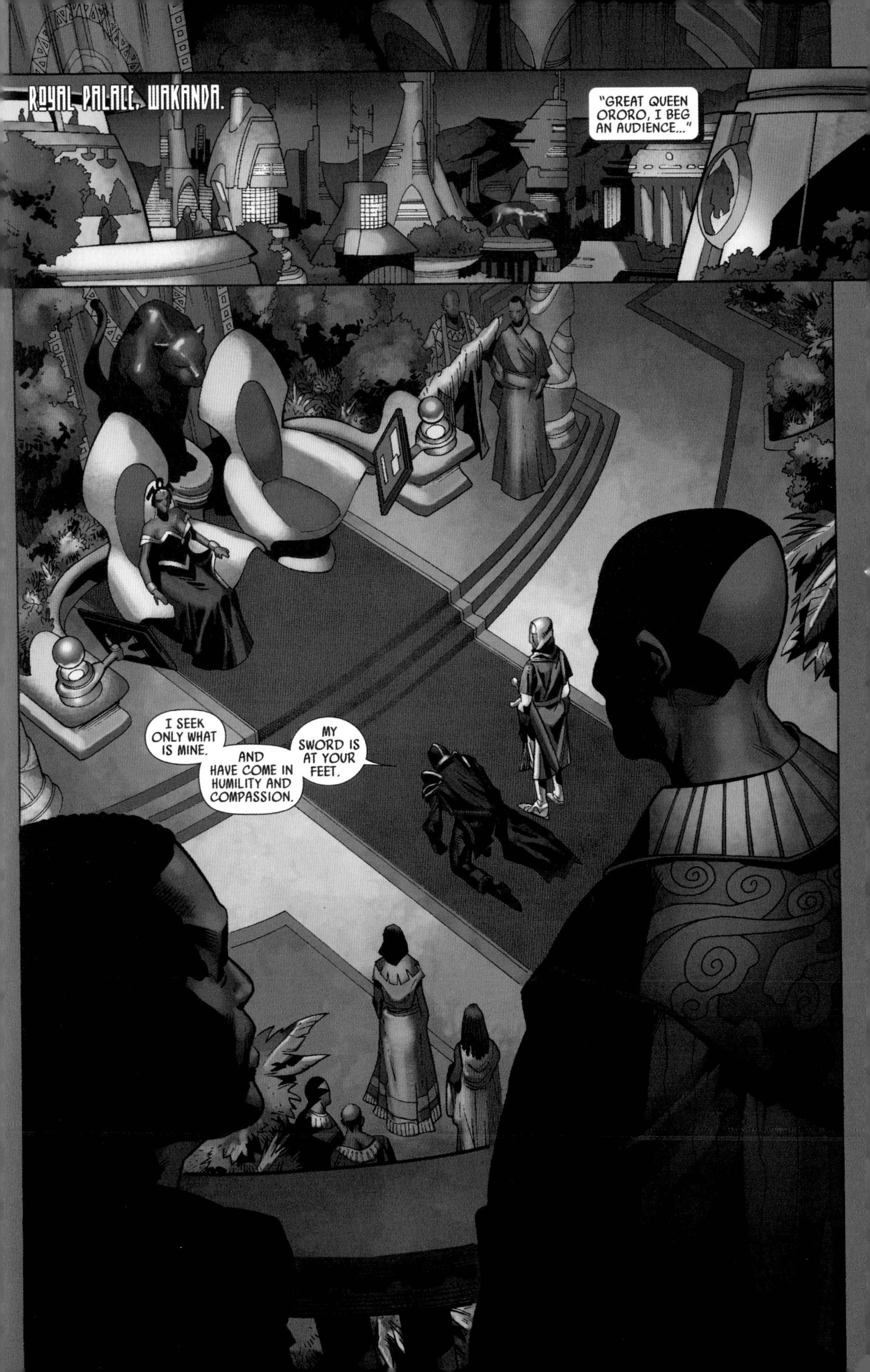
ROYAL PALACE, WAKANDA.
"GREAT QUEEN ORORO, I BEG AN AUDIENCE..."
I SEEK ONLY WHAT IS MINE.
AND HAVE COME IN HUMILITY AND COMPASSION.
MY SWORD IS AT YOUR FEET.

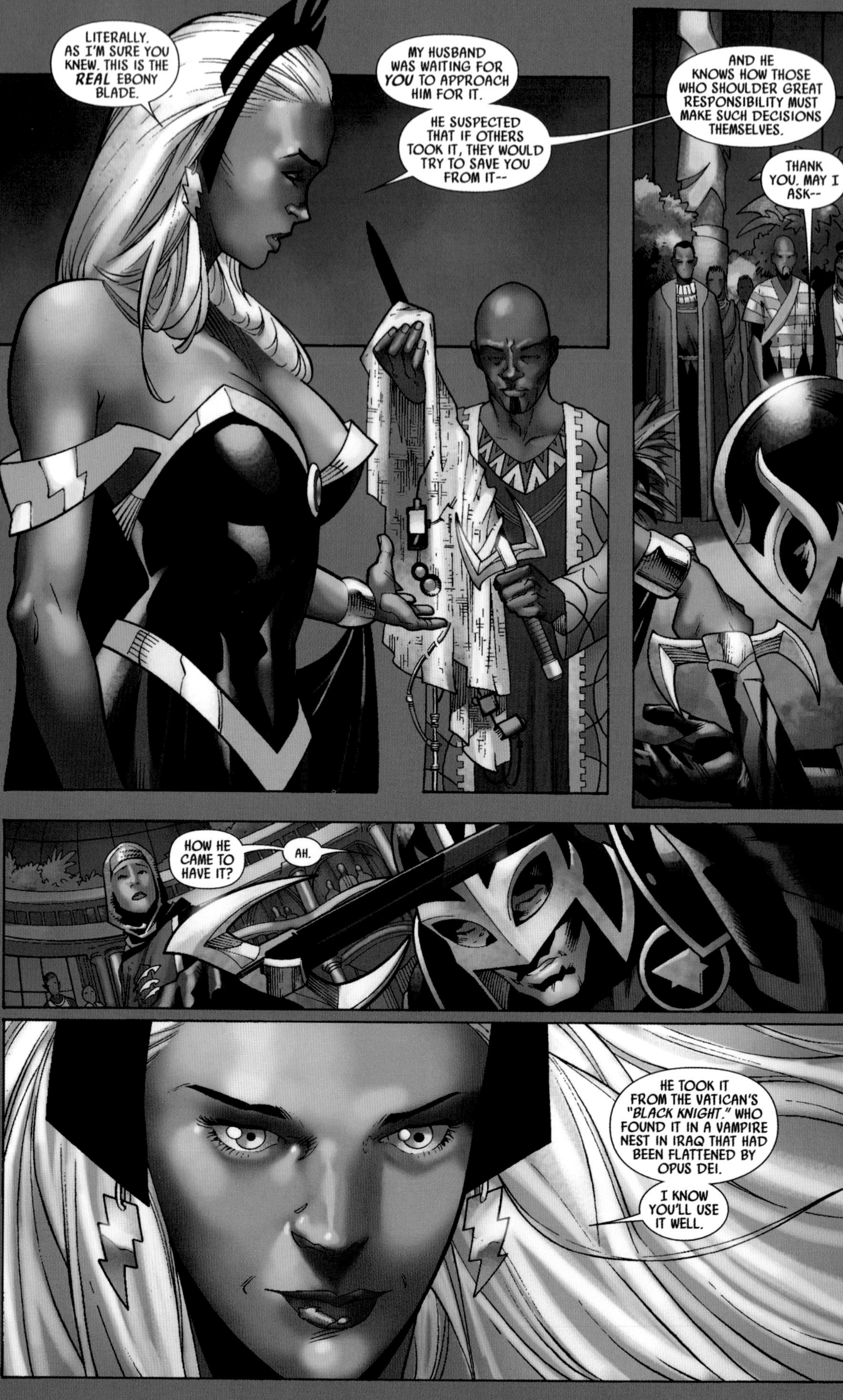
LITERALLY. AS I'M SURE YOU KNEW. THIS IS THE REAL EBONY BLADE.
MY HUSBAND WAS WAITING FOR YOU TO APPROACH HIM FOR IT.
HE SUSPECTED THAT IF OTHERS TOOK IT, THEY WOULD TRY TO SAVE YOU FROM IT--
AND HE KNOWS HOW THOSE WHO SHOULDER GREAT RESPONSIBILITY MUST MAKE SUCH DECISIONS THEMSELVES.
THANK YOU. MAY I ASK--
HOW HE CAME TO HAVE IT?
AH.
HE TOOK IT FROM THE VATICAN'S "BLACK KNIGHT," WHO FOUND IT IN A VAMPIRE NEST IN IRAQ THAT HAD BEEN FLATTENED BY OPUS DEI.
I KNOW YOU'LL USE IT WELL.

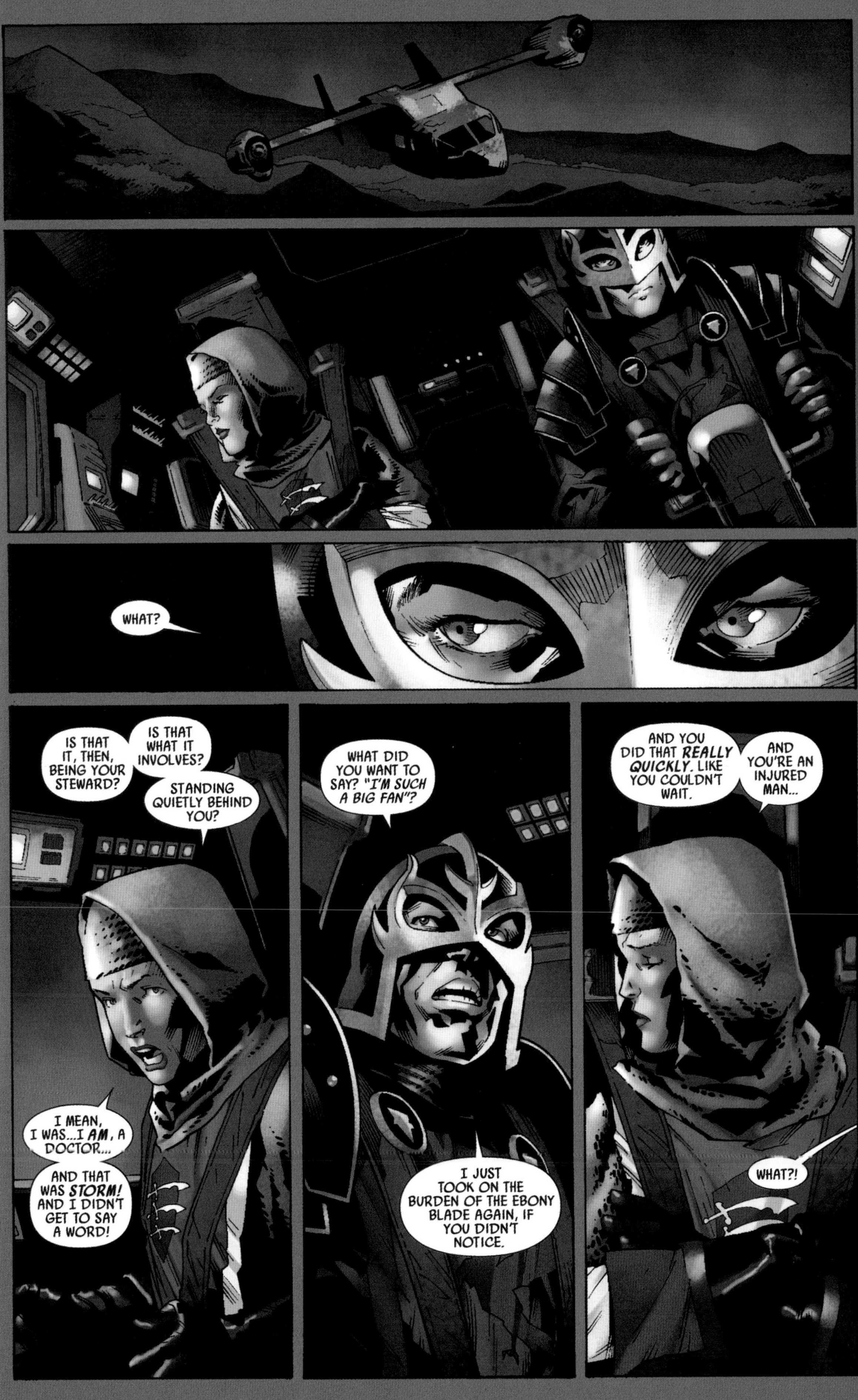

WHAT?
IS THAT IT, THEN, BEING YOUR STEWARD?
IS THAT WHAT IT INVOLVES?
STANDING QUIETLY BEHIND YOU?
I MEAN, I WAS...I AM, A DOCTOR...
AND THAT WAS STORM! AND I DIDN'T GET TO SAY A WORD!
WHAT DID YOU WANT TO SAY? "I'M SUCH A BIG FAN"?
I JUST TOOK ON THE BURDEN OF THE EBONY BLADE AGAIN, IF YOU DIDN'T NOTICE.
AND YOU DID THAT REALLY QUICKLY. LIKE YOU COULDN'T WAIT.
AND YOU'RE AN INJURED MAN...
WHAT?!

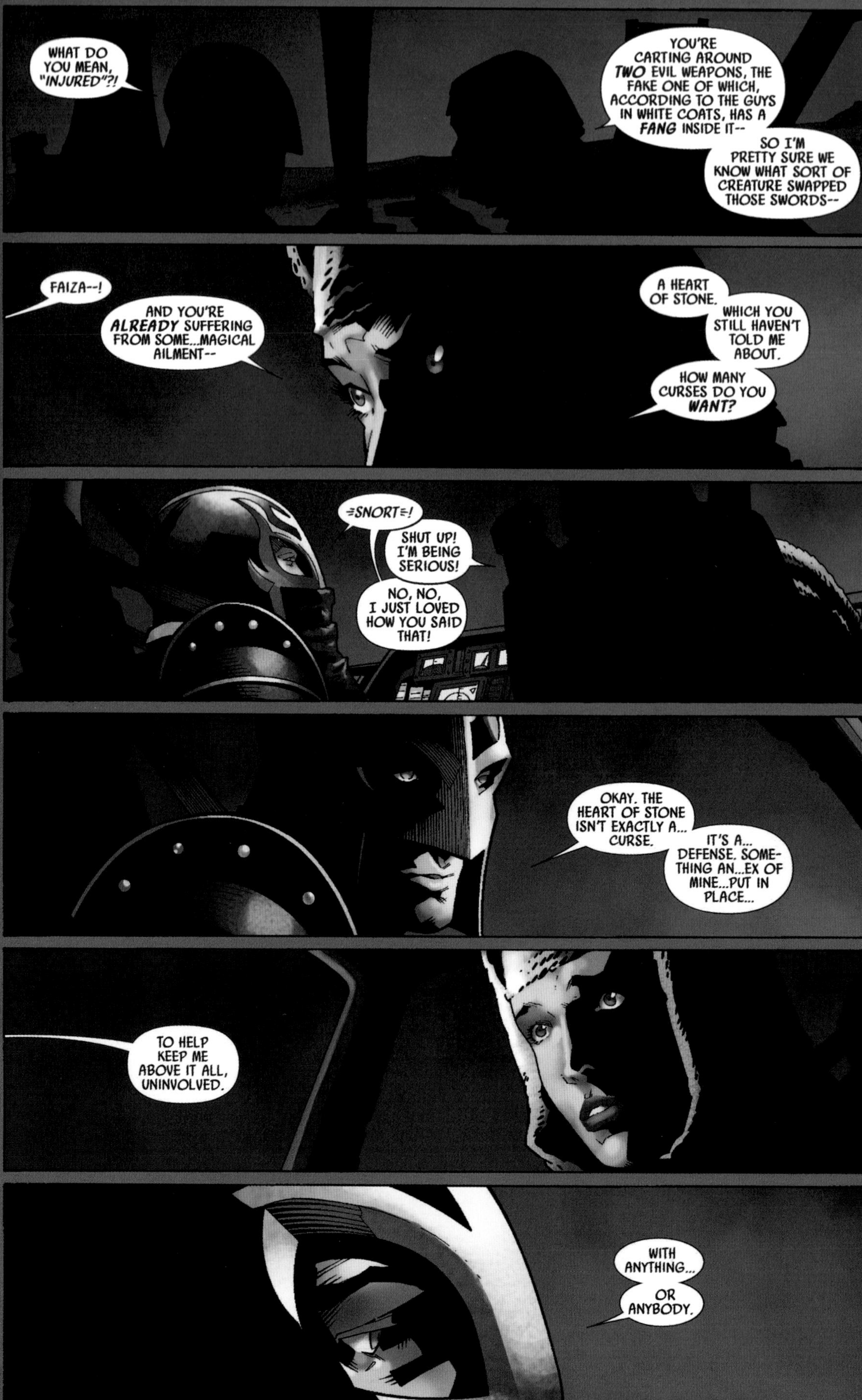
WHAT DO YOU MEAN, "INJURED"?!
YOU'RE CARTING AROUND TWO EVIL WEAPONS, THE FAKE ONE OF WHICH, ACCORDING TO THE GUYS IN WHITE COATS, HAS A FANG INSIDE IT--
SO I'M PRETTY SURE WE KNOW WHAT SORT OF CREATURE SWAPPED THOSE SWORDS--
FAIZA--!
AND YOU'RE ALREADY SUFFERING FROM SOME...MAGICAL AILMENT--
A HEART OF STONE.
WHICH YOU STILL HAVEN'T TOLD ME ABOUT.
HOW MANY CURSES DO YOU WANT?
SNORT!
SHUT UP! I'M BEING SERIOUS!
NO, NO, I JUST LOVED HOW YOU SAID THAT!
OKAY. THE HEART OF STONE ISN'T EXACTLY A... CURSE.
IT'S A... DEFENSE. SOMETHING AN...EX OF MINE...PUT IN PLACE...
TO HELP KEEP ME ABOVE IT ALL, UNINVOLVED.
WITH ANYTHING...
OR ANYBODY.

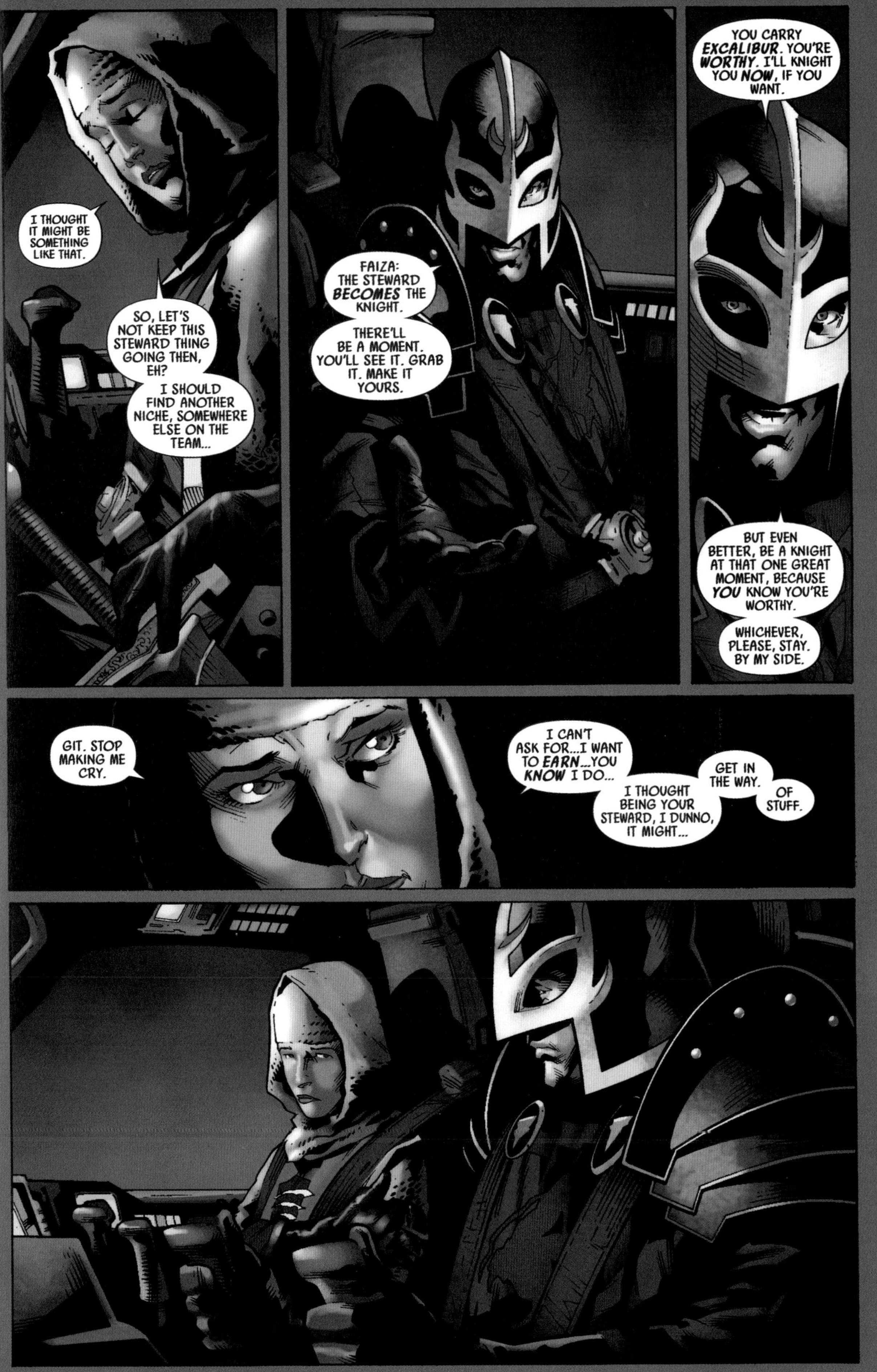
I THOUGHT IT MIGHT BE SOMETHING LIKE THAT.
SO, LET'S NOT KEEP THIS STEWARD THING GOING THEN, EH?
I SHOULD FIND ANOTHER NICHE, SOMEWHERE ELSE ON THE TEAM...
FAIZA: THE STEWARD BECOMES THE KNIGHT.
THERE'LL BE A MOMENT. YOU'LL SEE IT. GRAB IT. MAKE IT YOURS.
YOU CARRY EXCALIBUR. YOU'RE WORTHY. I'LL KNIGHT YOU NOW, IF YOU WANT.
BUT EVEN BETTER, BE A KNIGHT AT THAT ONE GREAT MOMENT, BECAUSE YOU KNOW YOU'RE WORTHY.
WHICHEVER, PLEASE, STAY. BY MY SIDE.
GIT. STOP MAKING ME CRY.
I CAN'T ASK FOR...I WANT TO EARN...YOU KNOW I DO...
I THOUGHT BEING YOUR STEWARD, I DUNNO, IT MIGHT...
GET IN THE WAY.
OF STUFF.

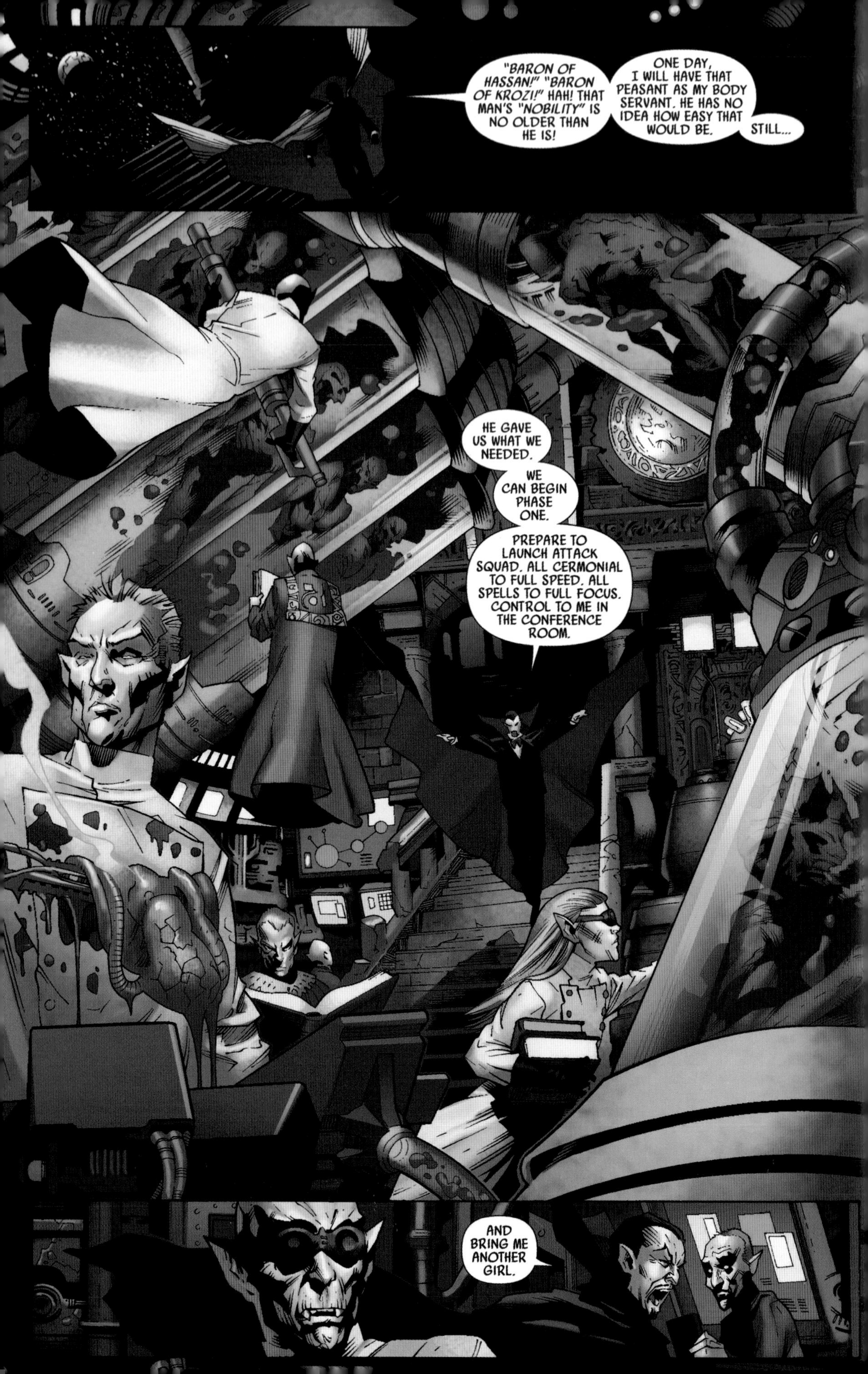
"BARON OF HASSAN!" "BARON OF KROZI!" HAH! THAT MAN'S "NOBILITY" IS NO OLDER THAN HE IS!
ONE DAY, I WILL HAVE THAT PEASANT AS MY BODY SERVANT. HE HAS NO IDEA HOW EASY THAT WOULD BE.
STILL...
HE GAVE US WHAT WE NEEDED.
WE CAN BEGIN PHASE ONE.
PREPARE TO LAUNCH ATTACK SQUAD. ALL CERMONIAL TO FULL SPEED. ALL SPELLS TO FULL FOCUS. CONTROL TO ME IN THE CONFERENCE ROOM.
AND BRING ME ANOTHER GIRL.

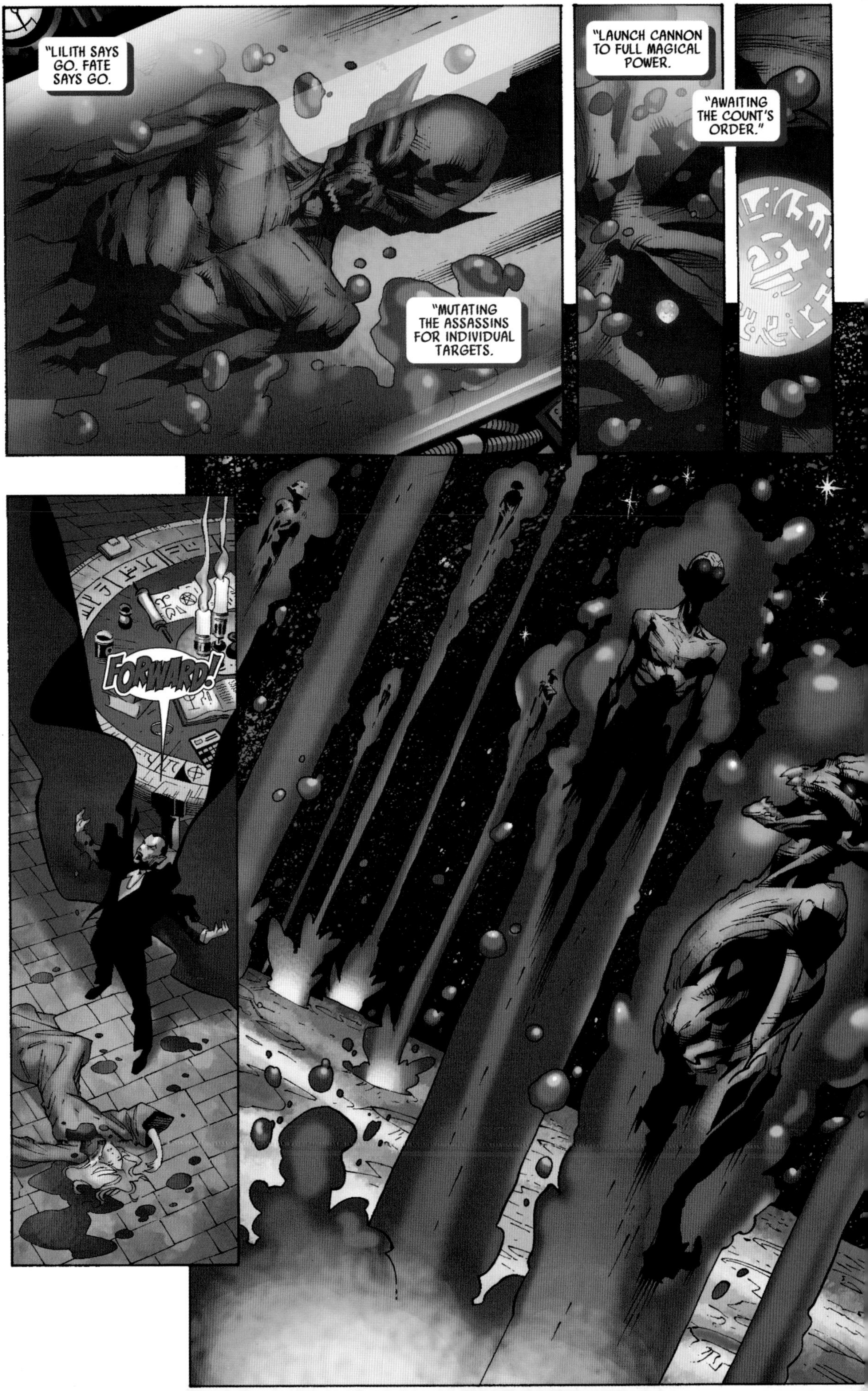
"LILITH SAYS GO. FATE SAYS GO.
"MUTATING THE ASSASSINS FOR INDIVIDUAL TARGETS.
"LAUNCH CANNON TO FULL MAGICAL POWER.
"AWAITING THE COUNT'S ORDER."
FORWARD!

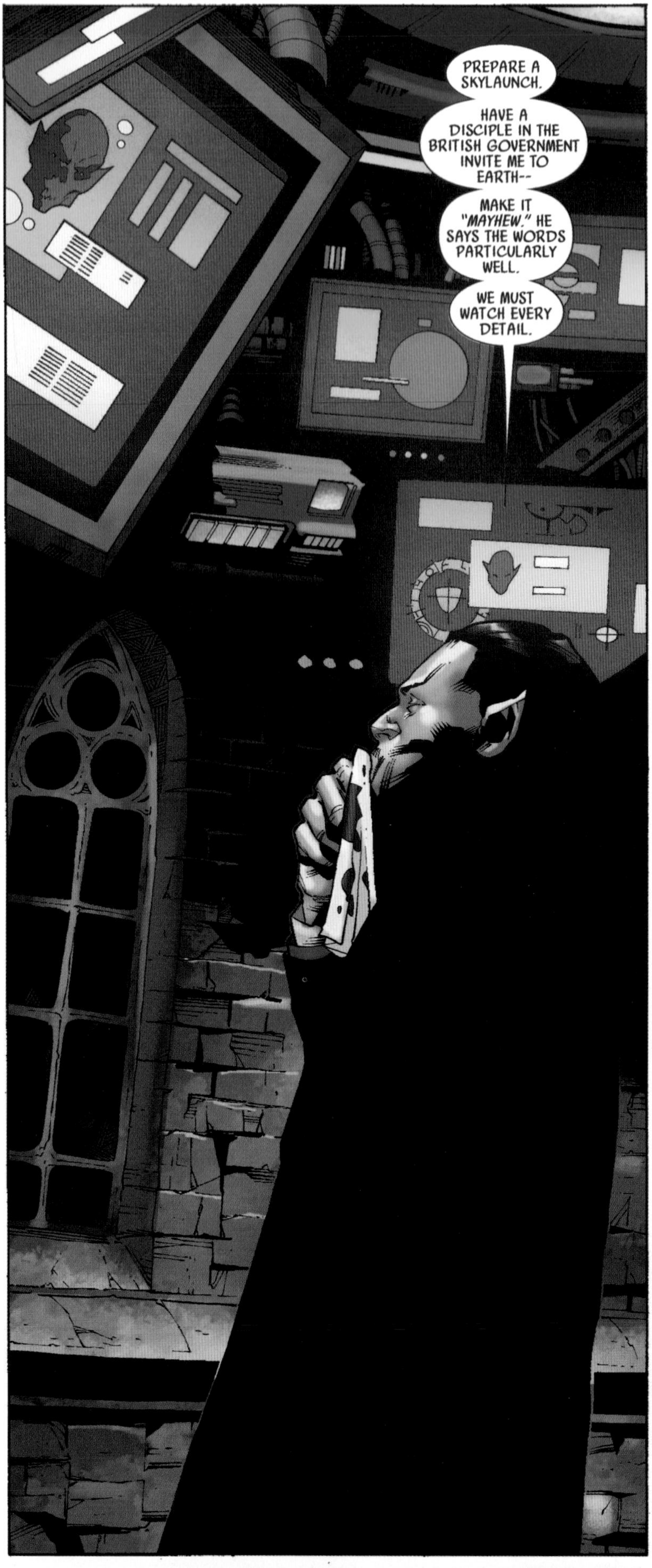
PREPARE A SKYLAUNCH.
HAVE A DISCIPLE IN THE BRITISH GOVERNMENT INVITE ME TO EARTH--
MAKE IT "*MAYHEW.*" HE SAYS THE WORDS PARTICULARLY WELL.
WE MUST WATCH EVERY DETAIL.

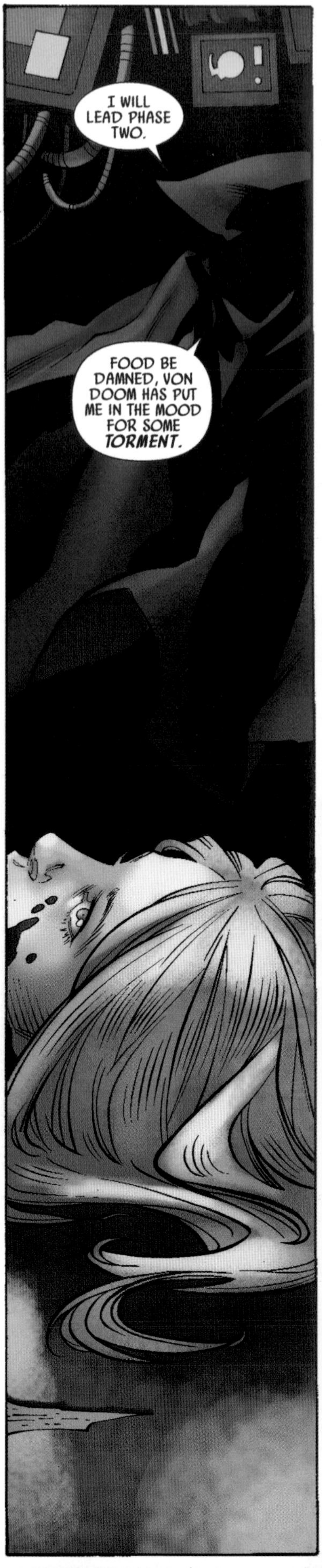
I WILL LEAD PHASE TWO.
FOOD BE DAMNED, VON DOOM HAS PUT ME IN THE MOOD FOR SOME ***TORMENT.***

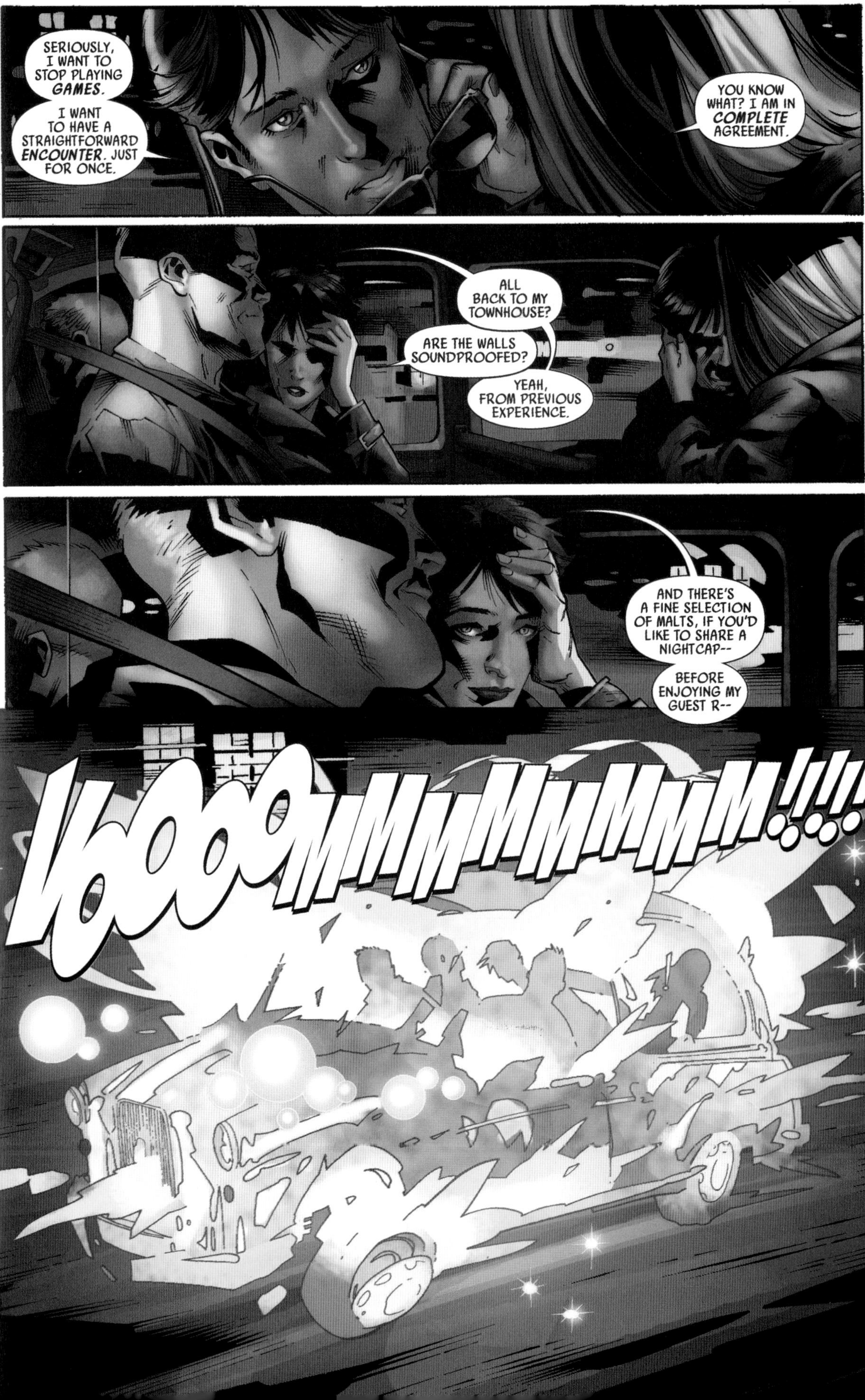
SERIOUSLY, I WANT TO STOP PLAYING **GAMES**.
I WANT TO HAVE A STRAIGHTFORWARD **ENCOUNTER**. JUST FOR ONCE.
YOU KNOW WHAT? I AM IN **COMPLETE** AGREEMENT.
ALL BACK TO MY TOWNHOUSE?
ARE THE WALLS SOUNDPROOFED?
YEAH, FROM PREVIOUS EXPERIENCE.
AND THERE'S A FINE SELECTION OF MALTS, IF YOU'D LIKE TO SHARE A NIGHTCAP--
BEFORE ENJOYING MY GUEST R--
VOOOOMMMMMMMMMMM!!!!!

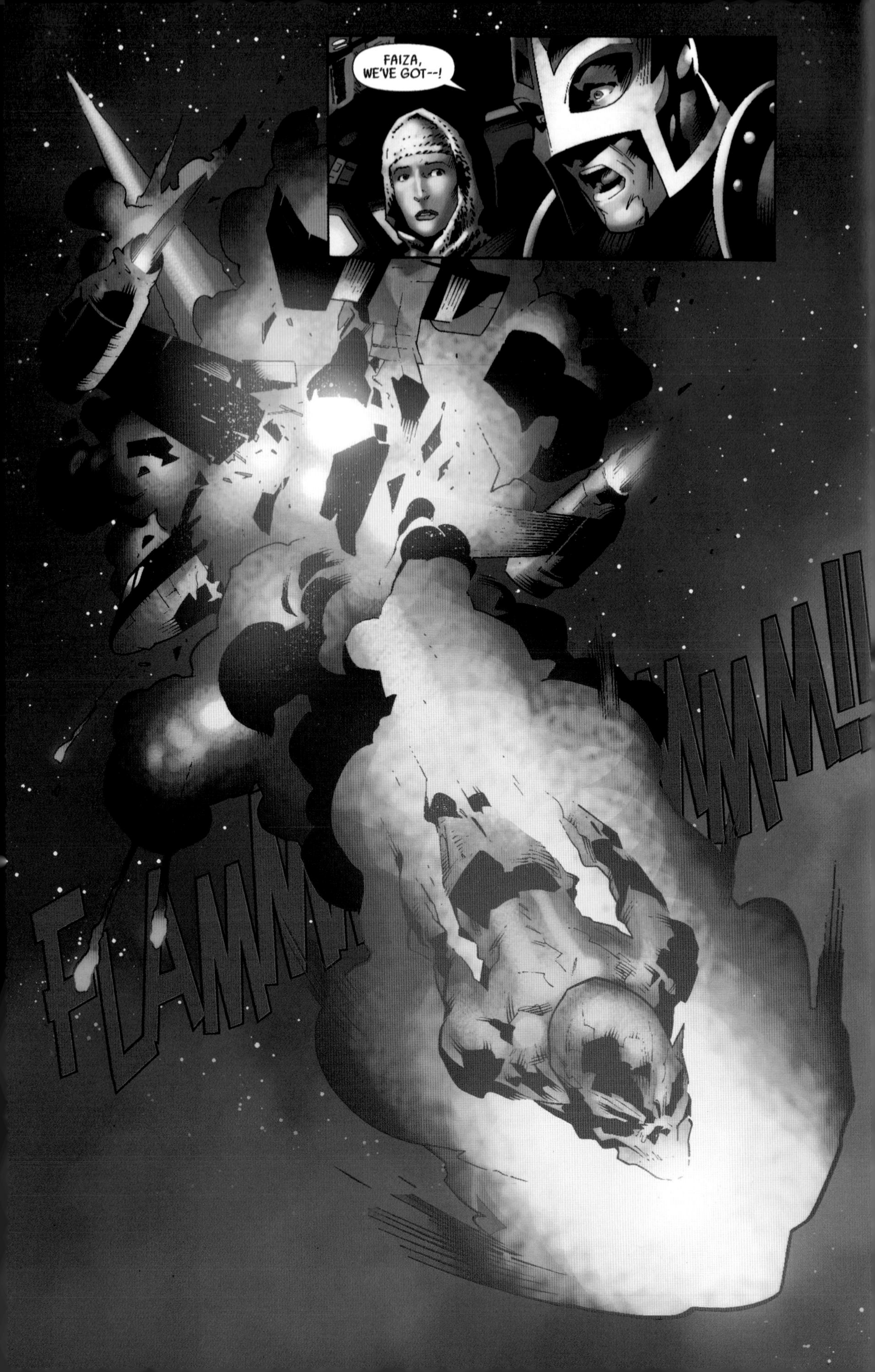
FAIZA, WE'VE GOT--!

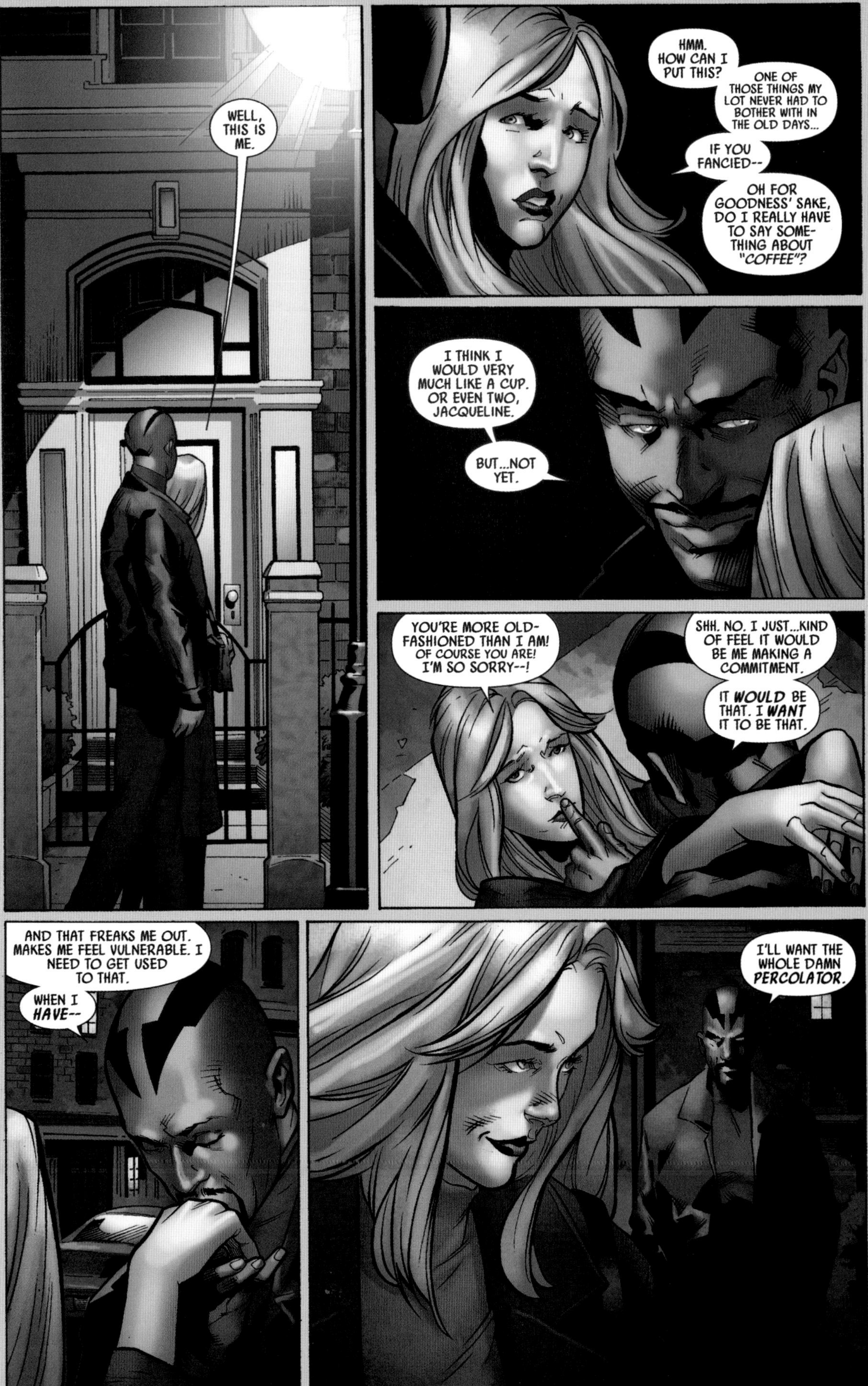
WELL, THIS IS ME.
HMM. HOW CAN I PUT THIS?
ONE OF THOSE THINGS MY LOT NEVER HAD TO BOTHER WITH IN THE OLD DAYS...
IF YOU FANCIED--
OH FOR GOODNESS' SAKE, DO I REALLY HAVE TO SAY SOME-THING ABOUT "COFFEE"?
I THINK I WOULD VERY MUCH LIKE A CUP. OR EVEN TWO, JACQUELINE.
BUT...NOT YET.
YOU'RE MORE OLD-FASHIONED THAN I AM! OF COURSE YOU ARE! I'M SO SORRY--!
SHH. NO. I JUST...KIND OF FEEL IT WOULD BE ME MAKING A COMMITMENT.
IT WOULD BE THAT. I WANT IT TO BE THAT.
AND THAT FREAKS ME OUT. MAKES ME FEEL VULNERABLE. I NEED TO GET USED TO THAT.
WHEN I HAVE--
I'LL WANT THE WHOLE DAMN PERCOLATOR.

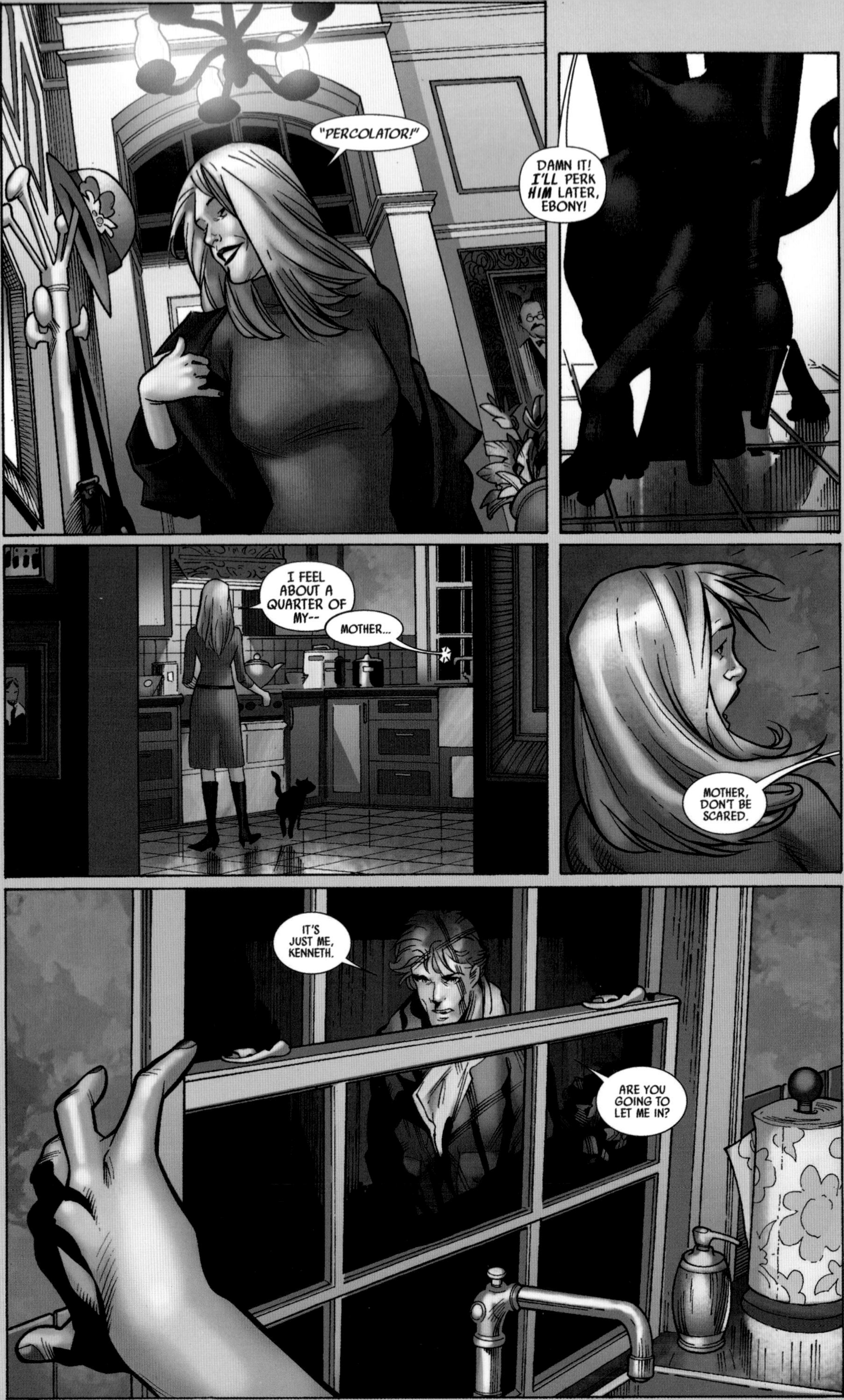
"PERCOLATOR!"
DAMN IT! I'LL PERK HIM LATER, EBONY!
I FEEL ABOUT A QUARTER OF MY--
MOTHER...
MOTHER, DON'T BE SCARED.
IT'S JUST ME, KENNETH.
ARE YOU GOING TO LET ME IN?

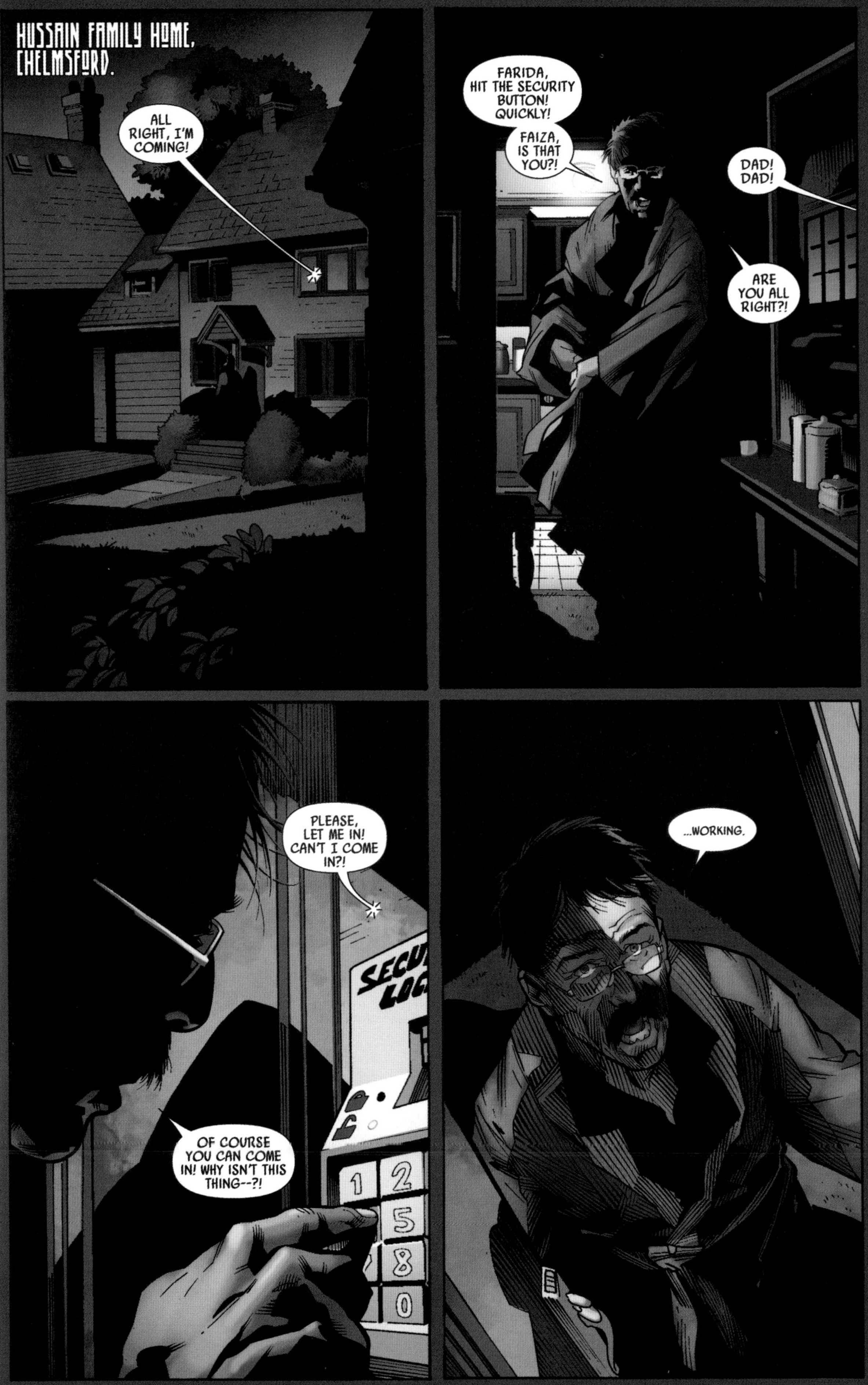
HUSSAIN FAMILY HOME, CHELMSFORD.
ALL RIGHT, I'M COMING!
FARIDA, HIT THE SECURITY BUTTON! QUICKLY!
FAIZA, IS THAT YOU?!
DAD! DAD!
ARE YOU ALL RIGHT?!
PLEASE, LET ME IN! CAN'T I COME IN?!
OF COURSE YOU CAN COME IN! WHY ISN'T THIS THING--?!
1
2
5
8
0
...WORKING.

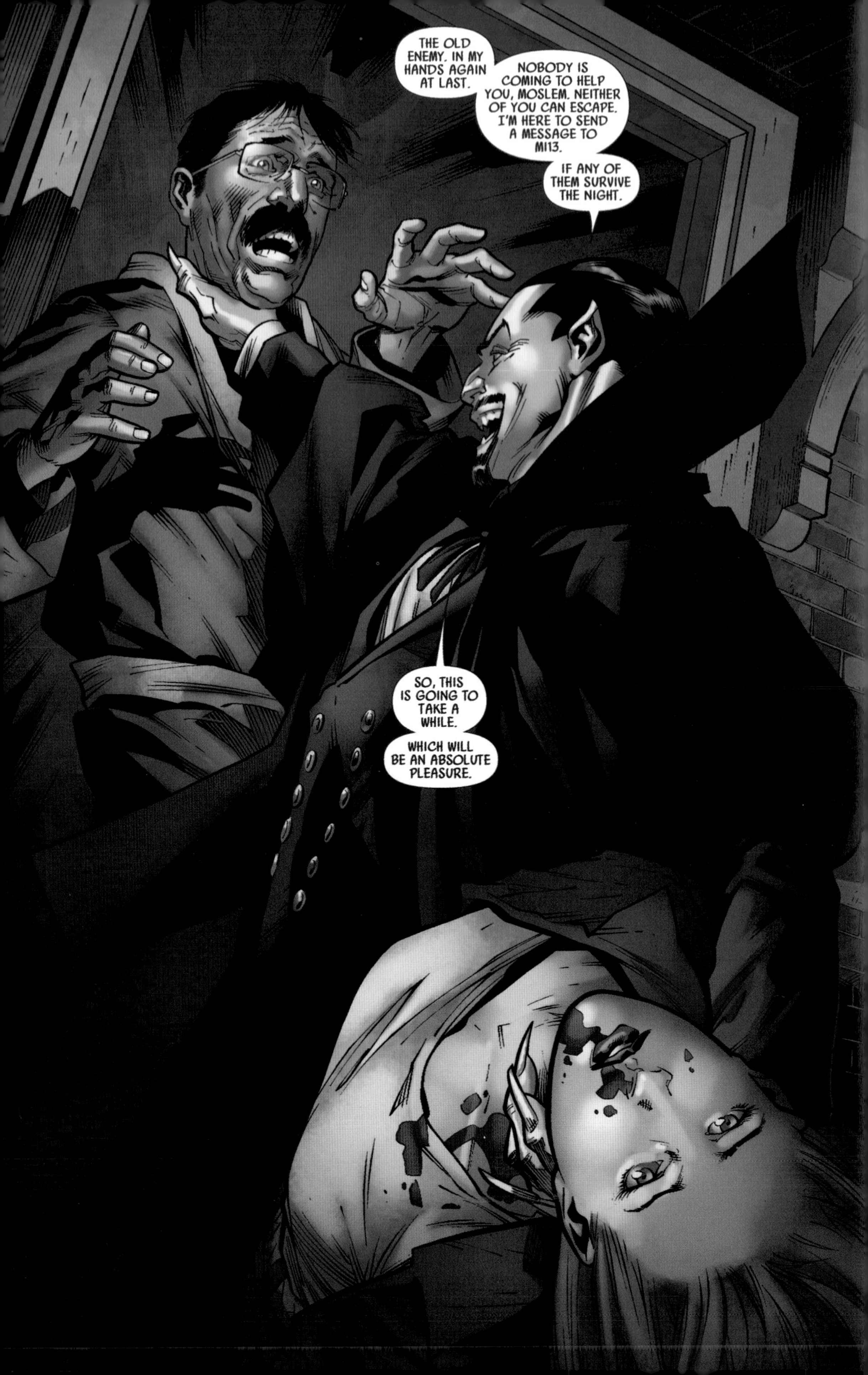
THE OLD ENEMY. IN MY HANDS AGAIN AT LAST.
NOBODY IS COMING TO HELP YOU, MOSLEM. NEITHER OF YOU CAN ESCAPE. I'M HERE TO SEND A MESSAGE TO MI13.
IF ANY OF THEM SURVIVE THE NIGHT.
SO, THIS IS GOING TO TAKE A WHILE.
WHICH WILL BE AN ABSOLUTE PLEASURE.

CAPTAIN BRITAIN AND MI13 #11
COVER ARTWORK

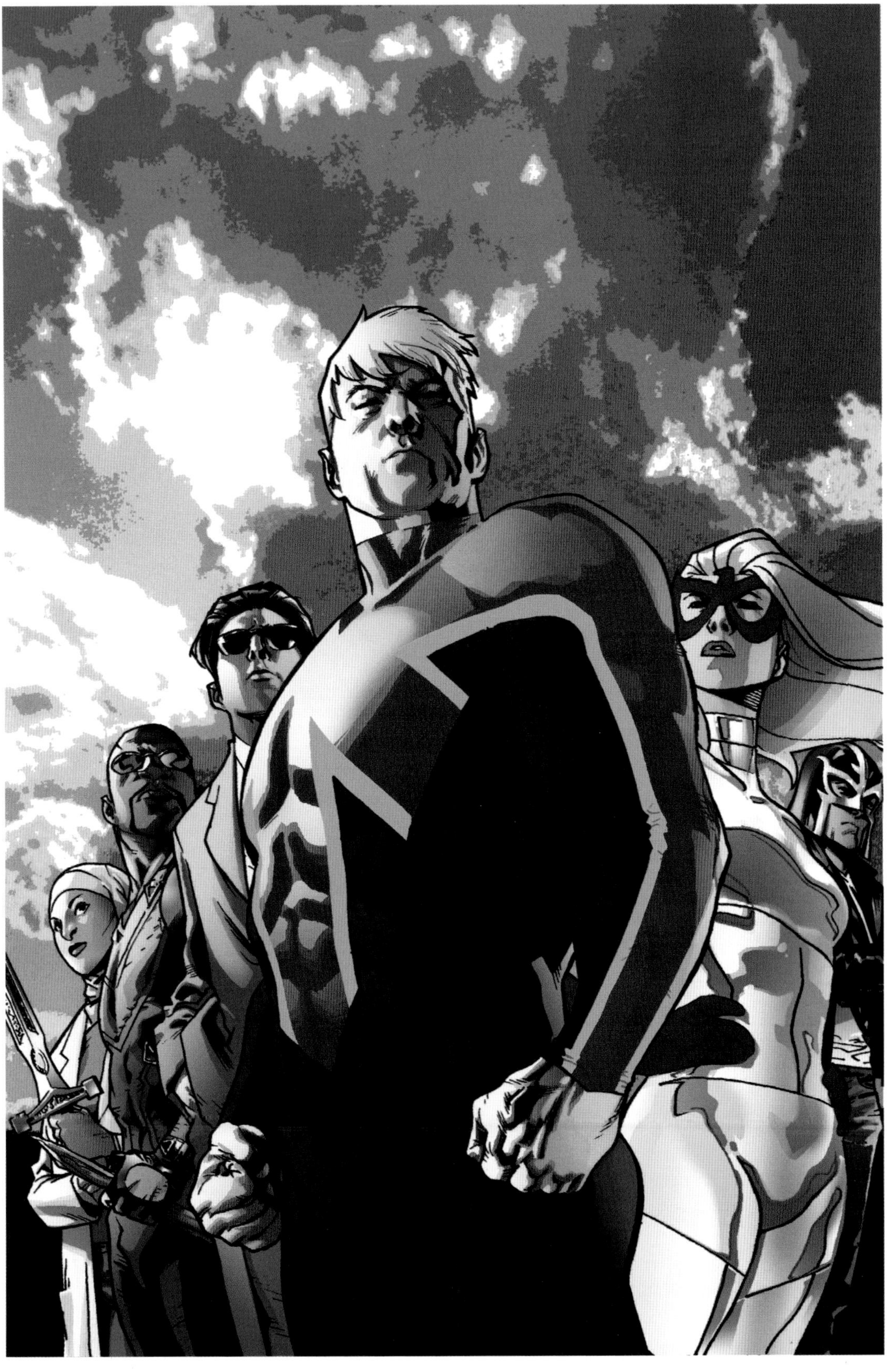

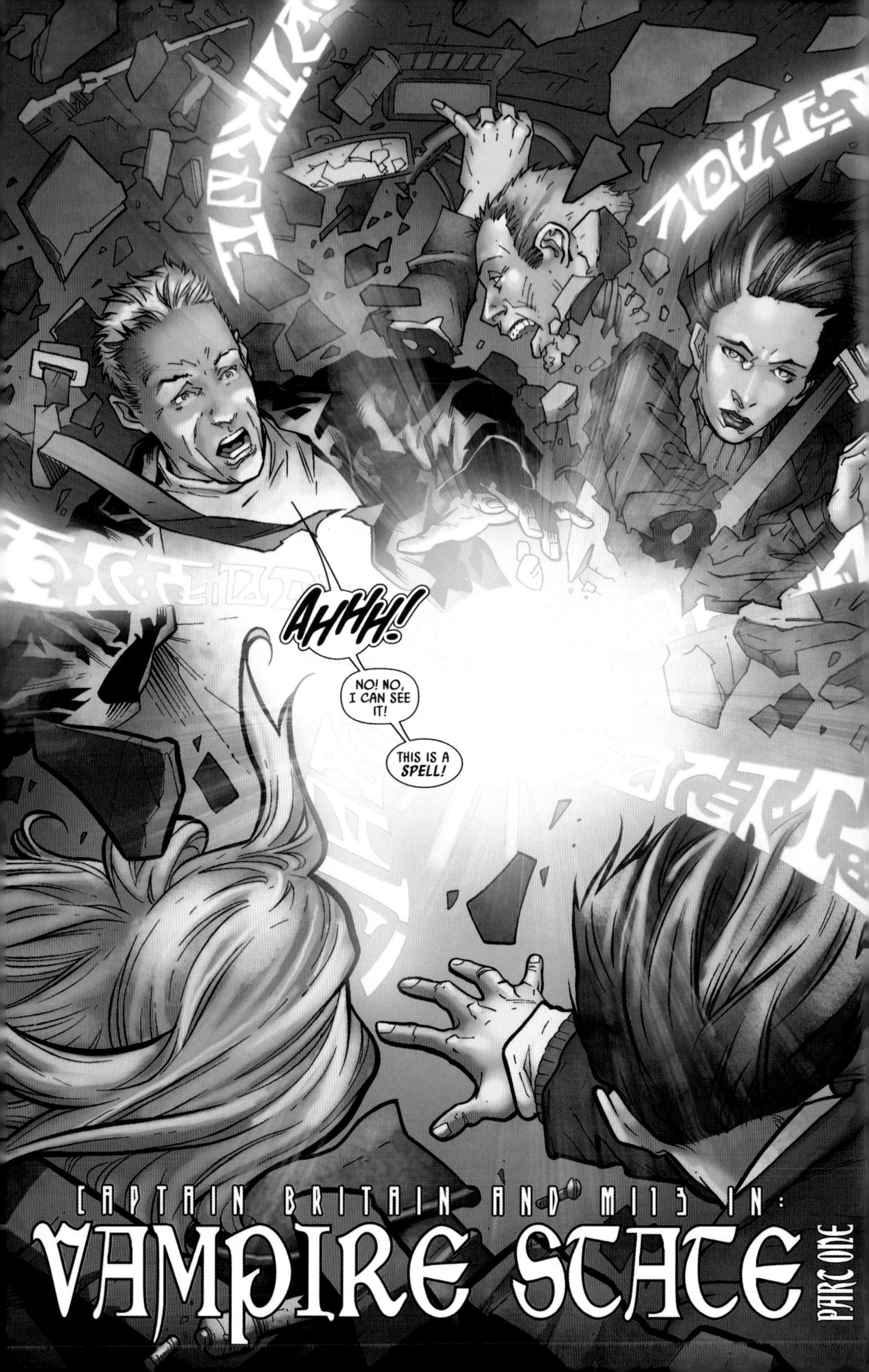
AHHH!
NO! NO, I CAN SEE IT!
THIS IS A SPELL!
CAPTAIN BRITAIN AND MI13 IN:
VAMPIRE STATE
PART ONE

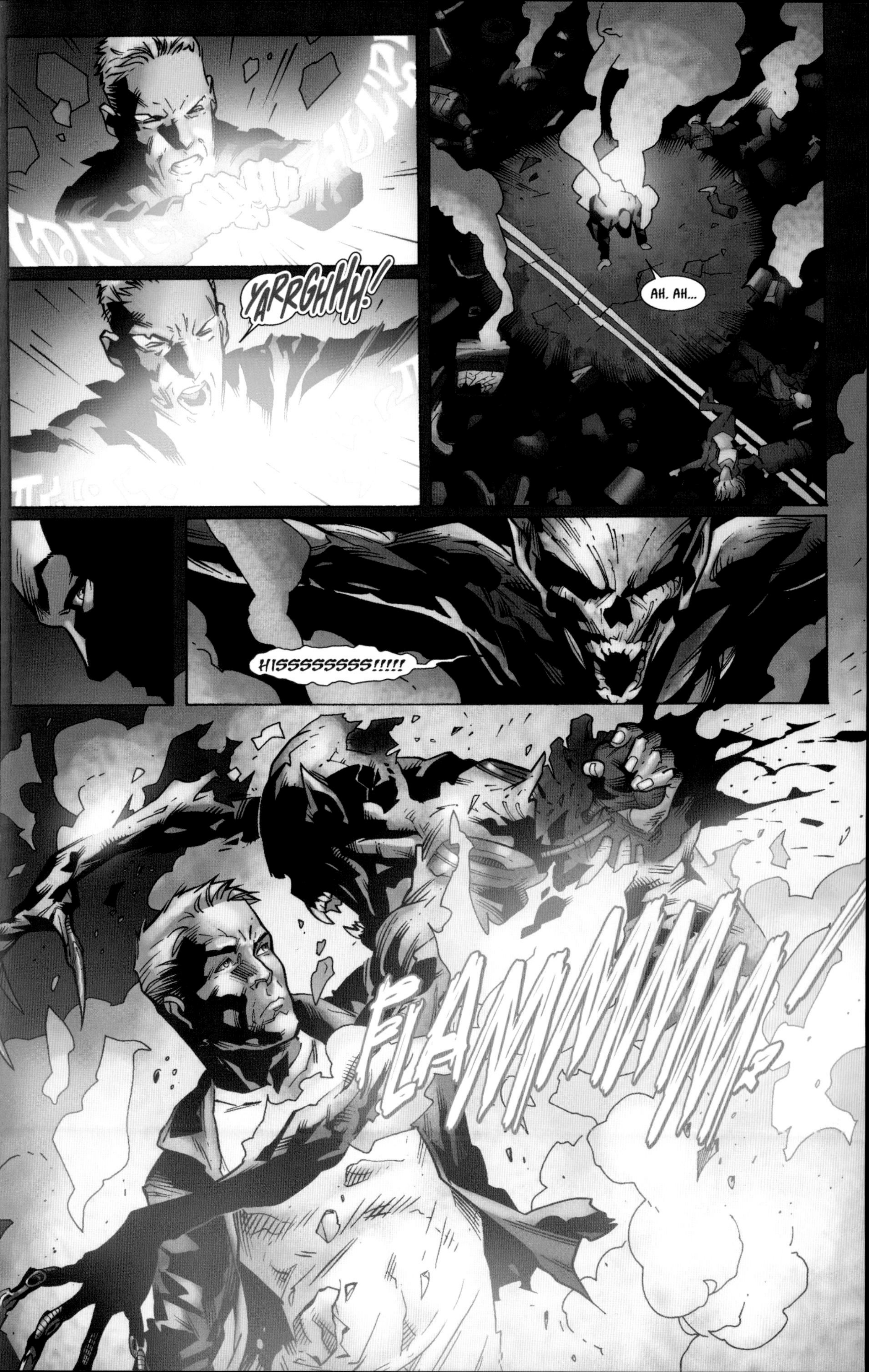
YARRGHHH!
AH, AH...
HISSSSSSSS!!!!!
FLAMMMMM!

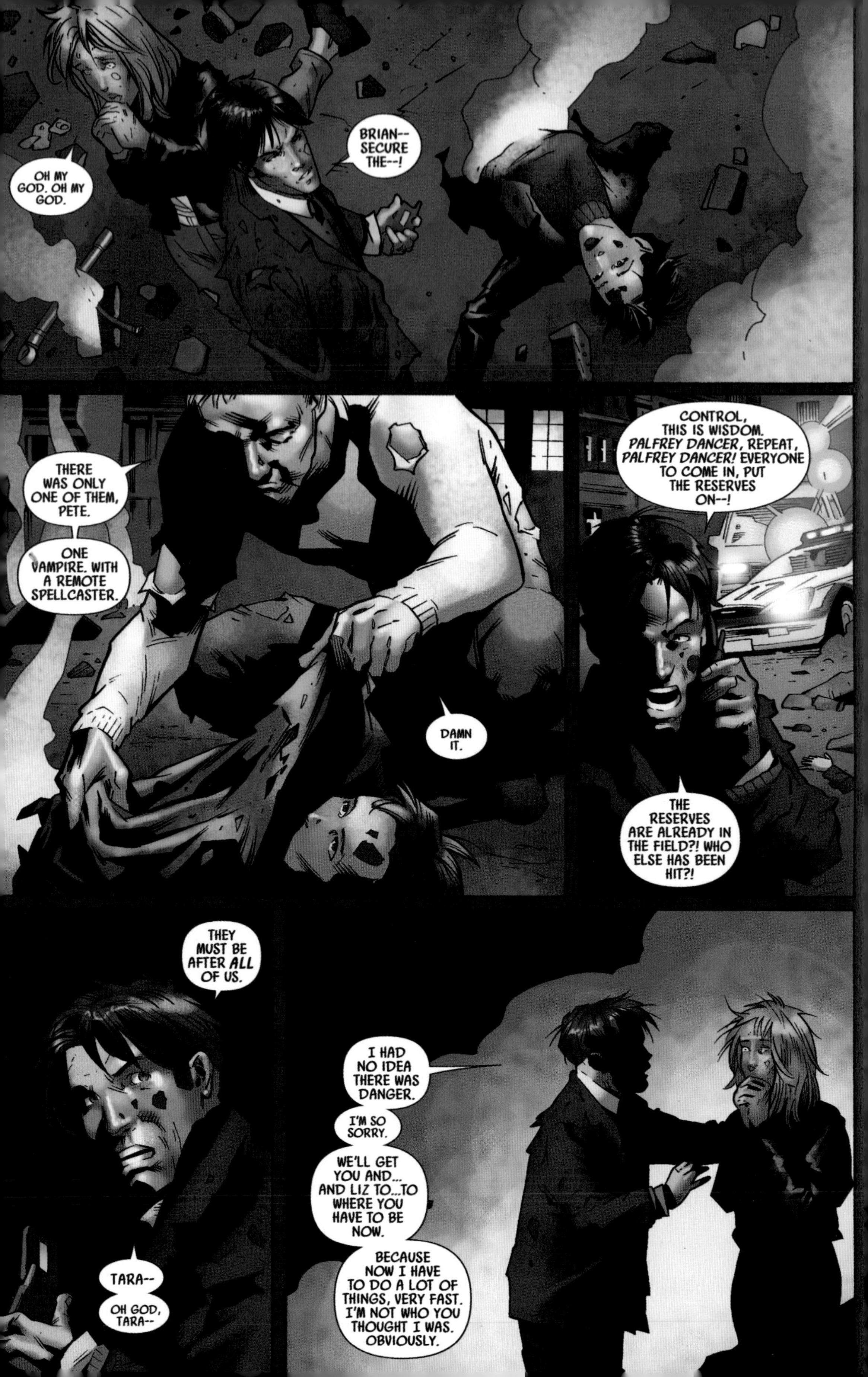
OH MY GOD. OH MY GOD.
BRIAN-- SECURE THE--!
THERE WAS ONLY ONE OF THEM, PETE.
ONE VAMPIRE. WITH A REMOTE SPELLCASTER.
DAMN IT.
CONTROL, THIS IS WISDOM. PALFREY DANCER, REPEAT, PALFREY DANCER! EVERYONE TO COME IN, PUT THE RESERVES ON--!
THE RESERVES ARE ALREADY IN THE FIELD?! WHO ELSE HAS BEEN HIT?!
THEY MUST BE AFTER ALL OF US.
TARA--
OH GOD, TARA--
I HAD NO IDEA THERE WAS DANGER.
I'M SO SORRY.
WE'LL GET YOU AND... AND LIZ TO...TO WHERE YOU HAVE TO BE NOW.
BECAUSE NOW I HAVE TO DO A LOT OF THINGS, VERY FAST. I'M NOT WHO YOU THOUGHT I WAS. OBVIOUSLY.

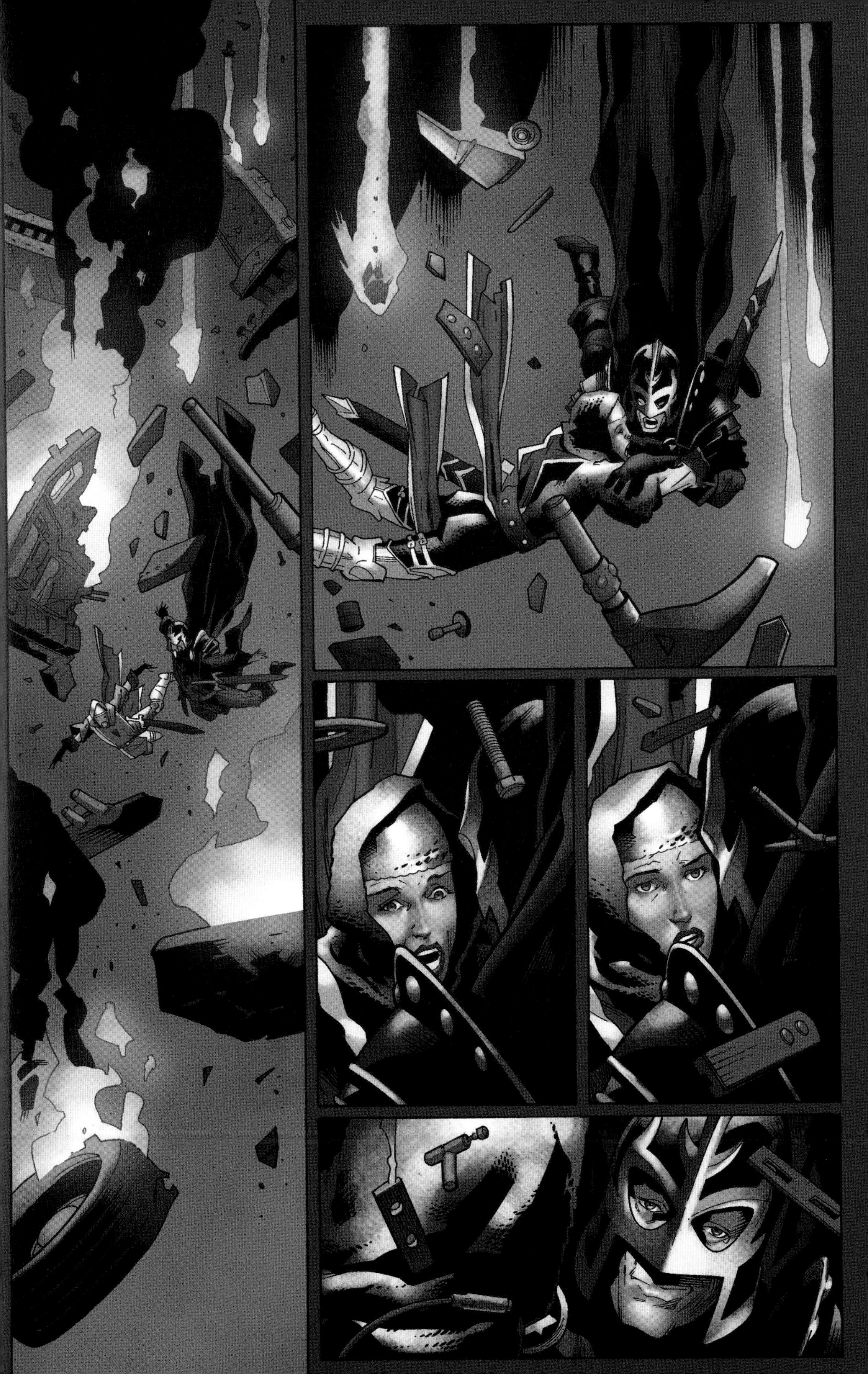

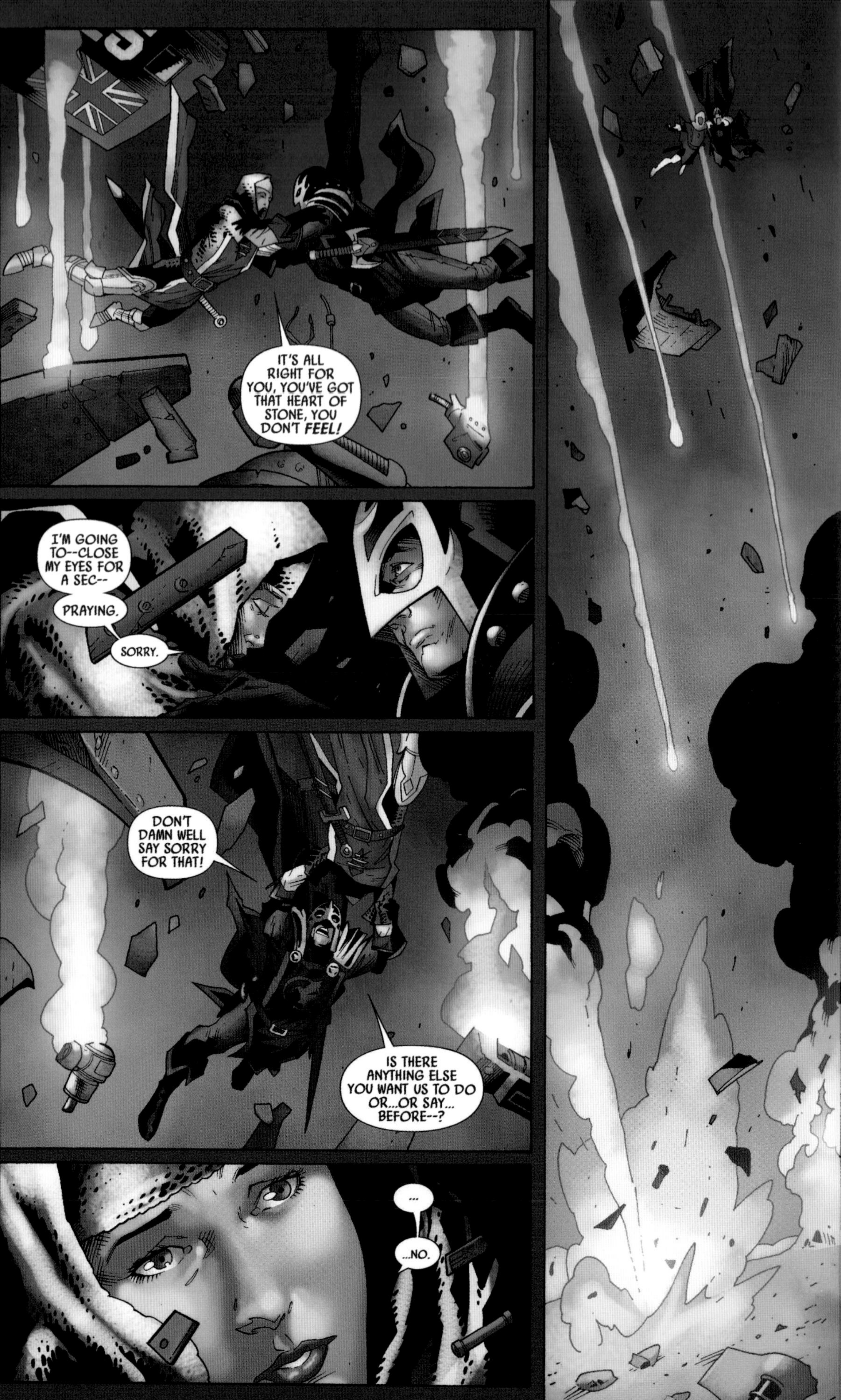
IT'S ALL RIGHT FOR YOU, YOU'VE GOT THAT HEART OF STONE, YOU DON'T FEEL!
I'M GOING TO--CLOSE MY EYES FOR A SEC--
PRAYING.
SORRY.
DON'T DAMN WELL SAY SORRY FOR THAT!
IS THERE ANYTHING ELSE YOU WANT US TO DO OR...OR SAY... BEFORE--?
...
...NO.

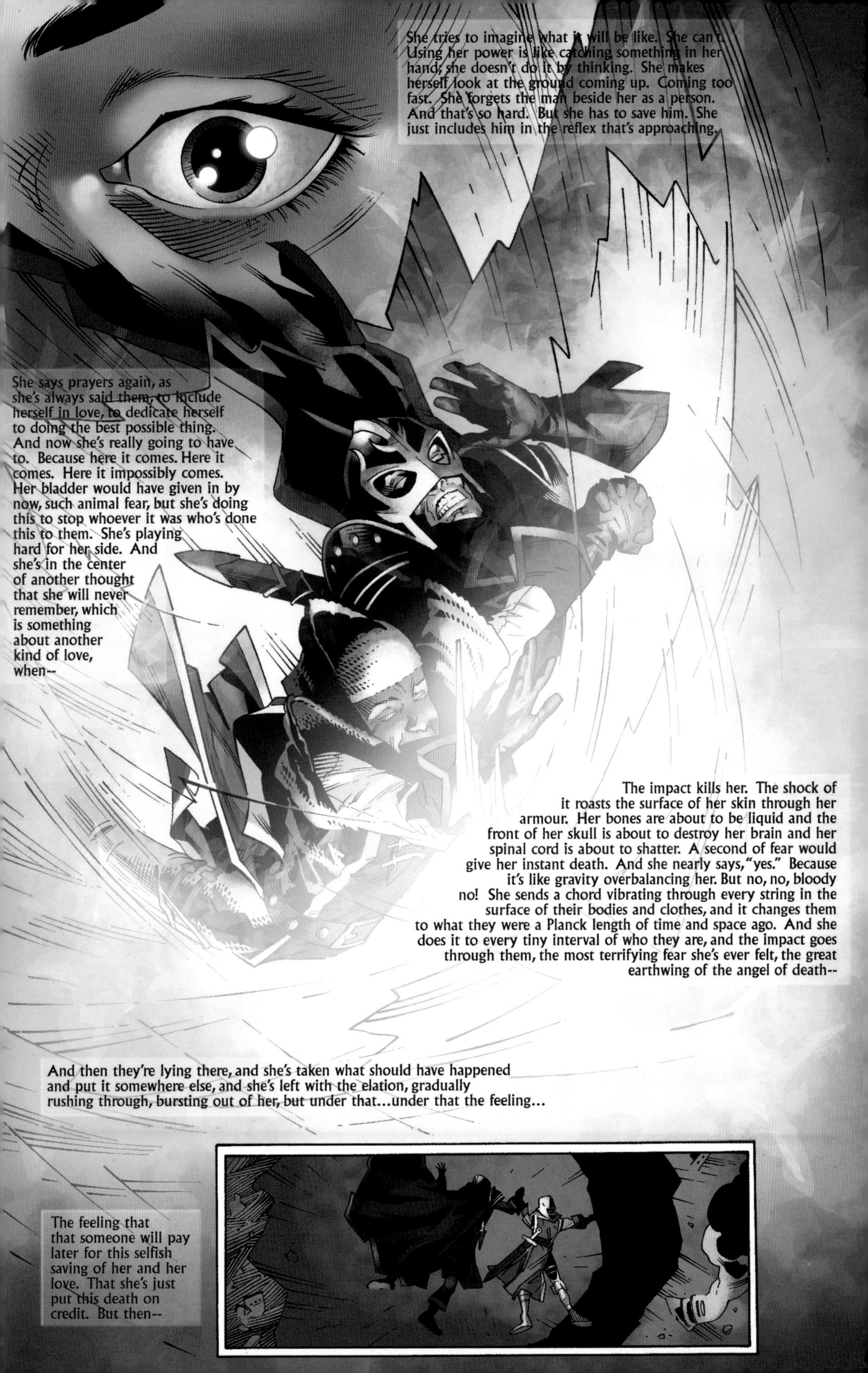
She tries to imagine what it will be like. She can't. Using her power is like catching something in her hand; she doesn't do it by thinking. She makes herself look at the ground coming up. Coming too fast. She forgets the man beside her as a person. And that's so hard. But she has to save him. She just includes him in the reflex that's approaching.
She says prayers again, as she's always said them, to include herself in love, to dedicate herself to doing the best possible thing. And now she's really going to have to. Because here it comes. Here it comes. Here it impossibly comes. Her bladder would have given in by now, such animal fear, but she's doing this to stop whoever it was who's done this to them. She's playing hard for her side. And she's in the center of another thought that she will never remember, which is something about another kind of love, when--
The impact kills her. The shock of it roasts the surface of her skin through her armour. Her bones are about to be liquid and the front of her skull is about to destroy her brain and her spinal cord is about to shatter. A second of fear would give her instant death. And she nearly says, "yes." Because it's like gravity overbalancing her. But no, no, bloody no! She sends a chord vibrating through every string in the surface of their bodies and clothes, and it changes them to what they were a Planck length of time and space ago. And she does it to every tiny interval of who they are, and the impact goes through them, the most terrifying fear she's ever felt, the great earthwing of the angel of death--
And then they're lying there, and she's taken what should have happened and put it somewhere else, and she's left with the elation, gradually rushing through, bursting out of her, but under that...under that the feeling...
The feeling that that someone will pay later for this selfish saving of her and her love. That she's just put this death on credit. But then--

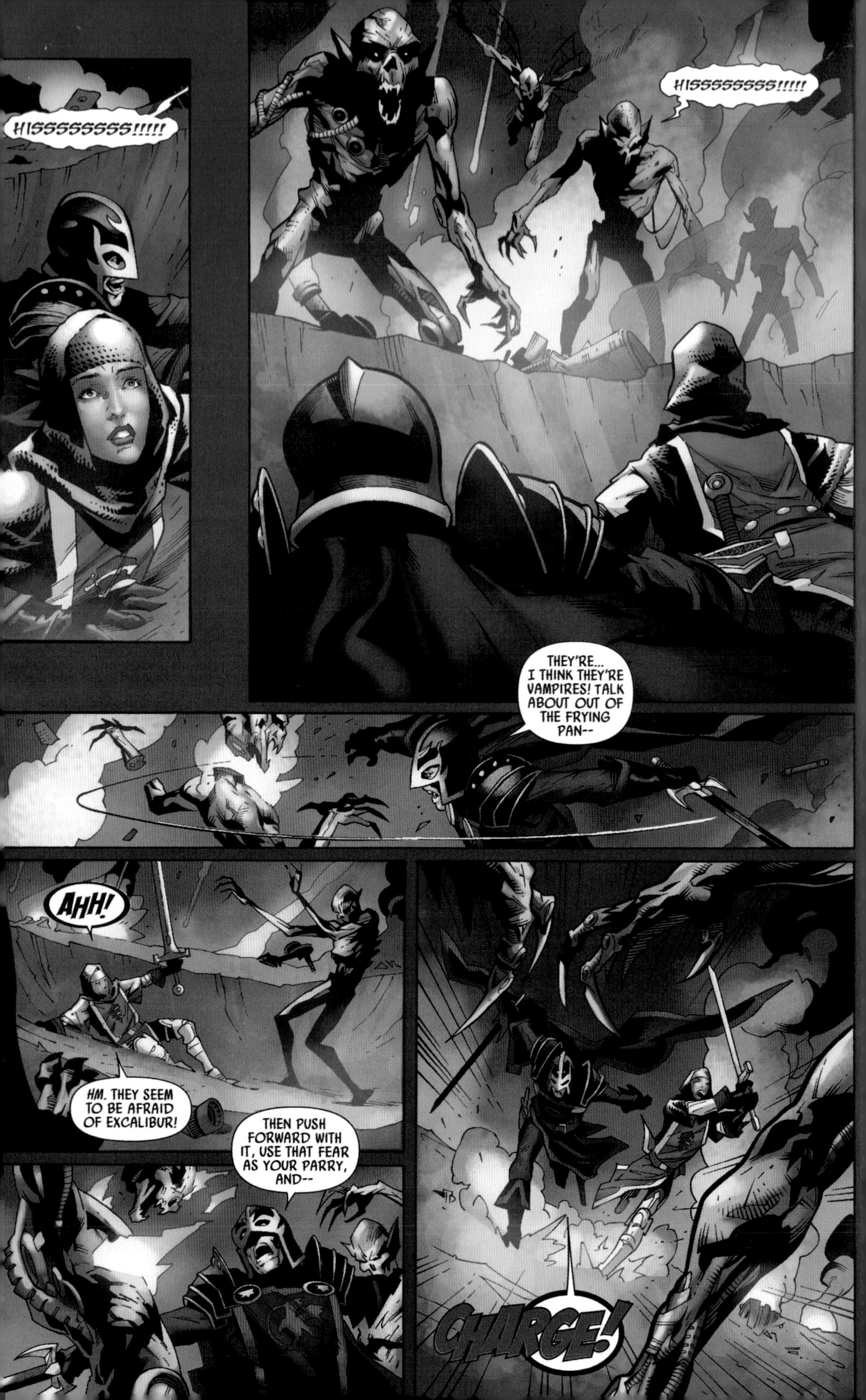
HISSSSSSSSS!!!!!
HISSSSSSSSS!!!!!
THEY'RE... I THINK THEY'RE VAMPIRES! TALK ABOUT OUT OF THE FRYING PAN--
AHH!
HM. THEY SEEM TO BE AFRAID OF EXCALIBUR!
THEN PUSH FORWARD WITH IT, USE THAT FEAR AS YOUR PARRY, AND--
CHARGE!

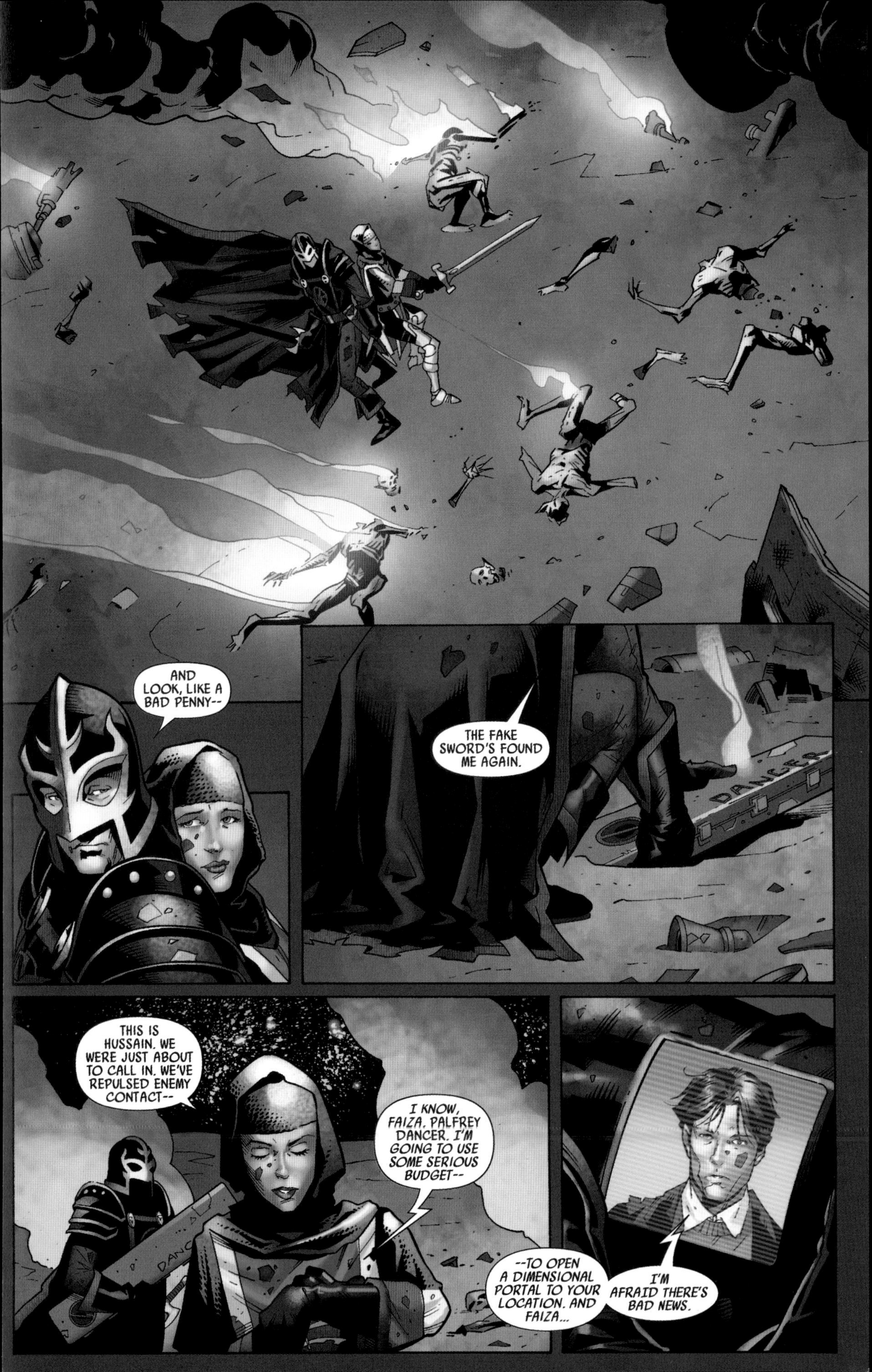
AND LOOK, LIKE A BAD PENNY--
THE FAKE SWORD'S FOUND ME AGAIN.
DANCER
THIS IS HUSSAIN. WE WERE JUST ABOUT TO CALL IN. WE'VE REPULSED ENEMY CONTACT--
I KNOW, FAIZA. PALFREY DANCER. I'M GOING TO USE SOME SERIOUS BUDGET--
--TO OPEN A DIMENSIONAL PORTAL TO YOUR LOCATION. AND FAIZA...
I'M AFRAID THERE'S BAD NEWS.

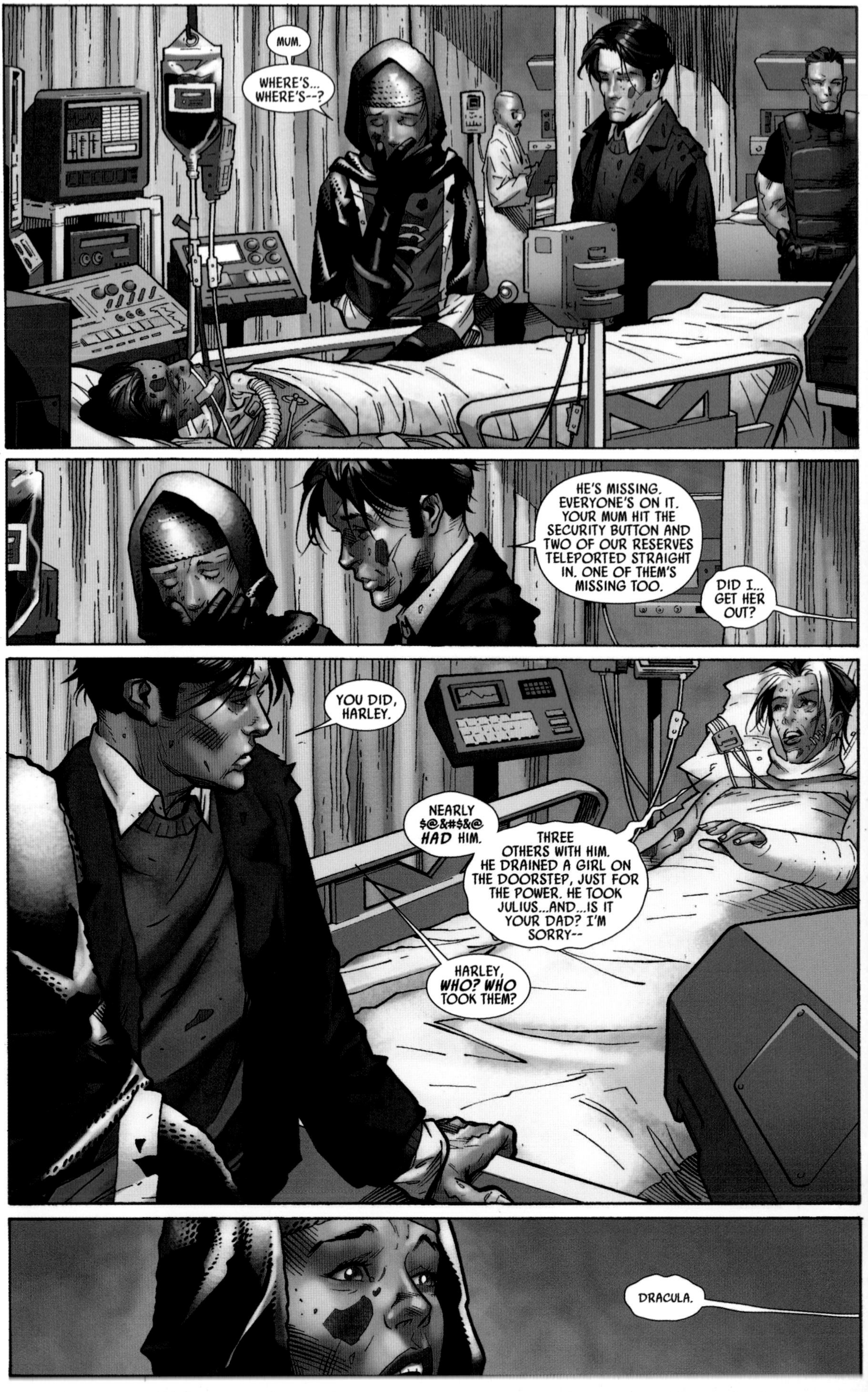
MUM.
WHERE'S... WHERE'S--?
HE'S MISSING. EVERYONE'S ON IT. YOUR MUM HIT THE SECURITY BUTTON AND TWO OF OUR RESERVES TELEPORTED STRAIGHT IN. ONE OF THEM'S MISSING TOO.
DID I... GET HER OUT?
YOU DID, HARLEY.
NEARLY $@&#$&@ HAD HIM.
THREE OTHERS WITH HIM. HE DRAINED A GIRL ON THE DOORSTEP, JUST FOR THE POWER. HE TOOK JULIUS...AND...IS IT YOUR DAD? I'M SORRY--
HARLEY, WHO? WHO TOOK THEM?
DRACULA.

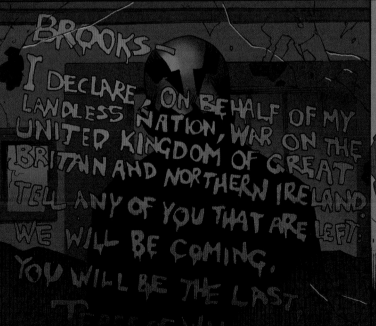

BROOKS

I DECLARE, ON BEHALF OF MY LAWLESS NATION, WAR ON THE UNITED KINGDOM OF GREAT BRITAIN AND NORTHERN IRELAND. TELL ANY OF YOU THAT ARE LEFT: WE WILL BE COMING. YOU WILL BE THE LAST.

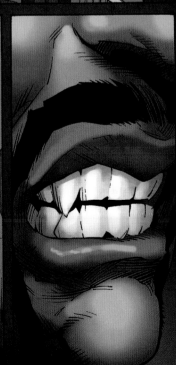

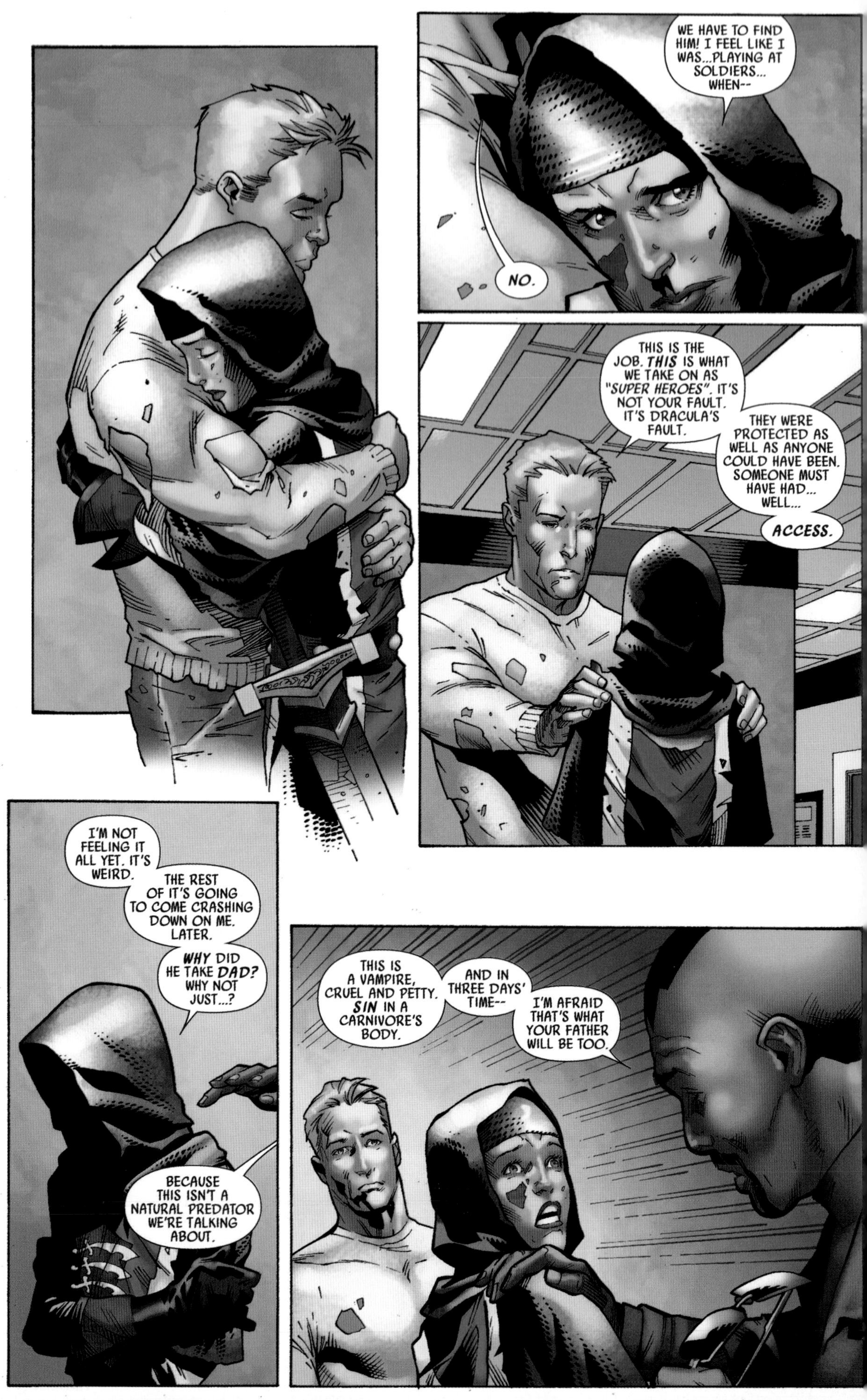
WE HAVE TO FIND HIM! I FEEL LIKE I WAS...PLAYING AT SOLDIERS... WHEN--
NO.
THIS IS THE JOB. THIS IS WHAT WE TAKE ON AS "SUPER HEROES". IT'S NOT YOUR FAULT. IT'S DRACULA'S FAULT.
THEY WERE PROTECTED AS WELL AS ANYONE COULD HAVE BEEN. SOMEONE MUST HAVE HAD... WELL...
ACCESS.
I'M NOT FEELING IT ALL YET. IT'S WEIRD.
THE REST OF IT'S GOING TO COME CRASHING DOWN ON ME. LATER.
WHY DID HE TAKE DAD? WHY NOT JUST...?
BECAUSE THIS ISN'T A NATURAL PREDATOR WE'RE TALKING ABOUT.
THIS IS A VAMPIRE, CRUEL AND PETTY. SIN IN A CARNIVORE'S BODY.
AND IN THREE DAYS' TIME--
I'M AFRAID THAT'S WHAT YOUR FATHER WILL BE TOO.

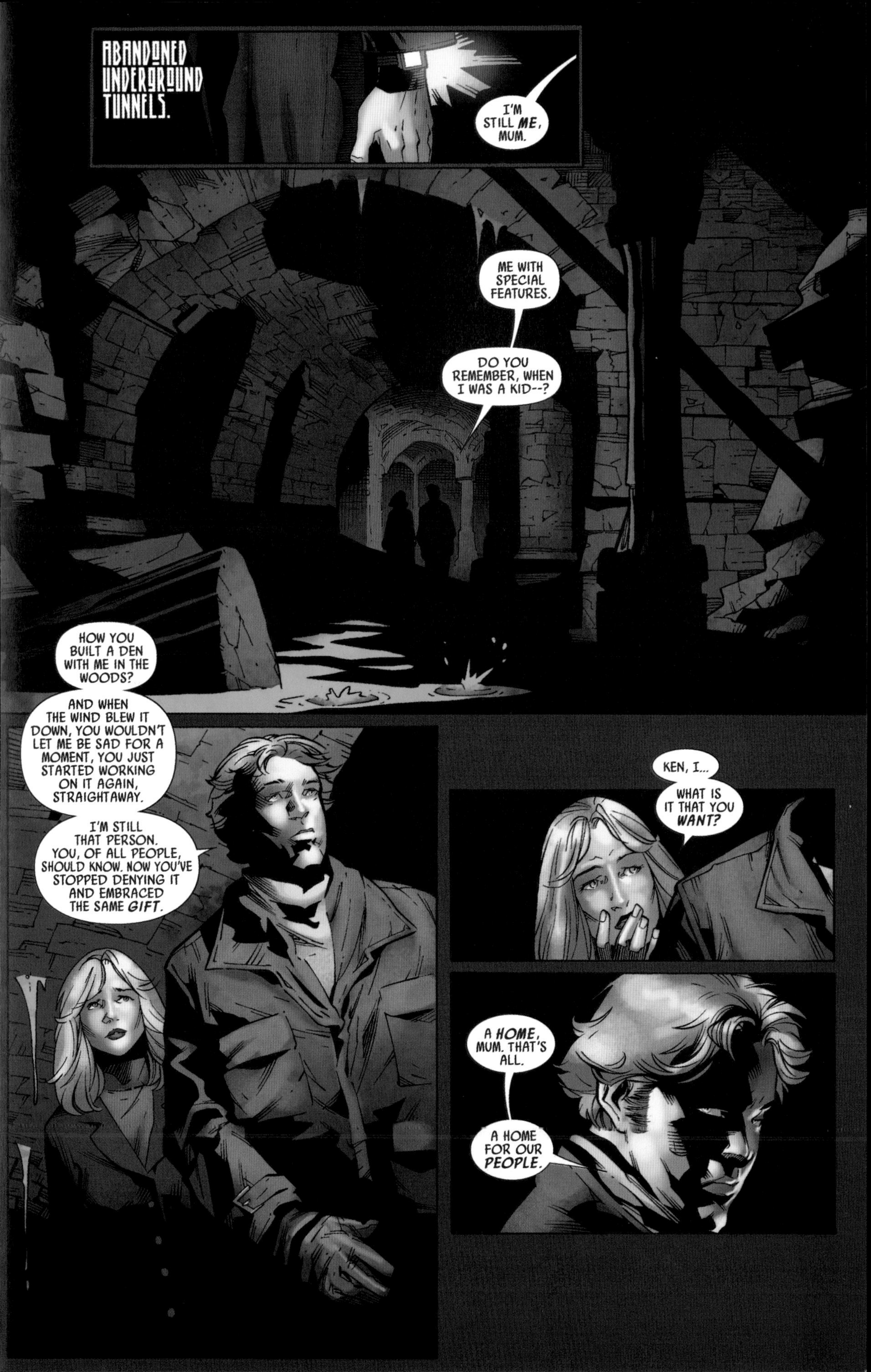
ABANDONED UNDERGROUND TUNNELS.
I'M STILL *ME*, MUM.
ME WITH SPECIAL FEATURES.
DO YOU REMEMBER, WHEN I WAS A KID--?
HOW YOU BUILT A DEN WITH ME IN THE WOODS?
AND WHEN THE WIND BLEW IT DOWN, YOU WOULDN'T LET ME BE SAD FOR A MOMENT, YOU JUST STARTED WORKING ON IT AGAIN, STRAIGHTAWAY.
I'M STILL THAT PERSON. YOU, OF ALL PEOPLE, SHOULD KNOW. NOW YOU'VE STOPPED DENYING IT AND EMBRACED THE SAME *GIFT*.
KEN, I...
WHAT IS IT THAT YOU *WANT?*
A *HOME*, MUM. THAT'S ALL.
A HOME FOR OUR *PEOPLE*.

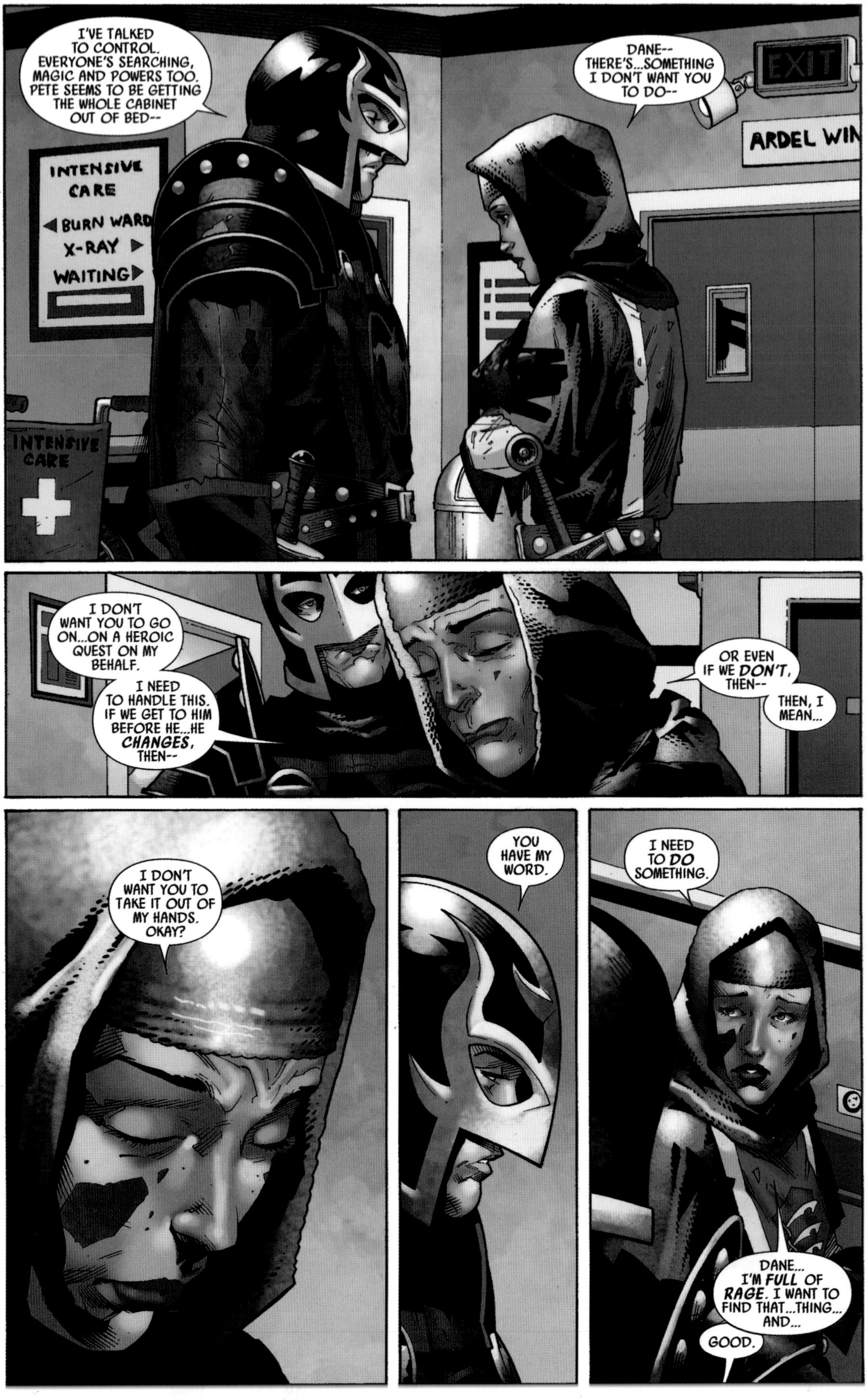
I'VE TALKED TO CONTROL. EVERYONE'S SEARCHING, MAGIC AND POWERS TOO. PETE SEEMS TO BE GETTING THE WHOLE CABINET OUT OF BED--
DANE-- THERE'S...SOMETHING I DON'T WANT YOU TO DO--
EXIT
ARDEL WIN
INTENSIVE CARE
BURN WARD
X-RAY
WAITING
INTENSIVE CARE
I DON'T WANT YOU TO GO ON...ON A HEROIC QUEST ON MY BEHALF.
I NEED TO HANDLE THIS. IF WE GET TO HIM BEFORE HE...HE CHANGES, THEN--
OR EVEN IF WE DON'T, THEN--
THEN, I MEAN...
I DON'T WANT YOU TO TAKE IT OUT OF MY HANDS. OKAY?
YOU HAVE MY WORD.
I NEED TO DO SOMETHING.
DANE... I'M FULL OF RAGE. I WANT TO FIND THAT...THING... AND...
GOOD.

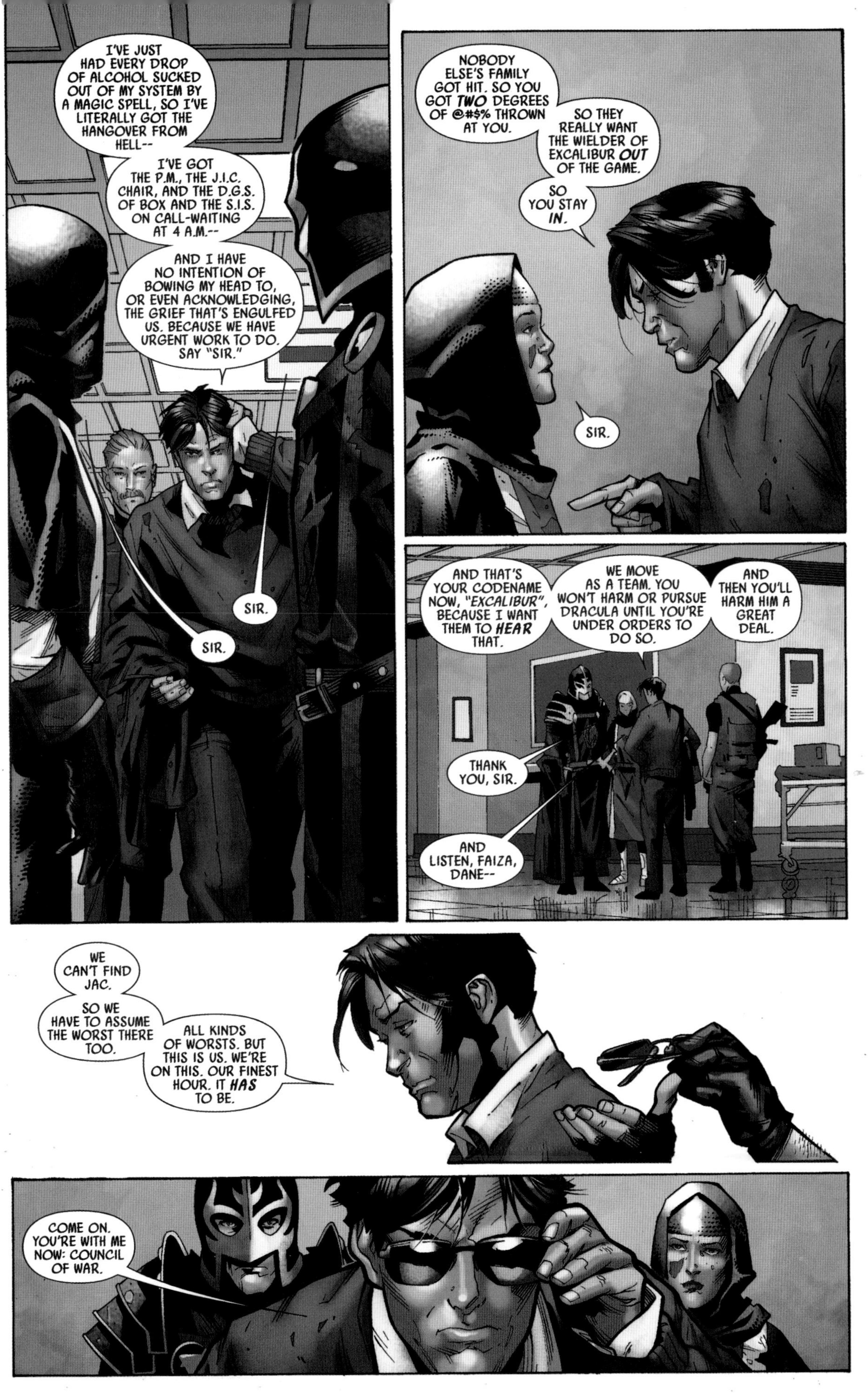
I'VE JUST HAD EVERY DROP OF ALCOHOL SUCKED OUT OF MY SYSTEM BY A MAGIC SPELL, SO I'VE LITERALLY GOT THE HANGOVER FROM HELL--
I'VE GOT THE P.M., THE J.I.C. CHAIR, AND THE D.G.S. OF BOX AND THE S.I.S. ON CALL-WAITING AT 4 A.M.--
AND I HAVE NO INTENTION OF BOWING MY HEAD TO, OR EVEN ACKNOWLEDGING, THE GRIEF THAT'S ENGULFED US. BECAUSE WE HAVE URGENT WORK TO DO. SAY "SIR."
SIR.
SIR.
NOBODY ELSE'S FAMILY GOT HIT. SO YOU GOT TWO DEGREES OF @#$% THROWN AT YOU.
SO THEY REALLY WANT THE WIELDER OF EXCALIBUR OUT OF THE GAME.
SO YOU STAY IN.
SIR.
AND THAT'S YOUR CODENAME NOW, "EXCALIBUR", BECAUSE I WANT THEM TO HEAR THAT.
WE MOVE AS A TEAM. YOU WON'T HARM OR PURSUE DRACULA UNTIL YOU'RE UNDER ORDERS TO DO SO.
AND THEN YOU'LL HARM HIM A GREAT DEAL.
THANK YOU, SIR.
AND LISTEN, FAIZA, DANE--
WE CAN'T FIND JAC.
SO WE HAVE TO ASSUME THE WORST THERE TOO.
ALL KINDS OF WORSTS. BUT THIS IS US. WE'RE ON THIS. OUR FINEST HOUR. IT HAS TO BE.
COME ON. YOU'RE WITH ME NOW: COUNCIL OF WAR.

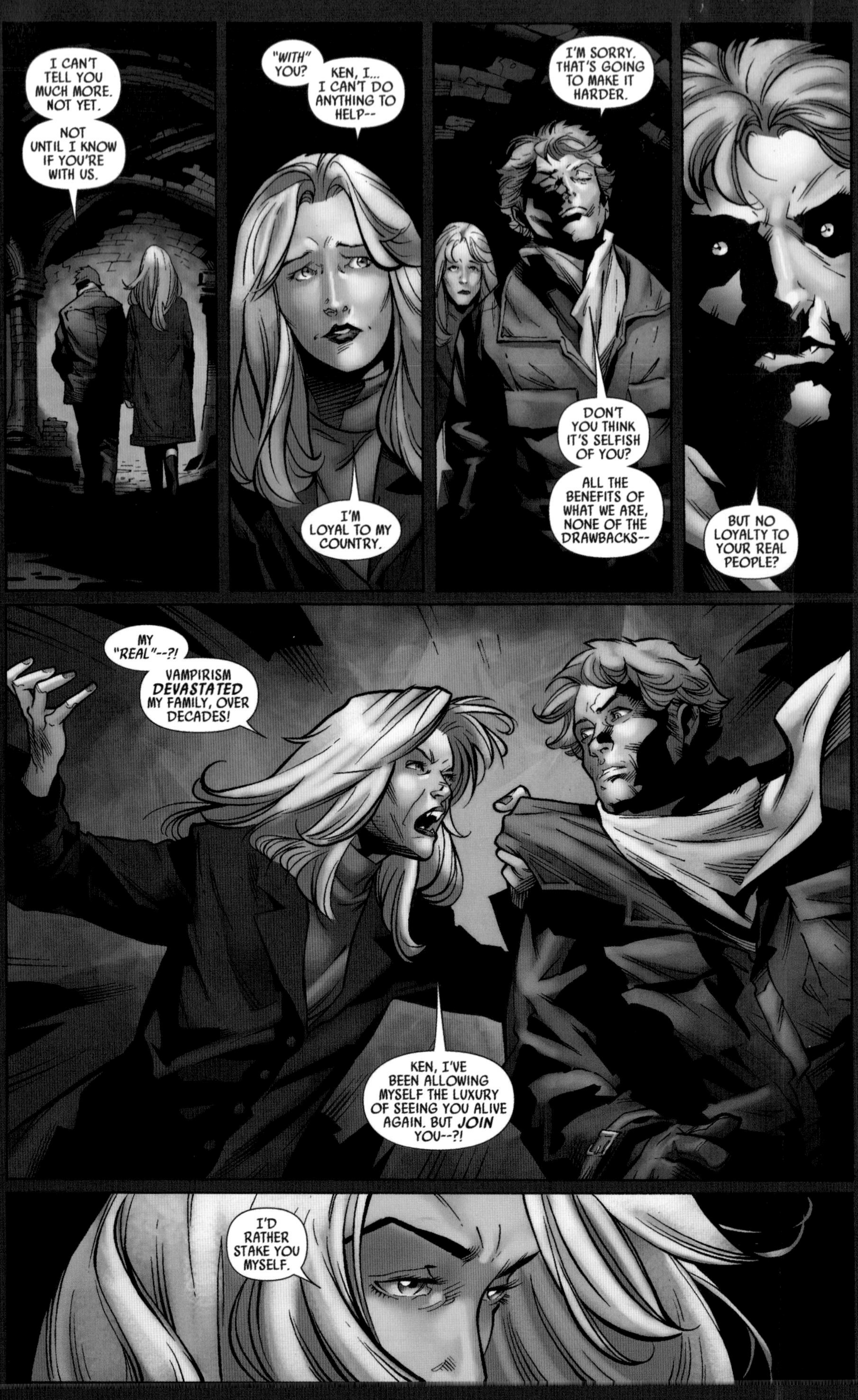
I CAN'T TELL YOU MUCH MORE. NOT YET.
NOT UNTIL I KNOW IF YOU'RE WITH US.
"WITH" YOU?
KEN, I... I CAN'T DO ANYTHING TO HELP--
I'M LOYAL TO MY COUNTRY.
I'M SORRY. THAT'S GOING TO MAKE IT HARDER.
DON'T YOU THINK IT'S SELFISH OF YOU?
ALL THE BENEFITS OF WHAT WE ARE, NONE OF THE DRAWBACKS--
BUT NO LOYALTY TO YOUR REAL PEOPLE?
MY "REAL"--?!
VAMPIRISM DEVASTATED MY FAMILY, OVER DECADES!
KEN, I'VE BEEN ALLOWING MYSELF THE LUXURY OF SEEING YOU ALIVE AGAIN. BUT JOIN YOU--?!
I'D RATHER STAKE YOU MYSELF.

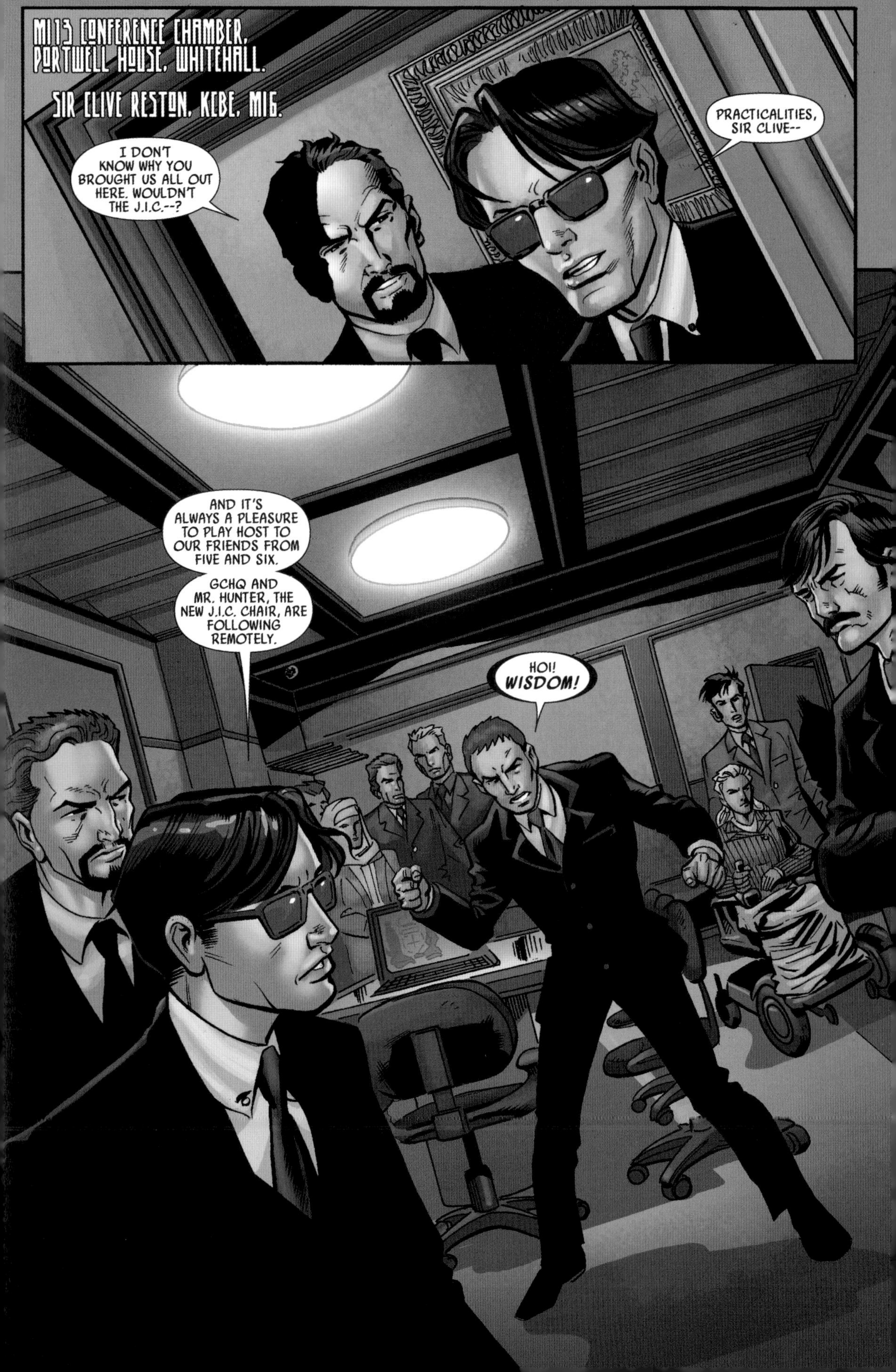
MI13 CONFERENCE CHAMBER, PORTWELL HOUSE, WHITEHALL.
SIR CLIVE RESTON, KCBE, MI6.
I DON'T KNOW WHY YOU BROUGHT US ALL OUT HERE. WOULDN'T THE J.I.C.--?
PRACTICALITIES, SIR CLIVE--
AND IT'S ALWAYS A PLEASURE TO PLAY HOST TO OUR FRIENDS FROM FIVE AND SIX.
GCHQ AND MR. HUNTER, THE NEW J.I.C. CHAIR, ARE FOLLOWING REMOTELY.
HOI! WISDOM!

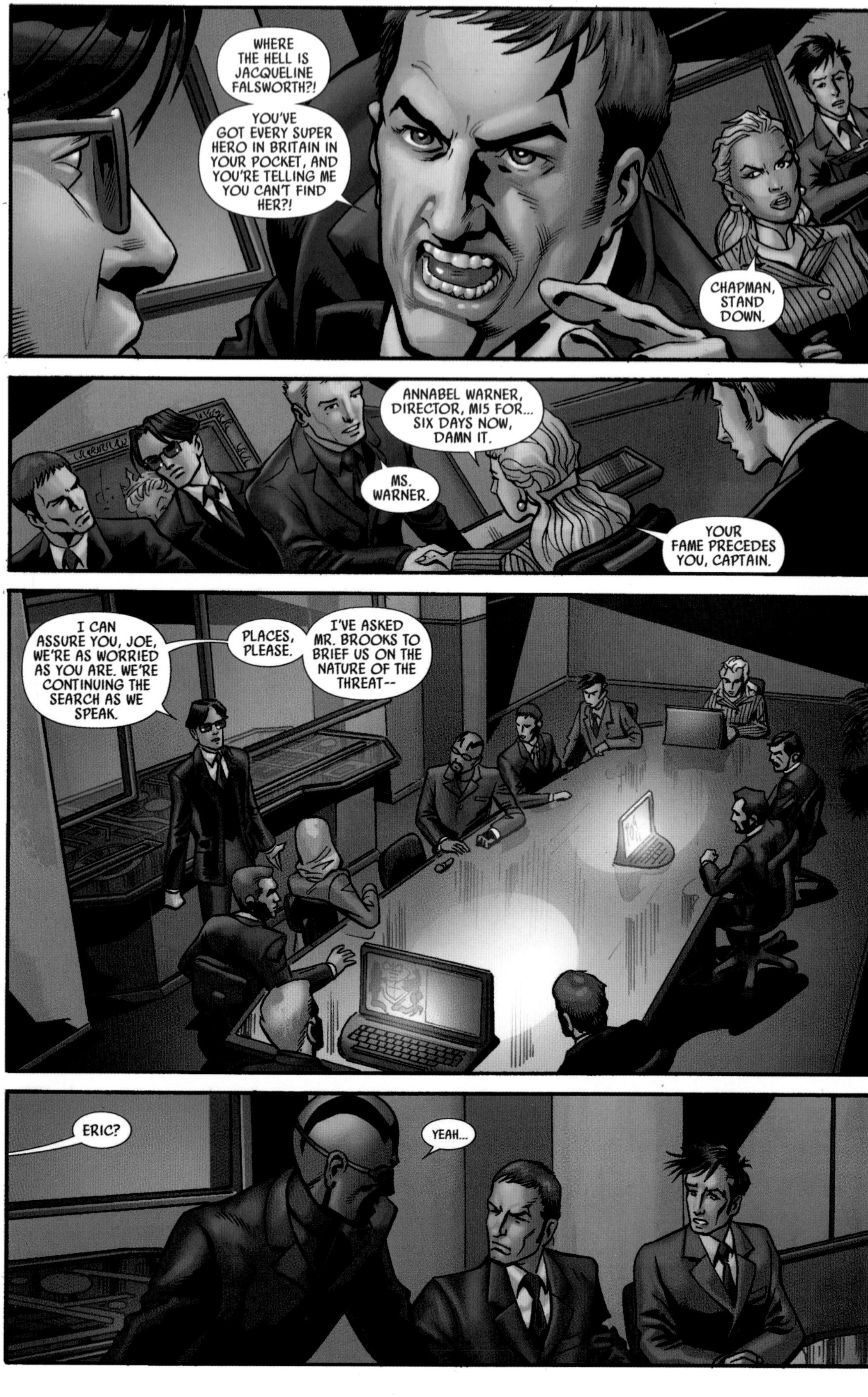
WHERE THE HELL IS JACQUELINE FALSWORTH?!
YOU'VE GOT EVERY SUPER HERO IN BRITAIN IN YOUR POCKET, AND YOU'RE TELLING ME YOU CAN'T FIND HER?!
CHAPMAN, STAND DOWN.
ANNABEL WARNER, DIRECTOR, MI5 FOR... SIX DAYS NOW, DAMN IT.
MS. WARNER.
YOUR FAME PRECEDES YOU, CAPTAIN.
I CAN ASSURE YOU, JOE, WE'RE AS WORRIED AS YOU ARE. WE'RE CONTINUING THE SEARCH AS WE SPEAK.
PLACES, PLEASE.
I'VE ASKED MR. BROOKS TO BRIEF US ON THE NATURE OF THE THREAT--
ERIC?
YEAH...

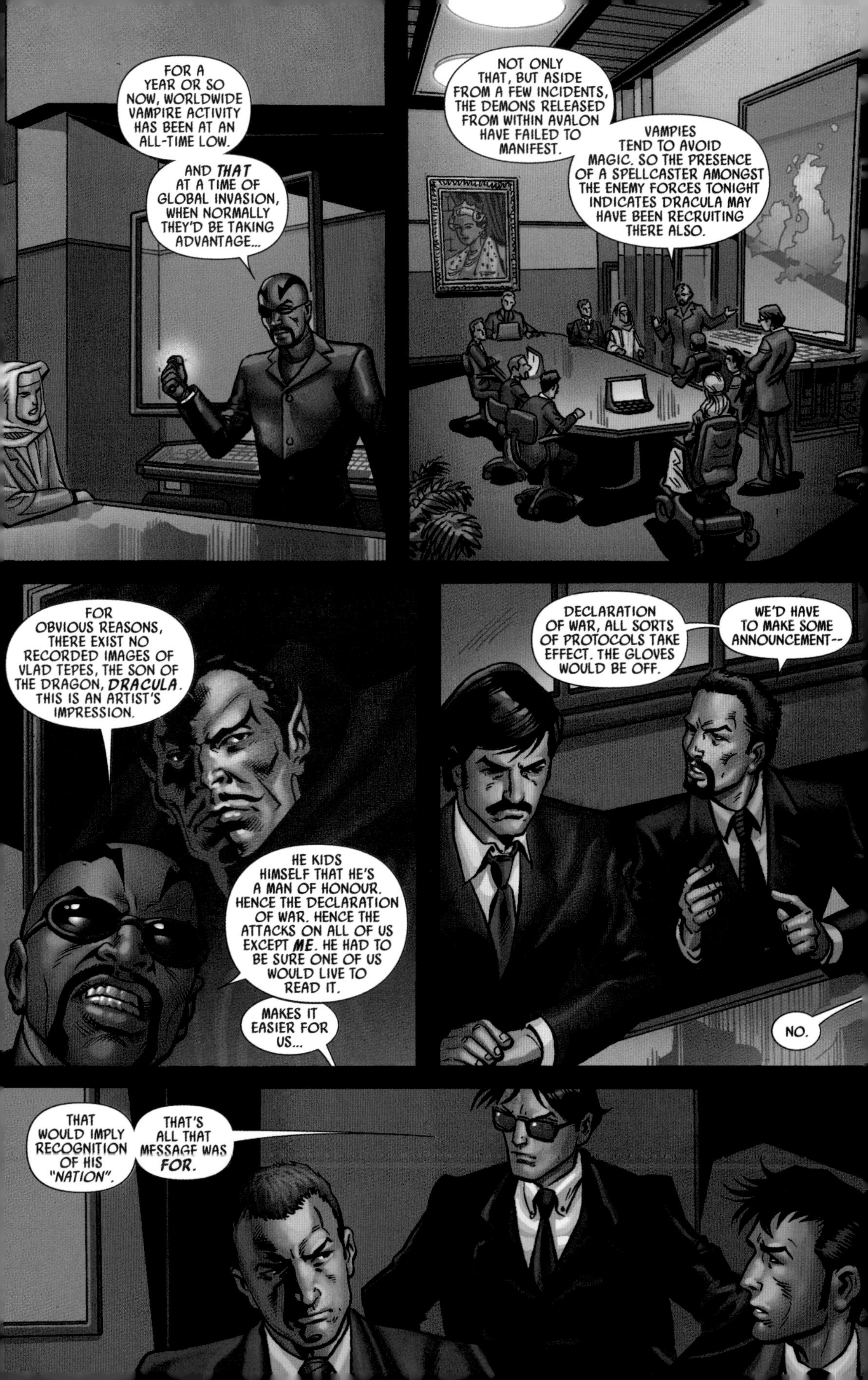
FOR A YEAR OR SO NOW, WORLDWIDE VAMPIRE ACTIVITY HAS BEEN AT AN ALL-TIME LOW.
AND *THAT* AT A TIME OF GLOBAL INVASION, WHEN NORMALLY THEY'D BE TAKING ADVANTAGE...
NOT ONLY THAT, BUT ASIDE FROM A FEW INCIDENTS, THE DEMONS RELEASED FROM WITHIN AVALON HAVE FAILED TO MANIFEST.
VAMPIES TEND TO AVOID MAGIC. SO THE PRESENCE OF A SPELLCASTER AMONGST THE ENEMY FORCES TONIGHT INDICATES DRACULA MAY HAVE BEEN RECRUITING THERE ALSO.
FOR OBVIOUS REASONS, THERE EXIST NO RECORDED IMAGES OF VLAD TEPES, THE SON OF THE DRAGON, *DRACULA*. THIS IS AN ARTIST'S IMPRESSION.
HE KIDS HIMSELF THAT HE'S A MAN OF HONOUR. HENCE THE DECLARATION OF WAR. HENCE THE ATTACKS ON ALL OF US EXCEPT *ME*. HE HAD TO BE SURE ONE OF US WOULD LIVE TO READ IT.
MAKES IT EASIER FOR US...
DECLARATION OF WAR, ALL SORTS OF PROTOCOLS TAKE EFFECT. THE GLOVES WOULD BE OFF.
WE'D HAVE TO MAKE SOME ANNOUNCEMENT--
NO.
THAT WOULD IMPLY RECOGNITION OF HIS *"NATION"*.
THAT'S ALL THAT MESSAGE WAS *FOR*.

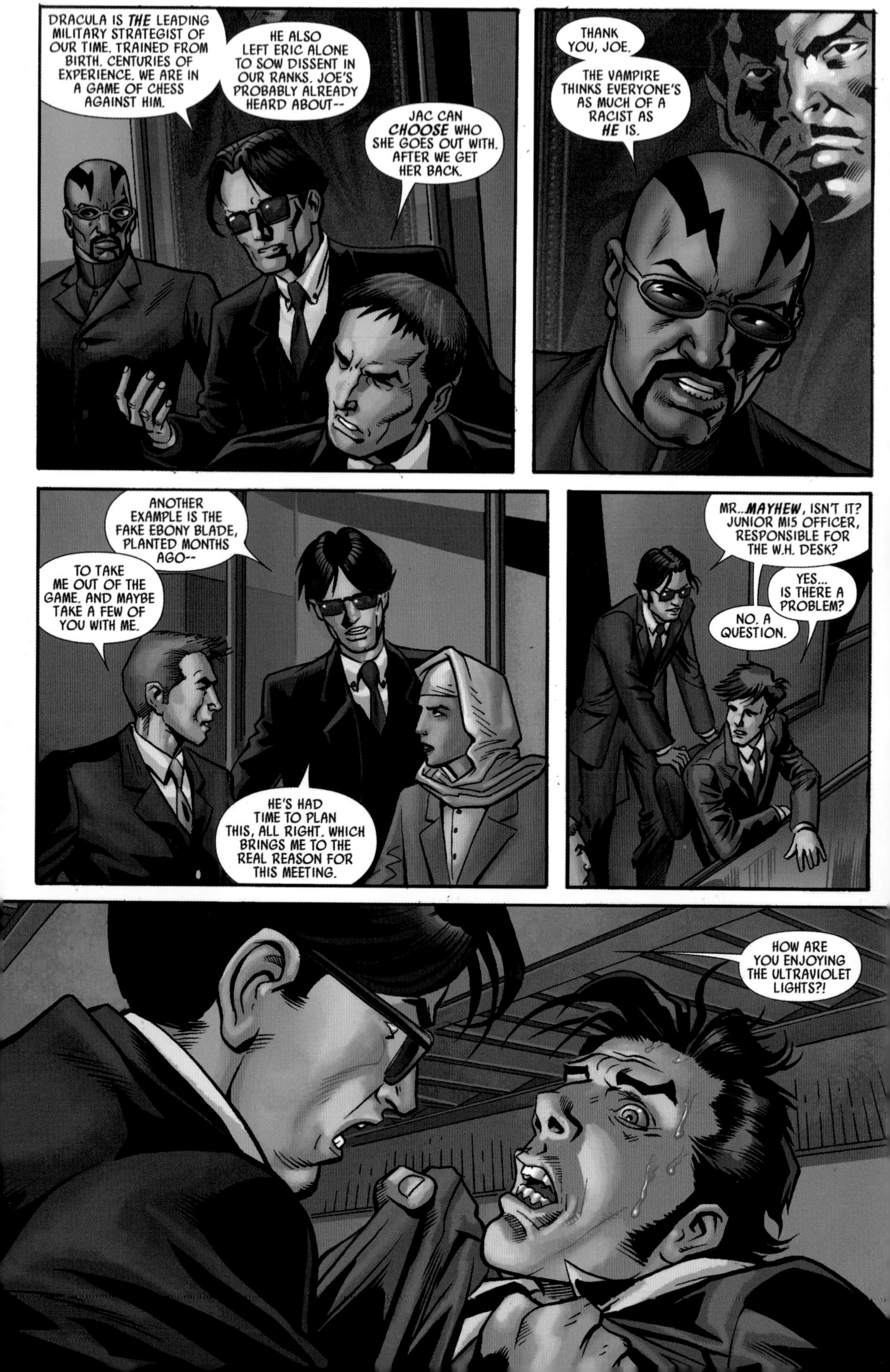
DRACULA IS THE LEADING MILITARY STRATEGIST OF OUR TIME. TRAINED FROM BIRTH. CENTURIES OF EXPERIENCE. WE ARE IN A GAME OF CHESS AGAINST HIM.
HE ALSO LEFT ERIC ALONE TO SOW DISSENT IN OUR RANKS. JOE'S PROBABLY ALREADY HEARD ABOUT--
JAC CAN CHOOSE WHO SHE GOES OUT WITH. AFTER WE GET HER BACK.
THANK YOU, JOE.
THE VAMPIRE THINKS EVERYONE'S AS MUCH OF A RACIST AS HE IS.
ANOTHER EXAMPLE IS THE FAKE EBONY BLADE, PLANTED MONTHS AGO--
TO TAKE ME OUT OF THE GAME. AND MAYBE TAKE A FEW OF YOU WITH ME.
HE'S HAD TIME TO PLAN THIS, ALL RIGHT. WHICH BRINGS ME TO THE REAL REASON FOR THIS MEETING.
MR.. MAYHEW, ISN'T IT? JUNIOR MI5 OFFICER, RESPONSIBLE FOR THE W.H. DESK?
YES... IS THERE A PROBLEM?
NO. A QUESTION.
HOW ARE YOU ENJOYING THE ULTRAVIOLET LIGHTS?!

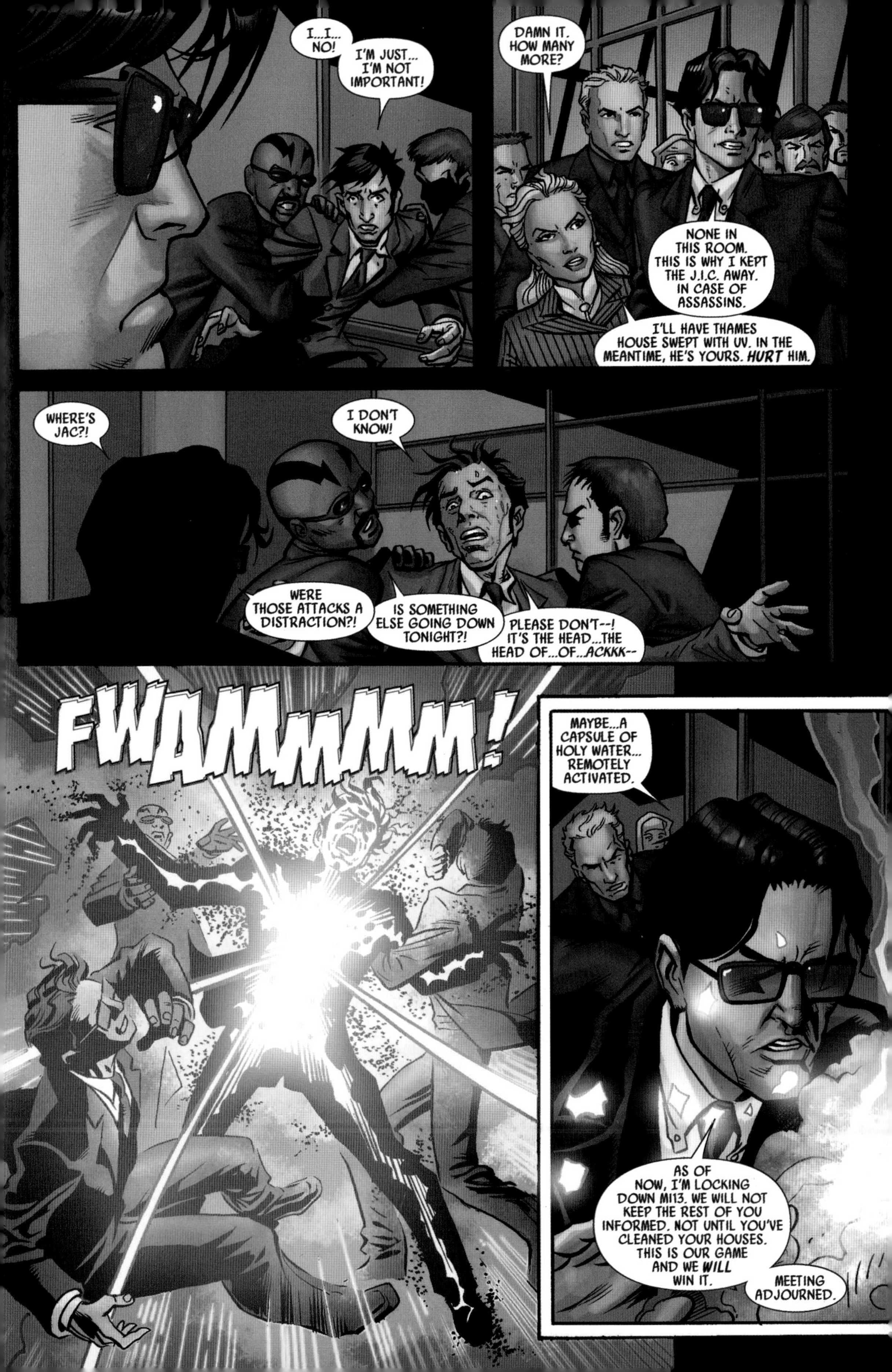
I...I... NO!
I'M JUST... I'M NOT IMPORTANT!
DAMN IT. HOW MANY MORE?
NONE IN THIS ROOM. THIS IS WHY I KEPT THE J.I.C. AWAY. IN CASE OF ASSASSINS.
I'LL HAVE THAMES HOUSE SWEPT WITH UV. IN THE MEANTIME, HE'S YOURS. HURT HIM.
WHERE'S JAC?!
I DON'T KNOW!
WERE THOSE ATTACKS A DISTRACTION?!
IS SOMETHING ELSE GOING DOWN TONIGHT?!
PLEASE DON'T--! IT'S THE HEAD...THE HEAD OF...OF...ACKKK--
FWAMMMM!
MAYBE...A CAPSULE OF HOLY WATER... REMOTELY ACTIVATED.
AS OF NOW, I'M LOCKING DOWN MI13. WE WILL NOT KEEP THE REST OF YOU INFORMED. NOT UNTIL YOU'VE CLEANED YOUR HOUSES. THIS IS OUR GAME AND WE WILL WIN IT.
MEETING ADJOURNED.

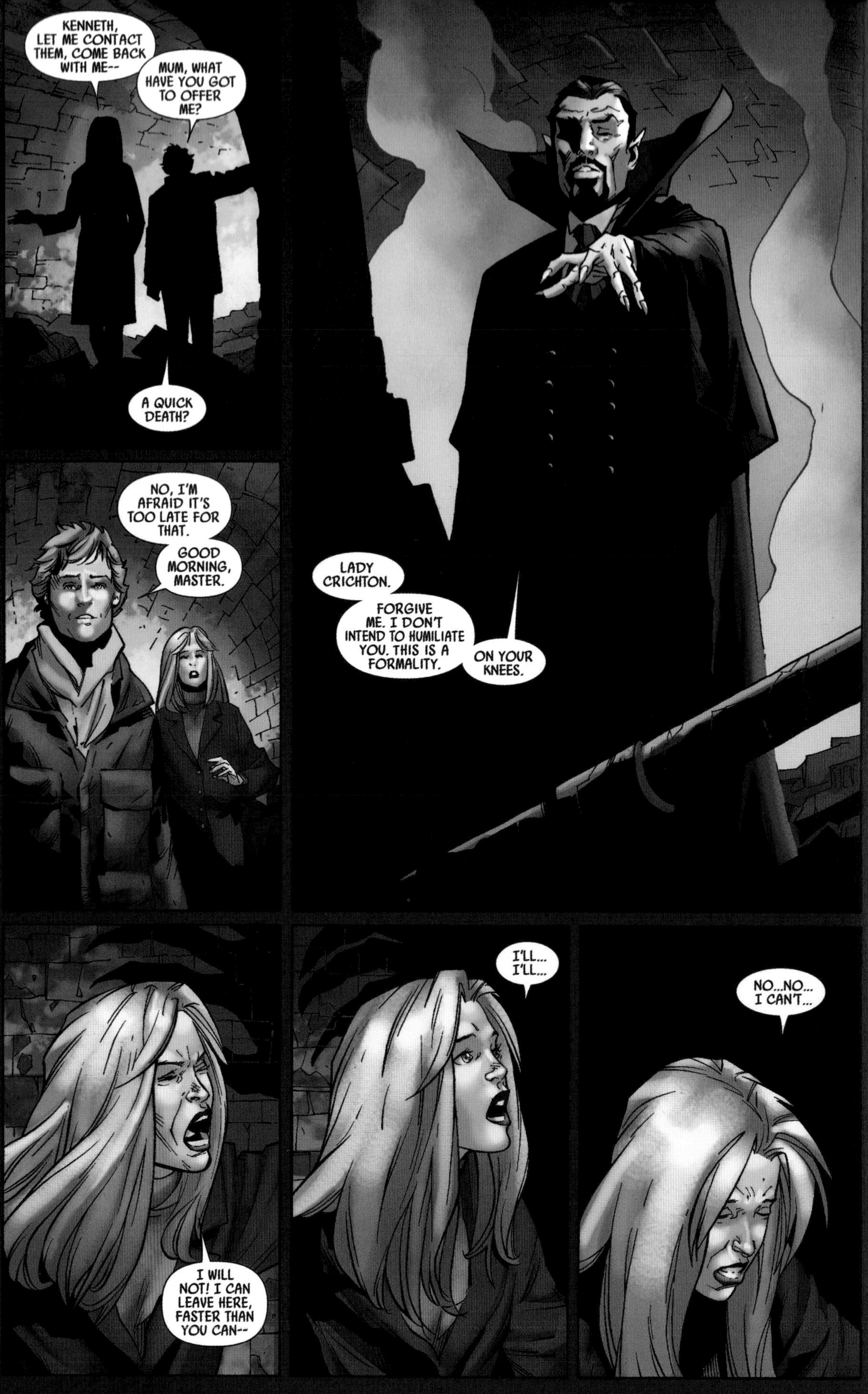
KENNETH, LET ME CONTACT THEM, COME BACK WITH ME--
MUM, WHAT HAVE YOU GOT TO OFFER ME?
A QUICK DEATH?
NO, I'M AFRAID IT'S TOO LATE FOR THAT.
GOOD MORNING, MASTER.
LADY CRICHTON.
FORGIVE ME. I DON'T INTEND TO HUMILIATE YOU. THIS IS A FORMALITY.
ON YOUR KNEES.
I WILL NOT! I CAN LEAVE HERE, FASTER THAN YOU CAN--
I'LL... I'LL...
NO...NO... I CAN'T...

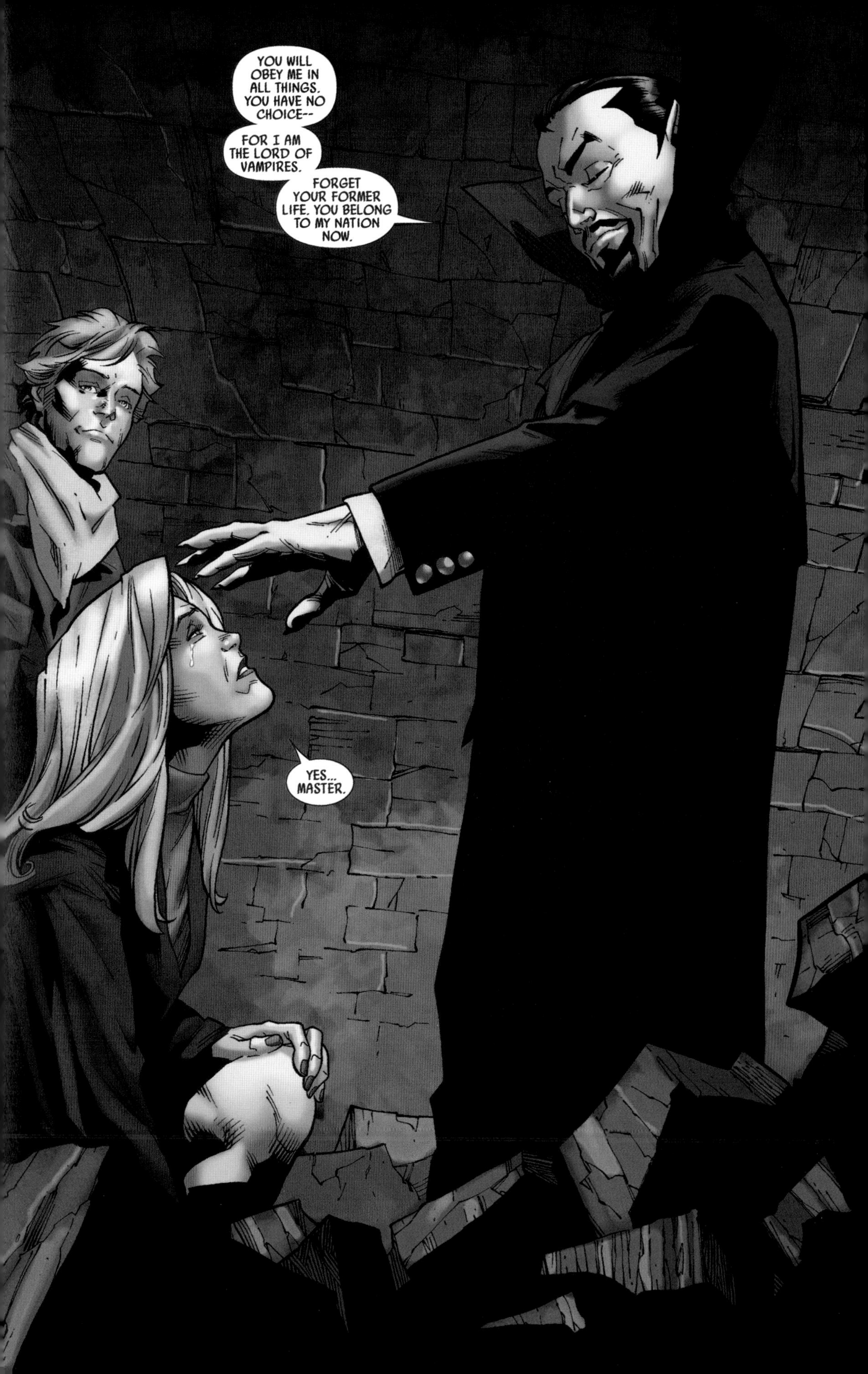
YOU WILL OBEY ME IN ALL THINGS. YOU HAVE NO CHOICE--
FOR I AM THE LORD OF VAMPIRES.
FORGET YOUR FORMER LIFE. YOU BELONG TO MY NATION NOW.
YES... MASTER.

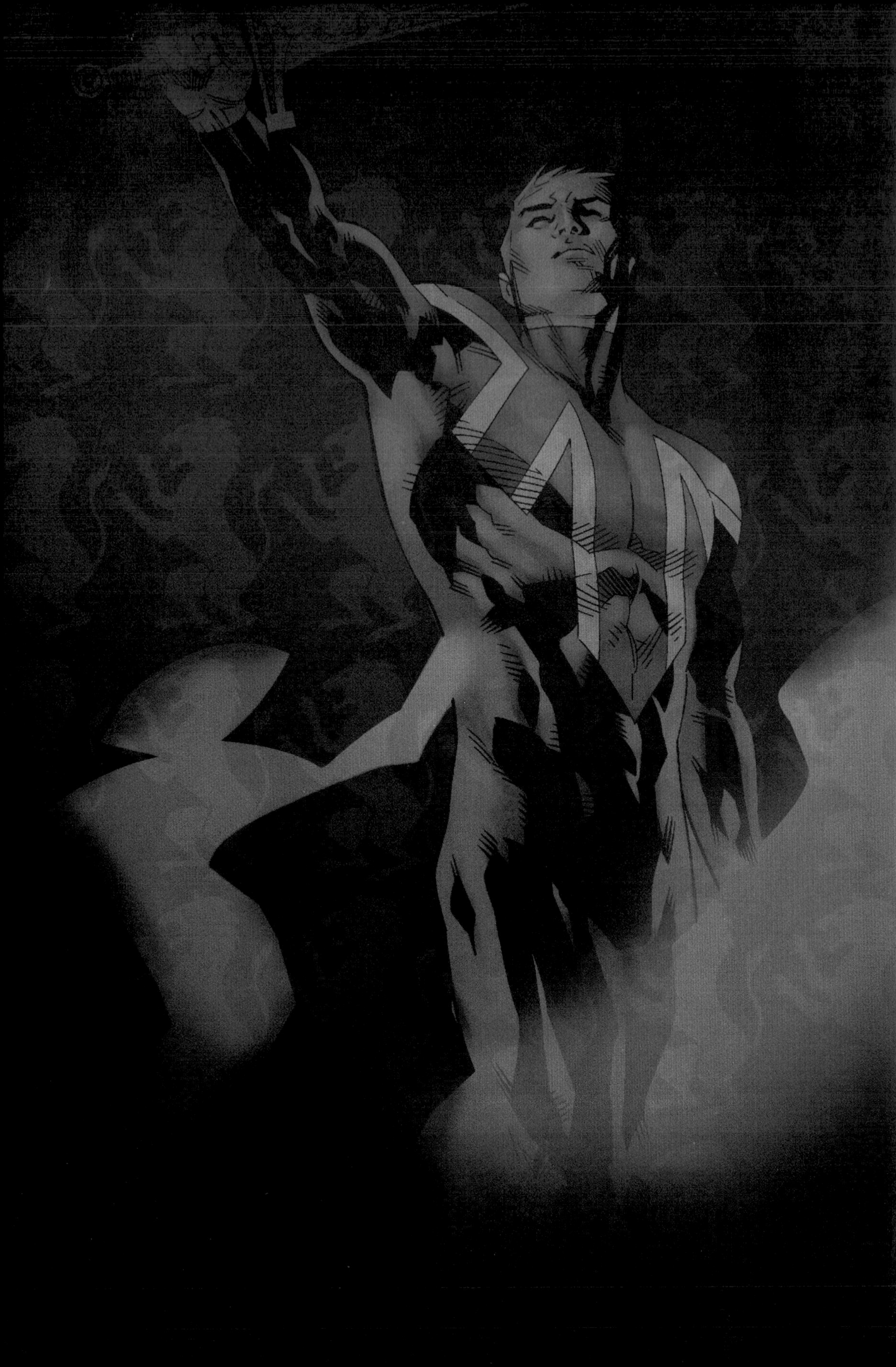

CAPTAIN BRITAIN AND MI13 #12
COVER ARTWORK

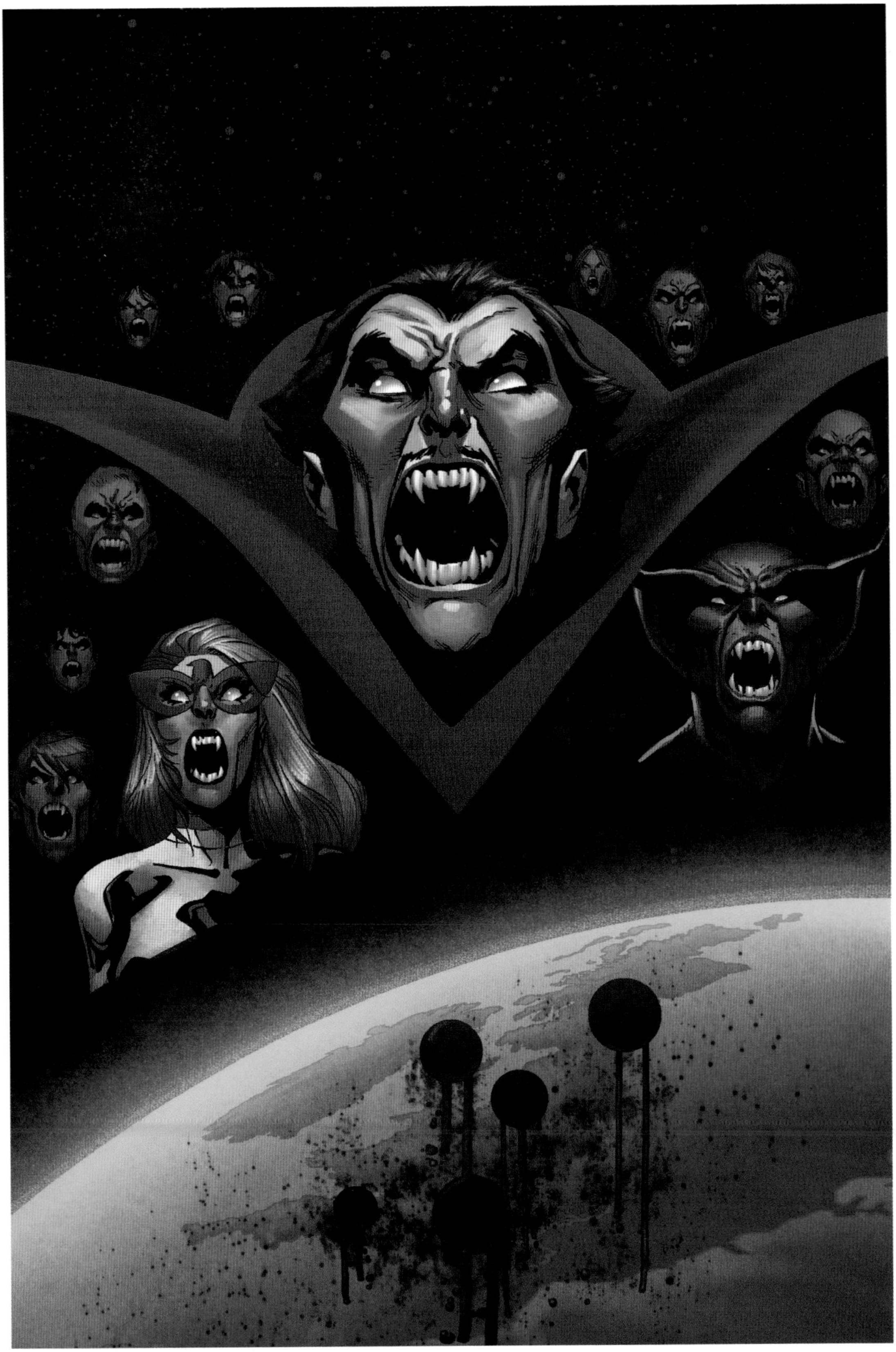

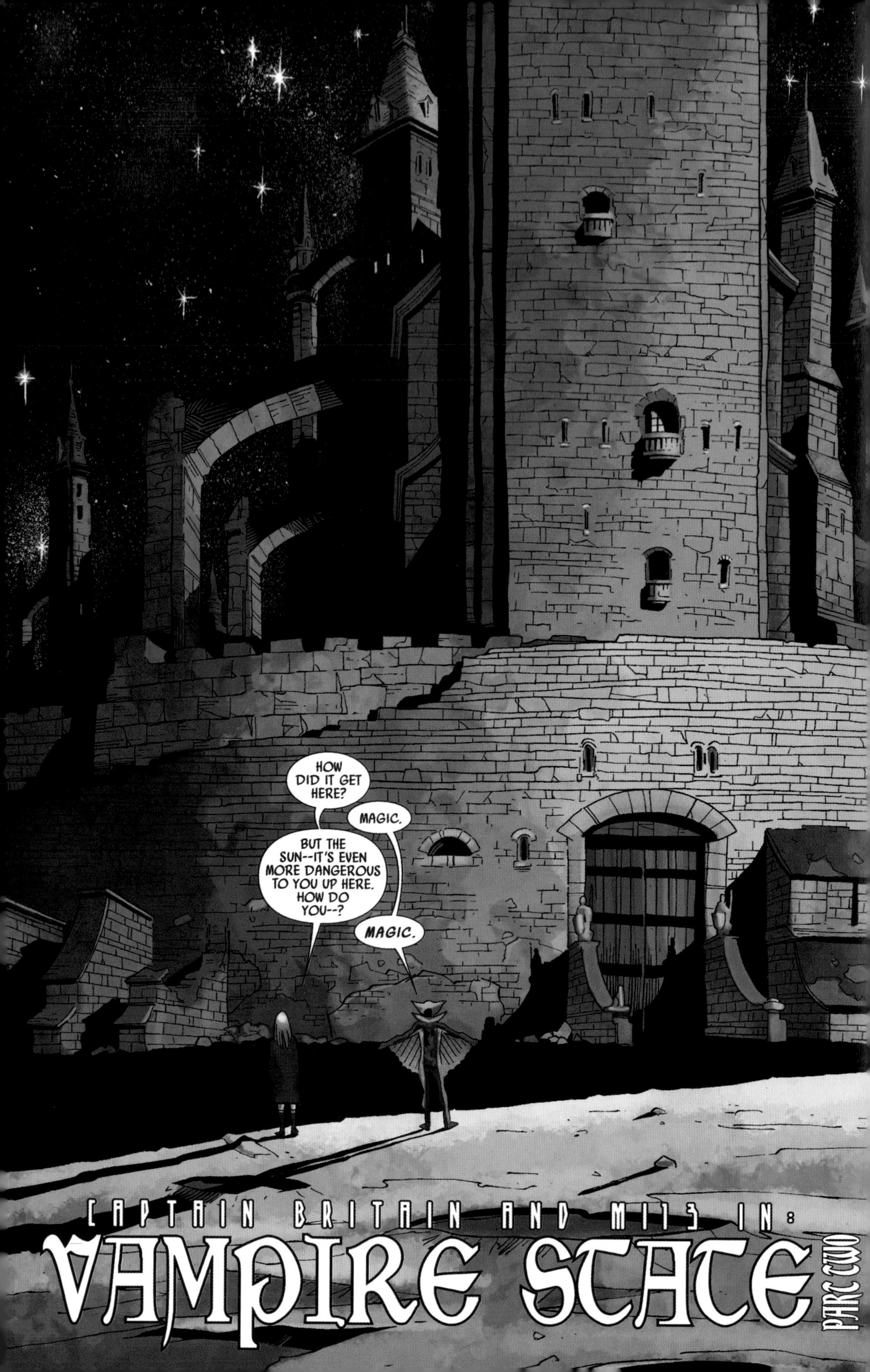
HOW DID IT GET HERE?
MAGIC.
BUT THE SUN--IT'S EVEN MORE DANGEROUS TO YOU UP HERE. HOW DO YOU--?
MAGIC.
CAPTAIN BRITAIN AND MI13 IN:
VAMPIRE STATE
PART TWO

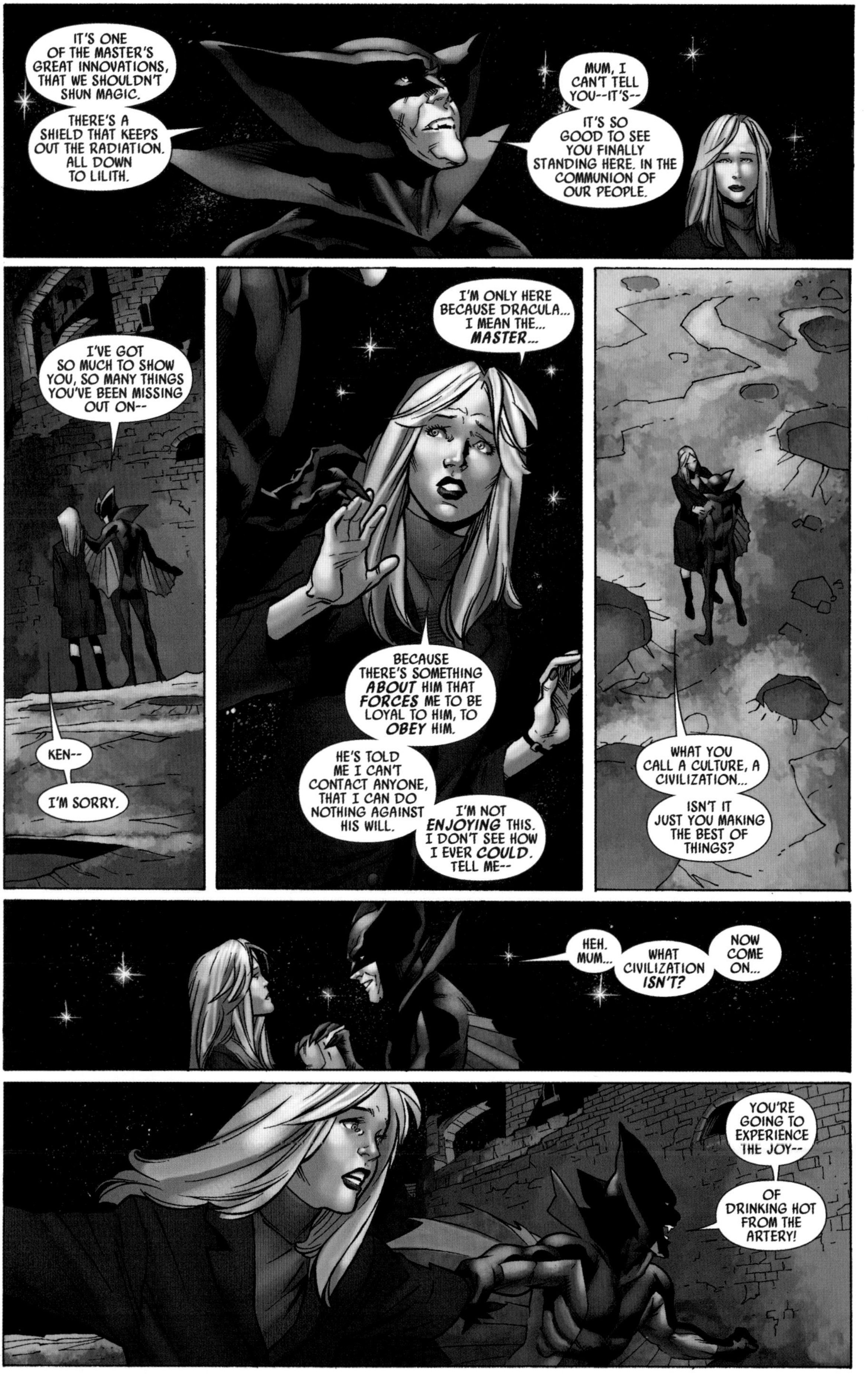
IT'S ONE OF THE MASTER'S GREAT INNOVATIONS, THAT WE SHOULDN'T SHUN MAGIC.
THERE'S A SHIELD THAT KEEPS OUT THE RADIATION. ALL DOWN TO LILITH.
MUM, I CAN'T TELL YOU--IT'S--
IT'S SO GOOD TO SEE YOU FINALLY STANDING HERE. IN THE COMMUNION OF OUR PEOPLE.
I'VE GOT SO MUCH TO SHOW YOU, SO MANY THINGS YOU'VE BEEN MISSING OUT ON--
KEN--
I'M SORRY.
I'M ONLY HERE BECAUSE DRACULA... I MEAN THE... MASTER...
BECAUSE THERE'S SOMETHING ABOUT HIM THAT FORCES ME TO BE LOYAL TO HIM, TO OBEY HIM.
HE'S TOLD ME I CAN'T CONTACT ANYONE, THAT I CAN DO NOTHING AGAINST HIS WILL.
I'M NOT ENJOYING THIS. I DON'T SEE HOW I EVER COULD. TELL ME--
WHAT YOU CALL A CULTURE, A CIVILIZATION...
ISN'T IT JUST YOU MAKING THE BEST OF THINGS?
HEH. MUM...
WHAT CIVILIZATION ISN'T?
NOW COME ON...
YOU'RE GOING TO EXPERIENCE THE JOY--
OF DRINKING HOT FROM THE ARTERY!

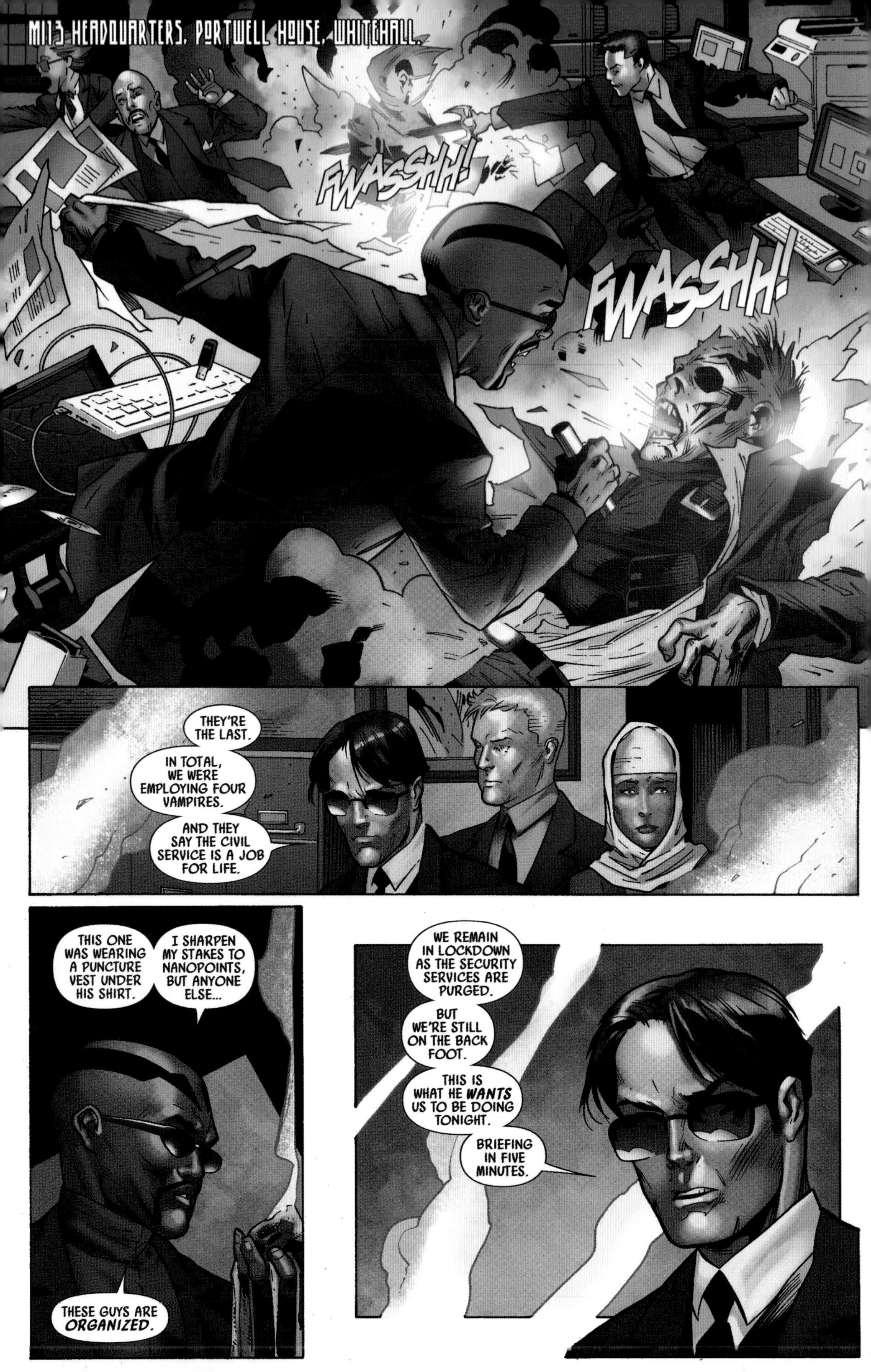
MI13 HEADQUARTERS, PORTWELL HOUSE, WHITEHALL.
FWASSHH!
FWASSHH!
THEY'RE THE LAST.
IN TOTAL, WE WERE EMPLOYING FOUR VAMPIRES.
AND THEY SAY THE CIVIL SERVICE IS A JOB FOR LIFE.
THIS ONE WAS WEARING A PUNCTURE VEST UNDER HIS SHIRT.
I SHARPEN MY STAKES TO NANOPOINTS, BUT ANYONE ELSE...
THESE GUYS ARE ORGANIZED.
WE REMAIN IN LOCKDOWN AS THE SECURITY SERVICES ARE PURGED.
BUT WE'RE STILL ON THE BACK FOOT.
THIS IS WHAT HE WANTS US TO BE DOING TONIGHT.
BRIEFING IN FIVE MINUTES.

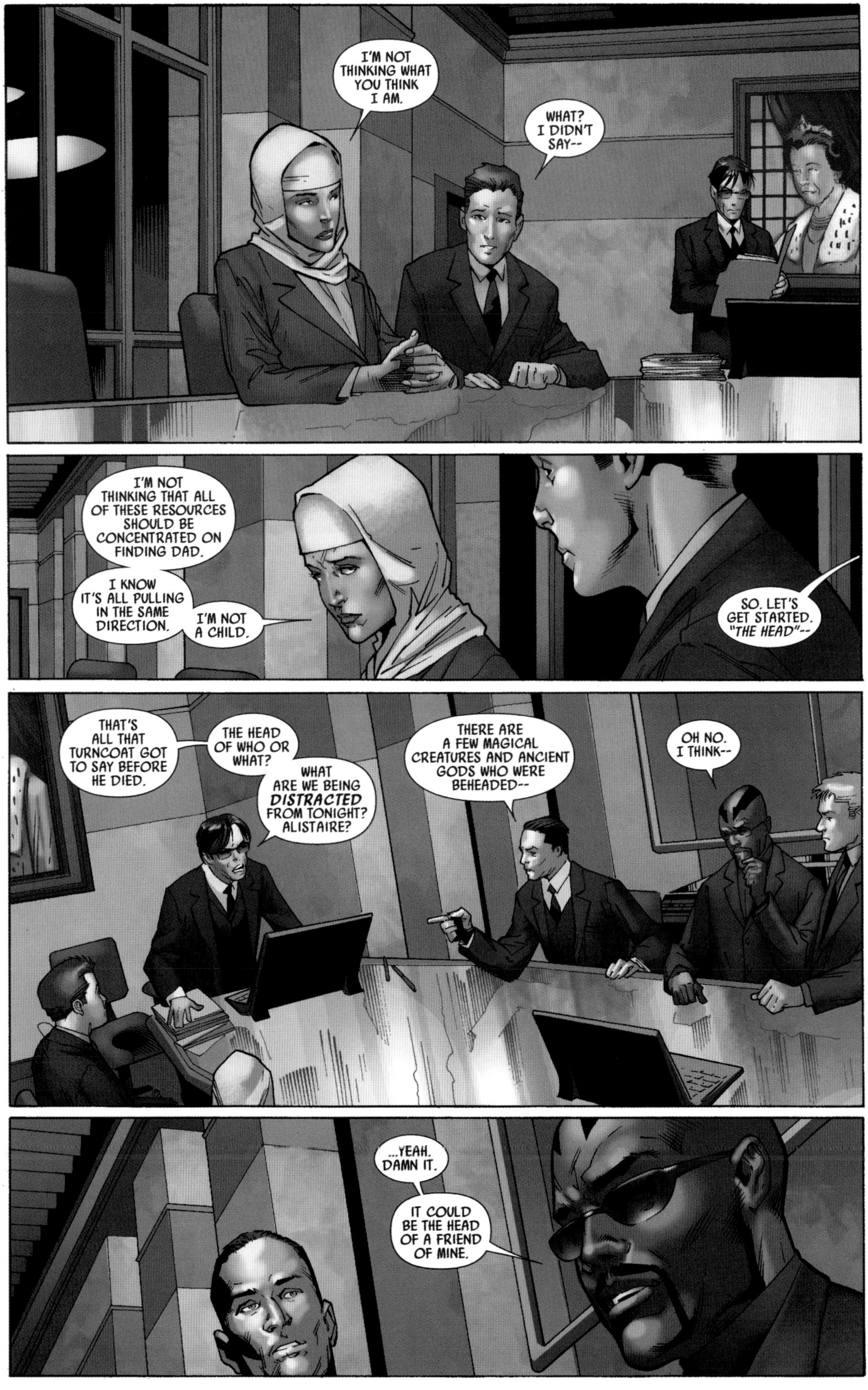
I'M NOT THINKING WHAT YOU THINK I AM.
WHAT? I DIDN'T SAY--
I'M NOT THINKING THAT ALL OF THESE RESOURCES SHOULD BE CONCENTRATED ON FINDING DAD.
I KNOW IT'S ALL PULLING IN THE SAME DIRECTION.
I'M NOT A CHILD.
SO. LET'S GET STARTED. "THE HEAD"--
THAT'S ALL THAT TURNCOAT GOT TO SAY BEFORE HE DIED.
THE HEAD OF WHO OR WHAT?
WHAT ARE WE BEING DISTRACTED FROM TONIGHT? ALISTAIRE?
THERE ARE A FEW MAGICAL CREATURES AND ANCIENT GODS WHO WERE BEHEADED--
OH NO. I THINK--
...YEAH. DAMN IT.
IT COULD BE THE HEAD OF A FRIEND OF MINE.

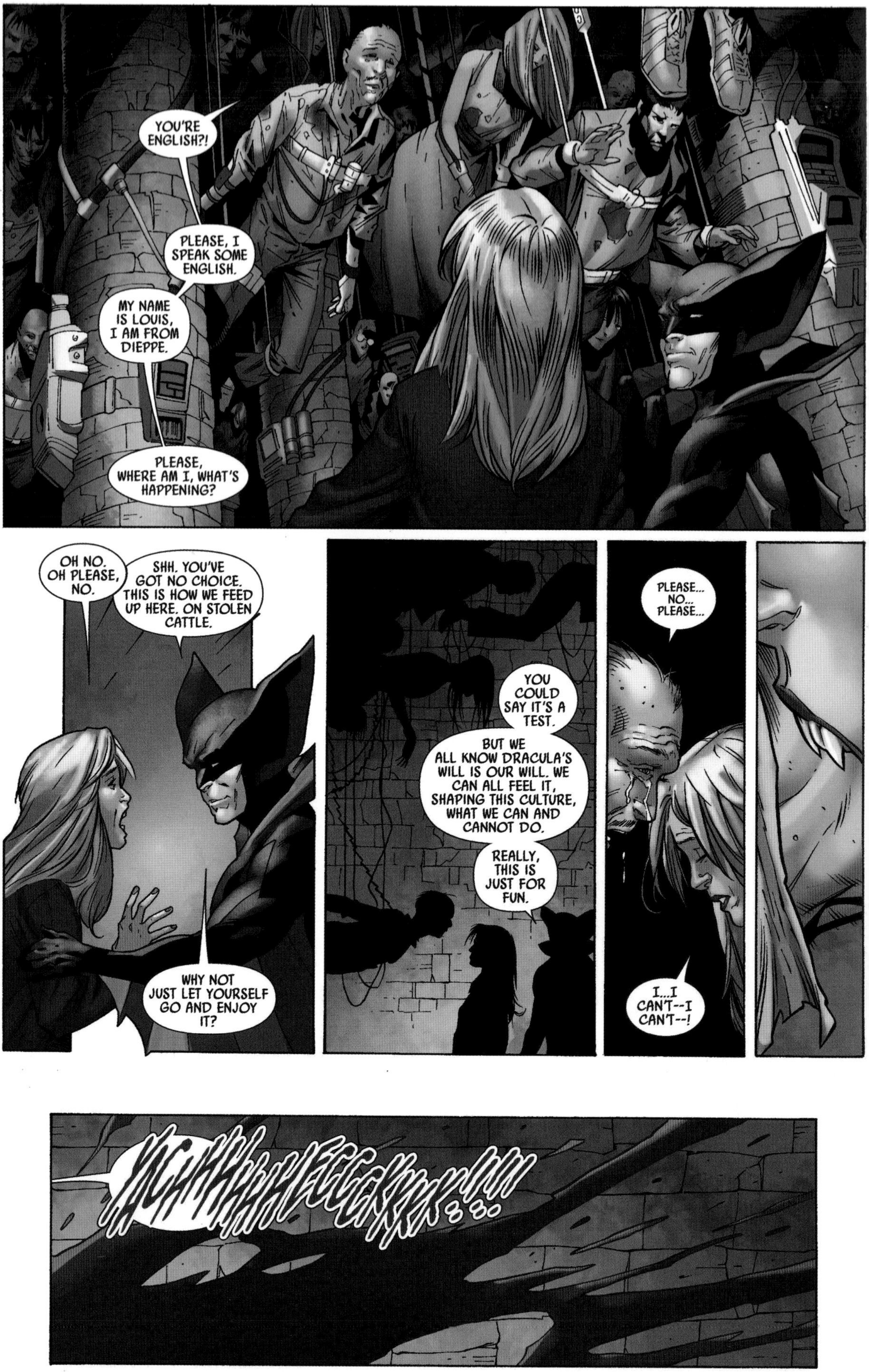
YOU'RE ENGLISH?!
PLEASE, I SPEAK SOME ENGLISH.
MY NAME IS LOUIS, I AM FROM DIEPPE.
PLEASE, WHERE AM I, WHAT'S HAPPENING?
OH NO. OH PLEASE, NO.
SHH. YOU'VE GOT NO CHOICE. THIS IS HOW WE FEED UP HERE. ON STOLEN CATTLE.
WHY NOT JUST LET YOURSELF GO AND ENJOY IT?
YOU COULD SAY IT'S A TEST.
BUT WE ALL KNOW DRACULA'S WILL IS OUR WILL. WE CAN ALL FEEL IT, SHAPING THIS CULTURE, WHAT WE CAN AND CANNOT DO.
REALLY, THIS IS JUST FOR FUN.
PLEASE... NO... PLEASE...
I...I CAN'T--I CAN'T--!

QUINCY HARKER. OLD COMRADE.

HE GAVE HIS LIFE TO DESTROY DRACULA. BROUGHT DOWN HIS CASTLE, USING EXPLOSIVES.

KILLED HIMSELF IN THE PROCESS.

WHAT *VERY* FEW PEOPLE KNOW IS, HE LEFT A *WILL*.

WITH SPECIFIC INSTRUCTIONS CONCERNING HIS EARTHLY REMAINS.

I THOUGHT YOU WERE A GADGET PERSON?

USUALLY. BUT AS WE'RE FINDING OUT: VAMPIRES USE COMPUTERS.

SO MY NOTEBOOK'S NOT A BLACKBERRY, BUT A PALIMPSEST, A BOOK WRITTEN OVER AN OLDER BOOK.

IN THIS CASE, A GIDEON BIBLE.

HERE IT IS...

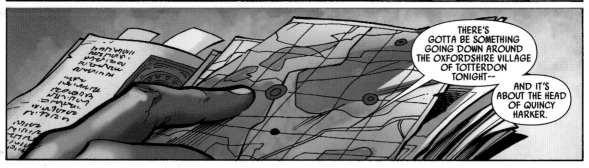

THERE'S GOTTA BE SOMETHING GOING DOWN AROUND THE OXFORDSHIRE VILLAGE OF TOTTERDON TONIGHT--

AND IT'S ABOUT THE HEAD OF QUINCY HARKER.

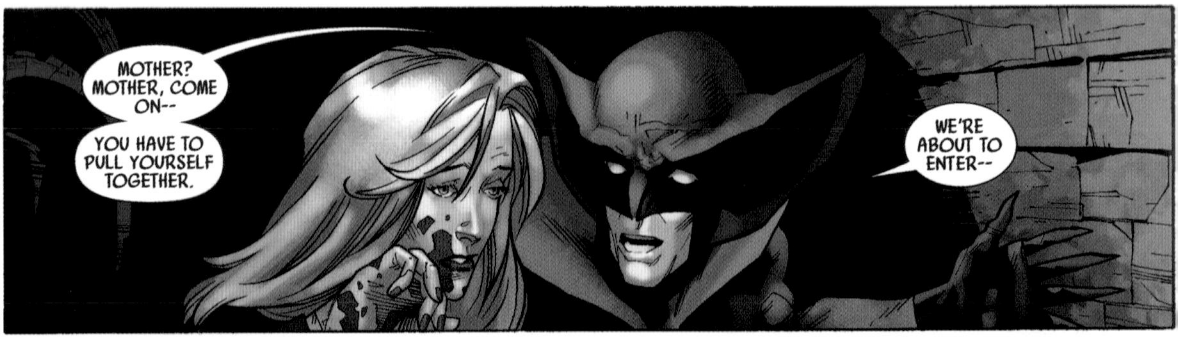
MOTHER? MOTHER, COME ON--
YOU HAVE TO PULL YOURSELF TOGETHER.
WE'RE ABOUT TO ENTER--

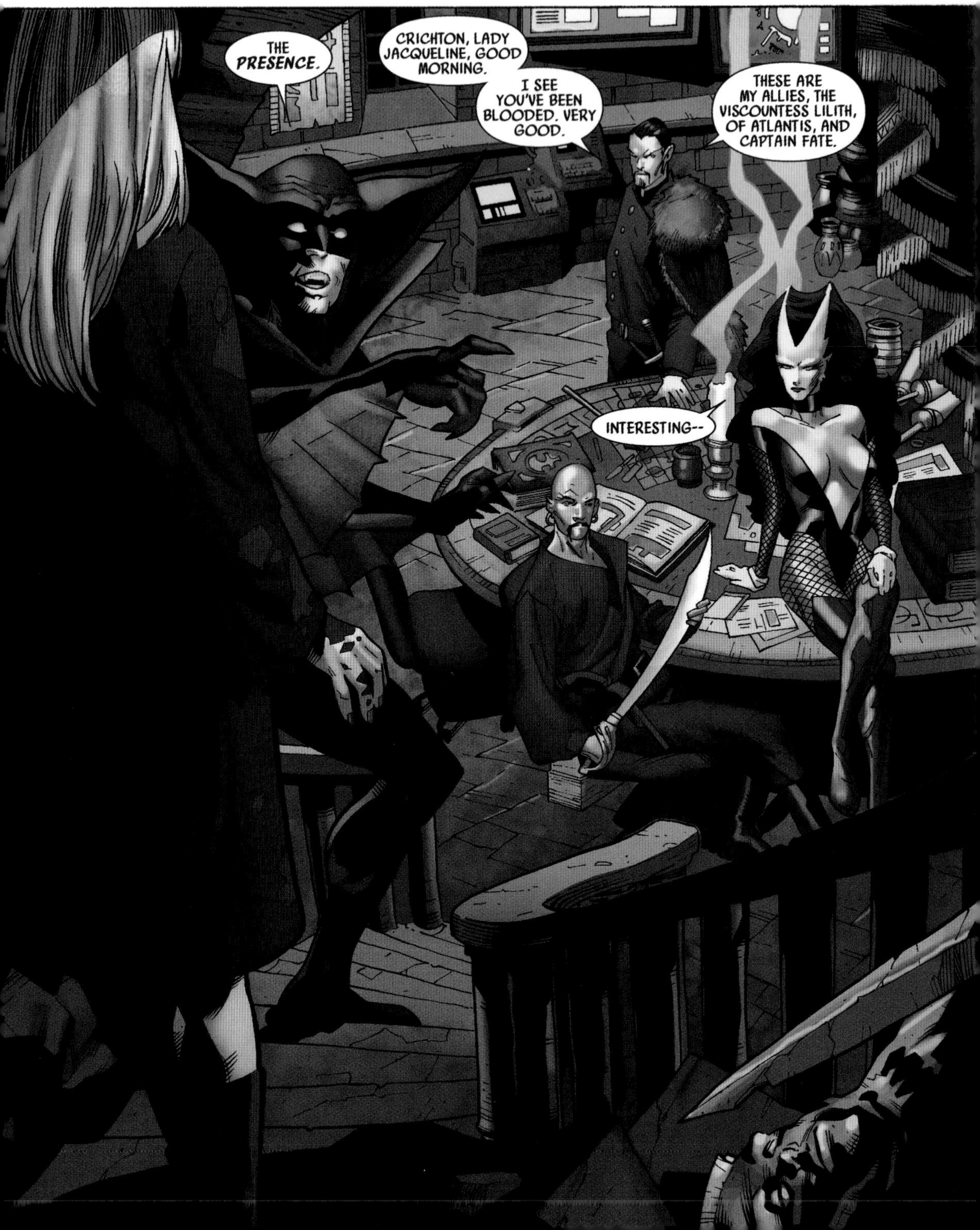
THE *PRESENCE*.
CRICHTON, LADY JACQUELINE, GOOD MORNING.
I SEE YOU'VE BEEN BLOODED. VERY GOOD.
THESE ARE MY ALLIES, THE VISCOUNTESS LILITH, OF ATLANTIS, AND CAPTAIN FATE.
INTERESTING--

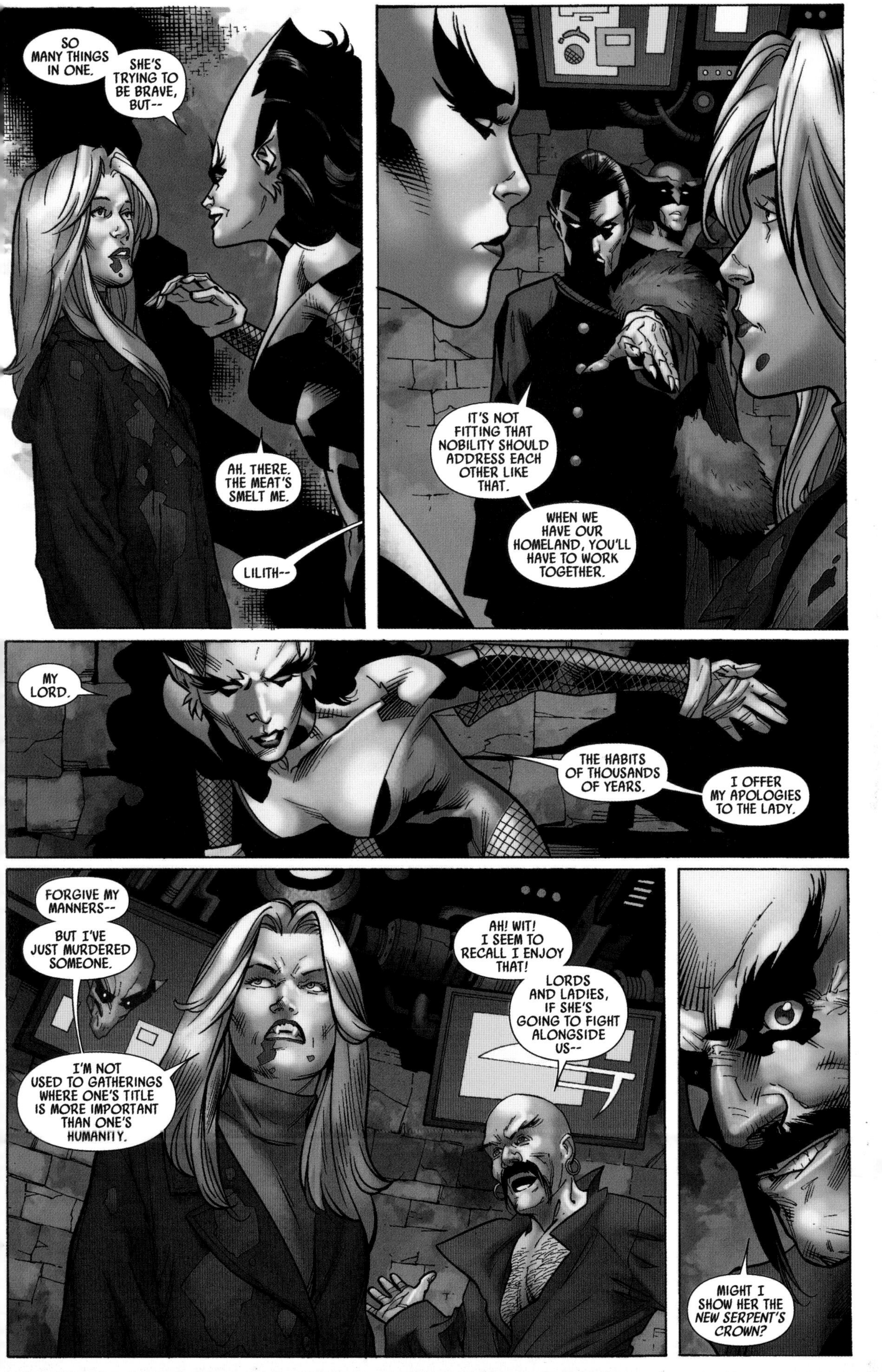
SO MANY THINGS IN ONE.
SHE'S TRYING TO BE BRAVE, BUT--
AH. THERE. THE MEAT'S SMELT ME.
LILITH--
IT'S NOT FITTING THAT NOBILITY SHOULD ADDRESS EACH OTHER LIKE THAT.
WHEN WE HAVE OUR HOMELAND, YOU'LL HAVE TO WORK TOGETHER.
MY LORD.
THE HABITS OF THOUSANDS OF YEARS.
I OFFER MY APOLOGIES TO THE LADY.
FORGIVE MY MANNERS--
BUT I'VE JUST MURDERED SOMEONE.
I'M NOT USED TO GATHERINGS WHERE ONE'S TITLE IS MORE IMPORTANT THAN ONE'S HUMANITY.
AH! WIT! I SEEM TO RECALL I ENJOY THAT!
LORDS AND LADIES, IF SHE'S GOING TO FIGHT ALONGSIDE US--
MIGHT I SHOW HER THE NEW SERPENT'S CROWN?

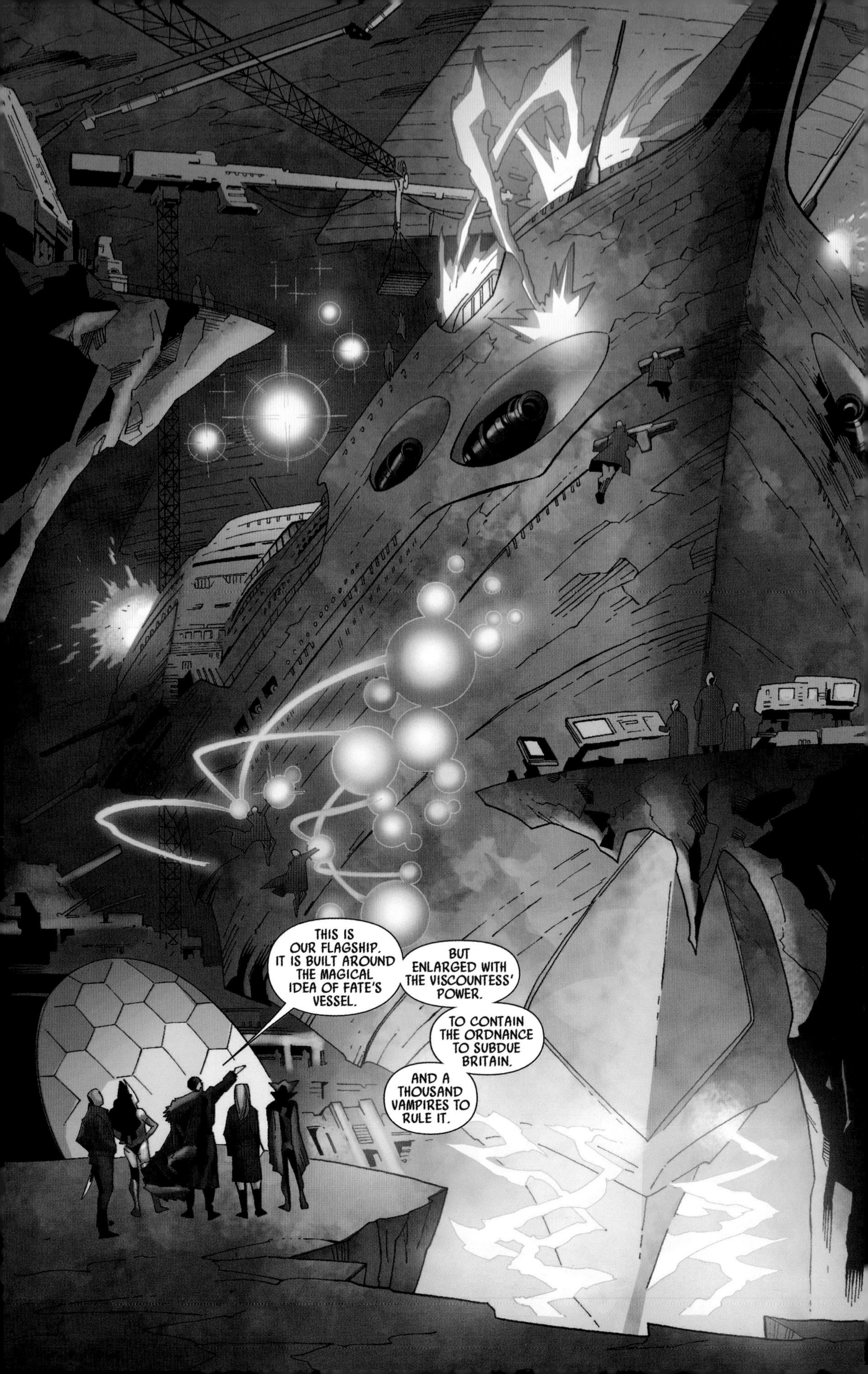
THIS IS OUR FLAGSHIP. IT IS BUILT AROUND THE MAGICAL IDEA OF FATE'S VESSEL.
BUT ENLARGED WITH THE VISCOUNTESS' POWER.
TO CONTAIN THE ORDNANCE TO SUBDUE BRITAIN.
AND A THOUSAND VAMPIRES TO RULE IT.

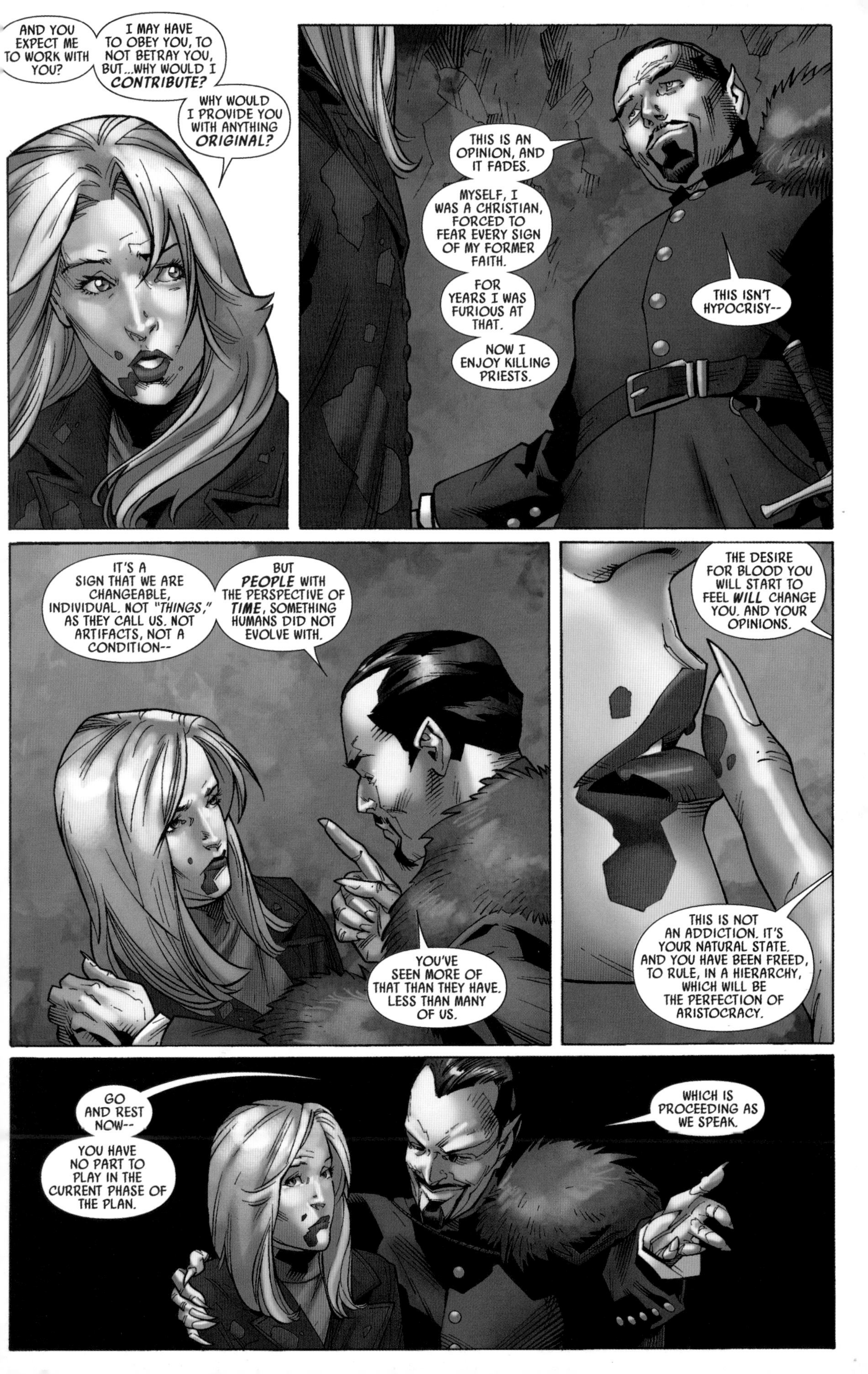
AND YOU EXPECT ME TO WORK WITH YOU?
I MAY HAVE TO OBEY YOU, TO NOT BETRAY YOU, BUT...WHY WOULD I CONTRIBUTE?
WHY WOULD I PROVIDE YOU WITH ANYTHING ORIGINAL?
THIS IS AN OPINION, AND IT FADES.
MYSELF, I WAS A CHRISTIAN, FORCED TO FEAR EVERY SIGN OF MY FORMER FAITH.
FOR YEARS I WAS FURIOUS AT THAT.
NOW I ENJOY KILLING PRIESTS.
THIS ISN'T HYPOCRISY--
IT'S A SIGN THAT WE ARE CHANGEABLE, INDIVIDUAL. NOT "THINGS," AS THEY CALL US. NOT ARTIFACTS, NOT A CONDITION--
BUT PEOPLE WITH THE PERSPECTIVE OF TIME, SOMETHING HUMANS DID NOT EVOLVE WITH.
YOU'VE SEEN MORE OF THAT THAN THEY HAVE. LESS THAN MANY OF US.
THE DESIRE FOR BLOOD YOU WILL START TO FEEL WILL CHANGE YOU. AND YOUR OPINIONS.
THIS IS NOT AN ADDICTION. IT'S YOUR NATURAL STATE. AND YOU HAVE BEEN FREED, TO RULE, IN A HIERARCHY, WHICH WILL BE THE PERFECTION OF ARISTOCRACY.
GO AND REST NOW--
YOU HAVE NO PART TO PLAY IN THE CURRENT PHASE OF THE PLAN.
WHICH IS PROCEEDING AS WE SPEAK.

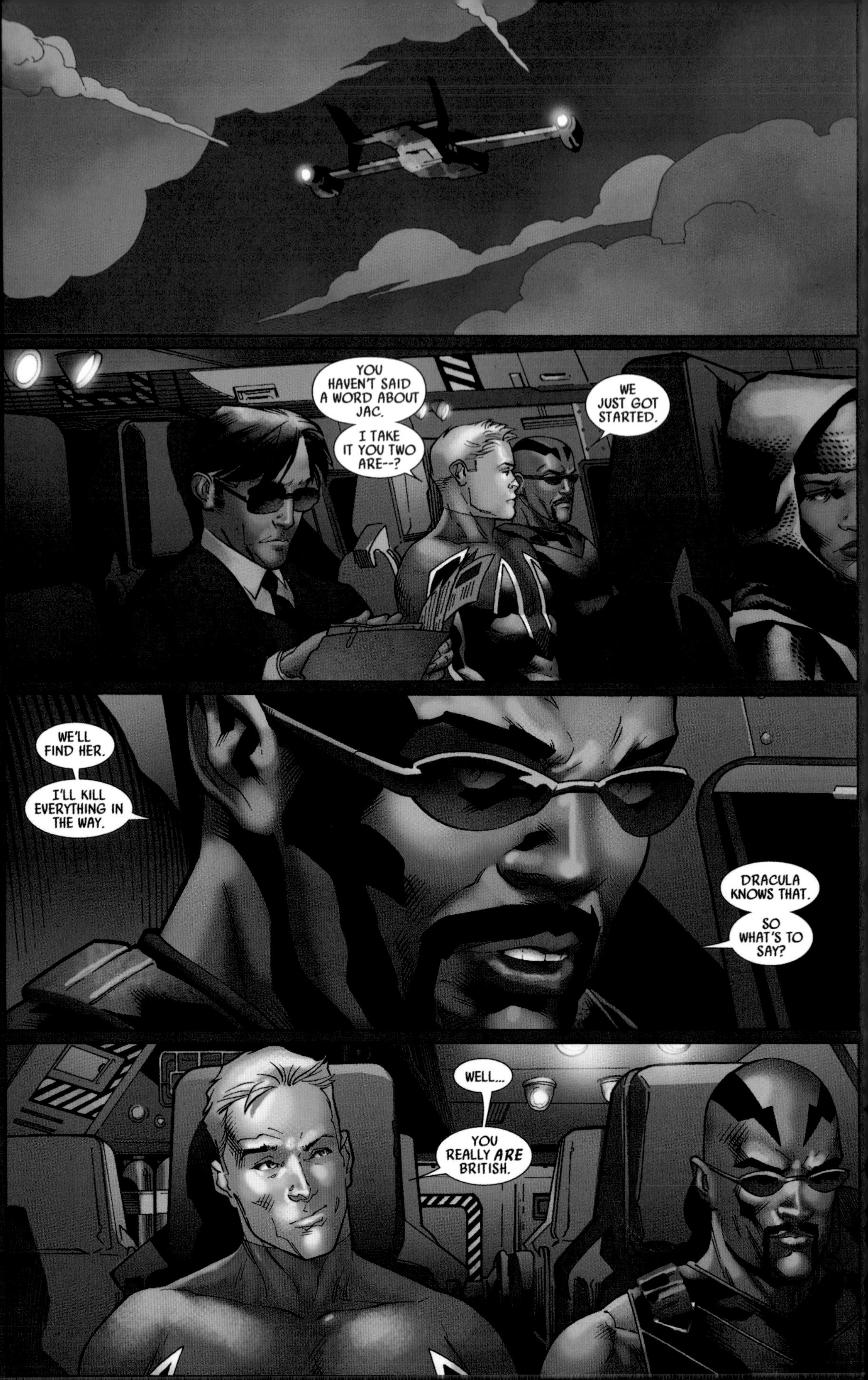

YOU HAVEN'T SAID A WORD ABOUT JAC.
I TAKE IT YOU TWO ARE--?
WE JUST GOT STARTED.
WE'LL FIND HER.
I'LL KILL EVERYTHING IN THE WAY.
DRACULA KNOWS THAT.
SO WHAT'S TO SAY?
WELL...
YOU REALLY *ARE* BRITISH.

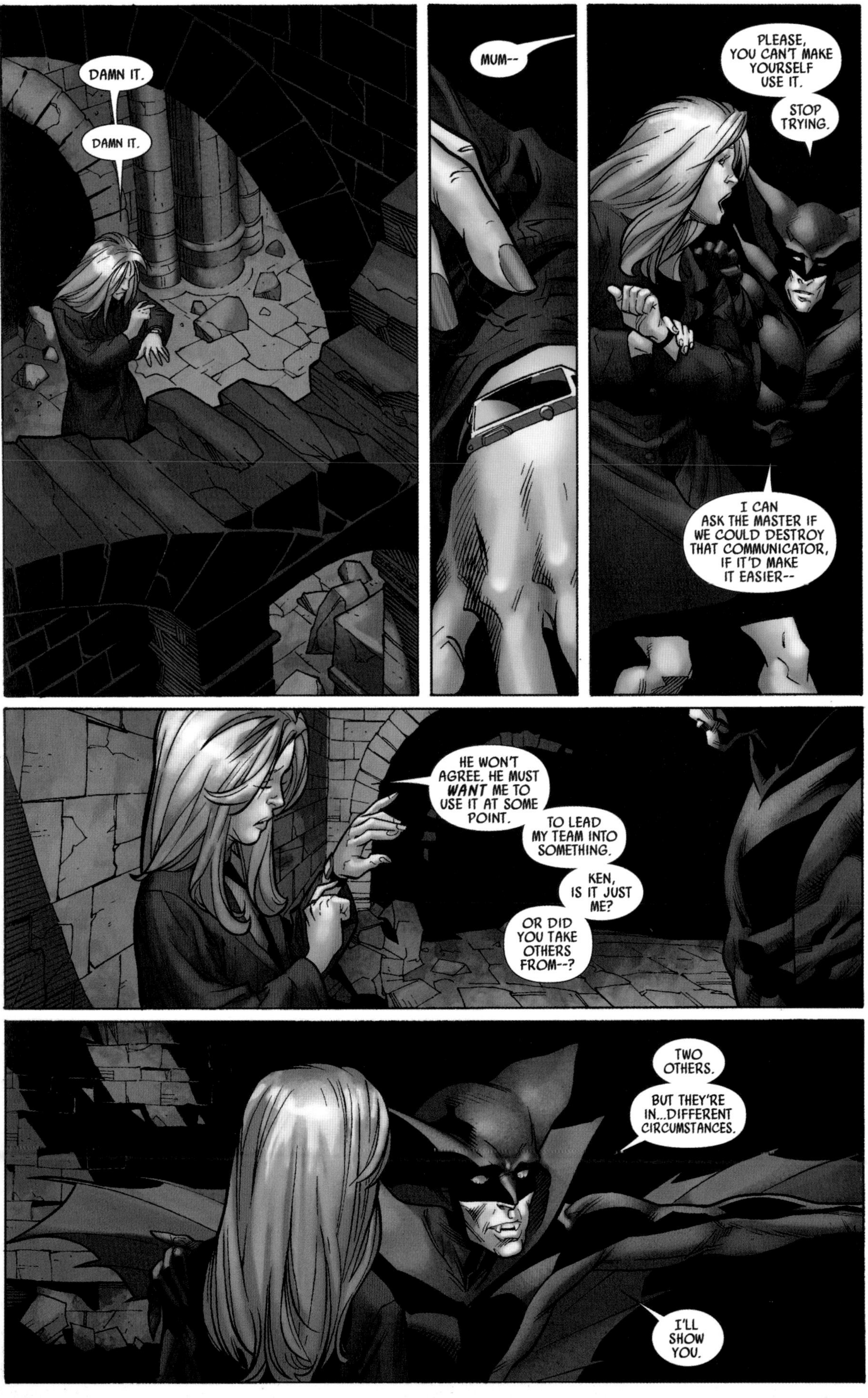
DAMN IT.
DAMN IT.
MUM--
PLEASE, YOU CAN'T MAKE YOURSELF USE IT.
STOP TRYING.
I CAN ASK THE MASTER IF WE COULD DESTROY THAT COMMUNICATOR, IF IT'D MAKE IT EASIER--
HE WON'T AGREE. HE MUST *WANT* ME TO USE IT AT SOME POINT.
TO LEAD MY TEAM INTO SOMETHING.
KEN, IS IT JUST ME?
OR DID YOU TAKE OTHERS FROM--?
TWO OTHERS.
BUT THEY'RE IN...DIFFERENT CIRCUMSTANCES.
I'LL SHOW YOU.

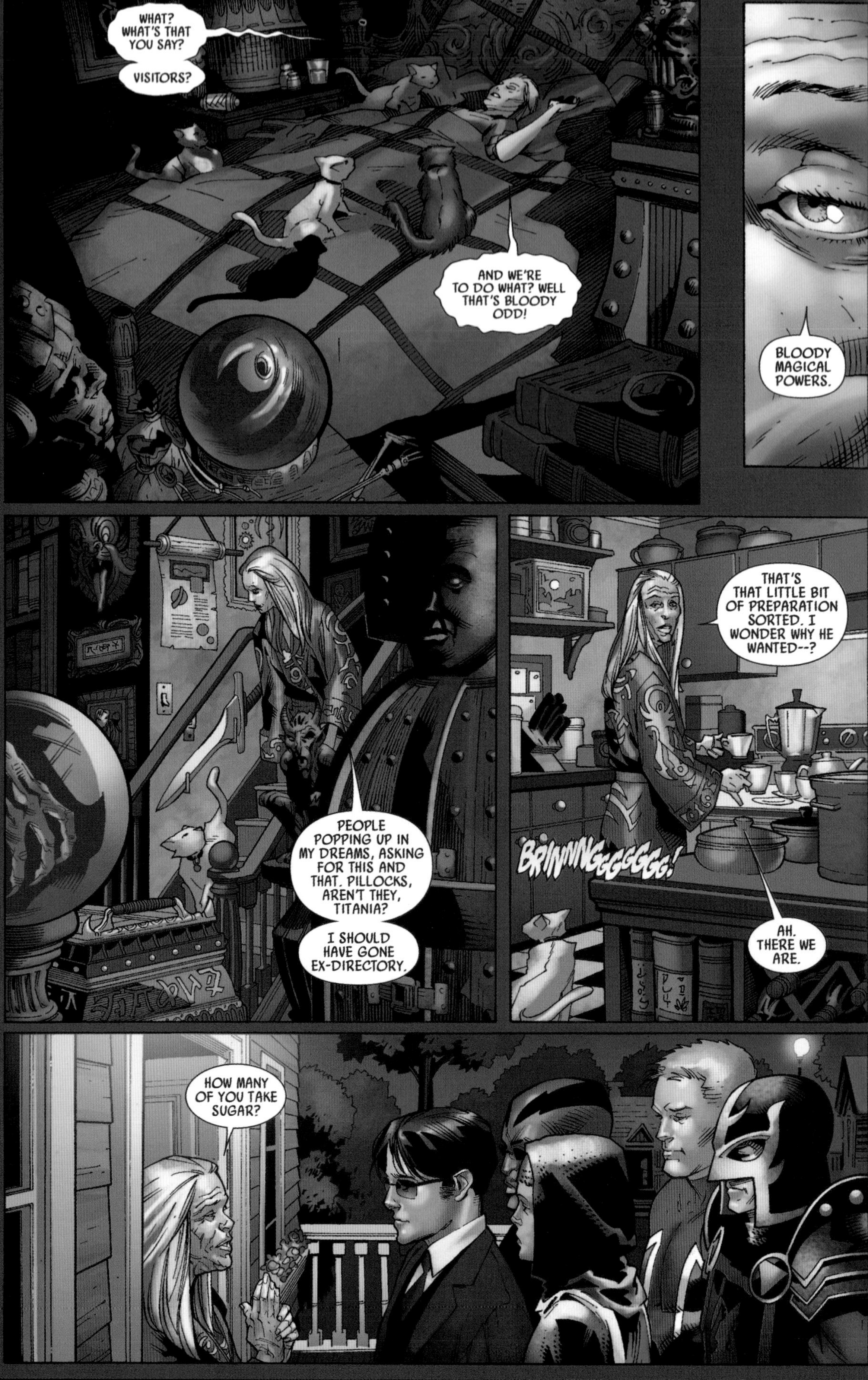
WHAT? WHAT'S THAT YOU SAY?
VISITORS?
AND WE'RE TO DO WHAT? WELL THAT'S BLOODY ODD!
BLOODY MAGICAL POWERS.
PEOPLE POPPING UP IN MY DREAMS, ASKING FOR THIS AND THAT. PILLOCKS, AREN'T THEY, TITANIA?
I SHOULD HAVE GONE EX-DIRECTORY.
THAT'S THAT LITTLE BIT OF PREPARATION SORTED. I WONDER WHY HE WANTED--?
BRINNNGGGGGG!
AH. THERE WE ARE.
HOW MANY OF YOU TAKE SUGAR?

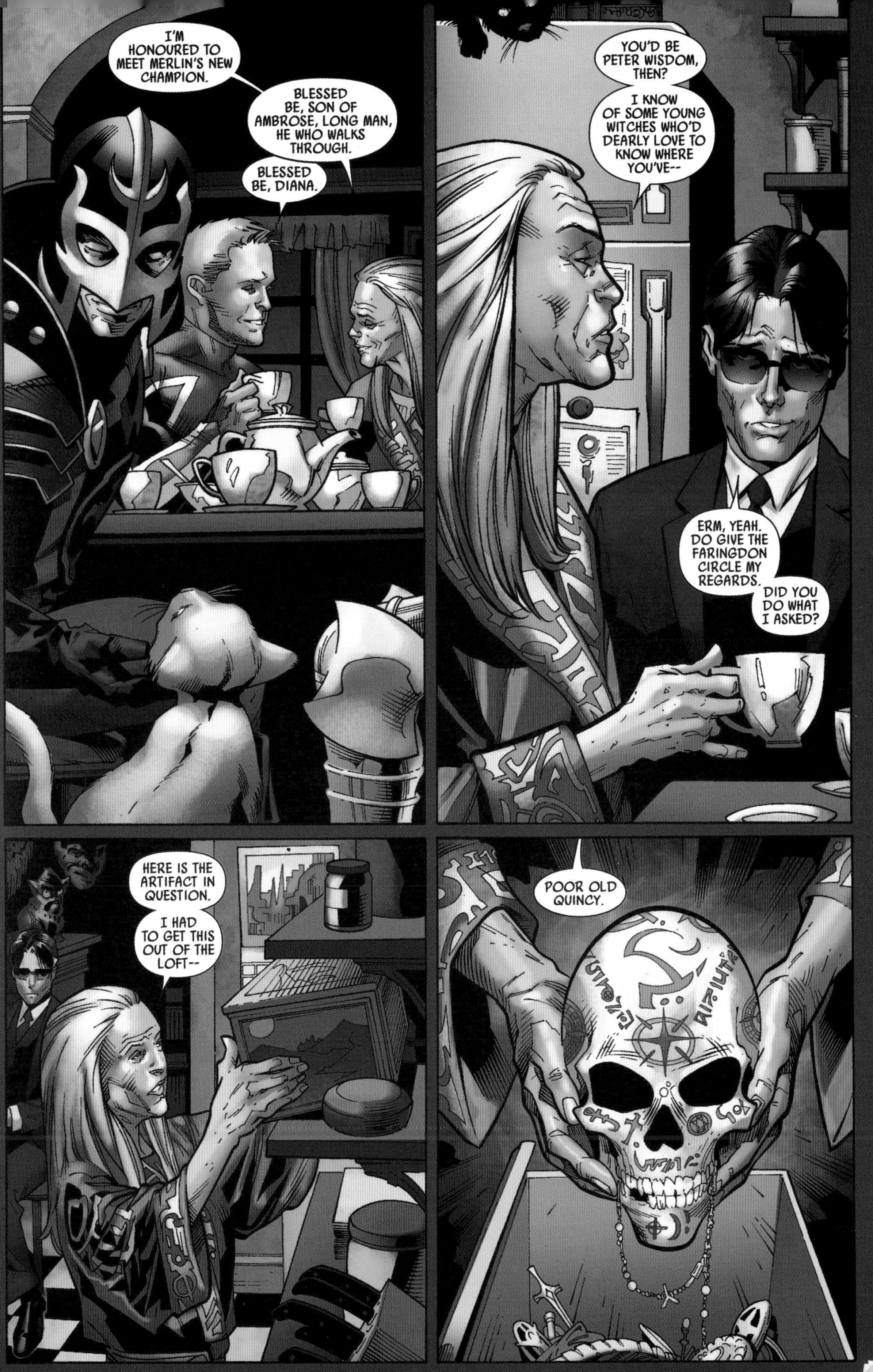
I'M HONOURED TO MEET MERLIN'S NEW CHAMPION.
BLESSED BE, SON OF AMBROSE, LONG MAN, HE WHO WALKS THROUGH.
BLESSED BE, DIANA.
YOU'D BE PETER WISDOM, THEN?
I KNOW OF SOME YOUNG WITCHES WHO'D DEARLY LOVE TO KNOW WHERE YOU'VE--
ERM, YEAH. DO GIVE THE FARINGDON CIRCLE MY REGARDS.
DID YOU DO WHAT I ASKED?
HERE IS THE ARTIFACT IN QUESTION.
I HAD TO GET THIS OUT OF THE LOFT--
POOR OLD QUINCY.

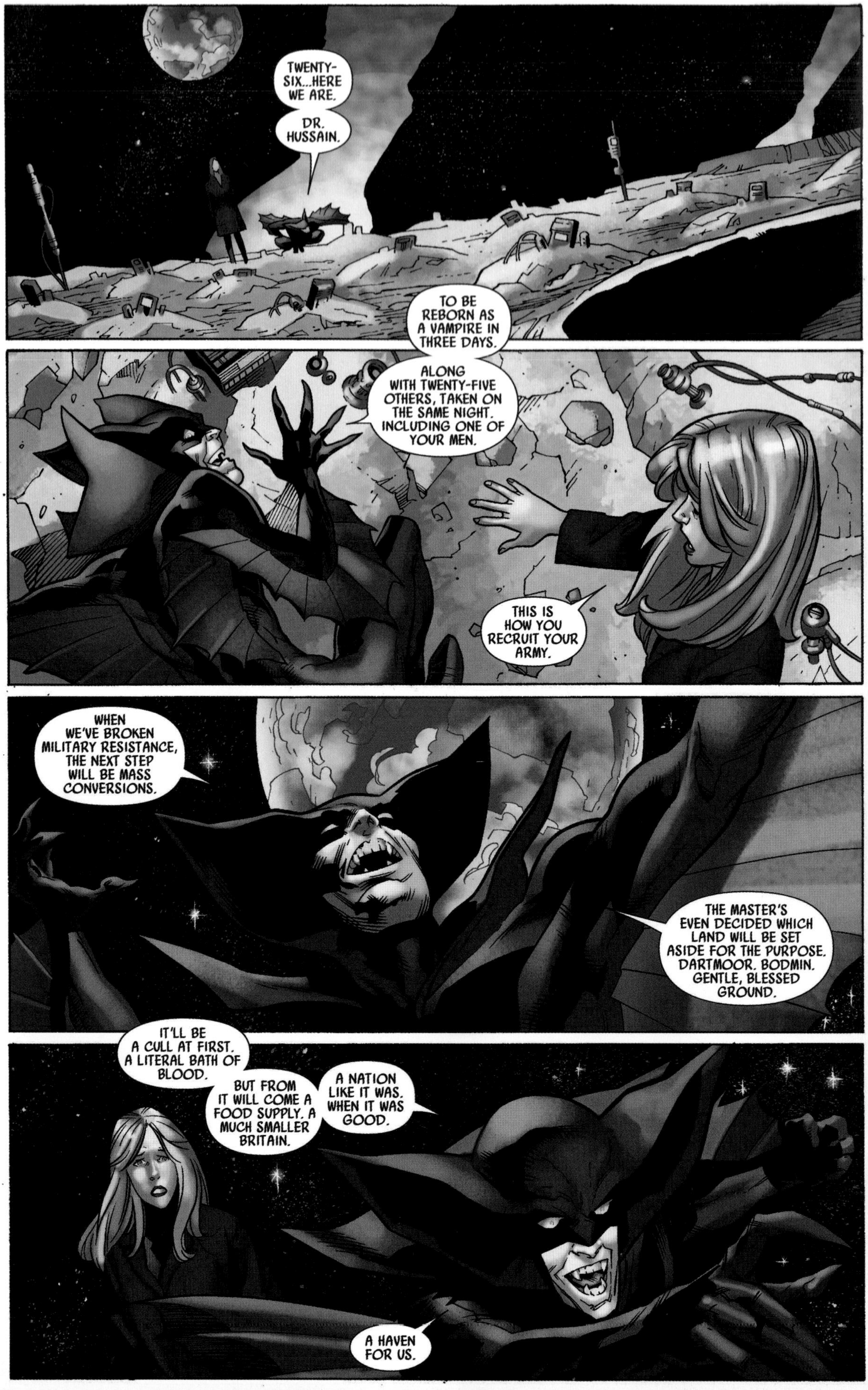

TWENTY-SIX...HERE WE ARE.
DR. HUSSAIN.
TO BE REBORN AS A VAMPIRE IN THREE DAYS.
ALONG WITH TWENTY-FIVE OTHERS, TAKEN ON THE SAME NIGHT. INCLUDING ONE OF YOUR MEN.
THIS IS HOW YOU RECRUIT YOUR ARMY.
WHEN WE'VE BROKEN MILITARY RESISTANCE, THE NEXT STEP WILL BE MASS CONVERSIONS.
THE MASTER'S EVEN DECIDED WHICH LAND WILL BE SET ASIDE FOR THE PURPOSE. DARTMOOR. BODMIN. GENTLE, BLESSED GROUND.
IT'LL BE A CULL AT FIRST. A LITERAL BATH OF BLOOD.
BUT FROM IT WILL COME A FOOD SUPPLY. A MUCH SMALLER BRITAIN.
A NATION LIKE IT WAS. WHEN IT WAS GOOD.
A HAVEN FOR US.

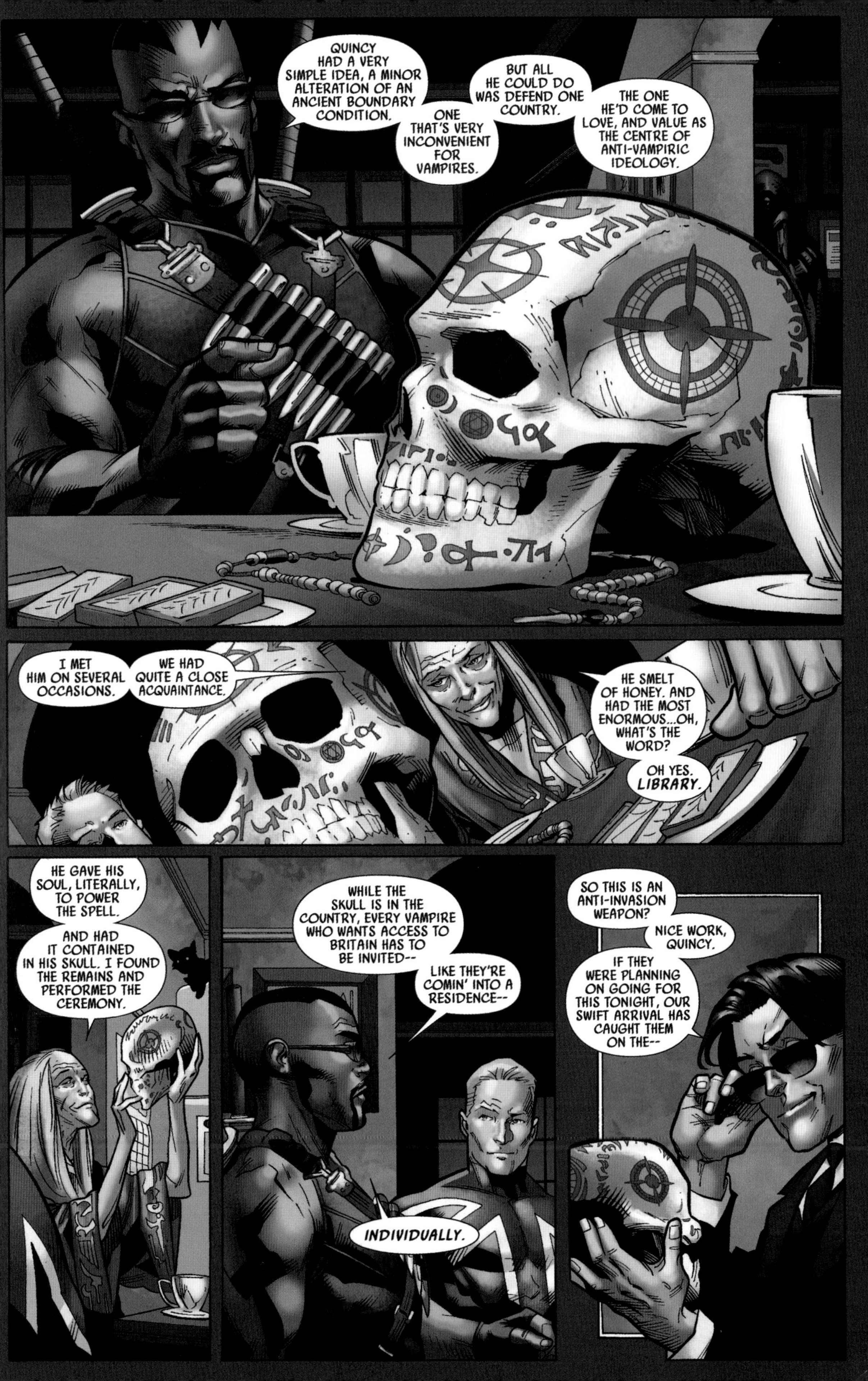
QUINCY HAD A VERY SIMPLE IDEA, A MINOR ALTERATION OF AN ANCIENT BOUNDARY CONDITION.
ONE THAT'S VERY INCONVENIENT FOR VAMPIRES.
BUT ALL HE COULD DO WAS DEFEND ONE COUNTRY.
THE ONE HE'D COME TO LOVE, AND VALUE AS THE CENTRE OF ANTI-VAMPIRIC IDEOLOGY.
I MET HIM ON SEVERAL OCCASIONS.
WE HAD QUITE A CLOSE ACQUAINTANCE.
HE SMELT OF HONEY. AND HAD THE MOST ENORMOUS...OH, WHAT'S THE WORD?
OH YES. LIBRARY.
HE GAVE HIS SOUL, LITERALLY, TO POWER THE SPELL.
AND HAD IT CONTAINED IN HIS SKULL. I FOUND THE REMAINS AND PERFORMED THE CEREMONY.
WHILE THE SKULL IS IN THE COUNTRY, EVERY VAMPIRE WHO WANTS ACCESS TO BRITAIN HAS TO BE INVITED--
LIKE THEY'RE COMIN' INTO A RESIDENCE--
INDIVIDUALLY.
SO THIS IS AN ANTI-INVASION WEAPON?
NICE WORK, QUINCY.
IF THEY WERE PLANNING ON GOING FOR THIS TONIGHT, OUR SWIFT ARRIVAL HAS CAUGHT THEM ON THE--

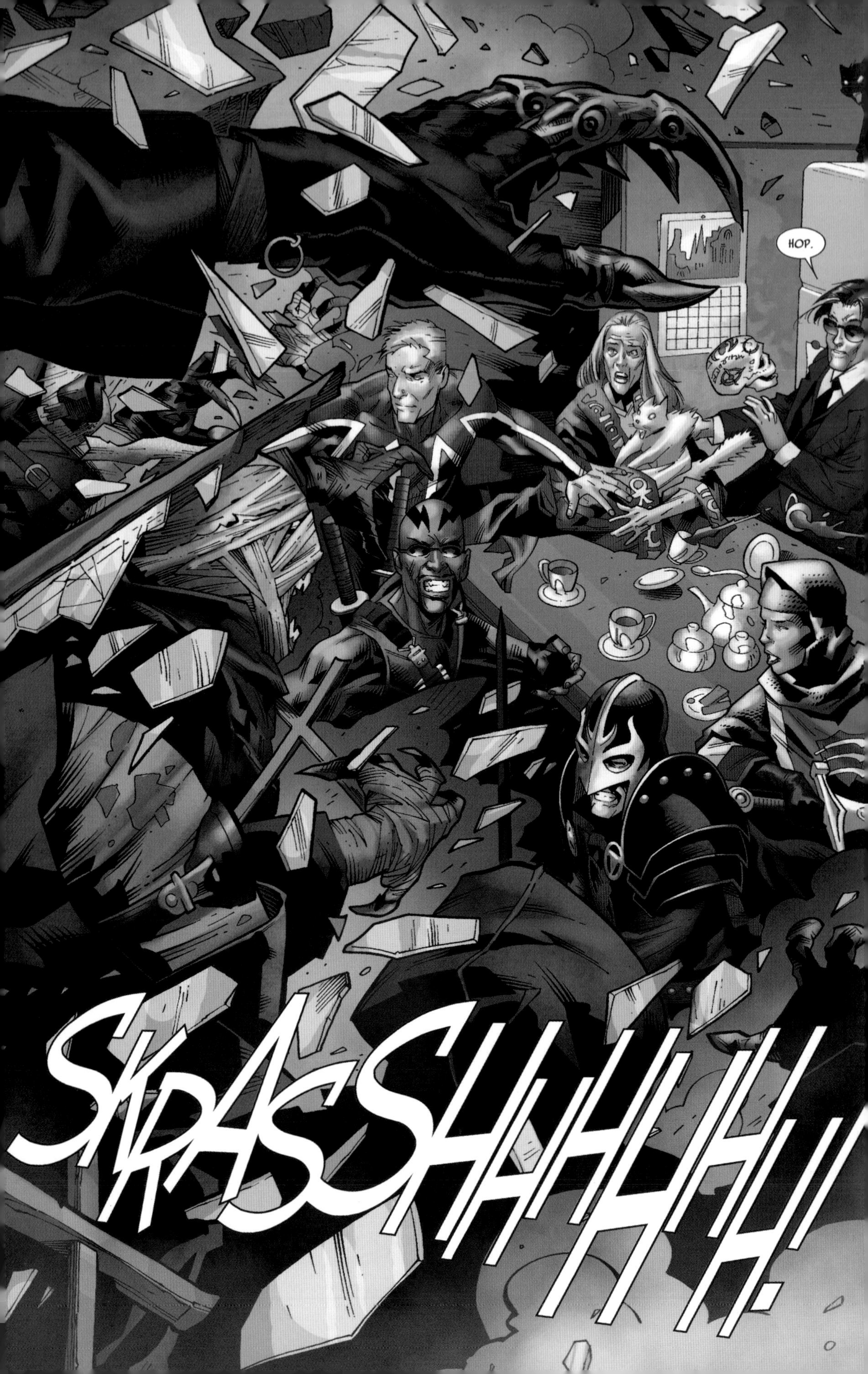
HOP.
SKRASSHHHHH!

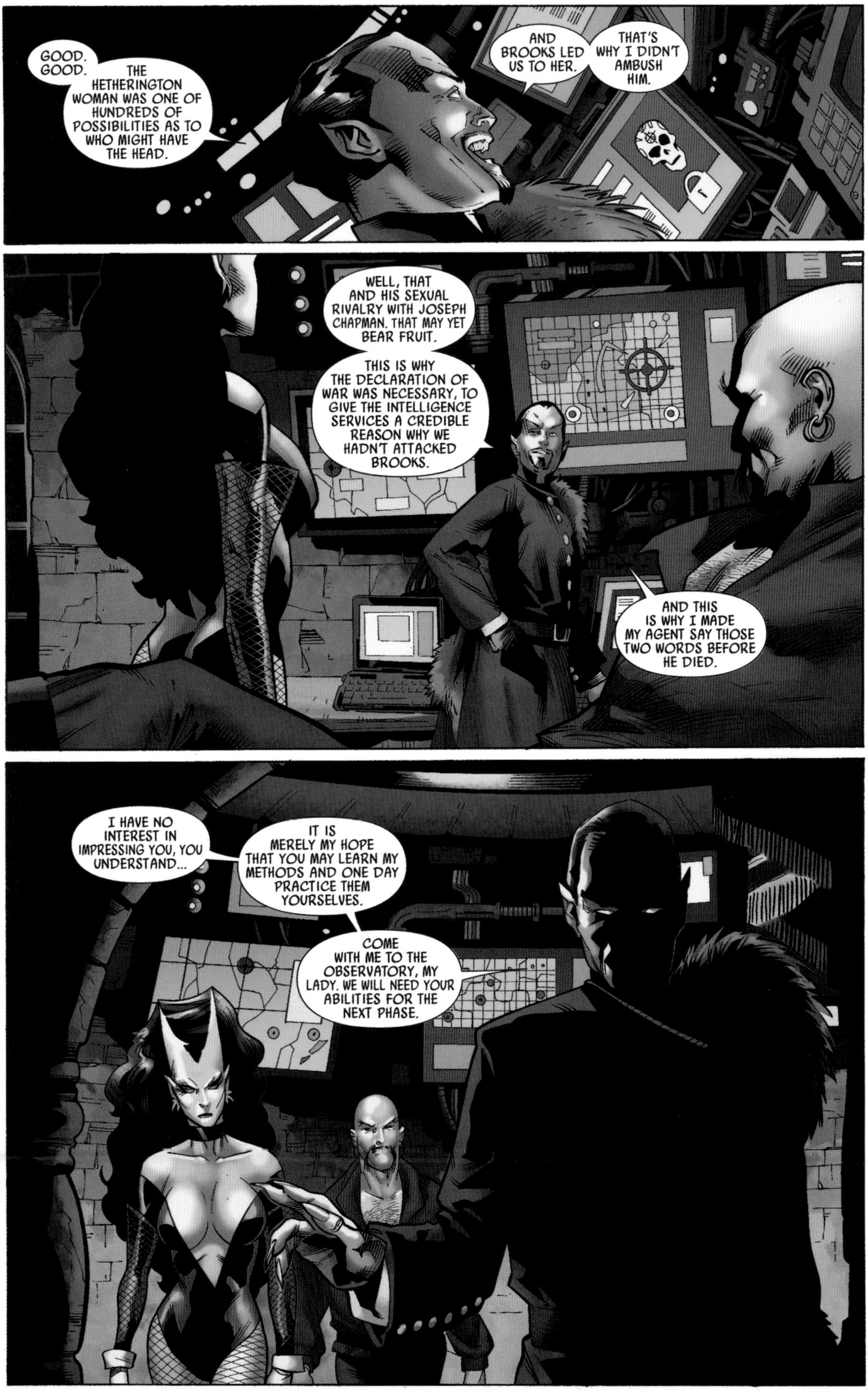
GOOD. GOOD.
THE HETHERINGTON WOMAN WAS ONE OF HUNDREDS OF POSSIBILITIES AS TO WHO MIGHT HAVE THE HEAD.
AND BROOKS LED US TO HER.
THAT'S WHY I DIDN'T AMBUSH HIM.
WELL, THAT AND HIS SEXUAL RIVALRY WITH JOSEPH CHAPMAN. THAT MAY YET BEAR FRUIT.
THIS IS WHY THE DECLARATION OF WAR WAS NECESSARY, TO GIVE THE INTELLIGENCE SERVICES A CREDIBLE REASON WHY WE HADN'T ATTACKED BROOKS.
AND THIS IS WHY I MADE MY AGENT SAY THOSE TWO WORDS BEFORE HE DIED.
I HAVE NO INTEREST IN IMPRESSING YOU, YOU UNDERSTAND...
IT IS MERELY MY HOPE THAT YOU MAY LEARN MY METHODS AND ONE DAY PRACTICE THEM YOURSELVES.
COME WITH ME TO THE OBSERVATORY, MY LADY. WE WILL NEED YOUR ABILITIES FOR THE NEXT PHASE.

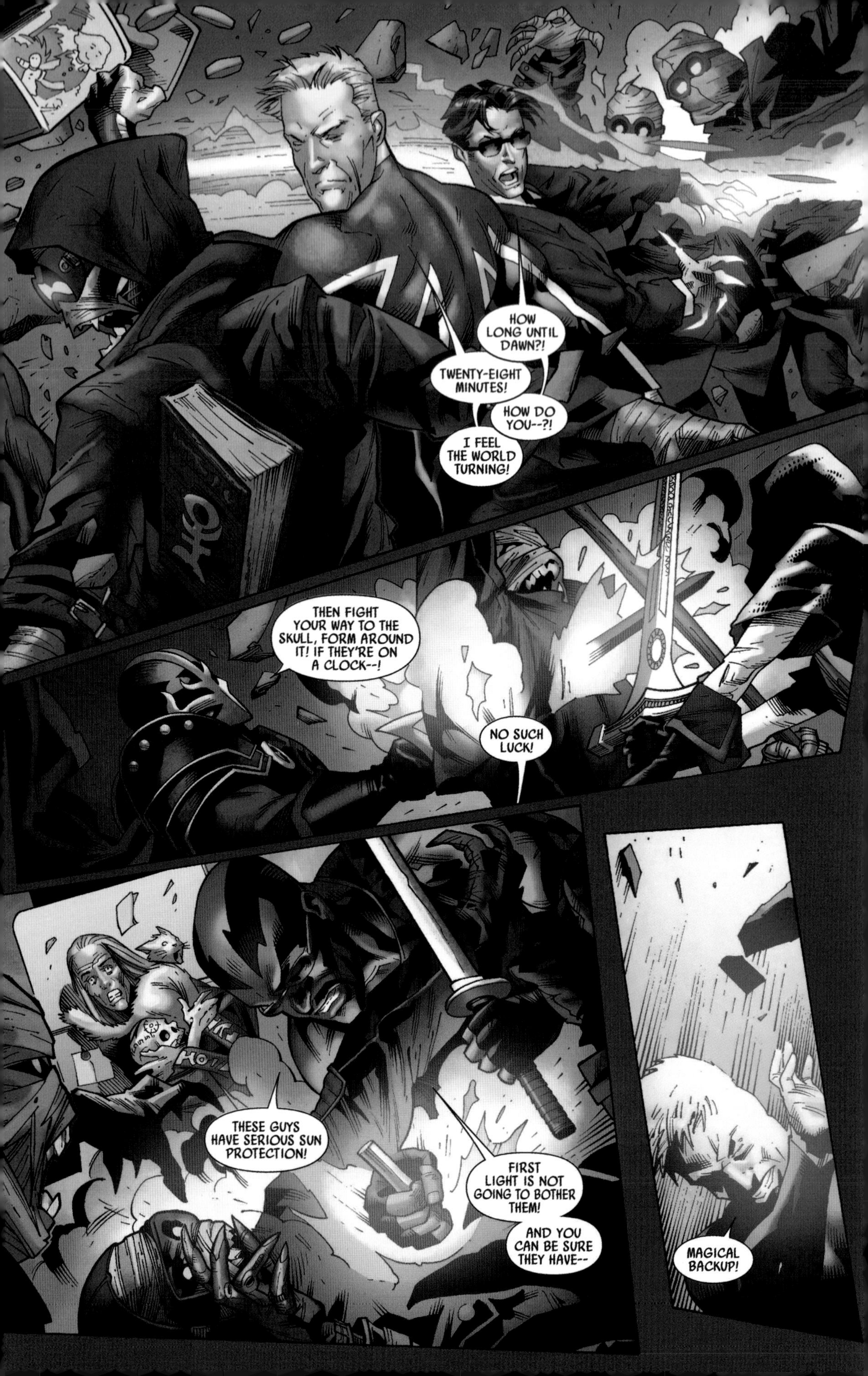
HOW LONG UNTIL DAWN?!
TWENTY-EIGHT MINUTES!
HOW DO YOU--?!
I FEEL THE WORLD TURNING!
THEN FIGHT YOUR WAY TO THE SKULL, FORM AROUND IT! IF THEY'RE ON A CLOCK--!
NO SUCH LUCK!
THESE GUYS HAVE SERIOUS SUN PROTECTION!
FIRST LIGHT IS NOT GOING TO BOTHER THEM!
AND YOU CAN BE SURE THEY HAVE--
MAGICAL BACKUP!

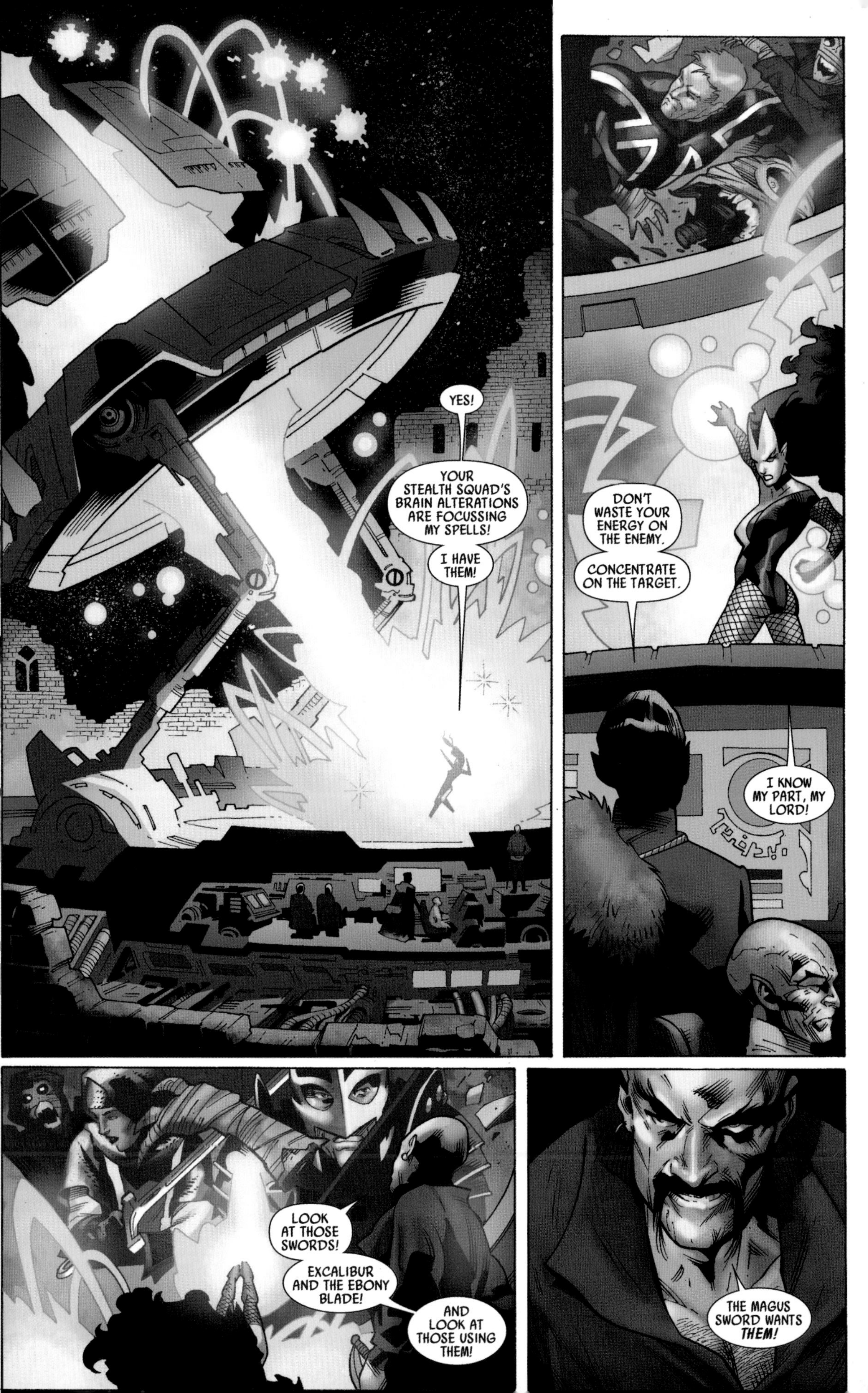
YES!
YOUR STEALTH SQUAD'S BRAIN ALTERATIONS ARE FOCUSSING MY SPELLS!
I HAVE THEM!
DON'T WASTE YOUR ENERGY ON THE ENEMY.
CONCENTRATE ON THE TARGET.
I KNOW MY PART, MY LORD!
LOOK AT THOSE SWORDS!
EXCALIBUR AND THE EBONY BLADE!
AND LOOK AT THOSE USING THEM!
THE MAGUS SWORD WANTS *THEM!*

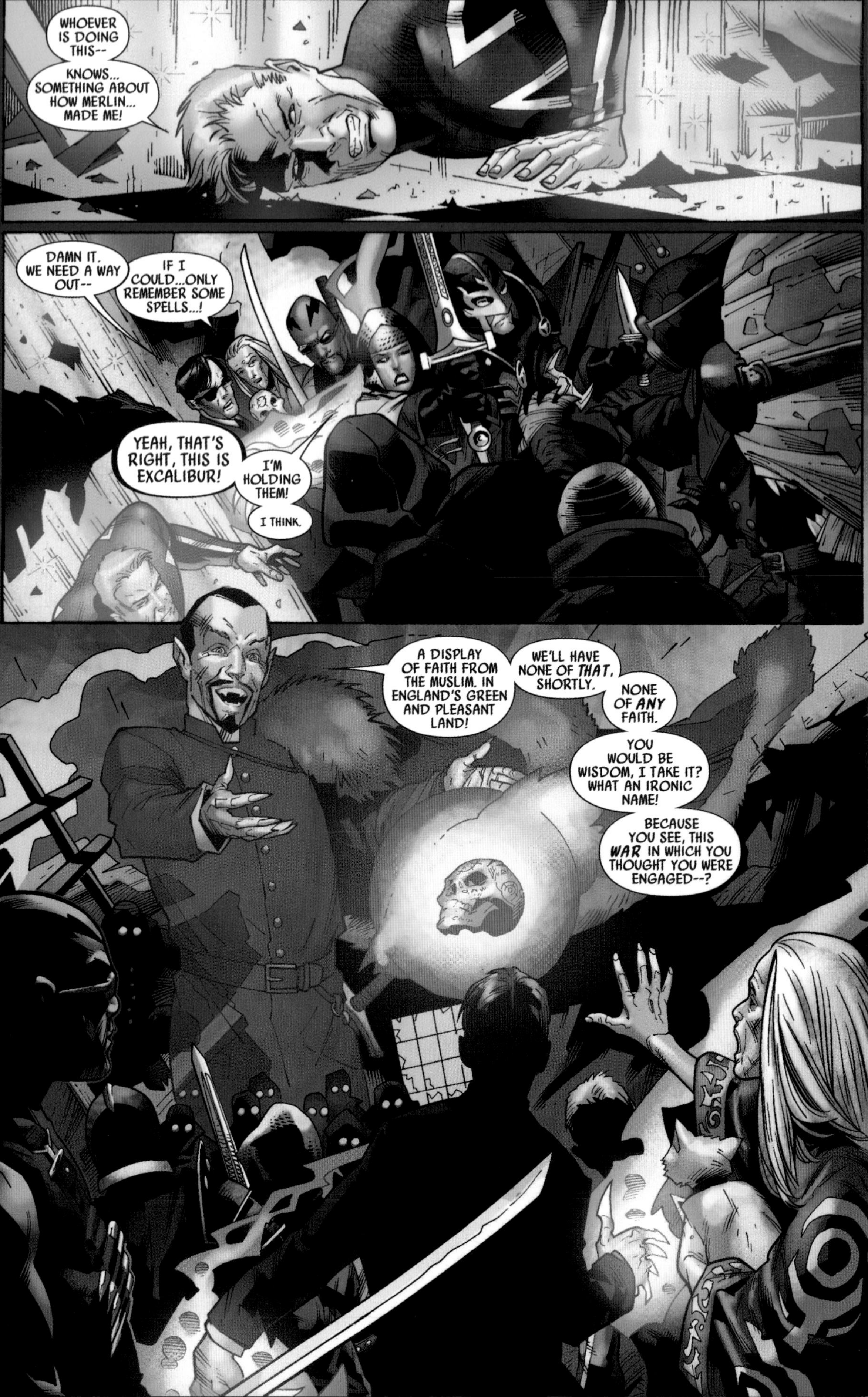
WHOEVER IS DOING THIS--
KNOWS... SOMETHING ABOUT HOW MERLIN... MADE ME!
DAMN IT. WE NEED A WAY OUT--
IF I COULD...ONLY REMEMBER SOME SPELLS...!
YEAH, THAT'S RIGHT, THIS IS EXCALIBUR!
I'M HOLDING THEM!
I THINK.
A DISPLAY OF FAITH FROM THE MUSLIM. IN ENGLAND'S GREEN AND PLEASANT LAND!
WE'LL HAVE NONE OF THAT, SHORTLY.
NONE OF ANY FAITH.
YOU WOULD BE WISDOM, I TAKE IT? WHAT AN IRONIC NAME!
BECAUSE YOU SEE, THIS WAR IN WHICH YOU THOUGHT YOU WERE ENGAGED--?

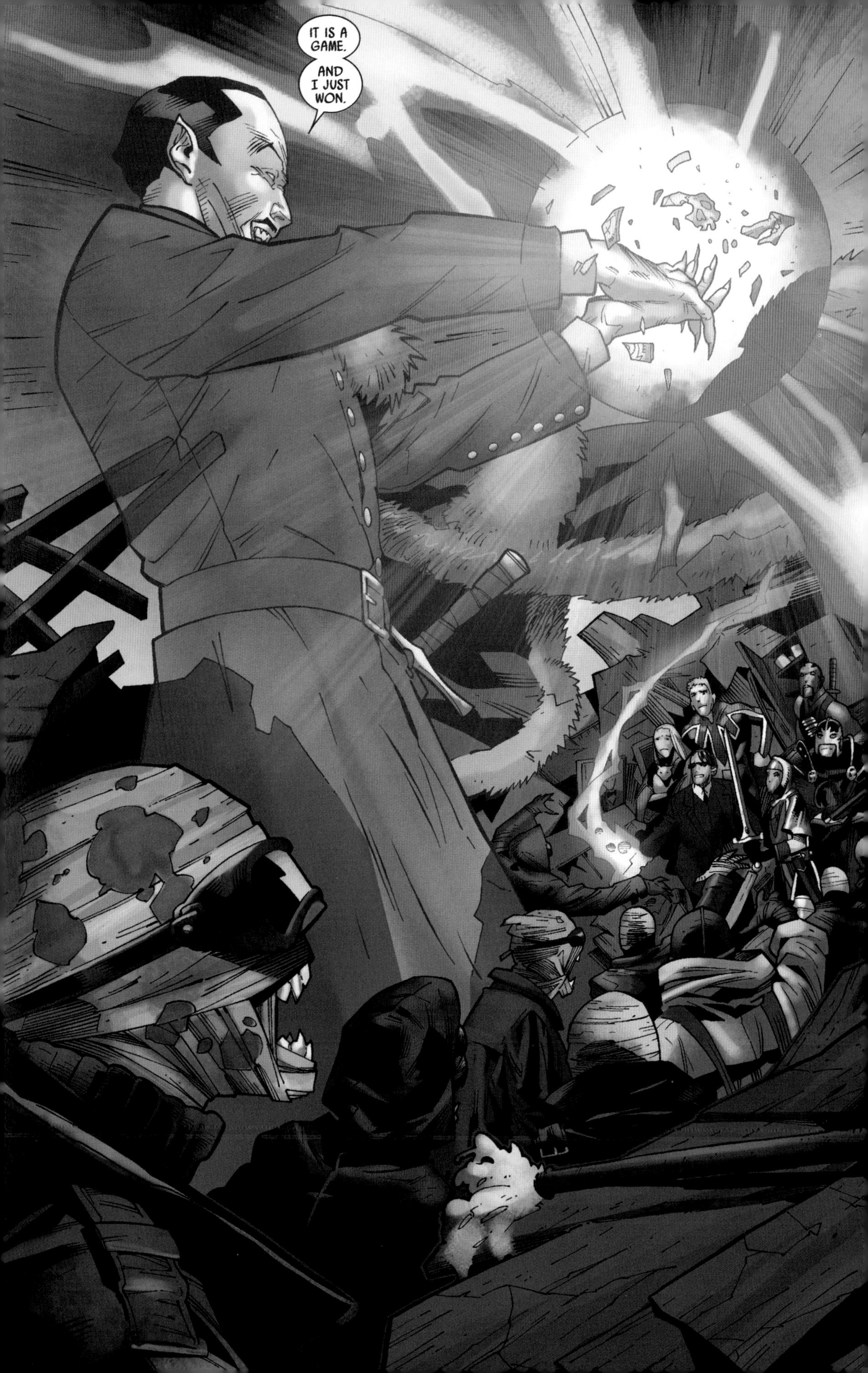
IT IS A GAME.
AND I JUST WON.

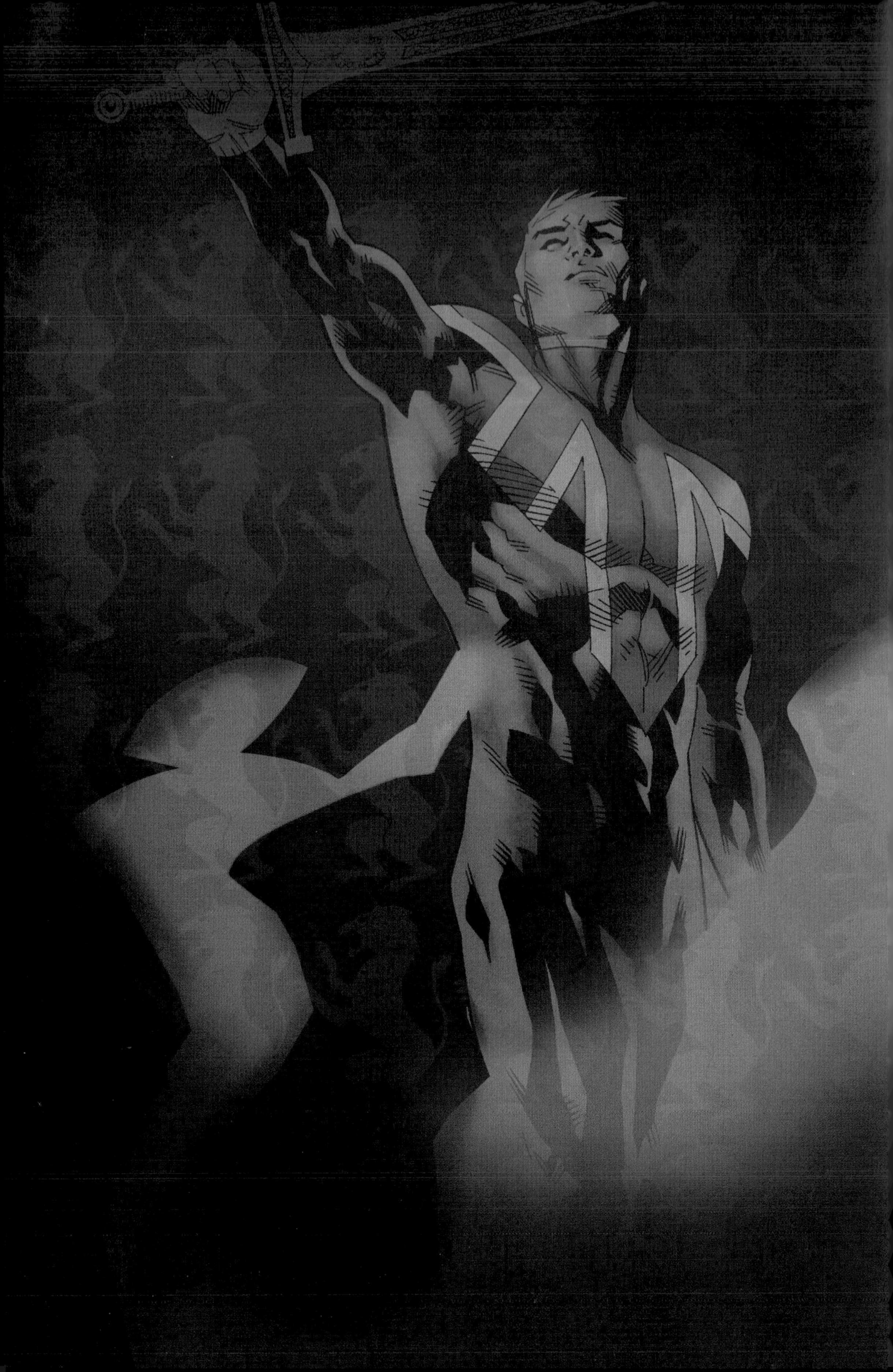

Captain Britain and MI13 #13
COVER ARTWORK

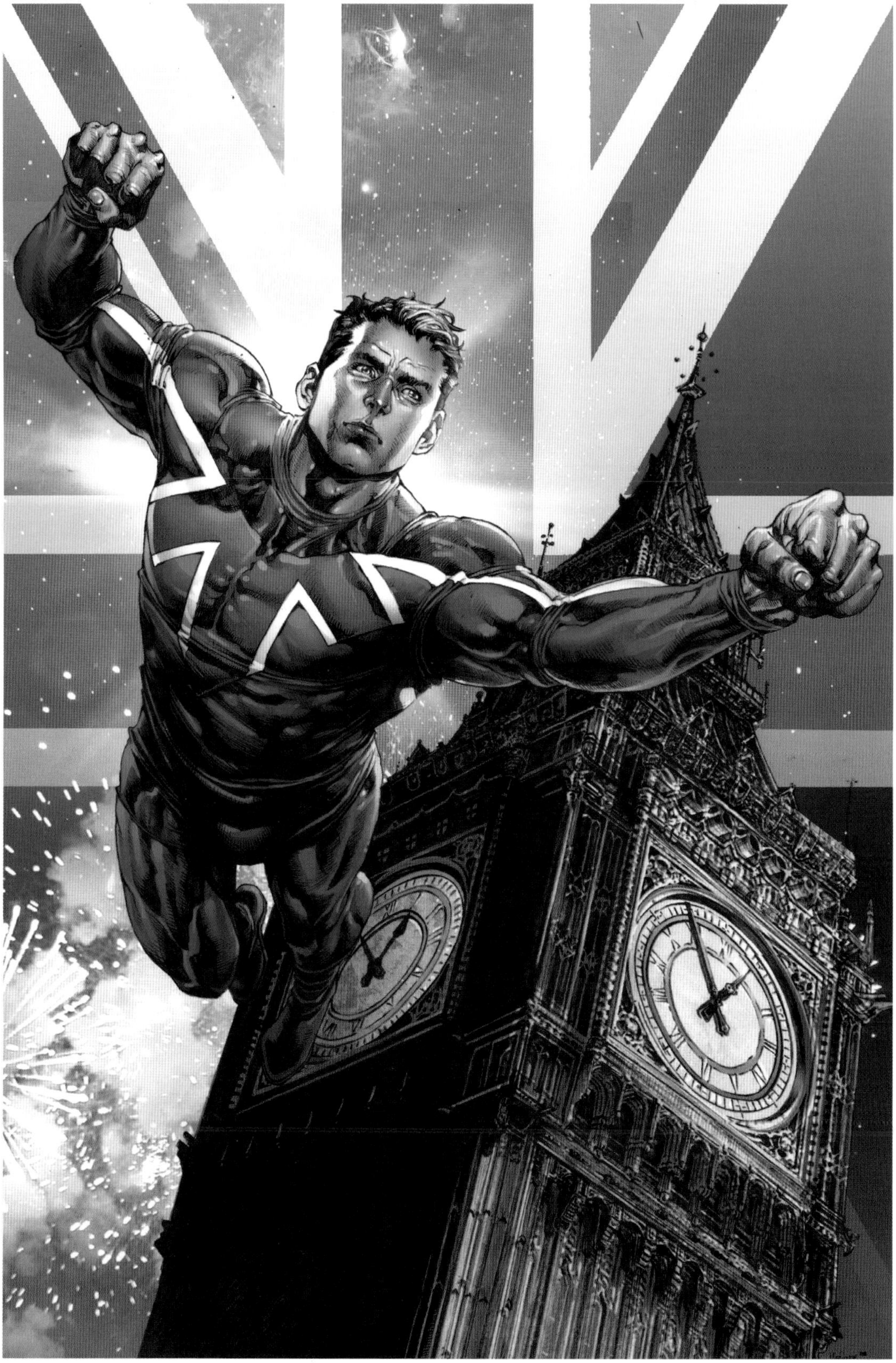

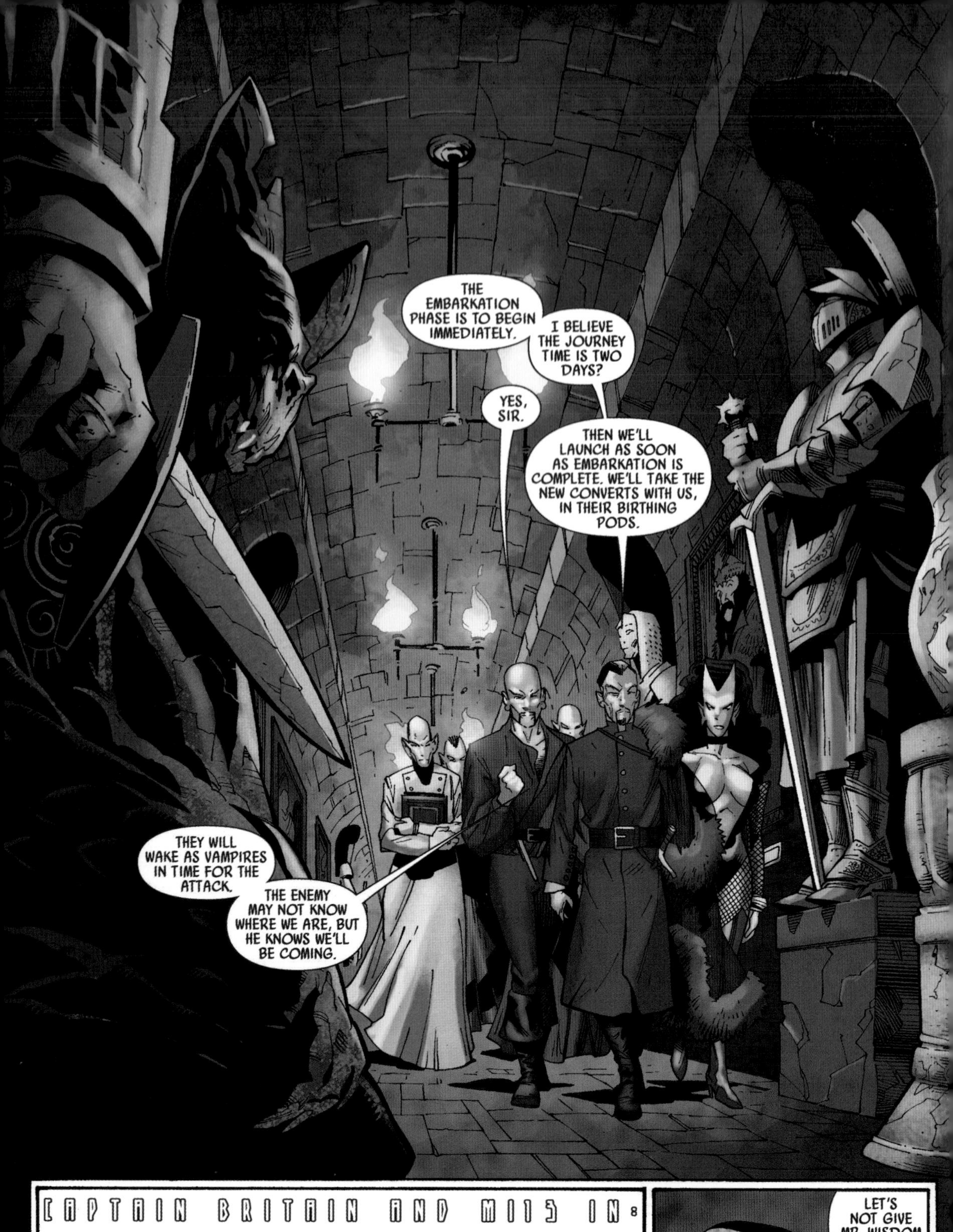
THE EMBARKATION PHASE IS TO BEGIN IMMEDIATELY.
I BELIEVE THE JOURNEY TIME IS TWO DAYS?
YES, SIR.
THEN WE'LL LAUNCH AS SOON AS EMBARKATION IS COMPLETE. WE'LL TAKE THE NEW CONVERTS WITH US, IN THEIR BIRTHING PODS.
THEY WILL WAKE AS VAMPIRES IN TIME FOR THE ATTACK.
THE ENEMY MAY NOT KNOW WHERE WE ARE, BUT HE KNOWS WE'LL BE COMING.

CAPTAIN BRITAIN AND MI13 IN:

VAMPIRE STATE

PART THREE

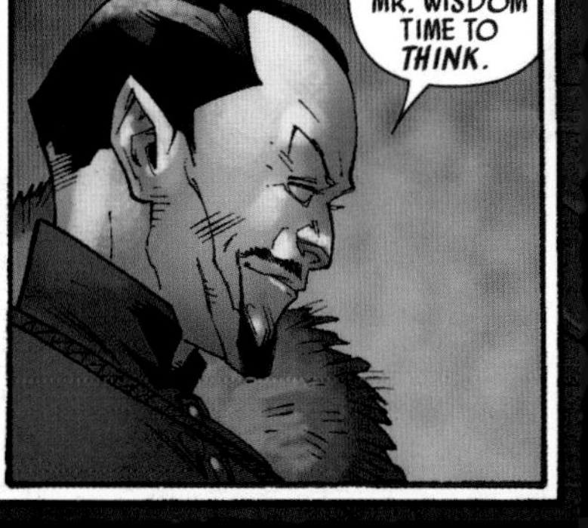
LET'S NOT GIVE MR. WISDOM TIME TO THINK.

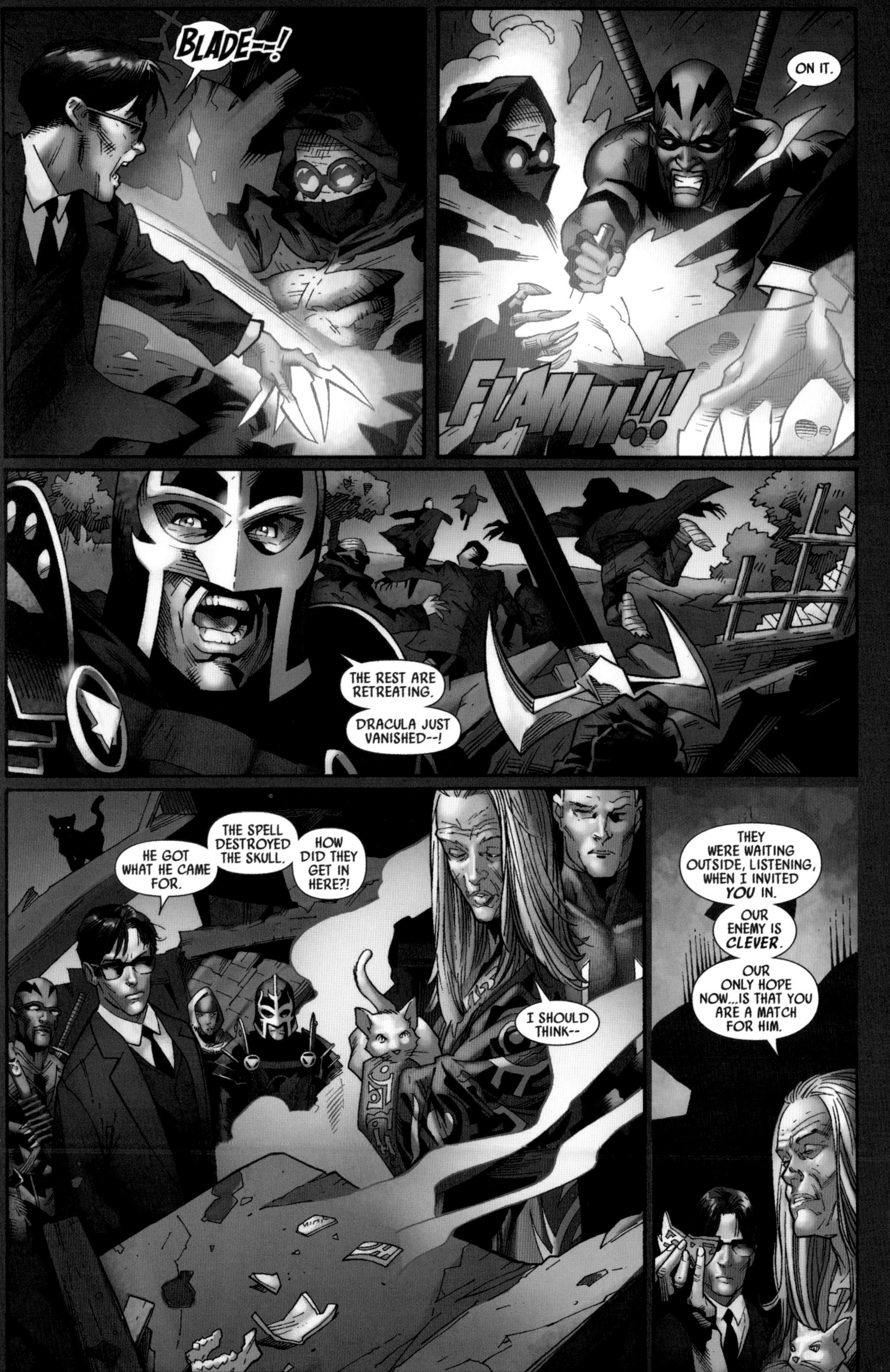
BLADE--!
ON IT.
FLAMM!!!
THE REST ARE RETREATING.
DRACULA JUST VANISHED--!
HE GOT WHAT HE CAME FOR.
THE SPELL DESTROYED THE SKULL.
HOW DID THEY GET IN HERE?!
I SHOULD THINK--
THEY WERE WAITING OUTSIDE, LISTENING, WHEN I INVITED YOU IN.
OUR ENEMY IS CLEVER.
OUR ONLY HOPE NOW...IS THAT YOU ARE A MATCH FOR HIM.

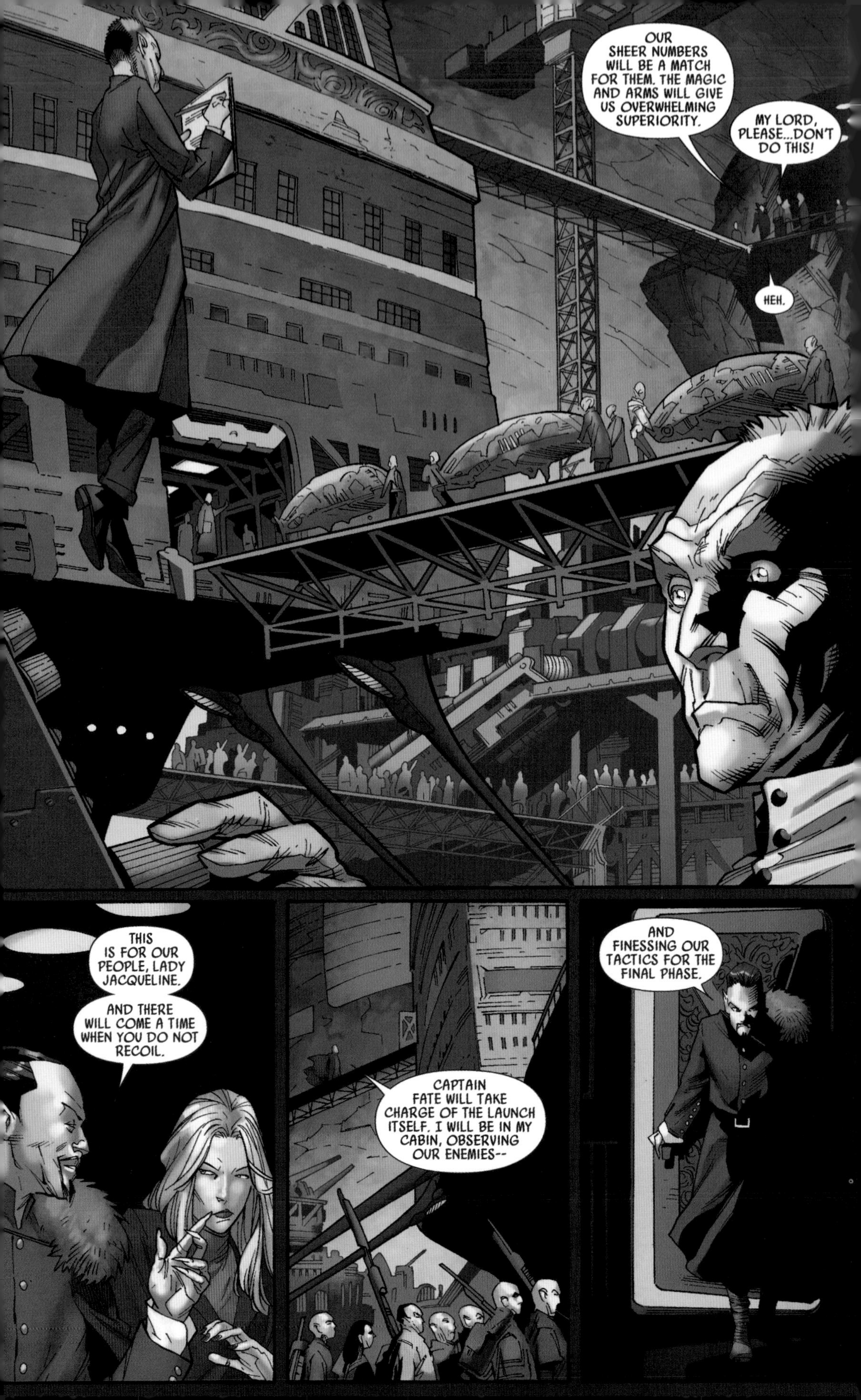
OUR SHEER NUMBERS WILL BE A MATCH FOR THEM. THE MAGIC AND ARMS WILL GIVE US OVERWHELMING SUPERIORITY.
MY LORD, PLEASE...DON'T DO THIS!
HEH.
THIS IS FOR OUR PEOPLE, LADY JACQUELINE.
AND THERE WILL COME A TIME WHEN YOU DO NOT RECOIL.
CAPTAIN FATE WILL TAKE CHARGE OF THE LAUNCH ITSELF. I WILL BE IN MY CABIN, OBSERVING OUR ENEMIES--
AND FINESSING OUR TACTICS FOR THE FINAL PHASE.

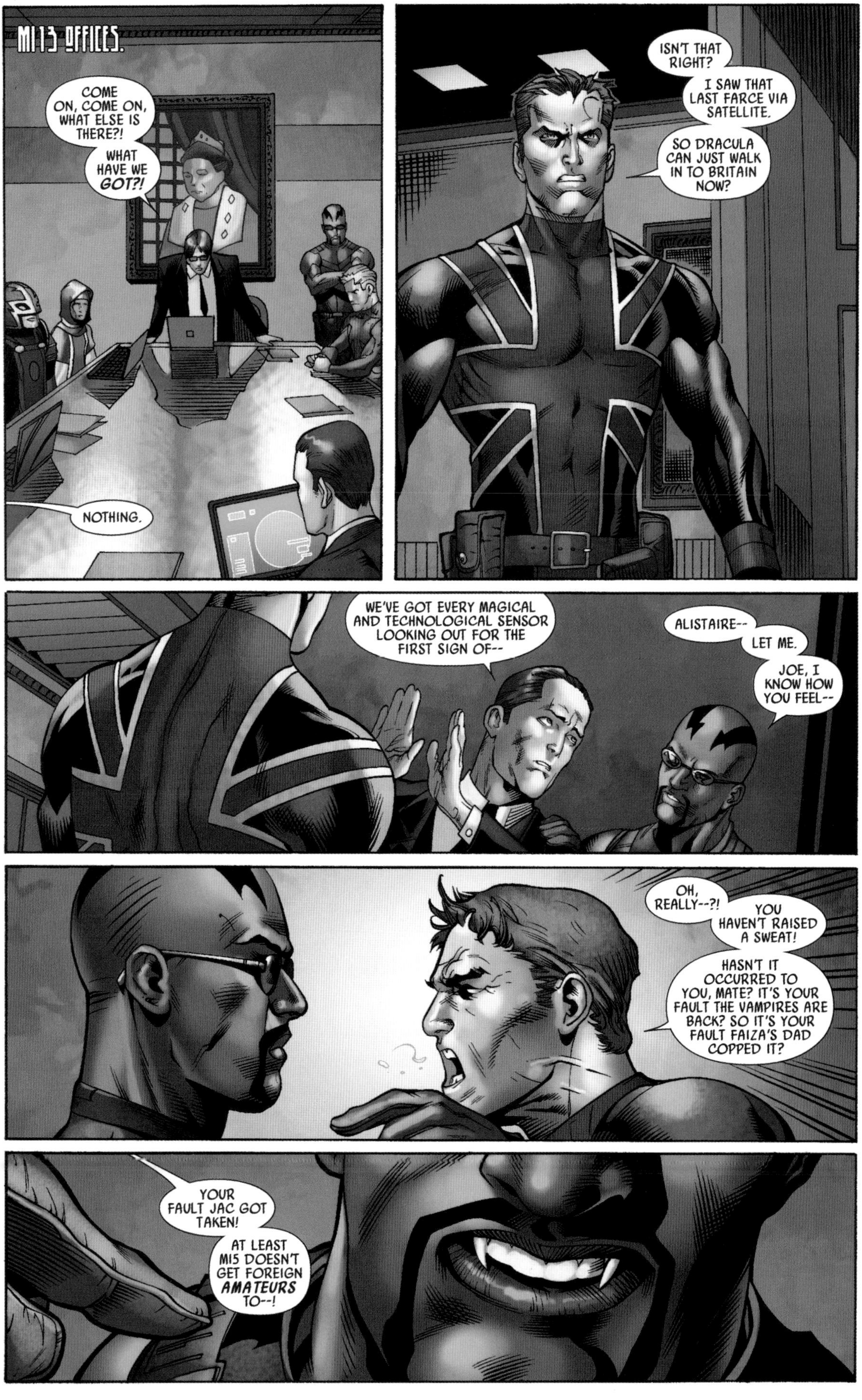
MI13 OFFICES.
COME ON, COME ON, WHAT ELSE IS THERE?!
WHAT HAVE WE GOT?!
NOTHING.
ISN'T THAT RIGHT?
I SAW THAT LAST FARCE VIA SATELLITE.
SO DRACULA CAN JUST WALK IN TO BRITAIN NOW?
WE'VE GOT EVERY MAGICAL AND TECHNOLOGICAL SENSOR LOOKING OUT FOR THE FIRST SIGN OF--
ALISTAIRE--
LET ME.
JOE, I KNOW HOW YOU FEEL--
OH, REALLY--?!
YOU HAVEN'T RAISED A SWEAT!
HASN'T IT OCCURRED TO YOU, MATE? IT'S YOUR FAULT THE VAMPIRES ARE BACK? SO IT'S YOUR FAULT FAIZA'S DAD COPPED IT?
YOUR FAULT JAC GOT TAKEN!
AT LEAST MI5 DOESN'T GET FOREIGN AMATEURS TO--!

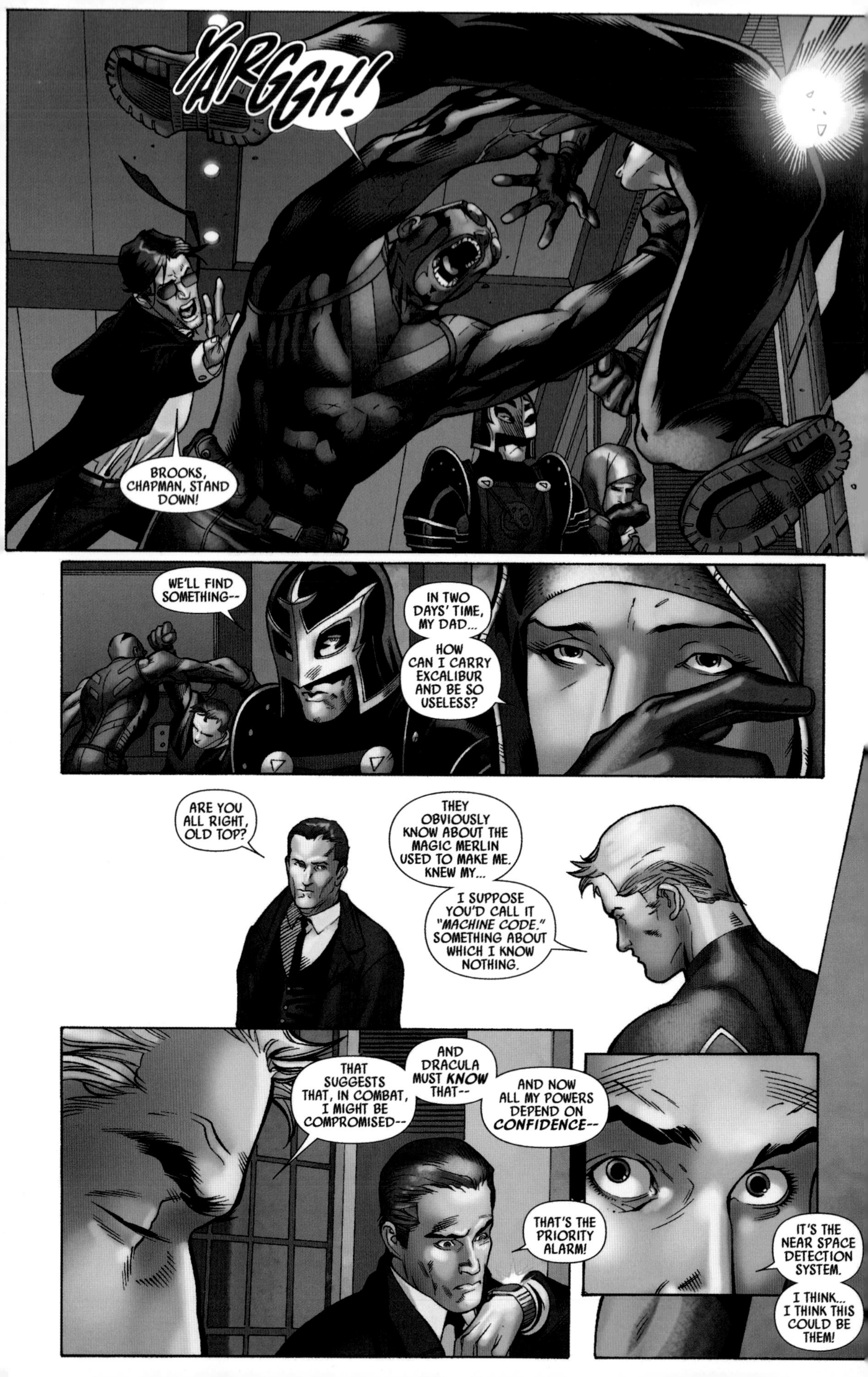
YARGGH!
BROOKS, CHAPMAN, STAND DOWN!
WE'LL FIND SOMETHING--
IN TWO DAYS' TIME, MY DAD...
HOW CAN I CARRY EXCALIBUR AND BE SO USELESS?
ARE YOU ALL RIGHT, OLD TOP?
THEY OBVIOUSLY KNOW ABOUT THE MAGIC MERLIN USED TO MAKE ME. KNEW MY...
I SUPPOSE YOU'D CALL IT "MACHINE CODE." SOMETHING ABOUT WHICH I KNOW NOTHING.
THAT SUGGESTS THAT, IN COMBAT, I MIGHT BE COMPROMISED--
AND DRACULA MUST KNOW THAT--
AND NOW ALL MY POWERS DEPEND ON CONFIDENCE--
THAT'S THE PRIORITY ALARM!
IT'S THE NEAR SPACE DETECTION SYSTEM.
I THINK... I THINK THIS COULD BE THEM!

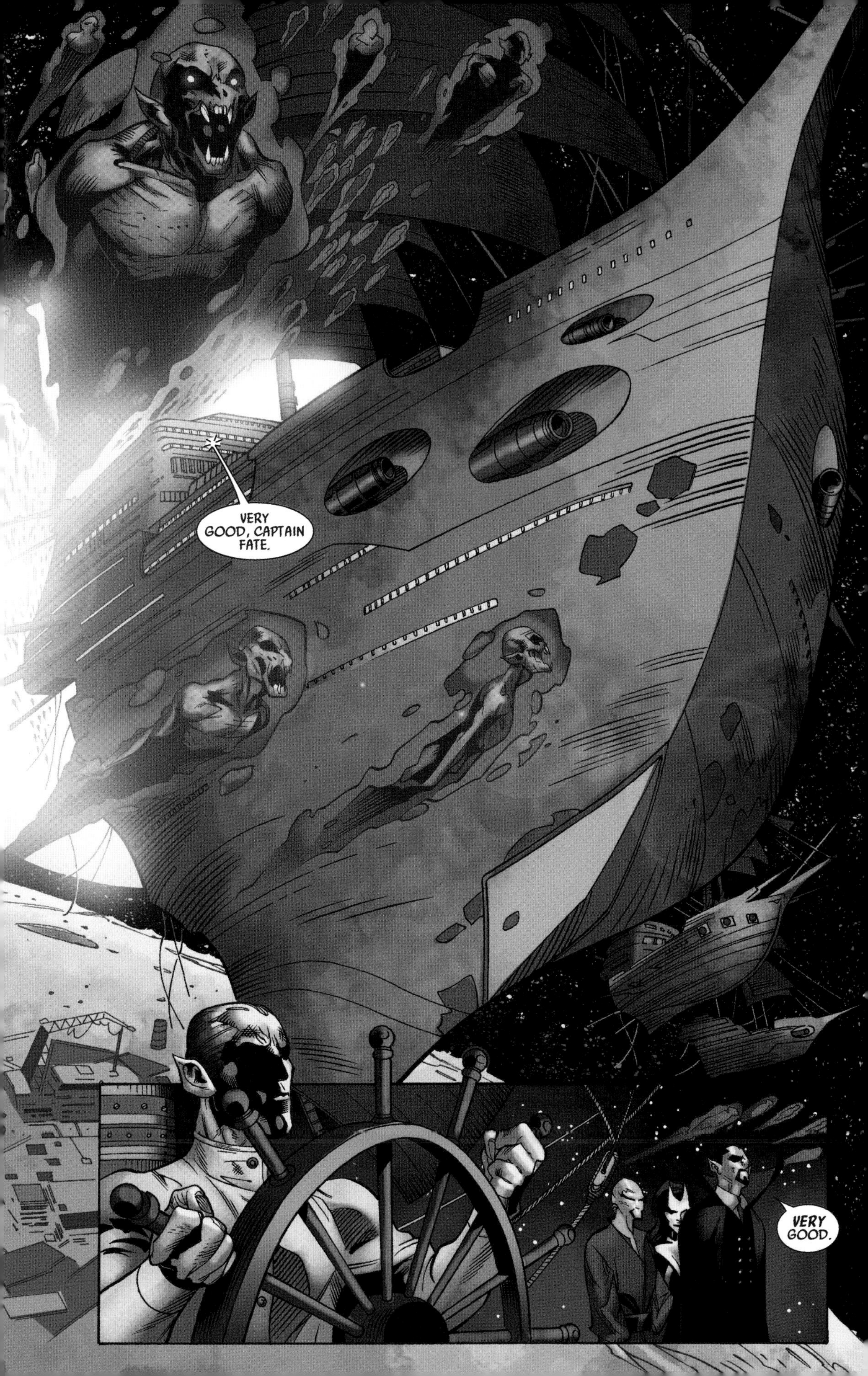
VERY GOOD, CAPTAIN FATE.
VERY GOOD.

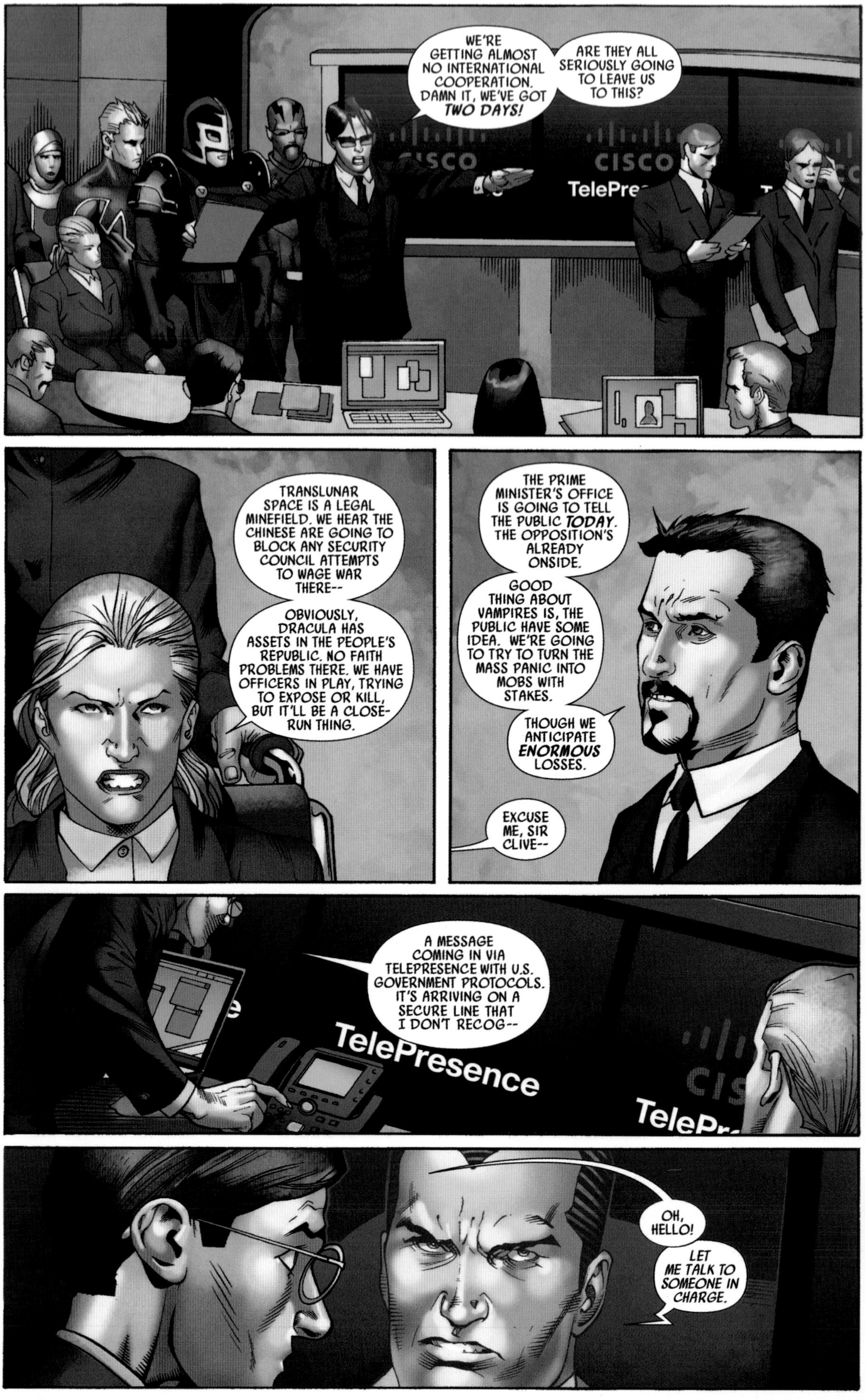
WE'RE GETTING ALMOST NO INTERNATIONAL COOPERATION. DAMN IT, WE'VE GOT TWO DAYS!
ARE THEY ALL SERIOUSLY GOING TO LEAVE US TO THIS?
CISCO
TelePresence
TRANSLUNAR SPACE IS A LEGAL MINEFIELD. WE HEAR THE CHINESE ARE GOING TO BLOCK ANY SECURITY COUNCIL ATTEMPTS TO WAGE WAR THERE--
OBVIOUSLY, DRACULA HAS ASSETS IN THE PEOPLE'S REPUBLIC. NO FAITH PROBLEMS THERE. WE HAVE OFFICERS IN PLAY, TRYING TO EXPOSE OR KILL, BUT IT'LL BE A CLOSE-RUN THING.
THE PRIME MINISTER'S OFFICE IS GOING TO TELL THE PUBLIC TODAY. THE OPPOSITION'S ALREADY ONSIDE.
GOOD THING ABOUT VAMPIRES IS, THE PUBLIC HAVE SOME IDEA. WE'RE GOING TO TRY TO TURN THE MASS PANIC INTO MOBS WITH STAKES.
THOUGH WE ANTICIPATE ENORMOUS LOSSES.
EXCUSE ME, SIR CLIVE--
A MESSAGE COMING IN VIA TELEPRESENCE WITH U.S. GOVERNMENT PROTOCOLS. IT'S ARRIVING ON A SECURE LINE THAT I DON'T RECOG--
TelePresence
OH, HELLO!
LET ME TALK TO SOMEONE IN CHARGE.

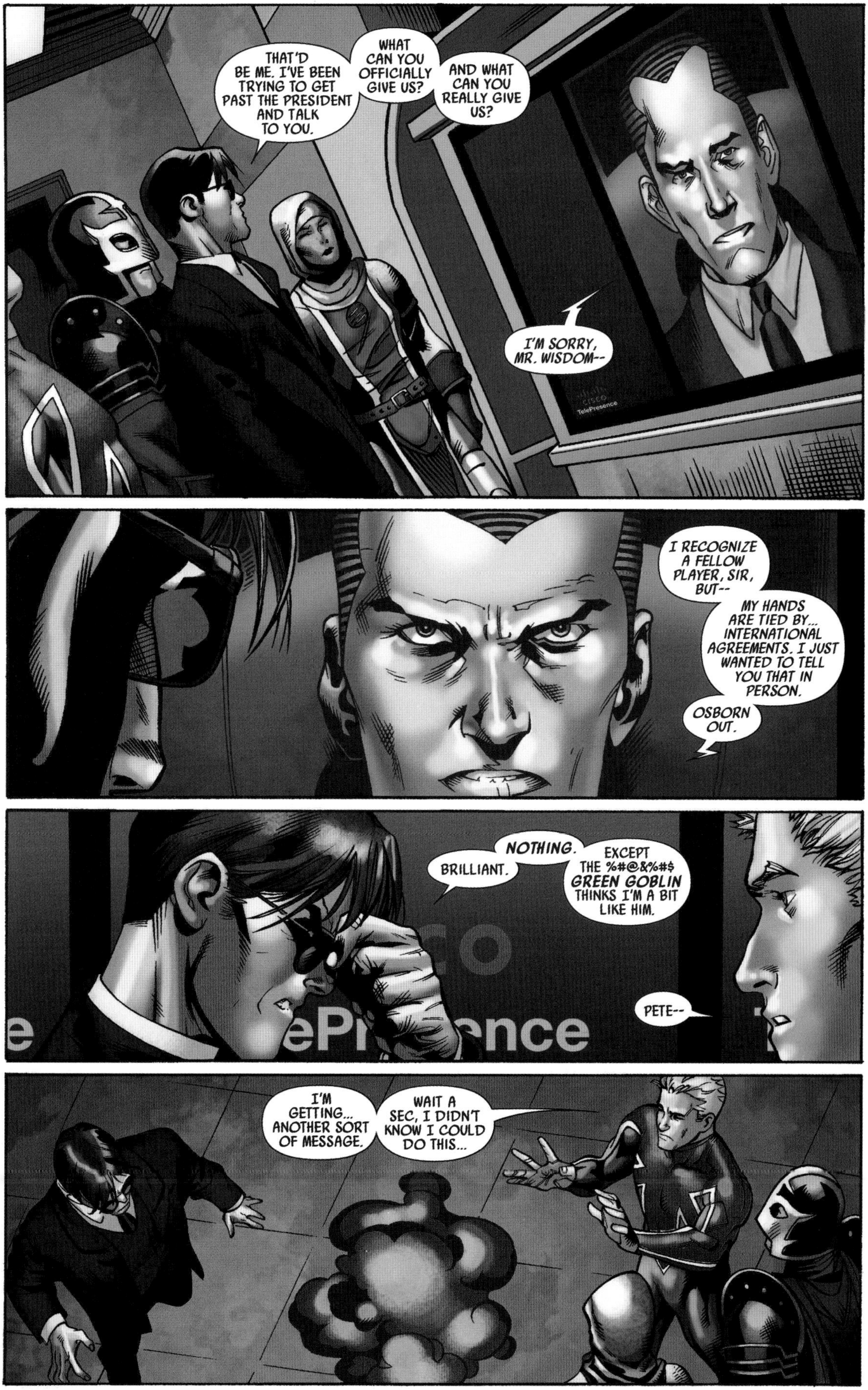
THAT'D BE ME. I'VE BEEN TRYING TO GET PAST THE PRESIDENT AND TALK TO YOU.
WHAT CAN YOU OFFICIALLY GIVE US?
AND WHAT CAN YOU REALLY GIVE US?
I'M SORRY, MR. WISDOM--
cisco
TelePresence
I RECOGNIZE A FELLOW PLAYER, SIR, BUT--
MY HANDS ARE TIED BY... INTERNATIONAL AGREEMENTS. I JUST WANTED TO TELL YOU THAT IN PERSON.
OSBORN OUT.
BRILLIANT.
NOTHING.
EXCEPT THE %#@&%#$ GREEN GOBLIN THINKS I'M A BIT LIKE HIM.
PETE--
I'M GETTING... ANOTHER SORT OF MESSAGE.
WAIT A SEC, I DIDN'T KNOW I COULD DO THIS...

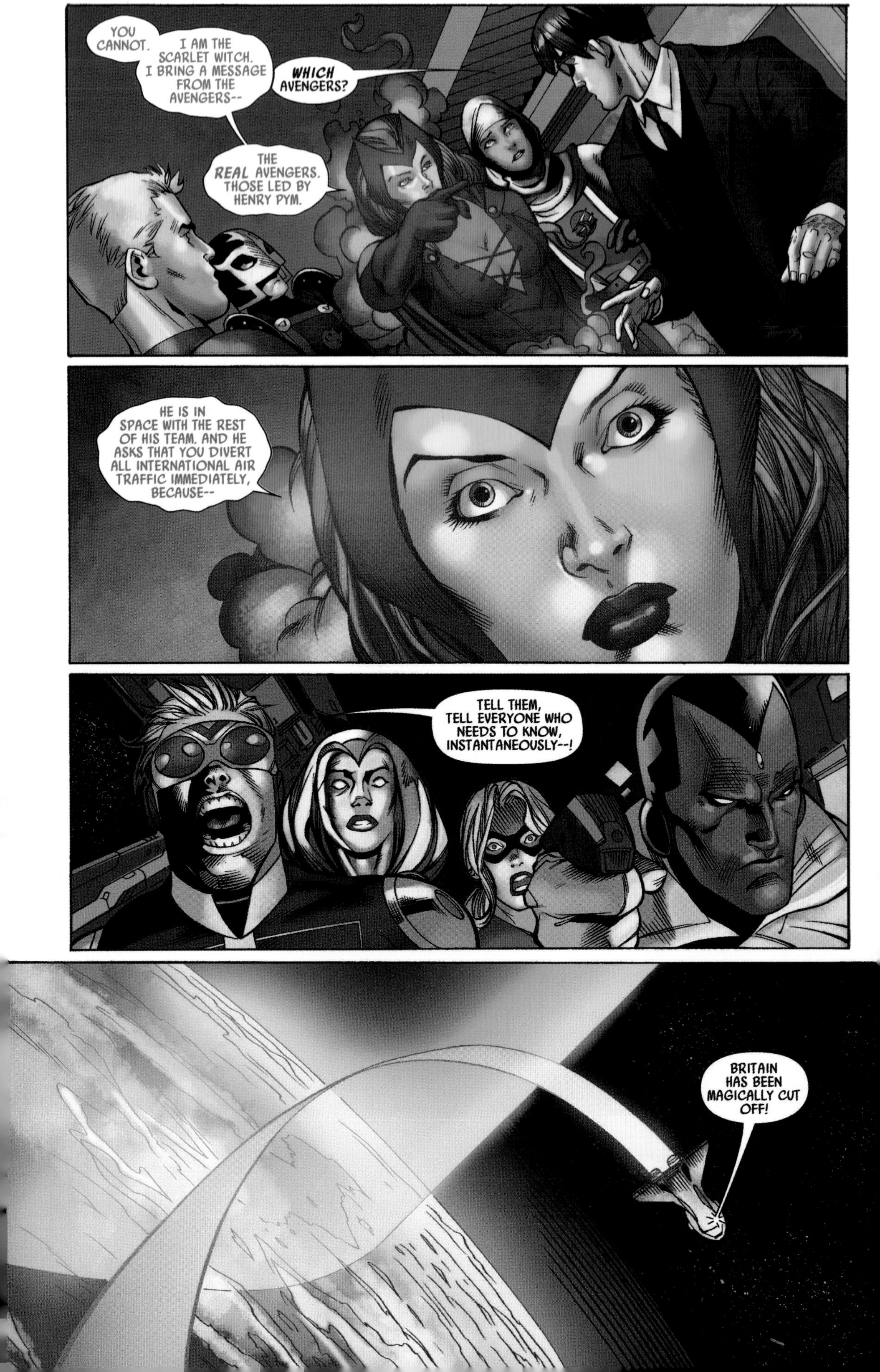
YOU CANNOT.
I AM THE SCARLET WITCH. I BRING A MESSAGE FROM THE AVENGERS--
WHICH AVENGERS?
THE REAL AVENGERS. THOSE LED BY HENRY PYM.
HE IS IN SPACE WITH THE REST OF HIS TEAM. AND HE ASKS THAT YOU DIVERT ALL INTERNATIONAL AIR TRAFFIC IMMEDIATELY, BECAUSE--
TELL THEM, TELL EVERYONE WHO NEEDS TO KNOW, INSTANTANEOUSLY--!
BRITAIN HAS BEEN MAGICALLY CUT OFF!

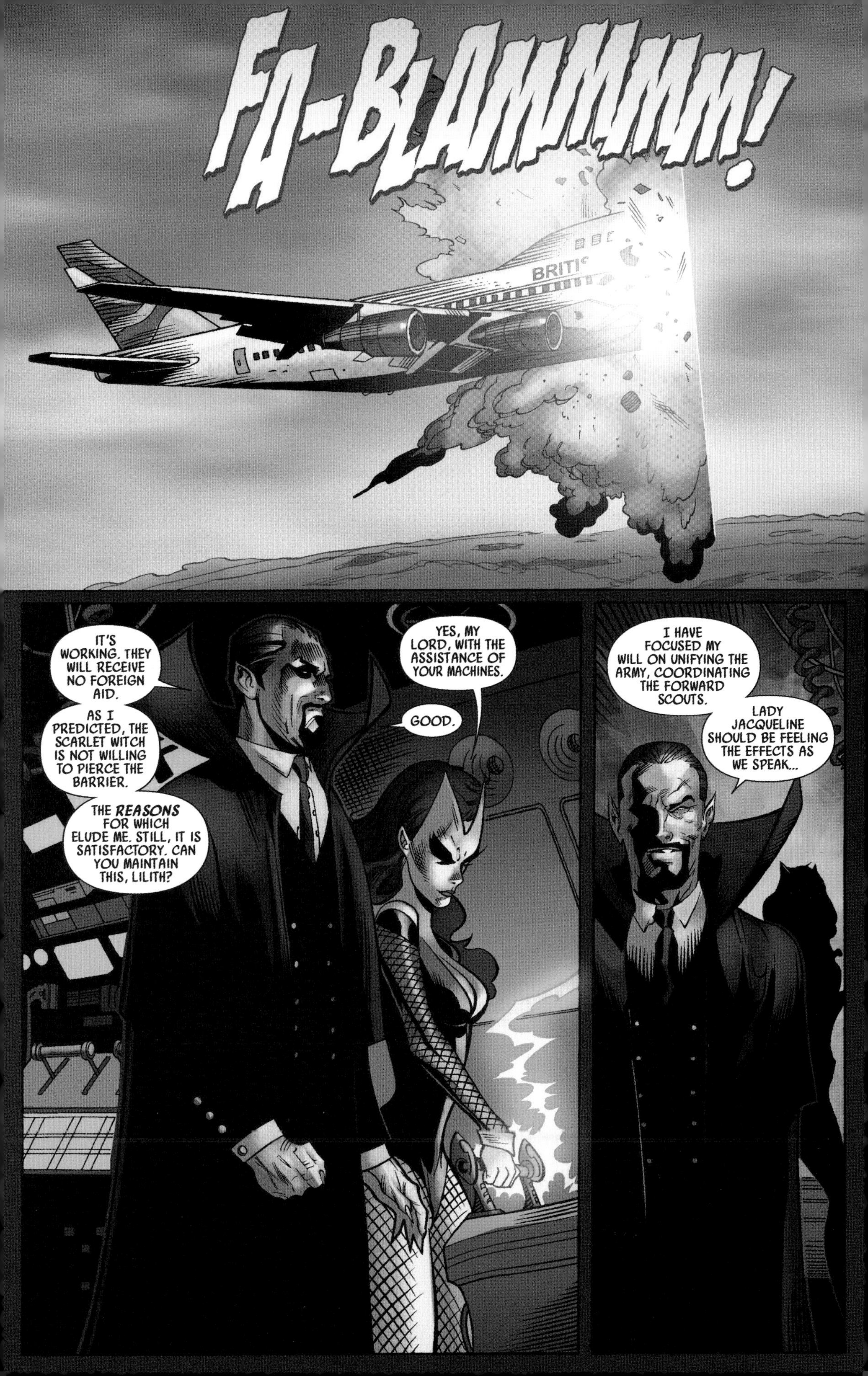
FA-BLAMMMM!
BRITIS
IT'S WORKING. THEY WILL RECEIVE NO FOREIGN AID.
AS I PREDICTED, THE SCARLET WITCH IS NOT WILLING TO PIERCE THE BARRIER.
THE *REASONS* FOR WHICH ELUDE ME. STILL, IT IS SATISFACTORY. CAN YOU MAINTAIN THIS, LILITH?
YES, MY LORD, WITH THE ASSISTANCE OF YOUR MACHINES.
GOOD.
I HAVE FOCUSED MY WILL ON UNIFYING THE ARMY, COORDINATING THE FORWARD SCOUTS.
LADY JACQUELINE SHOULD BE FEELING THE EFFECTS AS WE SPEAK...

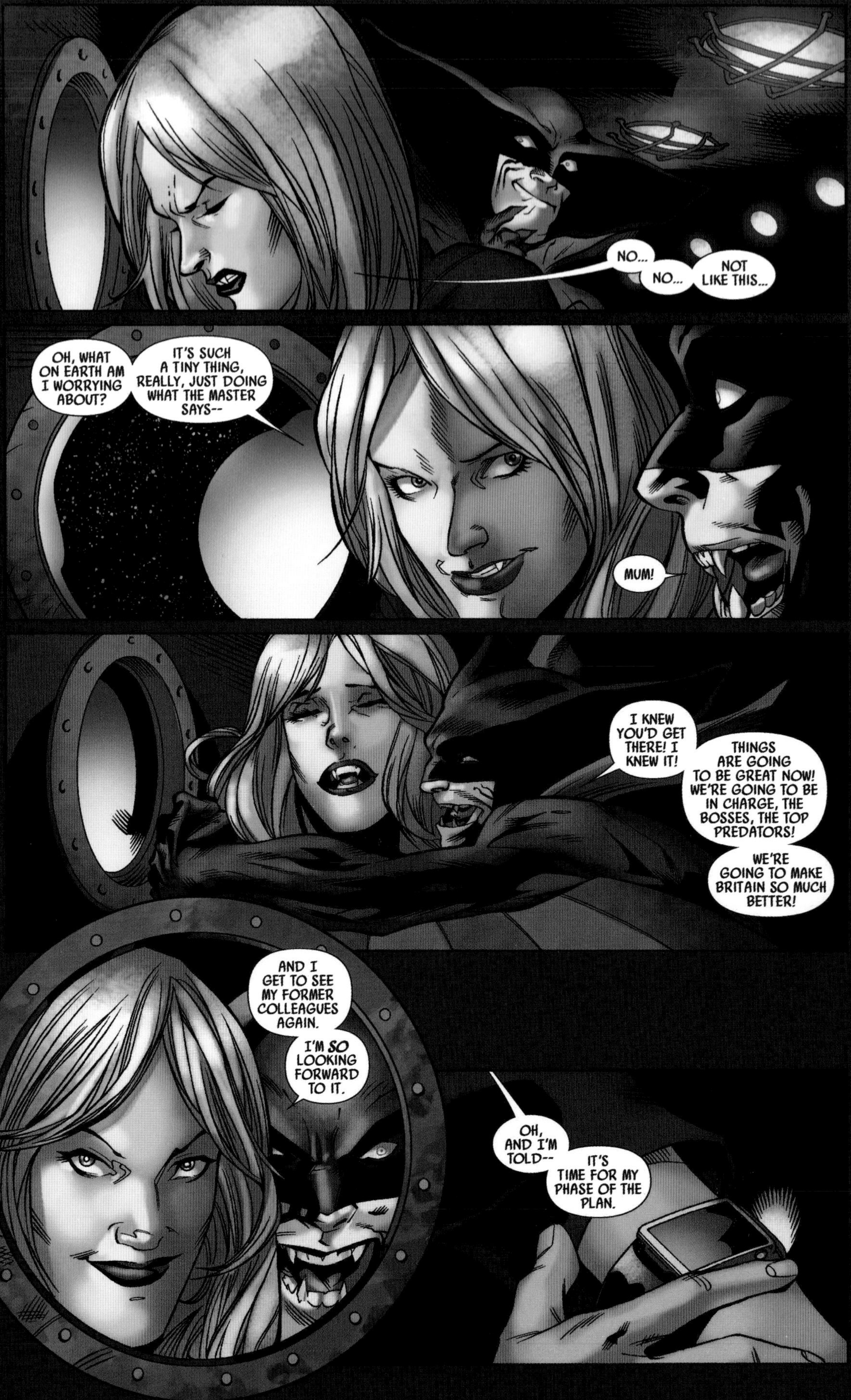
NO...
NO...
NOT LIKE THIS...
OH, WHAT ON EARTH AM I WORRYING ABOUT?
IT'S SUCH A TINY THING, REALLY, JUST DOING WHAT THE MASTER SAYS--
MUM!
I KNEW YOU'D GET THERE! I KNEW IT!
THINGS ARE GOING TO BE GREAT NOW! WE'RE GOING TO BE IN CHARGE, THE BOSSES, THE TOP PREDATORS!
WE'RE GOING TO MAKE BRITAIN SO MUCH BETTER!
AND I GET TO SEE MY FORMER COLLEAGUES AGAIN.
I'M SO LOOKING FORWARD TO IT.
OH, AND I'M TOLD--
IT'S TIME FOR MY PHASE OF THE PLAN.

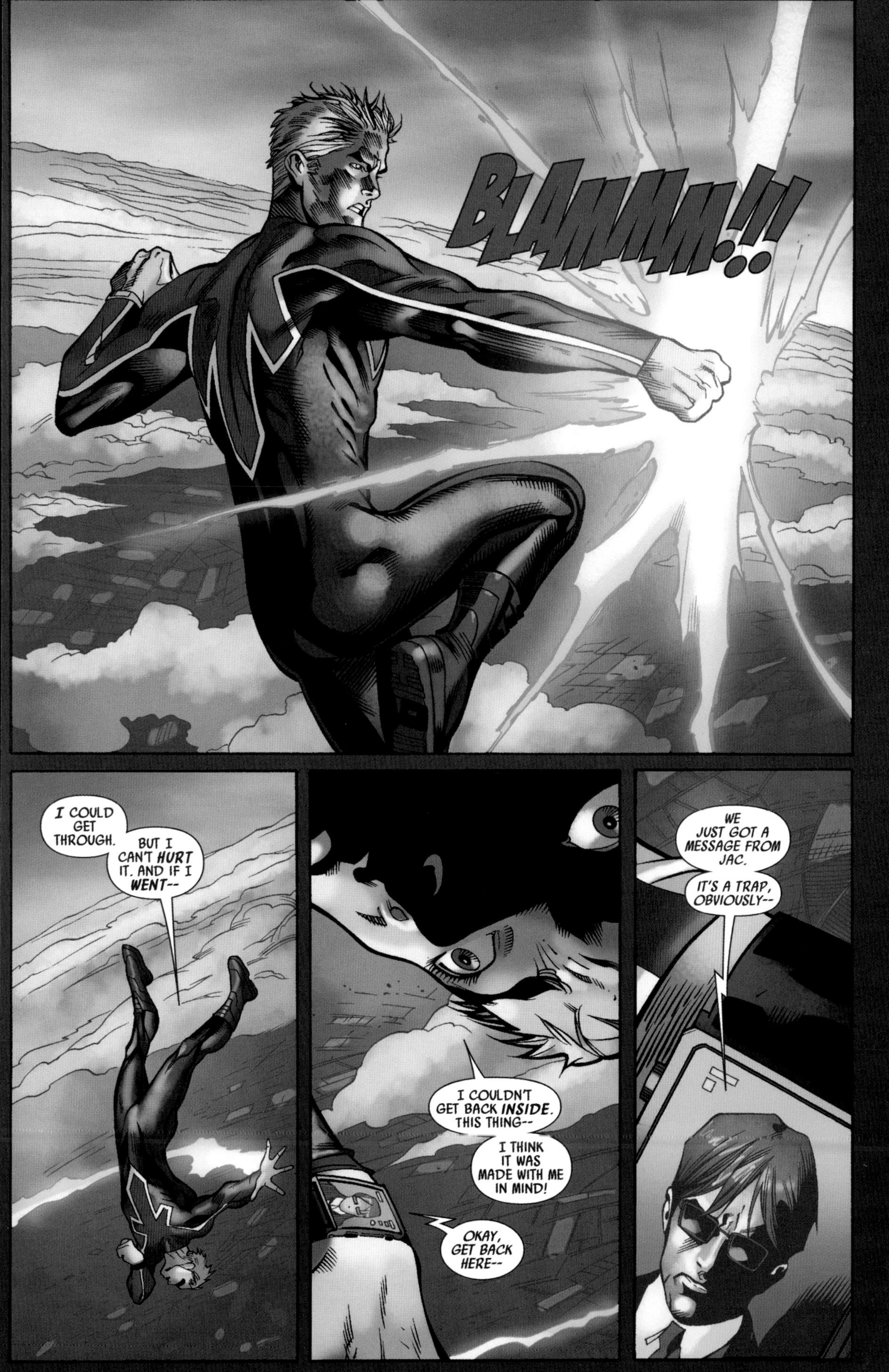
BLAMMMM!!!
I COULD GET THROUGH.
BUT I CAN'T HURT IT. AND IF I WENT--
I COULDN'T GET BACK INSIDE. THIS THING--
I THINK IT WAS MADE WITH ME IN MIND!
OKAY, GET BACK HERE--
WE JUST GOT A MESSAGE FROM JAC.
IT'S A TRAP, OBVIOUSLY--

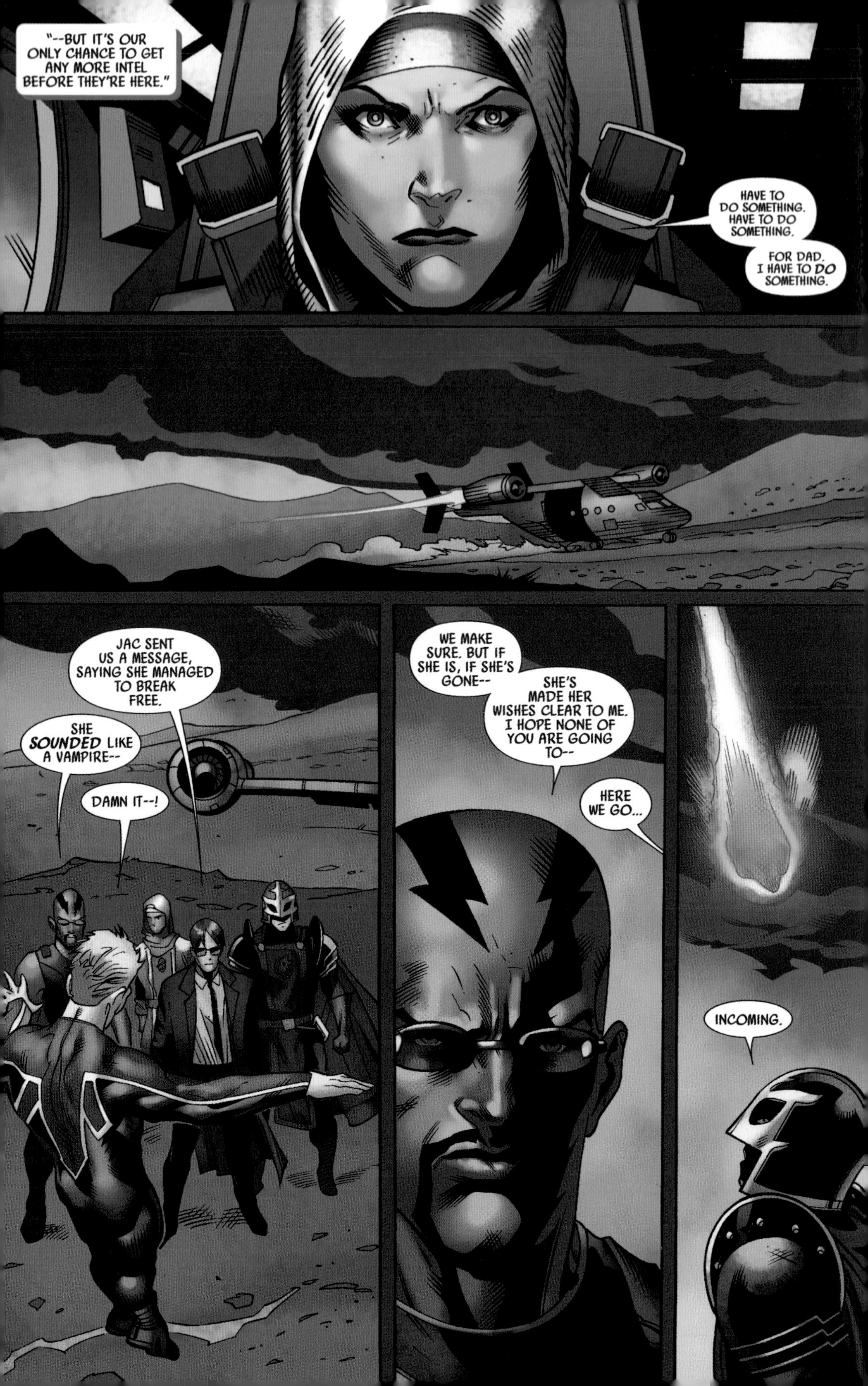
"--BUT IT'S OUR ONLY CHANCE TO GET ANY MORE INTEL BEFORE THEY'RE HERE."
HAVE TO DO SOMETHING. HAVE TO DO SOMETHING.
FOR DAD. I HAVE TO *DO* SOMETHING.
JAC SENT US A MESSAGE, SAYING SHE MANAGED TO BREAK FREE.
SHE ***SOUNDED*** LIKE A VAMPIRE--
DAMN IT--!
WE MAKE SURE. BUT IF SHE IS, IF SHE'S GONE--
SHE'S MADE HER WISHES CLEAR TO ME. I HOPE NONE OF YOU ARE GOING TO--
HERE WE GO...
INCOMING.

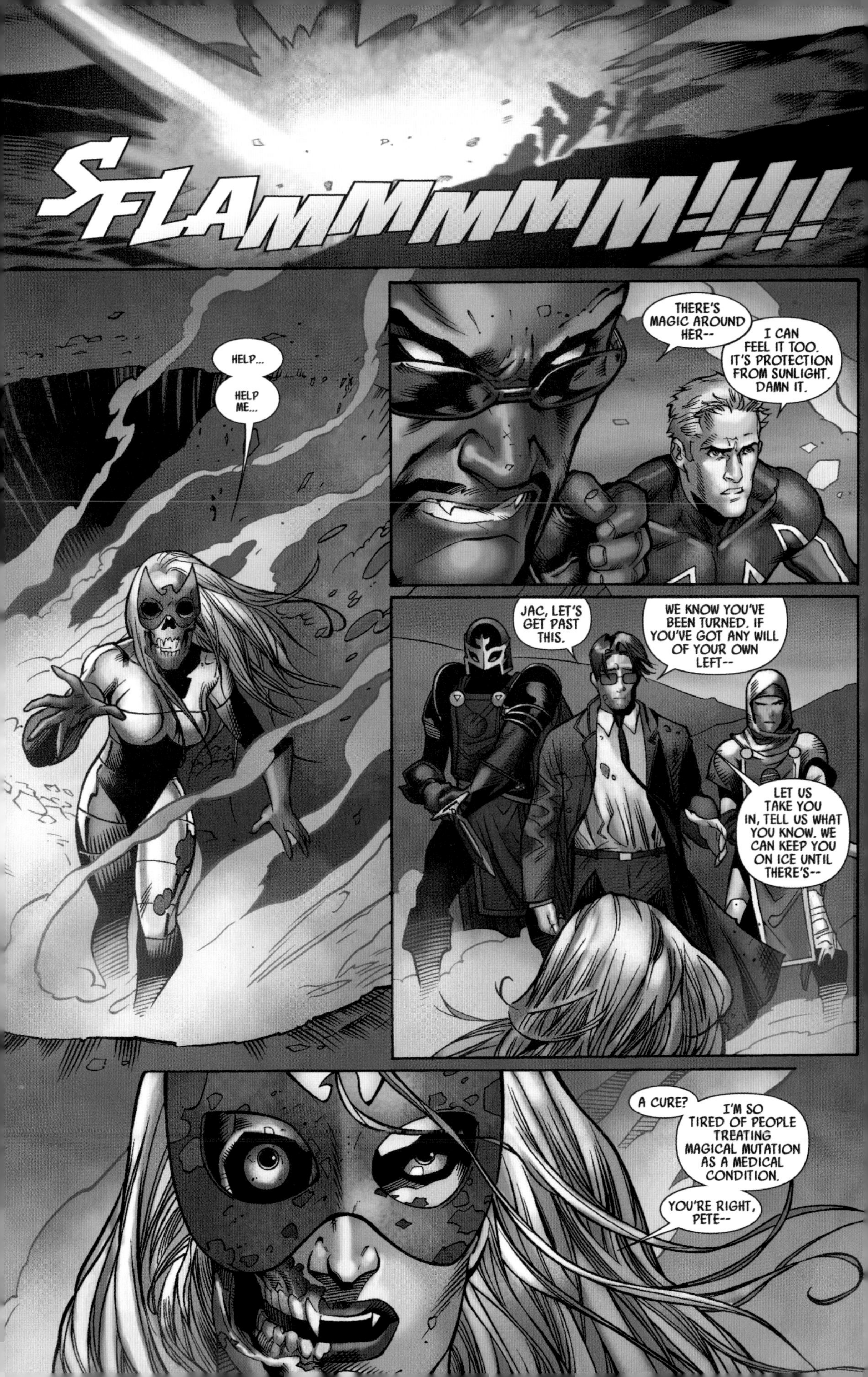
SFLAMMMMMM!!!!!
HELP...
HELP ME...
THERE'S MAGIC AROUND HER--
I CAN FEEL IT TOO. IT'S PROTECTION FROM SUNLIGHT. DAMN IT.
JAC, LET'S GET PAST THIS.
WE KNOW YOU'VE BEEN TURNED. IF YOU'VE GOT ANY WILL OF YOUR OWN LEFT--
LET US TAKE YOU IN, TELL US WHAT YOU KNOW. WE CAN KEEP YOU ON ICE UNTIL THERE'S--
A CURE?
I'M SO TIRED OF PEOPLE TREATING MAGICAL MUTATION AS A MEDICAL CONDITION.
YOU'RE RIGHT, PETE--

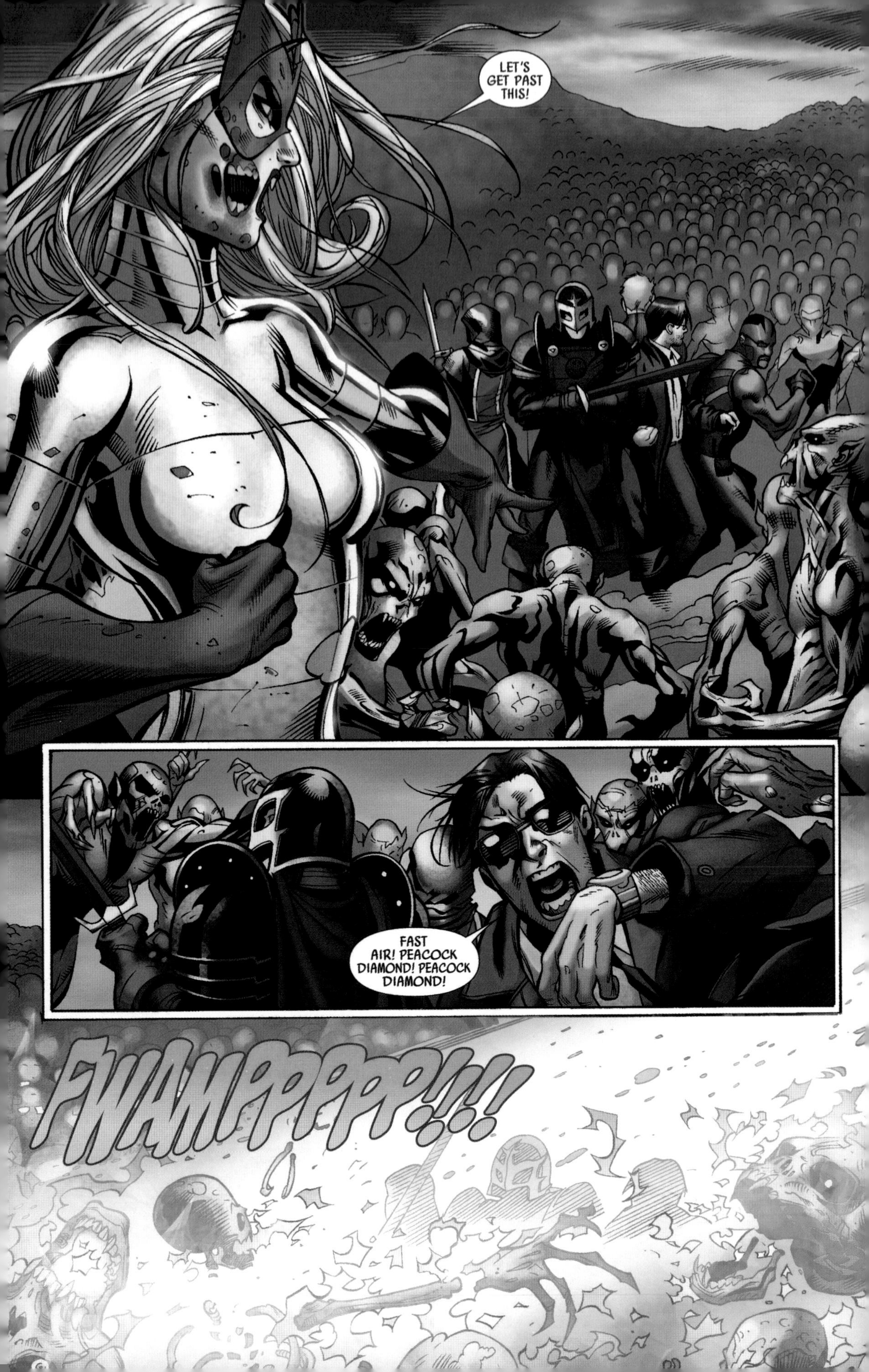
LET'S GET PAST THIS!
FAST AIR! PEACOCK DIAMOND! PEACOCK DIAMOND!
FWAMPPPPP!!!

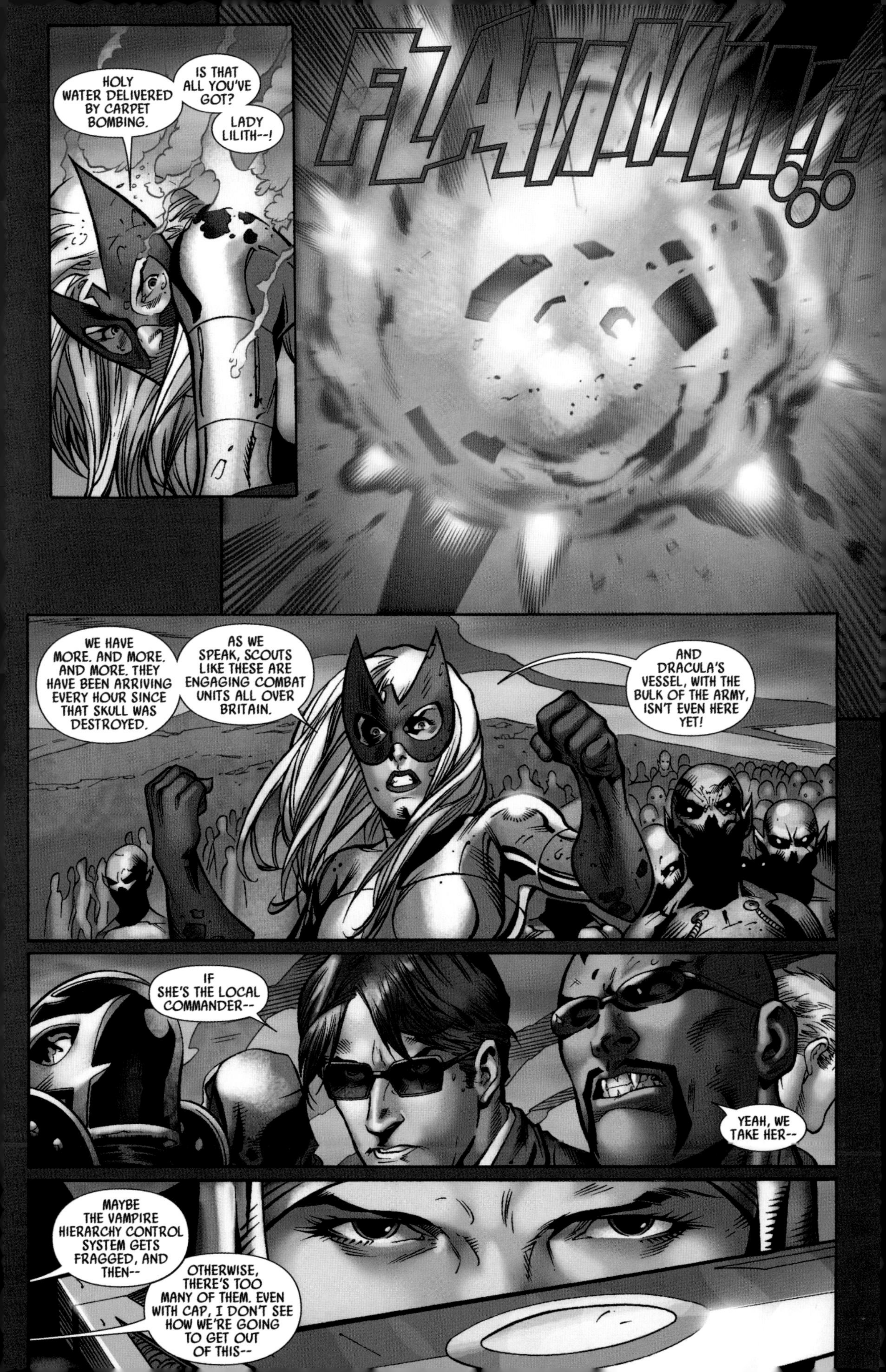
HOLY WATER DELIVERED BY CARPET BOMBING.
IS THAT ALL YOU'VE GOT?
LADY LILITH--!
FLAMMM!!
WE HAVE MORE. AND MORE. AND MORE. THEY HAVE BEEN ARRIVING EVERY HOUR SINCE THAT SKULL WAS DESTROYED.
AS WE SPEAK, SCOUTS LIKE THESE ARE ENGAGING COMBAT UNITS ALL OVER BRITAIN.
AND DRACULA'S VESSEL, WITH THE BULK OF THE ARMY, ISN'T EVEN HERE YET!
IF SHE'S THE LOCAL COMMANDER--
YEAH, WE TAKE HER--
MAYBE THE VAMPIRE HIERARCHY CONTROL SYSTEM GETS FRAGGED, AND THEN--
OTHERWISE, THERE'S TOO MANY OF THEM. EVEN WITH CAP, I DON'T SEE HOW WE'RE GOING TO GET OUT OF THIS--

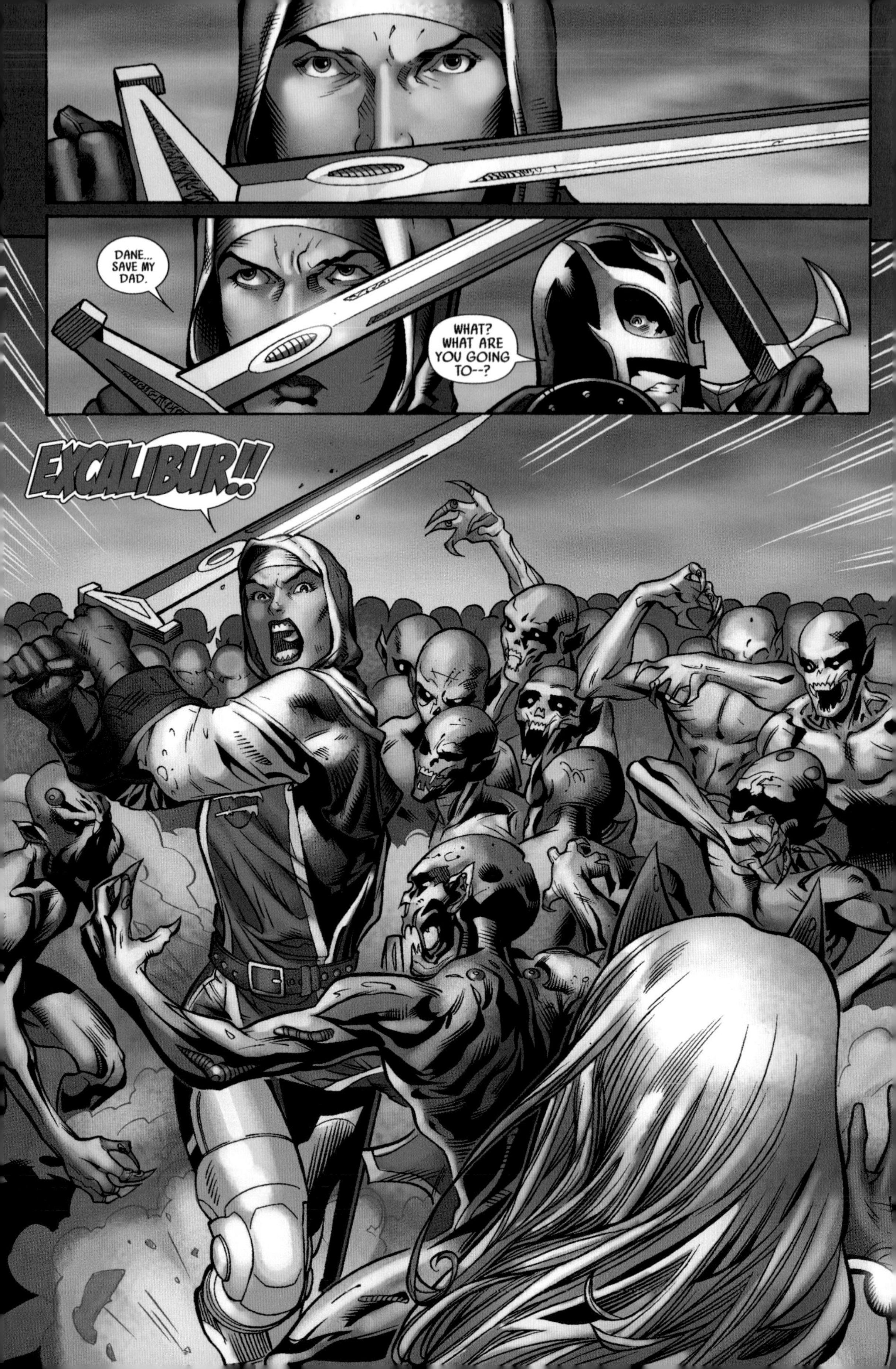

DANE... SAVE MY DAD.
WHAT? WHAT ARE YOU GOING TO--?
EXCALIBUR!!

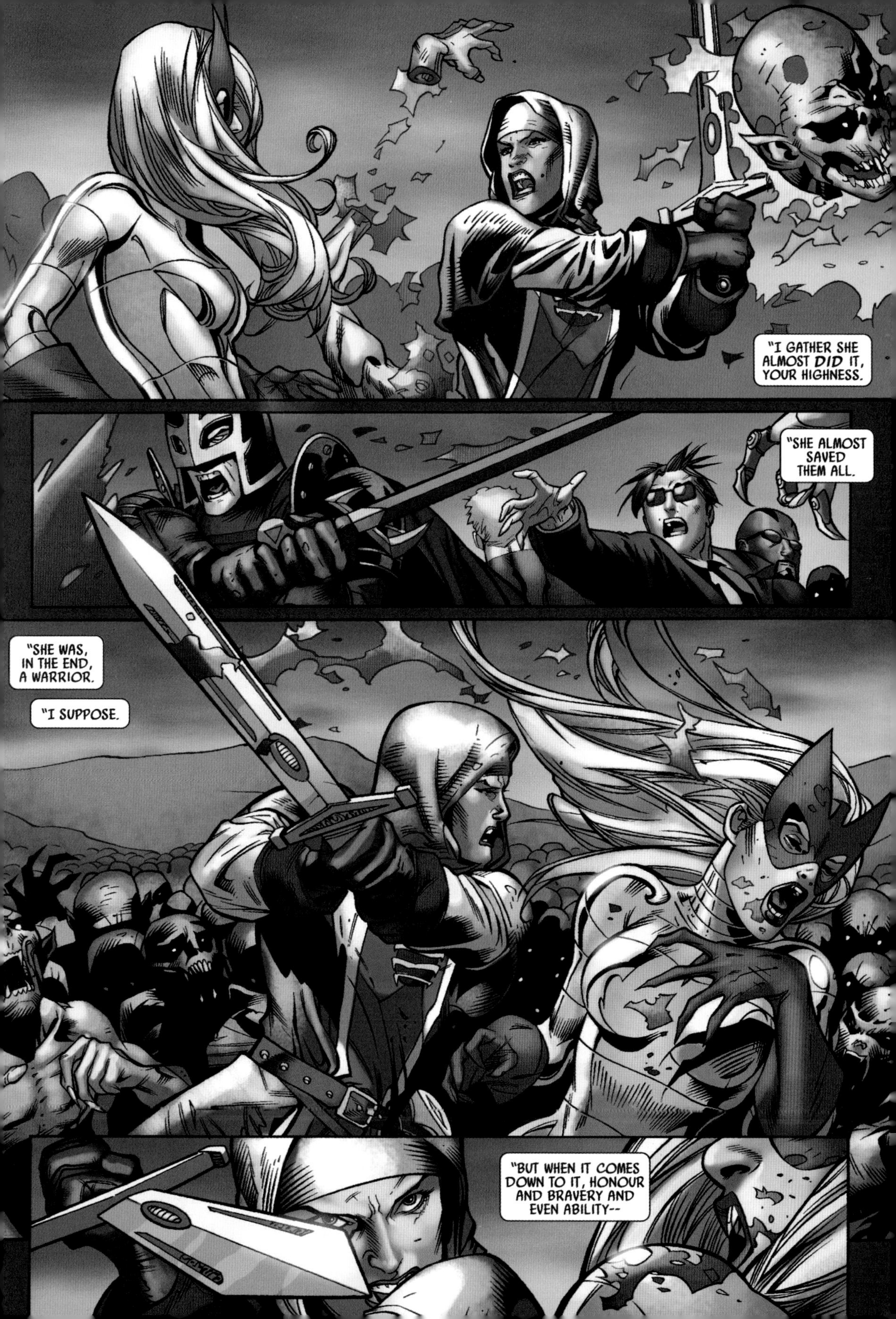
"I GATHER SHE ALMOST *DID* IT, YOUR HIGHNESS.
"SHE ALMOST SAVED THEM ALL.
"SHE WAS, IN THE END, A WARRIOR.
"I SUPPOSE.
"BUT WHEN IT COMES DOWN TO IT, HONOUR AND BRAVERY AND EVEN ABILITY--

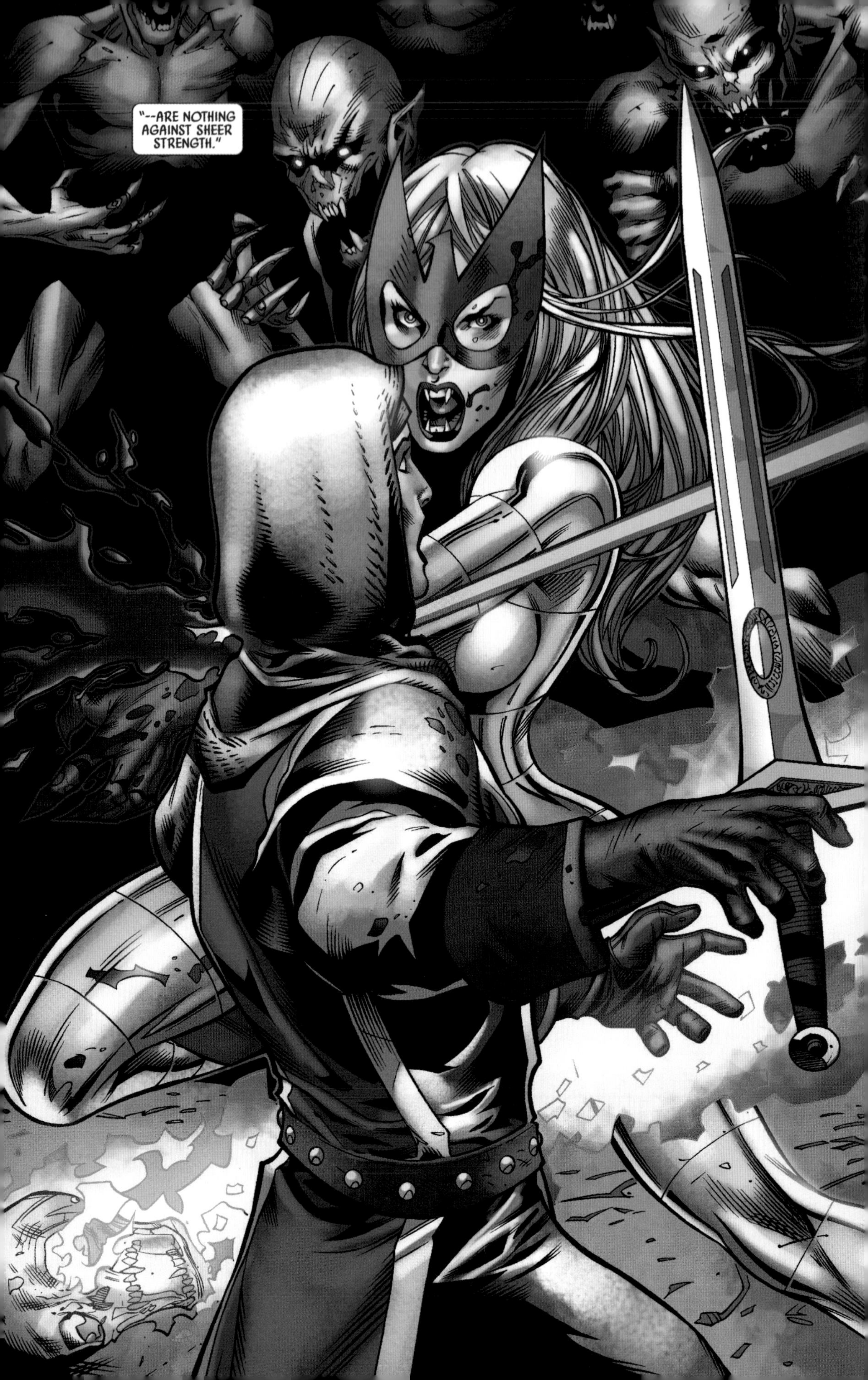
"--ARE NOTHING AGAINST SHEER STRENGTH."

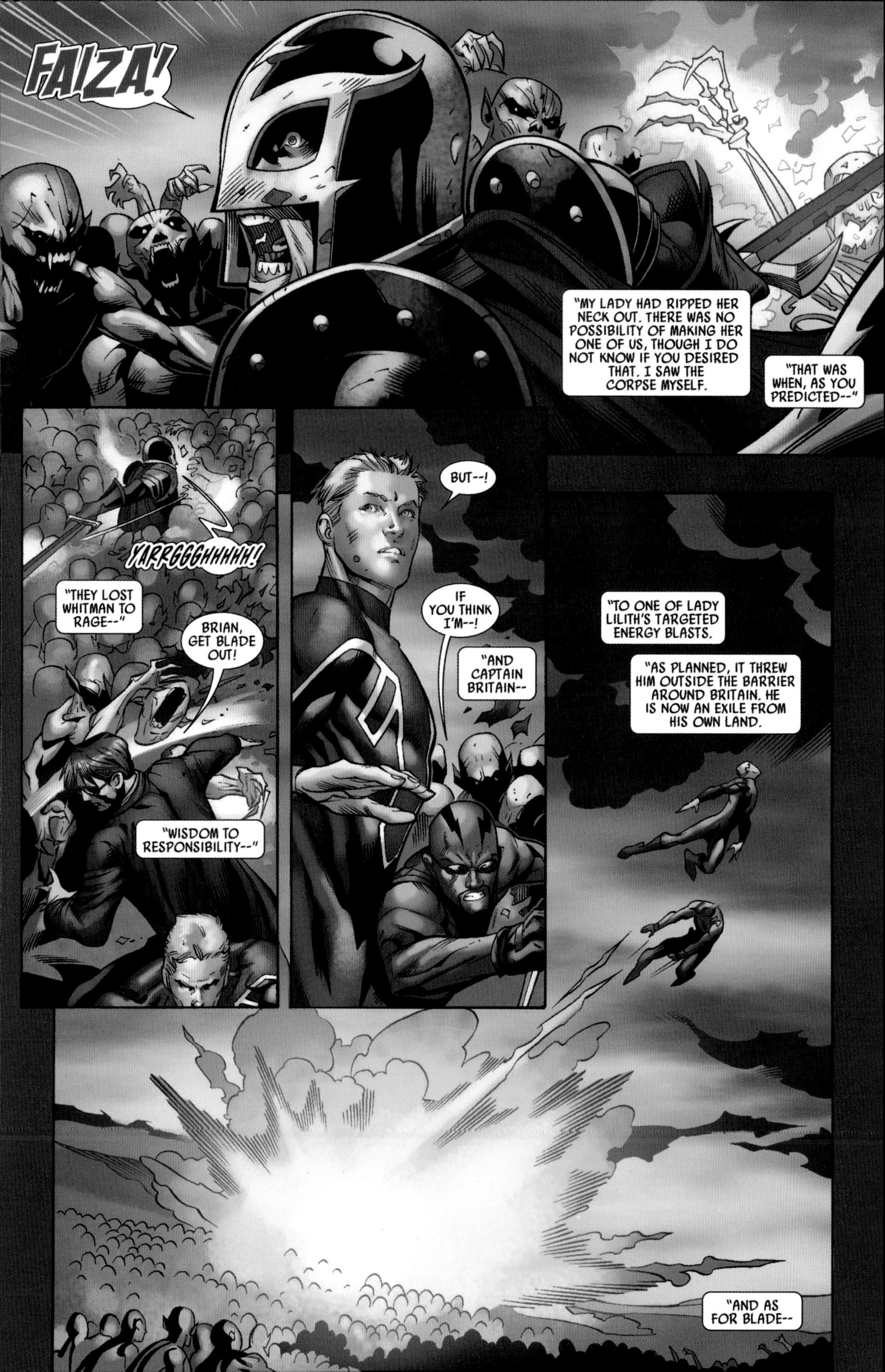
FAIZA!
"MY LADY HAD RIPPED HER NECK OUT. THERE WAS NO POSSIBILITY OF MAKING HER ONE OF US, THOUGH I DO NOT KNOW IF YOU DESIRED THAT. I SAW THE CORPSE MYSELF.
"THAT WAS WHEN, AS YOU PREDICTED--"
YARRGGGHHHHH!
"THEY LOST WHITMAN TO RAGE--"
BRIAN, GET BLADE OUT!
"WISDOM TO RESPONSIBILITY--"
BUT--!
IF YOU THINK I'M--!
"AND CAPTAIN BRITAIN--
"TO ONE OF LADY LILITH'S TARGETED ENERGY BLASTS.
"AS PLANNED, IT THREW HIM OUTSIDE THE BARRIER AROUND BRITAIN. HE IS NOW AN EXILE FROM HIS OWN LAND.
"AND AS FOR BLADE--

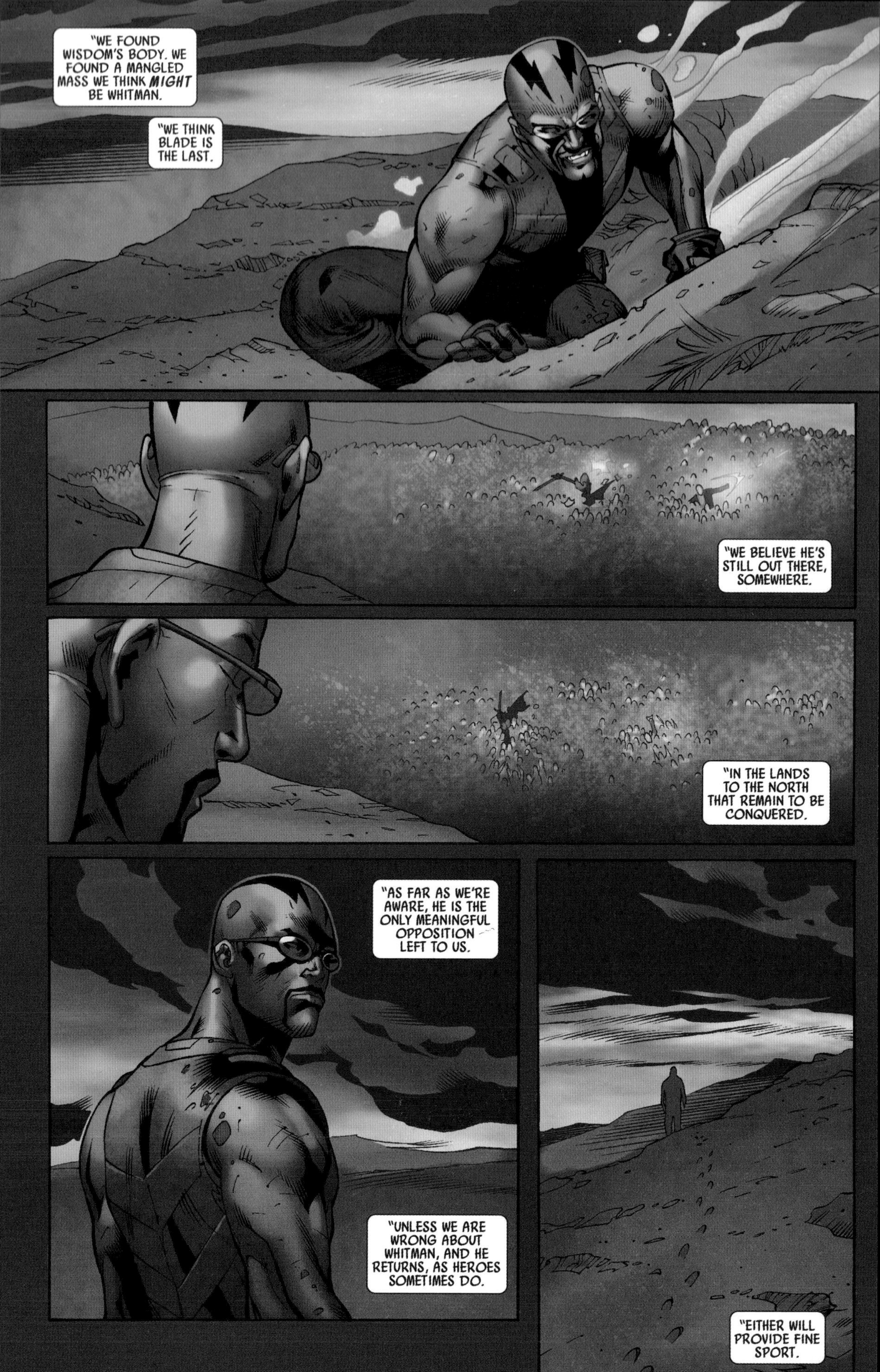
"WE FOUND WISDOM'S BODY. WE FOUND A MANGLED MASS WE THINK MIGHT BE WHITMAN.
"WE THINK BLADE IS THE LAST.
"WE BELIEVE HE'S STILL OUT THERE, SOMEWHERE.
"IN THE LANDS TO THE NORTH THAT REMAIN TO BE CONQUERED.
"AS FAR AS WE'RE AWARE, HE IS THE ONLY MEANINGFUL OPPOSITION LEFT TO US.
"UNLESS WE ARE WRONG ABOUT WHITMAN, AND HE RETURNS, AS HEROES SOMETIMES DO.
"EITHER WILL PROVIDE FINE SPORT.

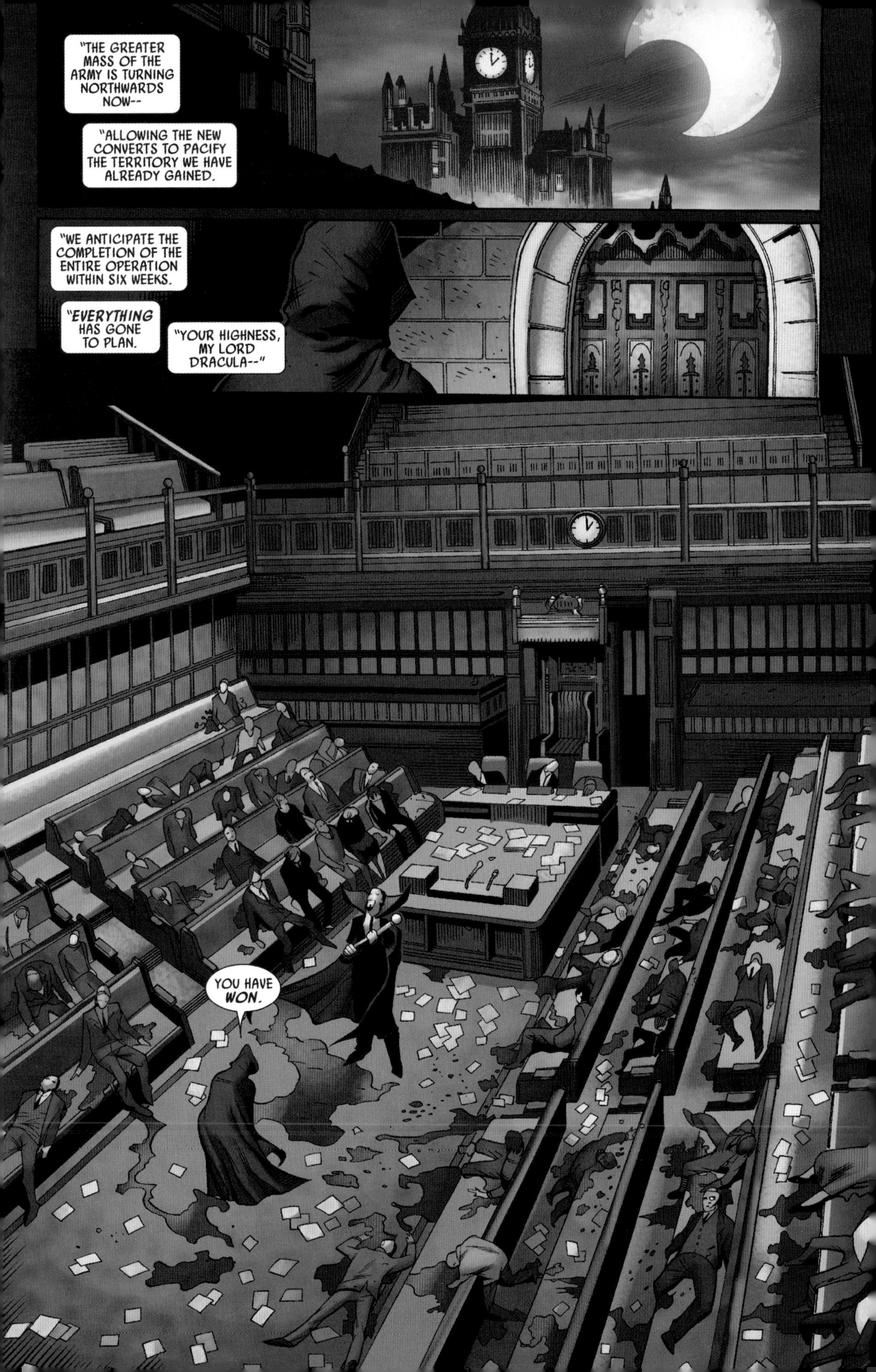
"THE GREATER MASS OF THE ARMY IS TURNING NORTHWARDS NOW--
"ALLOWING THE NEW CONVERTS TO PACIFY THE TERRITORY WE HAVE ALREADY GAINED.
"WE ANTICIPATE THE COMPLETION OF THE ENTIRE OPERATION WITHIN SIX WEEKS.
"EVERYTHING HAS GONE TO PLAN.
"YOUR HIGHNESS, MY LORD DRACULA--"
YOU HAVE WON.

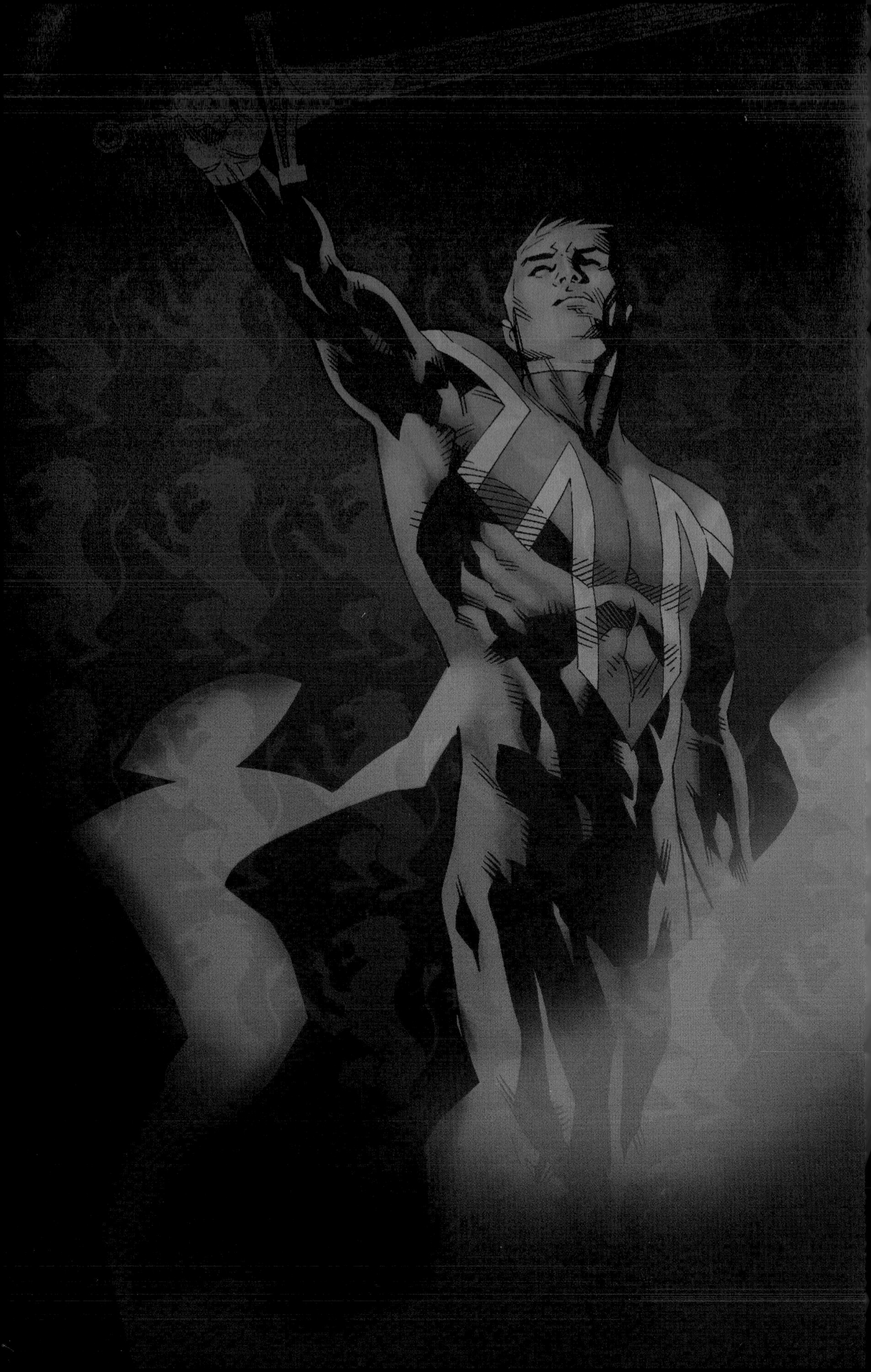

CAPTAIN BRITAIN AND MI13 ANNUAL #1
COVER ARTWORK

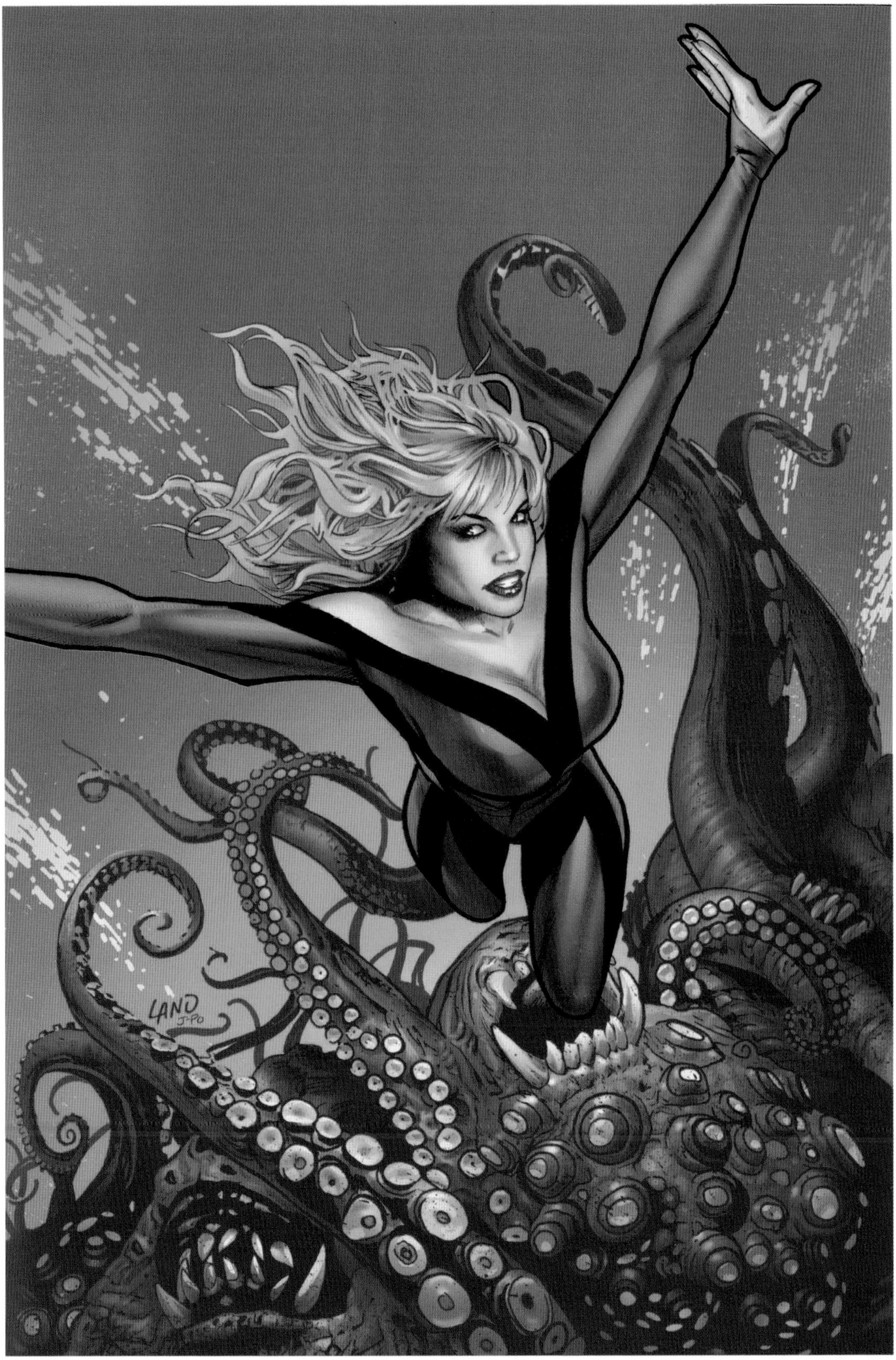
LAND
J-PO

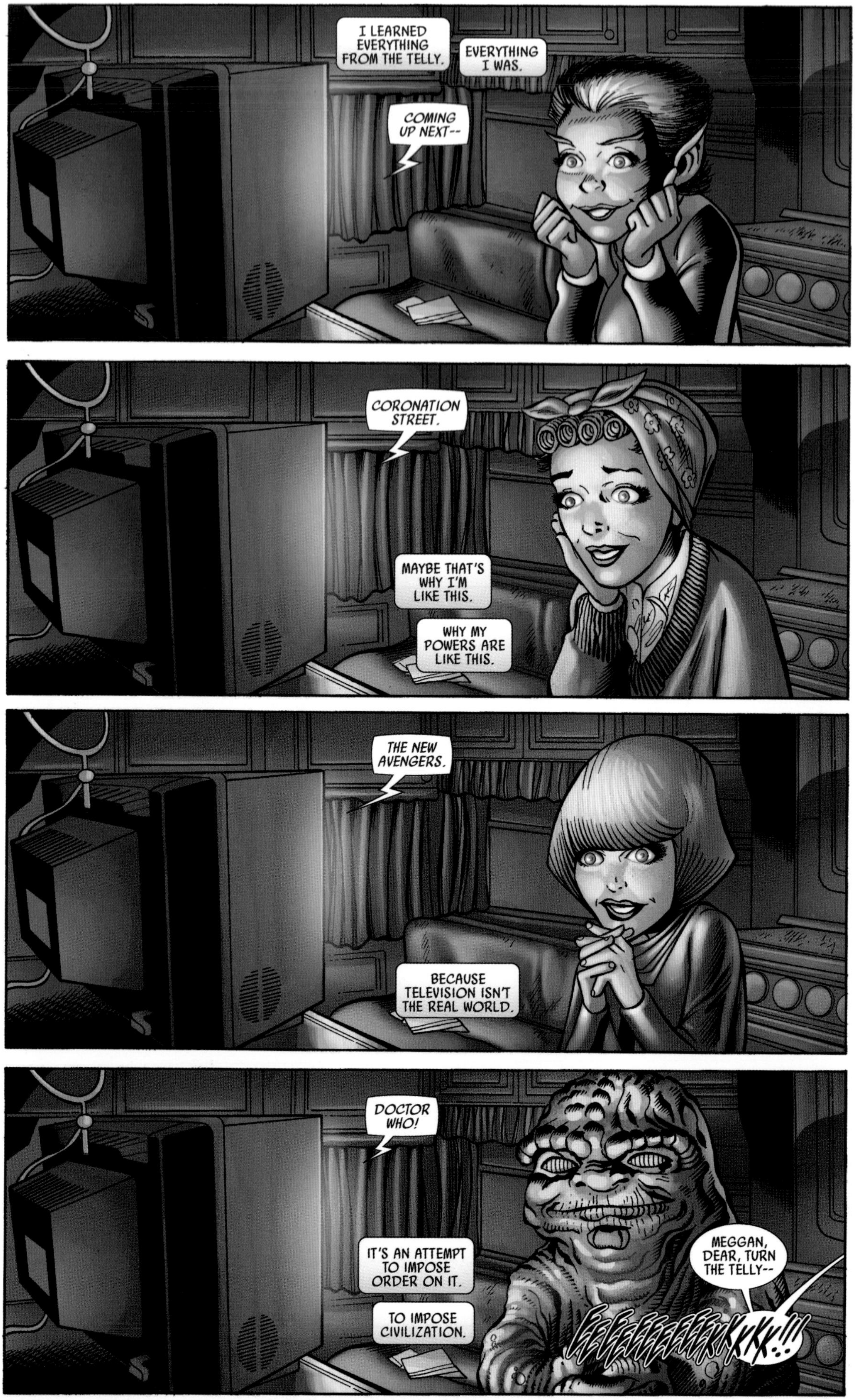
I LEARNED EVERYTHING FROM THE TELLY.
EVERYTHING I WAS.
COMING UP NEXT--
CORONATION STREET.
MAYBE THAT'S WHY I'M LIKE THIS.
WHY MY POWERS ARE LIKE THIS.
THE NEW AVENGERS.
BECAUSE TELEVISION ISN'T THE REAL WORLD.
DOCTOR WHO!
IT'S AN ATTEMPT TO IMPOSE ORDER ON IT.
TO IMPOSE CIVILIZATION.
MEGGAN, DEAR, TURN THE TELLY--
EEEEEEEEEEEEKKKK!!!

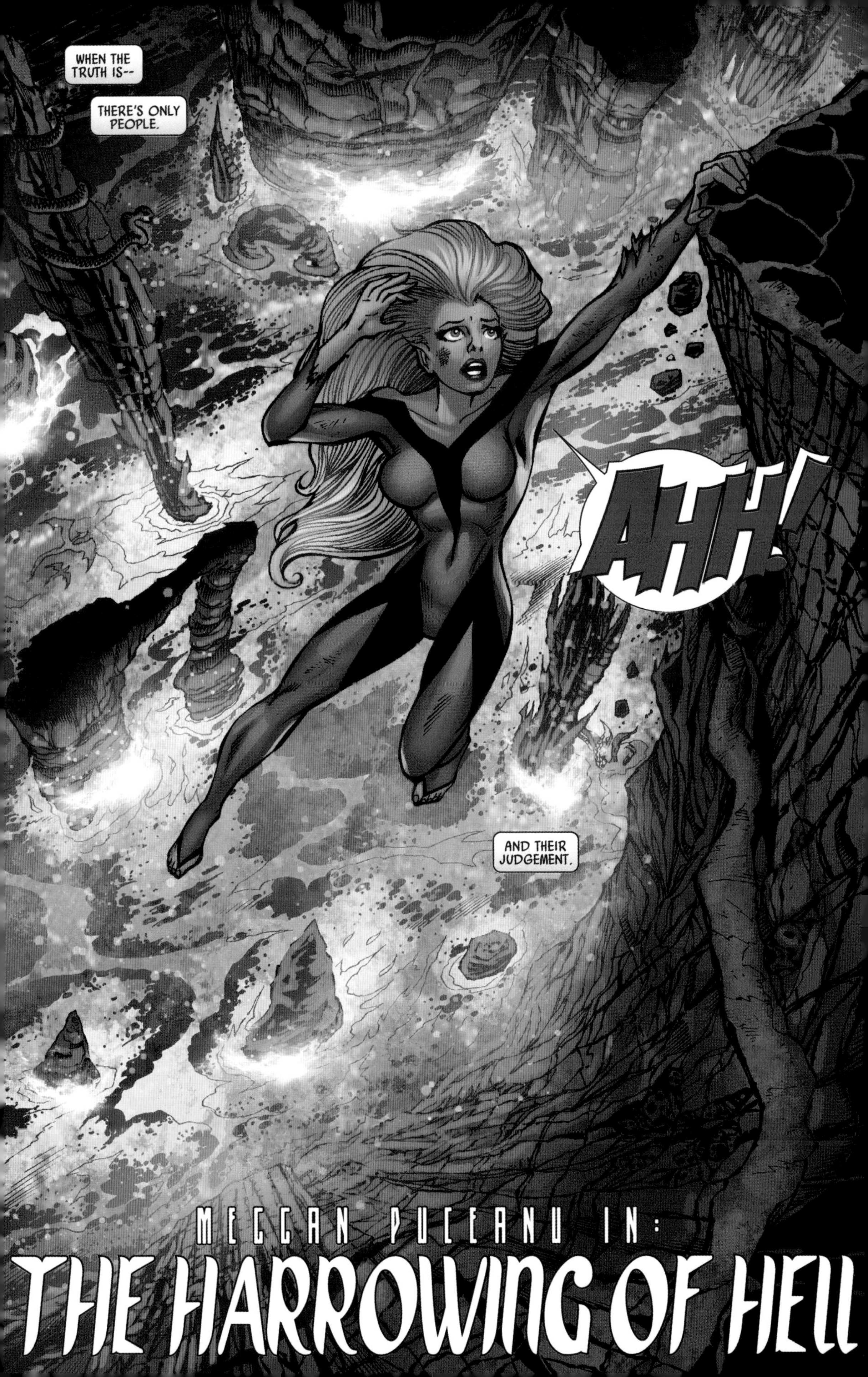
WHEN THE TRUTH IS--
THERE'S ONLY PEOPLE.
AHH!
AND THEIR JUDGEMENT.
MEGGAN PUCEANU IN:
THE HARROWING OF HELL

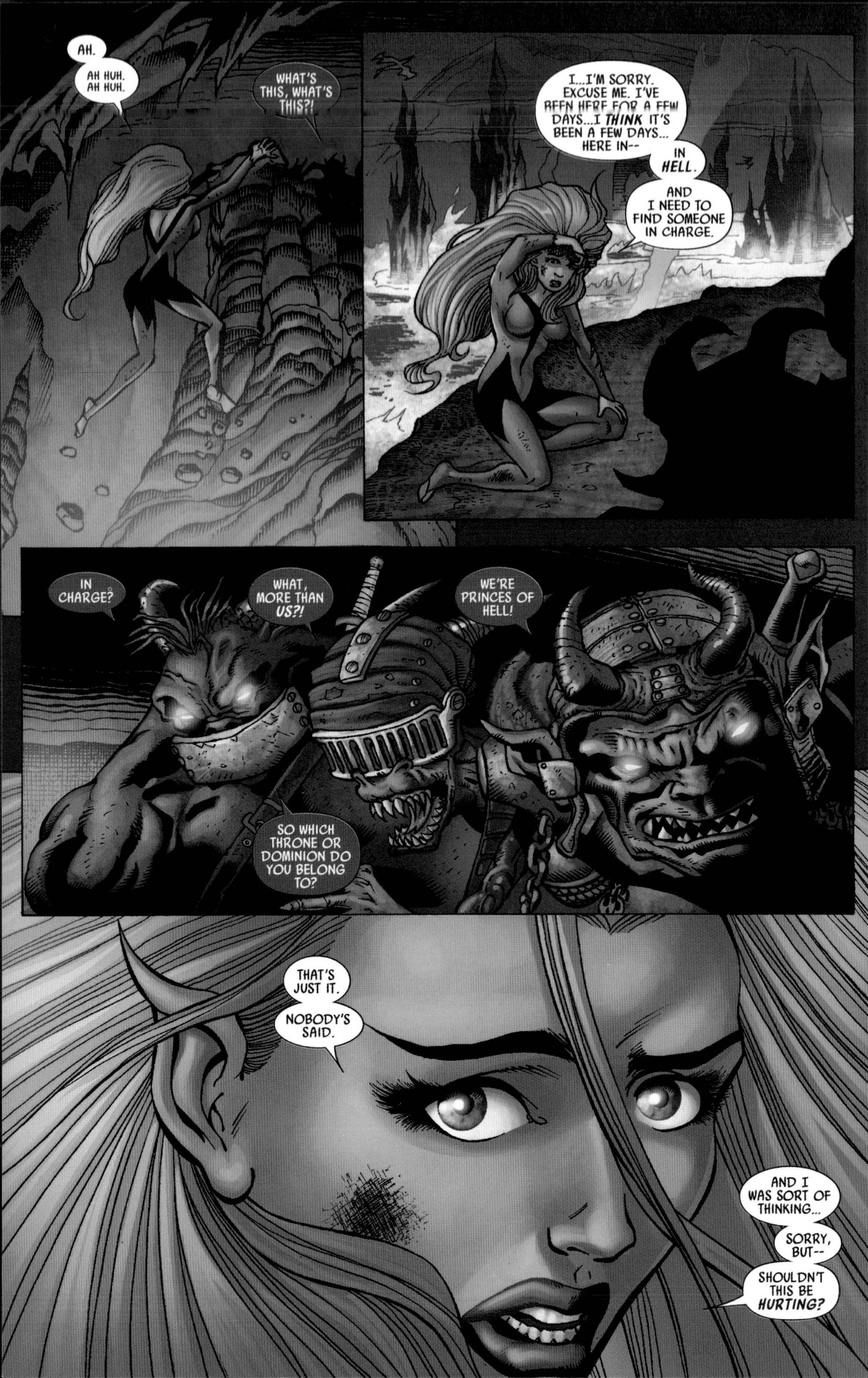
AH.
AH HUH. AH HUH.
WHAT'S THIS, WHAT'S THIS?!
I...I'M SORRY. EXCUSE ME. I'VE BEEN HERE FOR A FEW DAYS...I THINK IT'S BEEN A FEW DAYS... HERE IN--
IN HELL.
AND I NEED TO FIND SOMEONE IN CHARGE.
IN CHARGE?
WHAT, MORE THAN US?!
WE'RE PRINCES OF HELL!
SO WHICH THRONE OR DOMINION DO YOU BELONG TO?
THAT'S JUST IT.
NOBODY'S SAID.
AND I WAS SORT OF THINKING...
SORRY, BUT--
SHOULDN'T THIS BE HURTING?

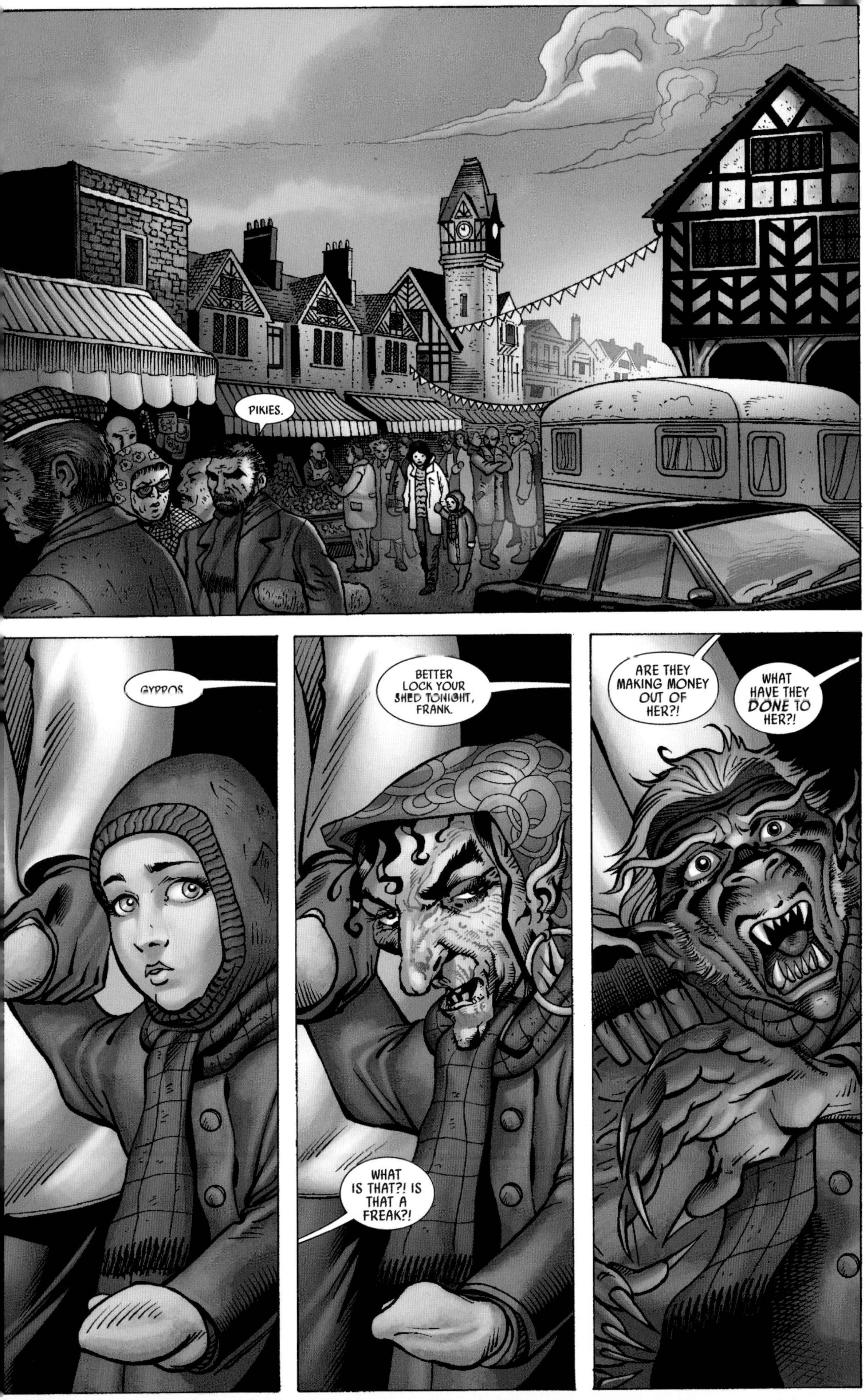
PIKIES.
GYPPOS
BETTER LOCK YOUR SHED TONIGHT, FRANK.
WHAT IS THAT?! IS THAT A FREAK?!
ARE THEY MAKING MONEY OUT OF HER?!
WHAT HAVE THEY DONE TO HER?!

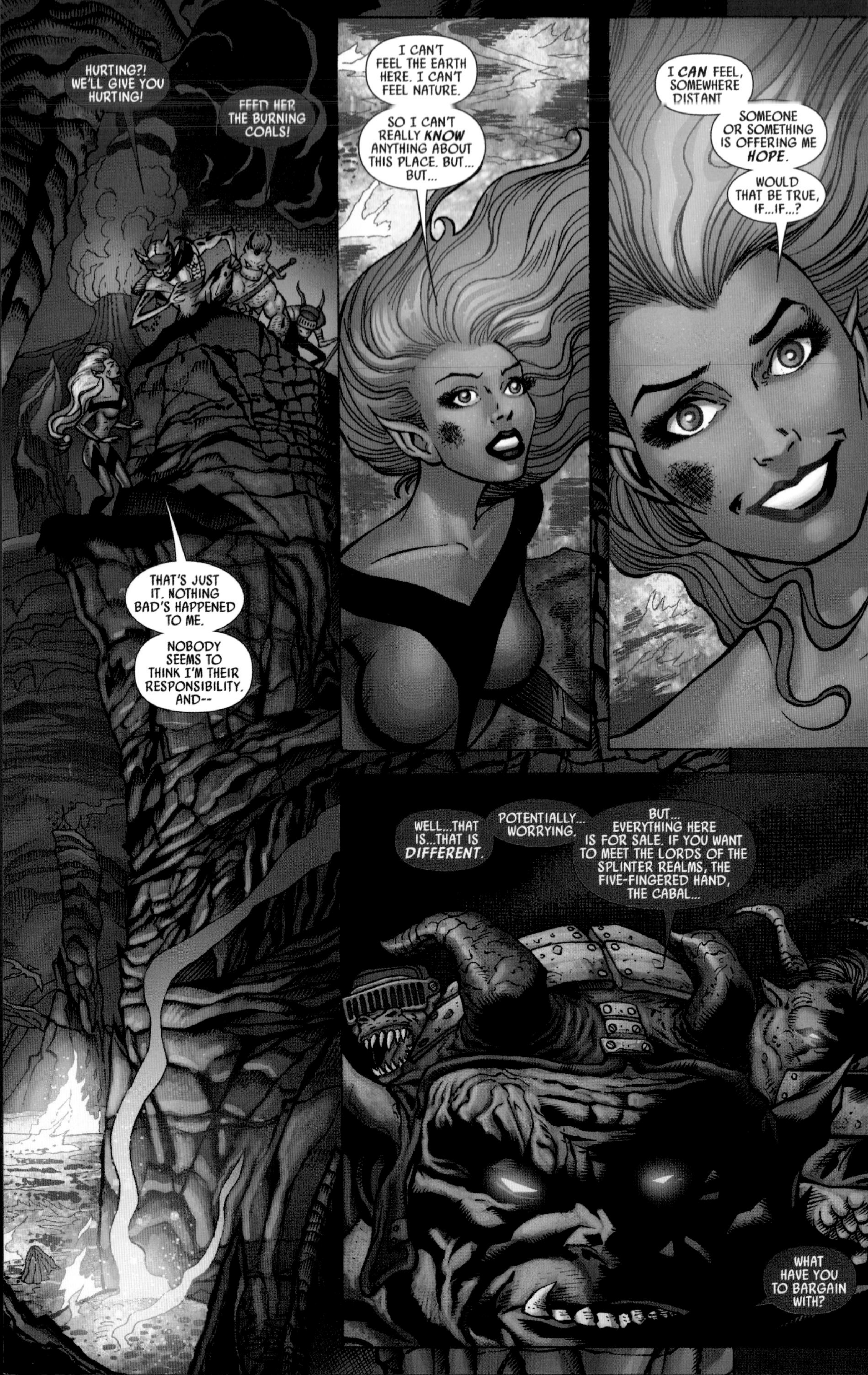
HURTING?! WE'LL GIVE YOU HURTING!
FEED HER THE BURNING COALS!
THAT'S JUST IT. NOTHING BAD'S HAPPENED TO ME.
NOBODY SEEMS TO THINK I'M THEIR RESPONSIBILITY. AND--
I CAN'T FEEL THE EARTH HERE. I CAN'T FEEL NATURE.
SO I CAN'T REALLY KNOW ANYTHING ABOUT THIS PLACE. BUT... BUT...
I CAN FEEL, SOMEWHERE DISTANT
SOMEONE OR SOMETHING IS OFFERING ME HOPE.
WOULD THAT BE TRUE, IF...IF...?
WELL...THAT IS...THAT IS DIFFERENT.
POTENTIALLY... WORRYING.
BUT... EVERYTHING HERE IS FOR SALE. IF YOU WANT TO MEET THE LORDS OF THE SPLINTER REALMS, THE FIVE-FINGERED HAND, THE CABAL...
WHAT HAVE YOU TO BARGAIN WITH?

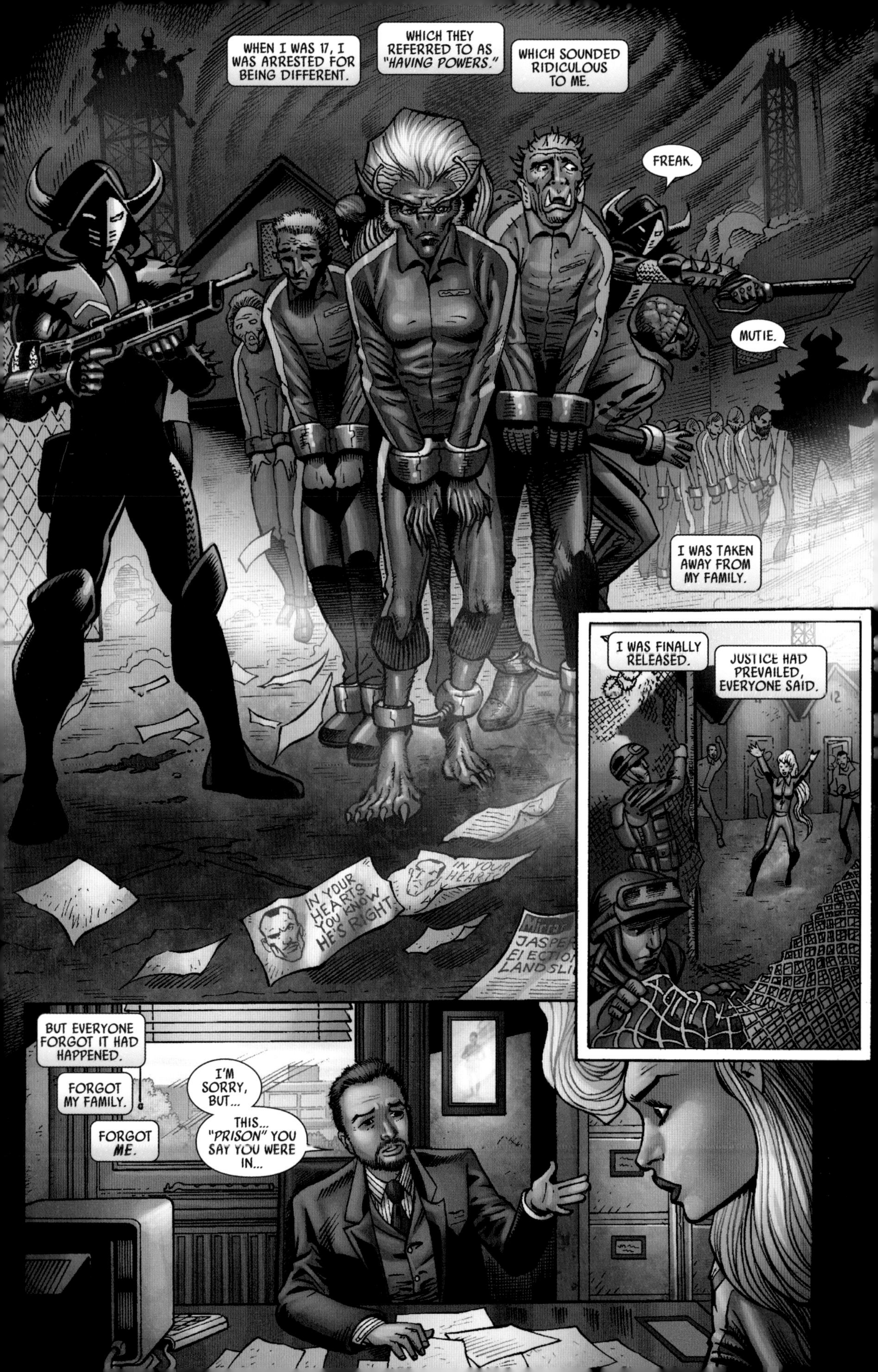
WHEN I WAS 17, I WAS ARRESTED FOR BEING DIFFERENT.
WHICH THEY REFERRED TO AS "HAVING POWERS."
WHICH SOUNDED RIDICULOUS TO ME.
FREAK.
MUTIE.
I WAS TAKEN AWAY FROM MY FAMILY.
IN YOUR HEARTS YOU KNOW HE'S RIGHT
I WAS FINALLY RELEASED.
JUSTICE HAD PREVAILED, EVERYONE SAID.
BUT EVERYONE FORGOT IT HAD HAPPENED.
FORGOT MY FAMILY.
FORGOT *ME*.
I'M SORRY, BUT...
THIS... "PRISON" YOU SAY YOU WERE IN...

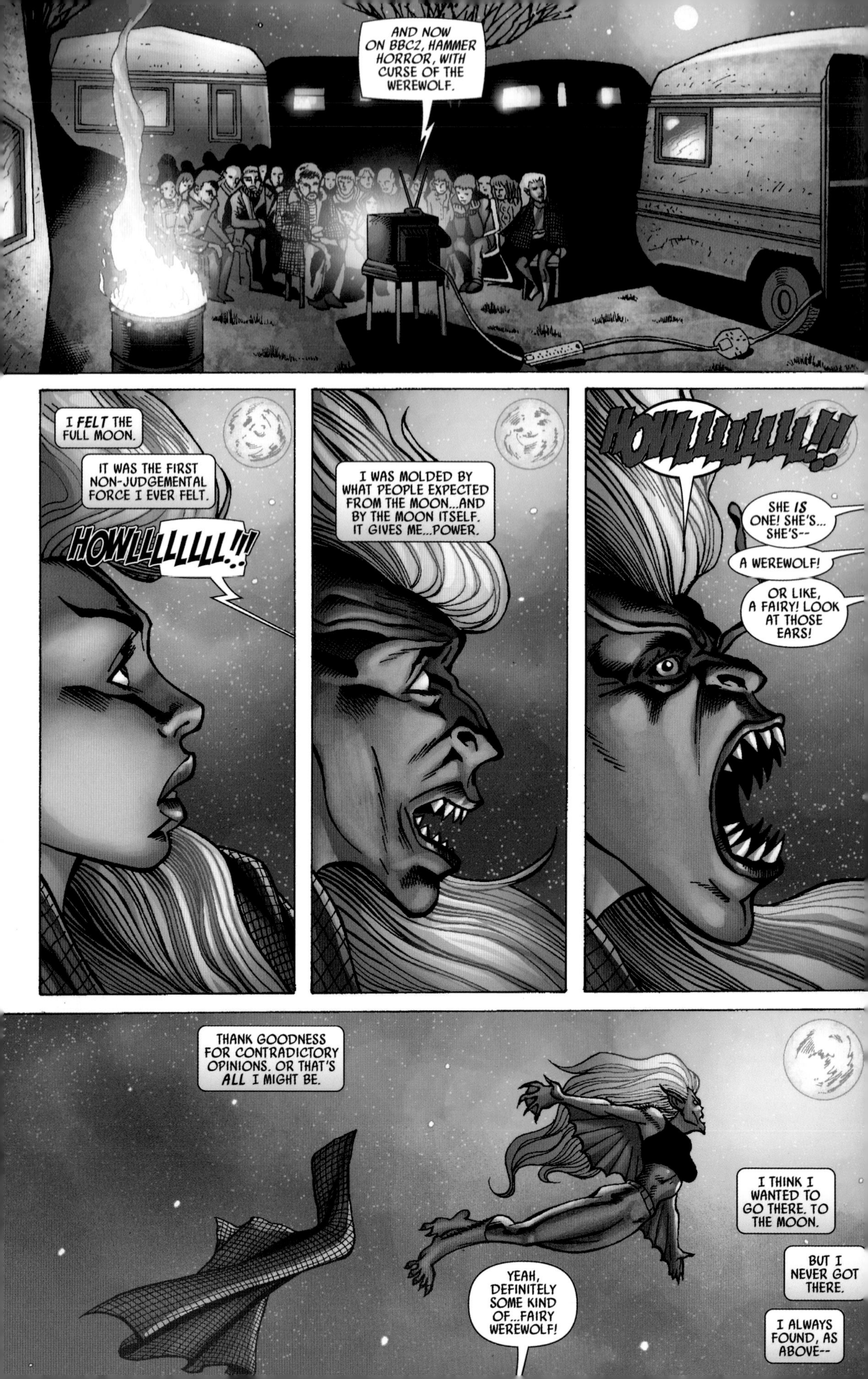

AND NOW ON BBC2, HAMMER HORROR, WITH CURSE OF THE WEREWOLF.
I FELT THE FULL MOON.
IT WAS THE FIRST NON-JUDGEMENTAL FORCE I EVER FELT.
HOWLLLLLLLL!!!
I WAS MOLDED BY WHAT PEOPLE EXPECTED FROM THE MOON...AND BY THE MOON ITSELF. IT GIVES ME...POWER.
HOWLLLLLLLL!!!
SHE IS ONE! SHE'S... SHE'S--
A WEREWOLF!
OR LIKE, A FAIRY! LOOK AT THOSE EARS!
THANK GOODNESS FOR CONTRADICTORY OPINIONS. OR THAT'S ALL I MIGHT BE.
I THINK I WANTED TO GO THERE. TO THE MOON.
BUT I NEVER GOT THERE.
I ALWAYS FOUND, AS ABOVE--
YEAH, DEFINITELY SOME KIND OF...FAIRY WEREWOLF!

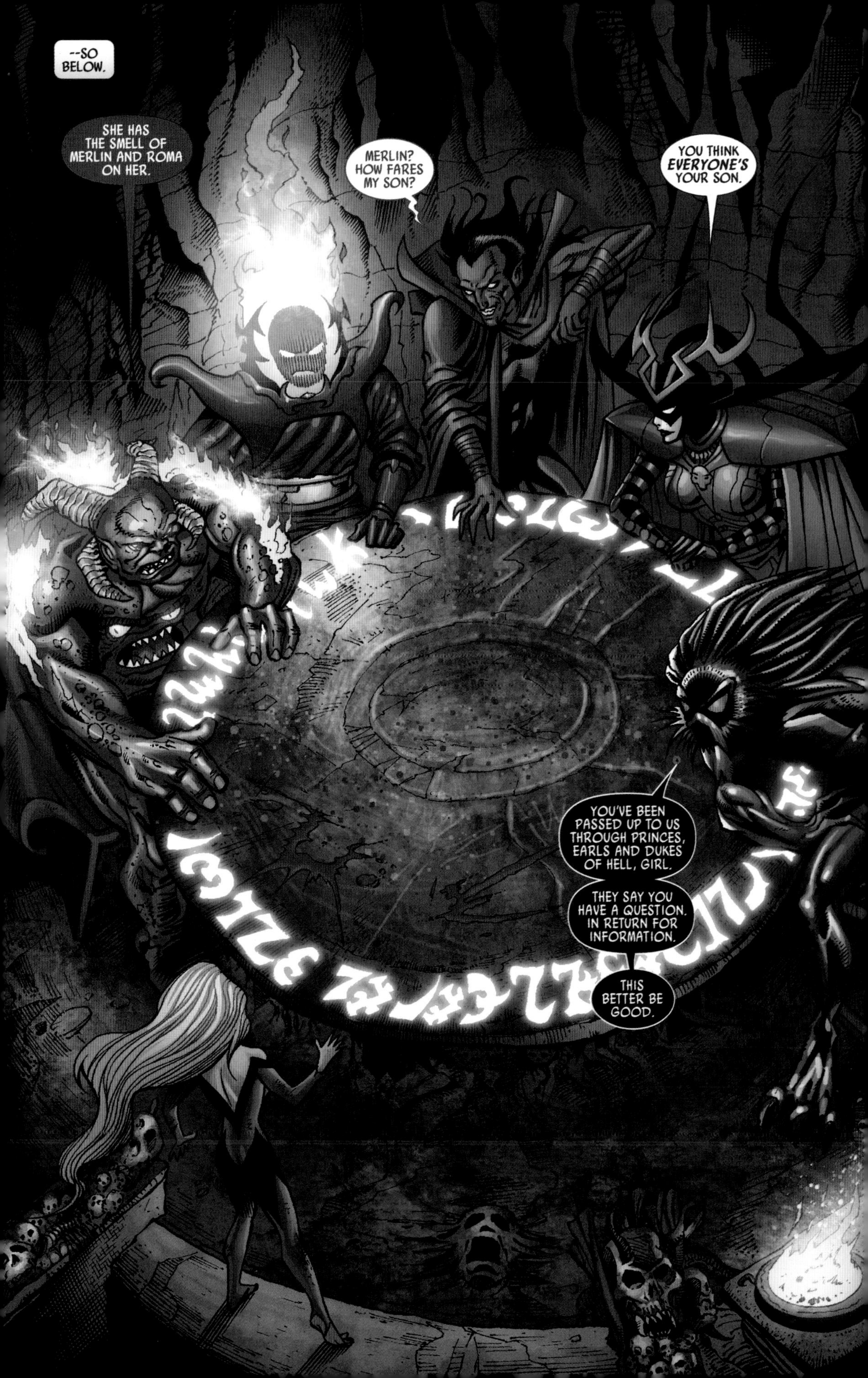
--SO BELOW.
SHE HAS THE SMELL OF MERLIN AND ROMA ON HER.
MERLIN? HOW FARES MY SON?
YOU THINK *EVERYONE'S* YOUR SON.
YOU'VE BEEN PASSED UP TO US THROUGH PRINCES, EARLS AND DUKES OF HELL, GIRL.
THEY SAY YOU HAVE A QUESTION. IN RETURN FOR INFORMATION.
THIS BETTER BE GOOD.

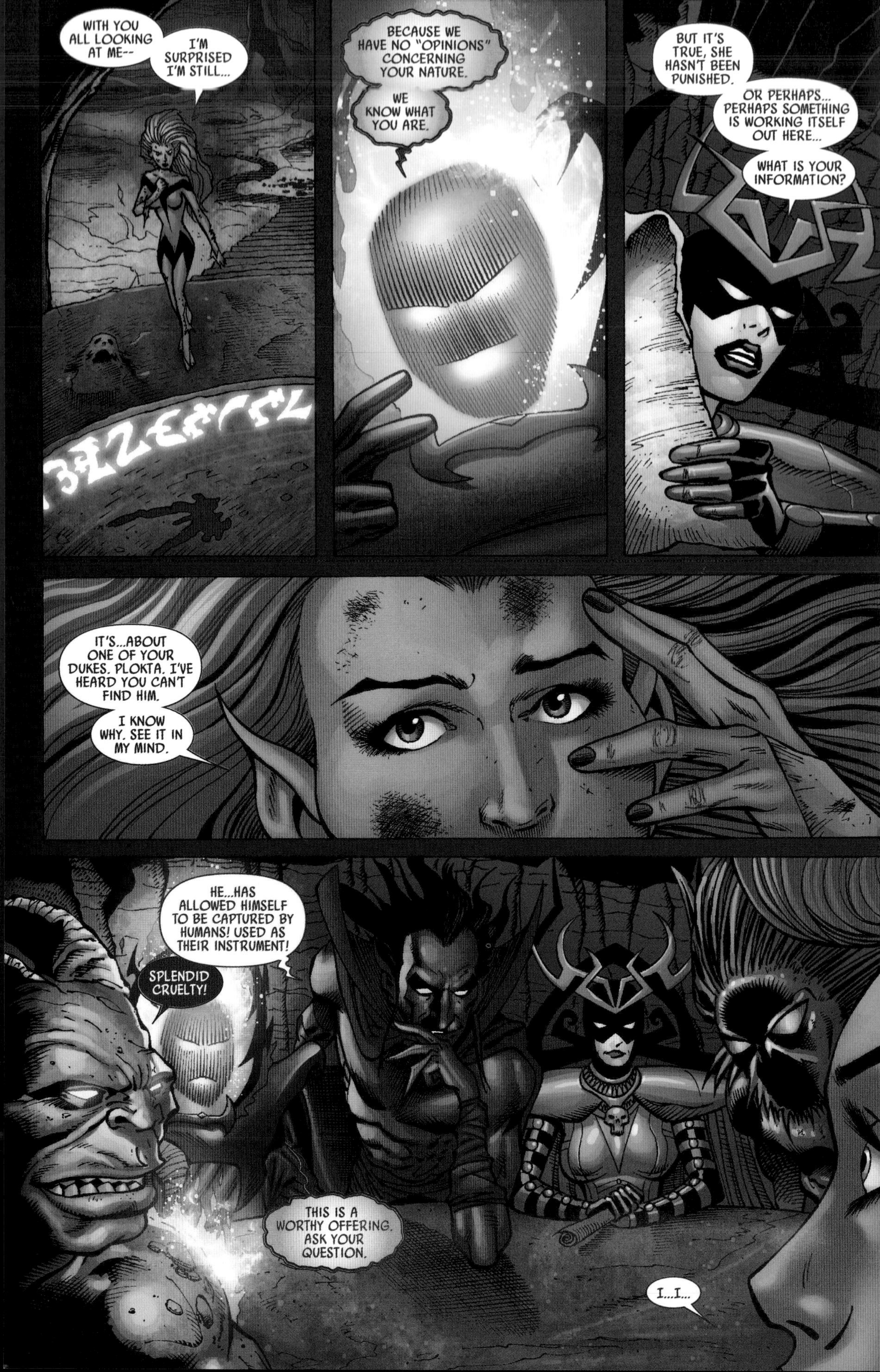

WITH YOU ALL LOOKING AT ME--
I'M SURPRISED I'M STILL...
BECAUSE WE HAVE NO "OPINIONS" CONCERNING YOUR NATURE.
WE KNOW WHAT YOU ARE.
BUT IT'S TRUE, SHE HASN'T BEEN PUNISHED.
OR PERHAPS... PERHAPS SOMETHING IS WORKING ITSELF OUT HERE...
WHAT IS YOUR INFORMATION?
IT'S...ABOUT ONE OF YOUR DUKES. PLOKTA. I'VE HEARD YOU CAN'T FIND HIM.
I KNOW WHY. SEE IT IN MY MIND.
HE...HAS ALLOWED HIMSELF TO BE CAPTURED BY HUMANS! USED AS THEIR INSTRUMENT!
SPLENDID CRUELTY!
THIS IS A WORTHY OFFERING. ASK YOUR QUESTION.
I...I...

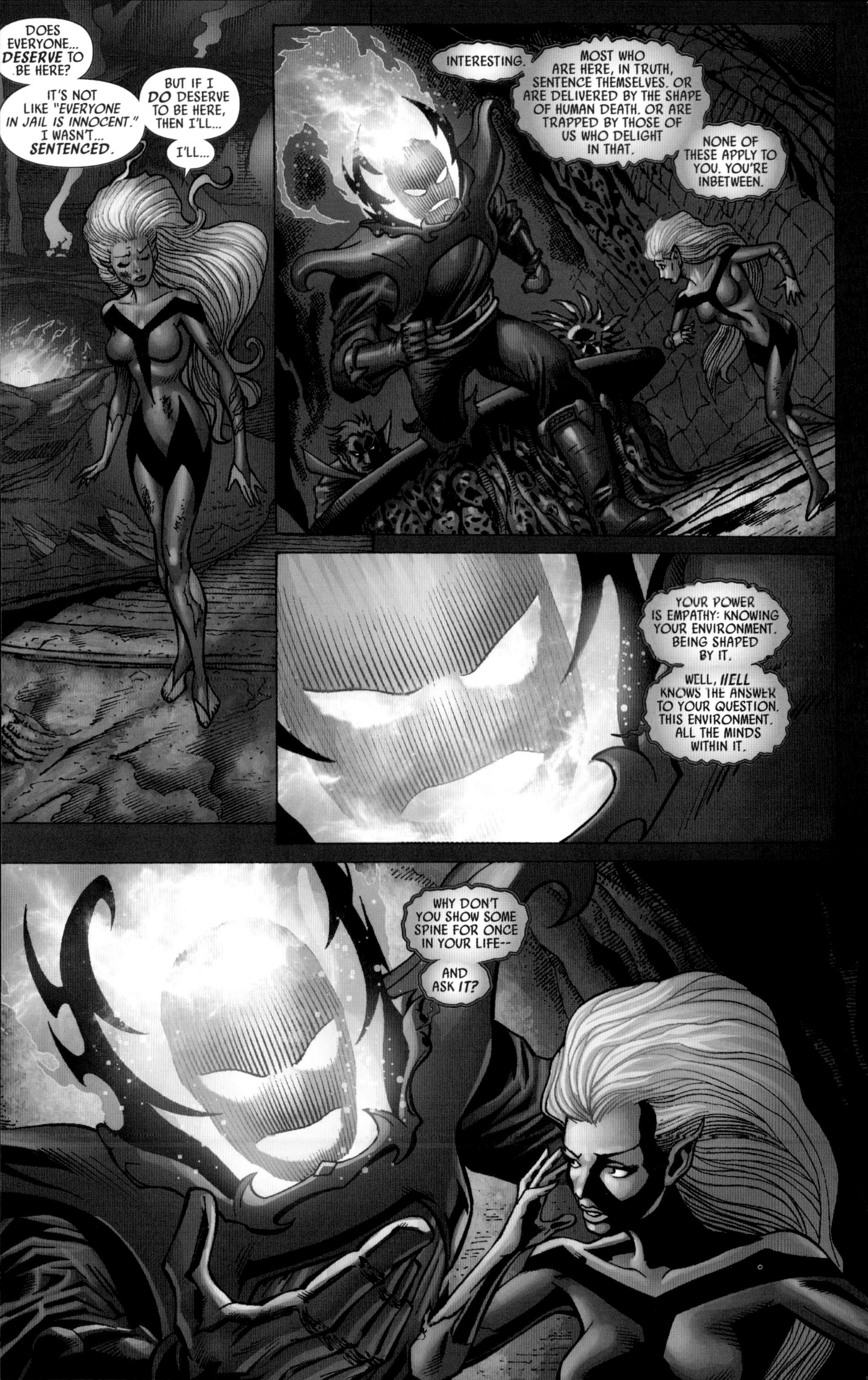

DOES EVERYONE... DESERVE TO BE HERE?
IT'S NOT LIKE "EVERYONE IN JAIL IS INNOCENT." I WASN'T... SENTENCED.
BUT IF I DO DESERVE TO BE HERE, THEN I'LL...
I'LL...
INTERESTING.
MOST WHO ARE HERE, IN TRUTH, SENTENCE THEMSELVES. OR ARE DELIVERED BY THE SHAPE OF HUMAN DEATH. OR ARE TRAPPED BY THOSE OF US WHO DELIGHT IN THAT.
NONE OF THESE APPLY TO YOU. YOU'RE INBETWEEN.
YOUR POWER IS EMPATHY: KNOWING YOUR ENVIRONMENT. BEING SHAPED BY IT.
WELL, HELL KNOWS THE ANSWER TO YOUR QUESTION. THIS ENVIRONMENT. ALL THE MINDS WITHIN IT.
WHY DON'T YOU SHOW SOME SPINE FOR ONCE IN YOUR LIFE--
AND ASK IT?

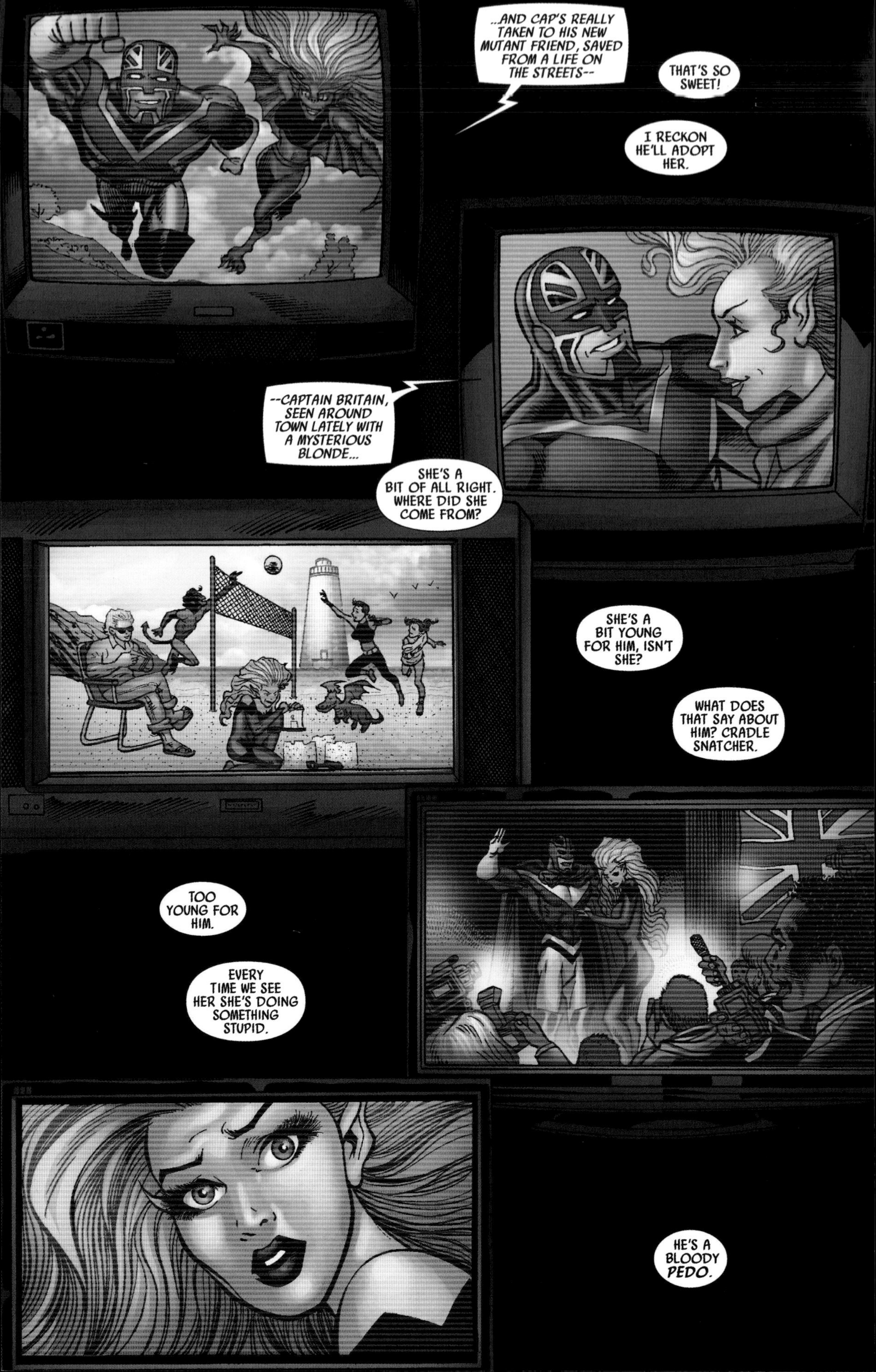
..AND CAP'S REALLY TAKEN TO HIS NEW MUTANT FRIEND, SAVED FROM A LIFE ON THE STREETS--
THAT'S SO SWEET!
I RECKON HE'LL ADOPT HER.
--CAPTAIN BRITAIN, SEEN AROUND TOWN LATELY WITH A MYSTERIOUS BLONDE...
SHE'S A BIT OF ALL RIGHT. WHERE DID SHE COME FROM?
SHE'S A BIT YOUNG FOR HIM, ISN'T SHE?
WHAT DOES THAT SAY ABOUT HIM? CRADLE SNATCHER.
TOO YOUNG FOR HIM.
EVERY TIME WE SEE HER SHE'S DOING SOMETHING STUPID.
HE'S A BLOODY PEDO.

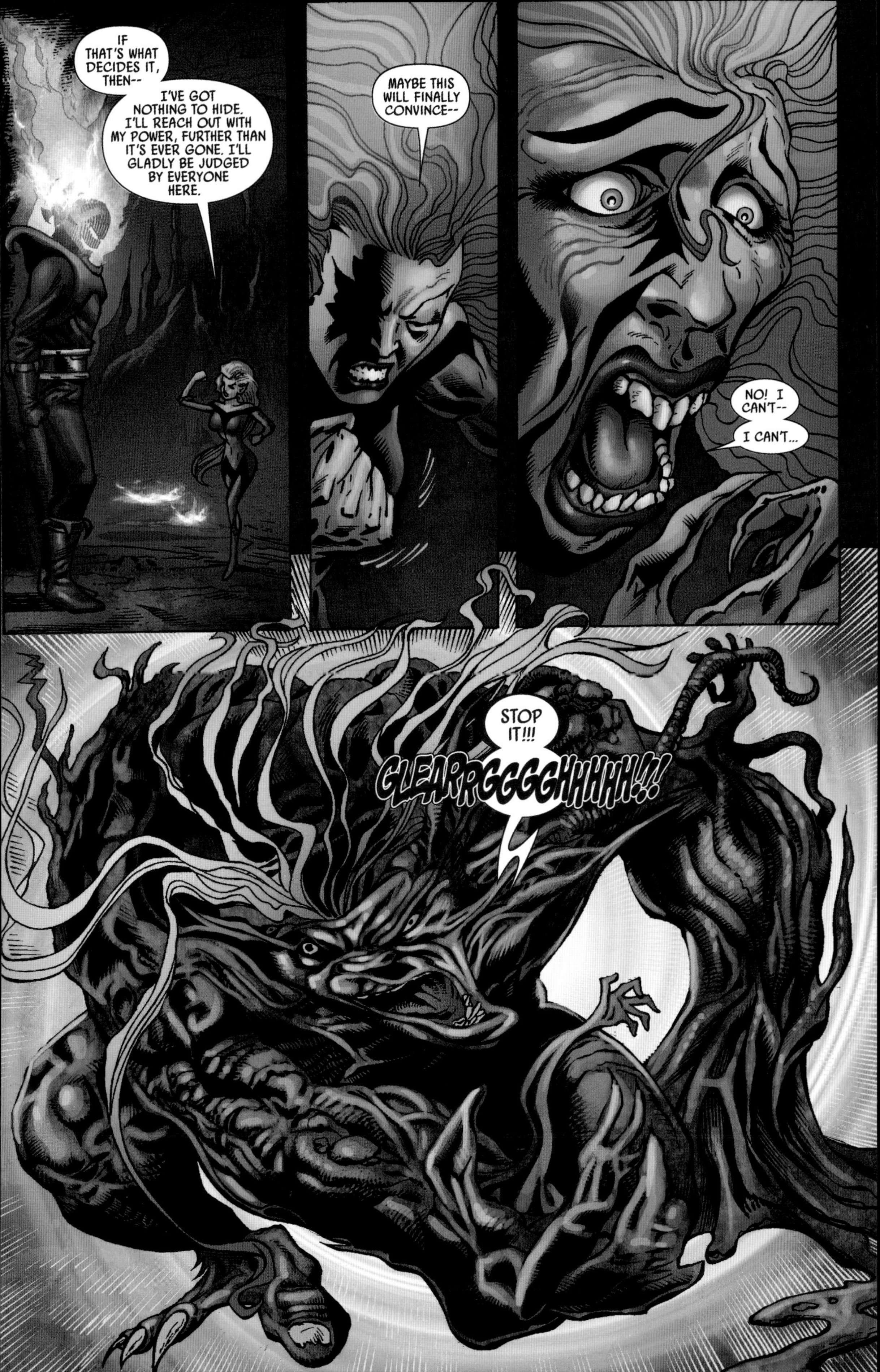
IF THAT'S WHAT DECIDES IT, THEN--
I'VE GOT NOTHING TO HIDE. I'LL REACH OUT WITH MY POWER, FURTHER THAN IT'S EVER GONE. I'LL GLADLY BE JUDGED BY EVERYONE HERE.
MAYBE THIS WILL FINALLY CONVINCE--
NO! I CAN'T--
I CAN'T...
STOP IT!!!
GLEARRGGGGHHHHH!!!

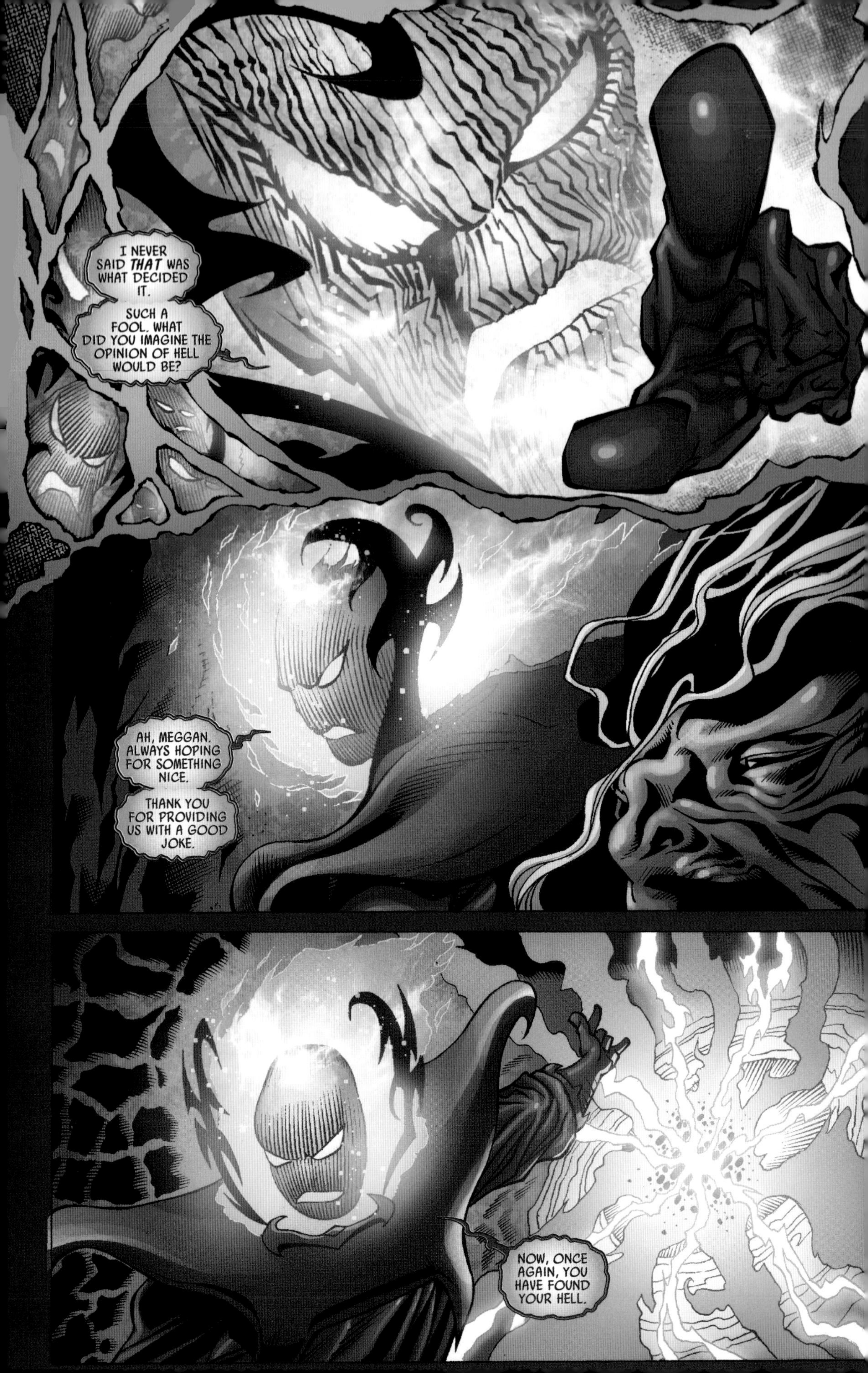
I NEVER SAID *THAT* WAS WHAT DECIDED IT.
SUCH A FOOL. WHAT DID YOU IMAGINE THE OPINION OF HELL WOULD BE?
AH, MEGGAN. ALWAYS HOPING FOR SOMETHING NICE.
THANK YOU FOR PROVIDING US WITH A GOOD JOKE.
NOW, ONCE AGAIN, YOU HAVE FOUND YOUR HELL.

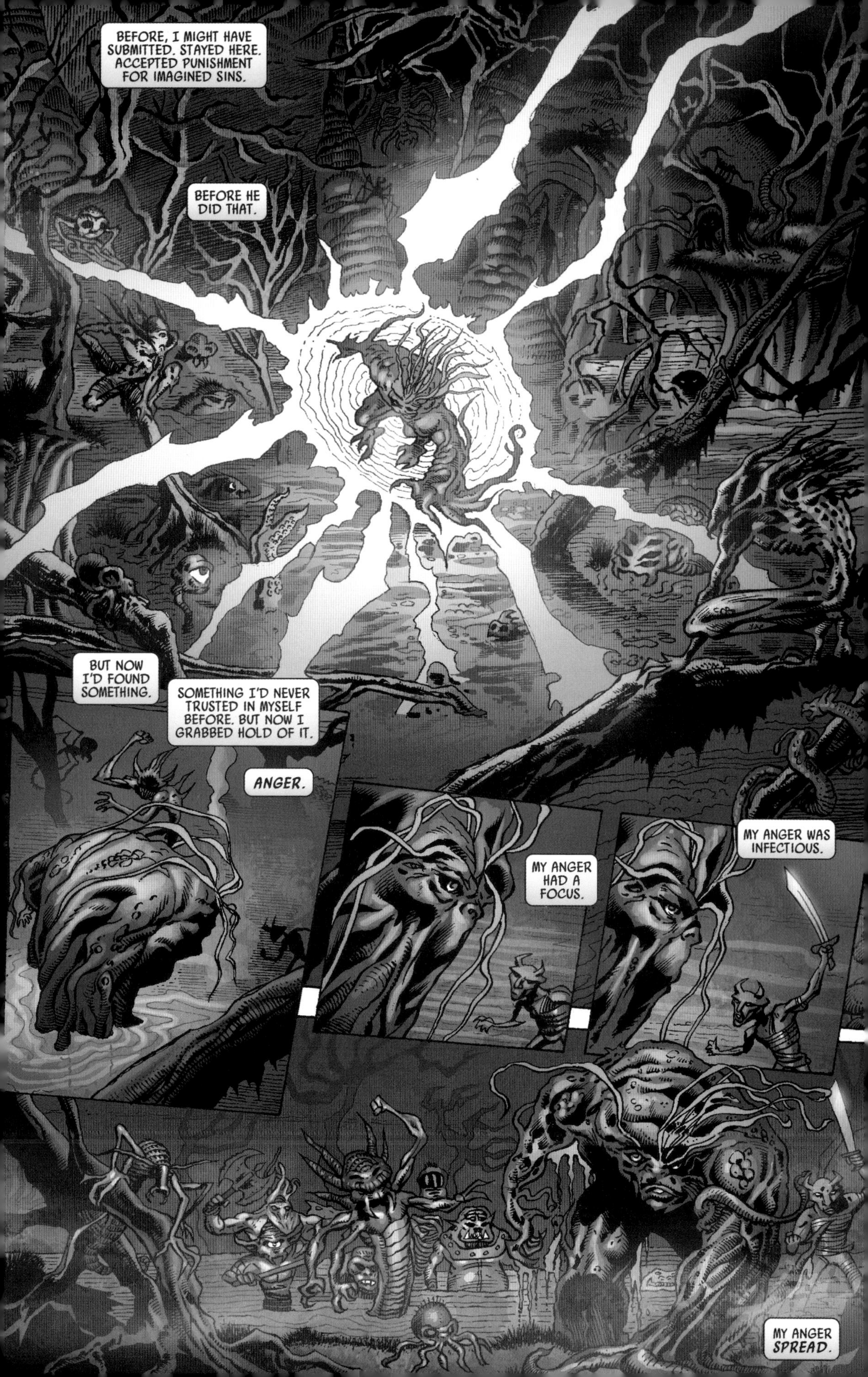
BEFORE, I MIGHT HAVE SUBMITTED. STAYED HERE. ACCEPTED PUNISHMENT FOR IMAGINED SINS.
BEFORE HE DID THAT.
BUT NOW I'D FOUND SOMETHING.
SOMETHING I'D NEVER TRUSTED IN MYSELF BEFORE. BUT NOW I GRABBED HOLD OF IT.
ANGER.
MY ANGER HAD A FOCUS.
MY ANGER WAS INFECTIOUS.
MY ANGER SPREAD.

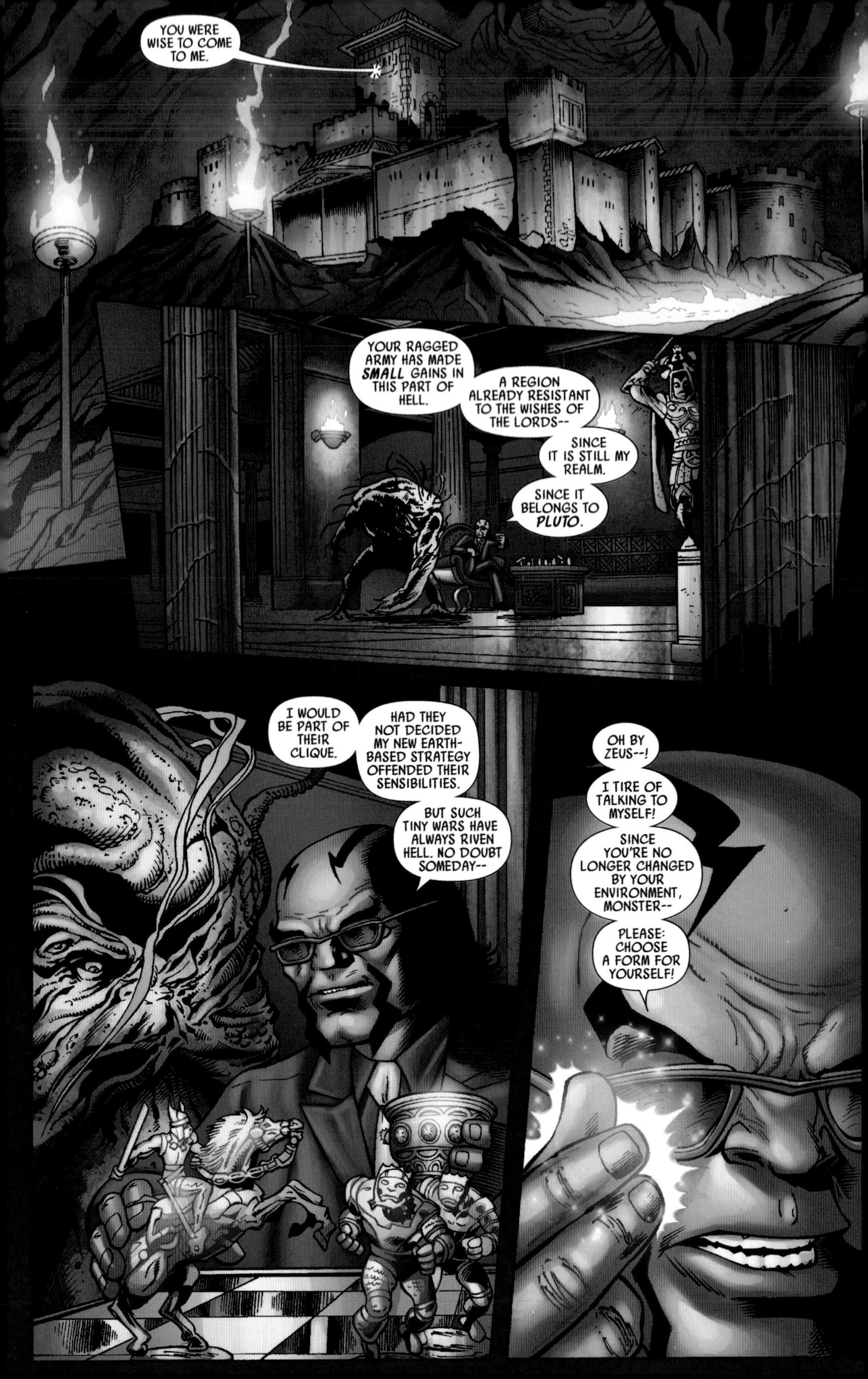
YOU WERE WISE TO COME TO ME.
YOUR RAGGED ARMY HAS MADE SMALL GAINS IN THIS PART OF HELL.
A REGION ALREADY RESISTANT TO THE WISHES OF THE LORDS--
SINCE IT IS STILL MY REALM.
SINCE IT BELONGS TO PLUTO.
I WOULD BE PART OF THEIR CLIQUE.
HAD THEY NOT DECIDED MY NEW EARTH-BASED STRATEGY OFFENDED THEIR SENSIBILITIES.
BUT SUCH TINY WARS HAVE ALWAYS RIVEN HELL. NO DOUBT SOMEDAY--
OH BY ZEUS--!
I TIRE OF TALKING TO MYSELF!
SINCE YOU'RE NO LONGER CHANGED BY YOUR ENVIRONMENT, MONSTER--
PLEASE: CHOOSE A FORM FOR YOURSELF!

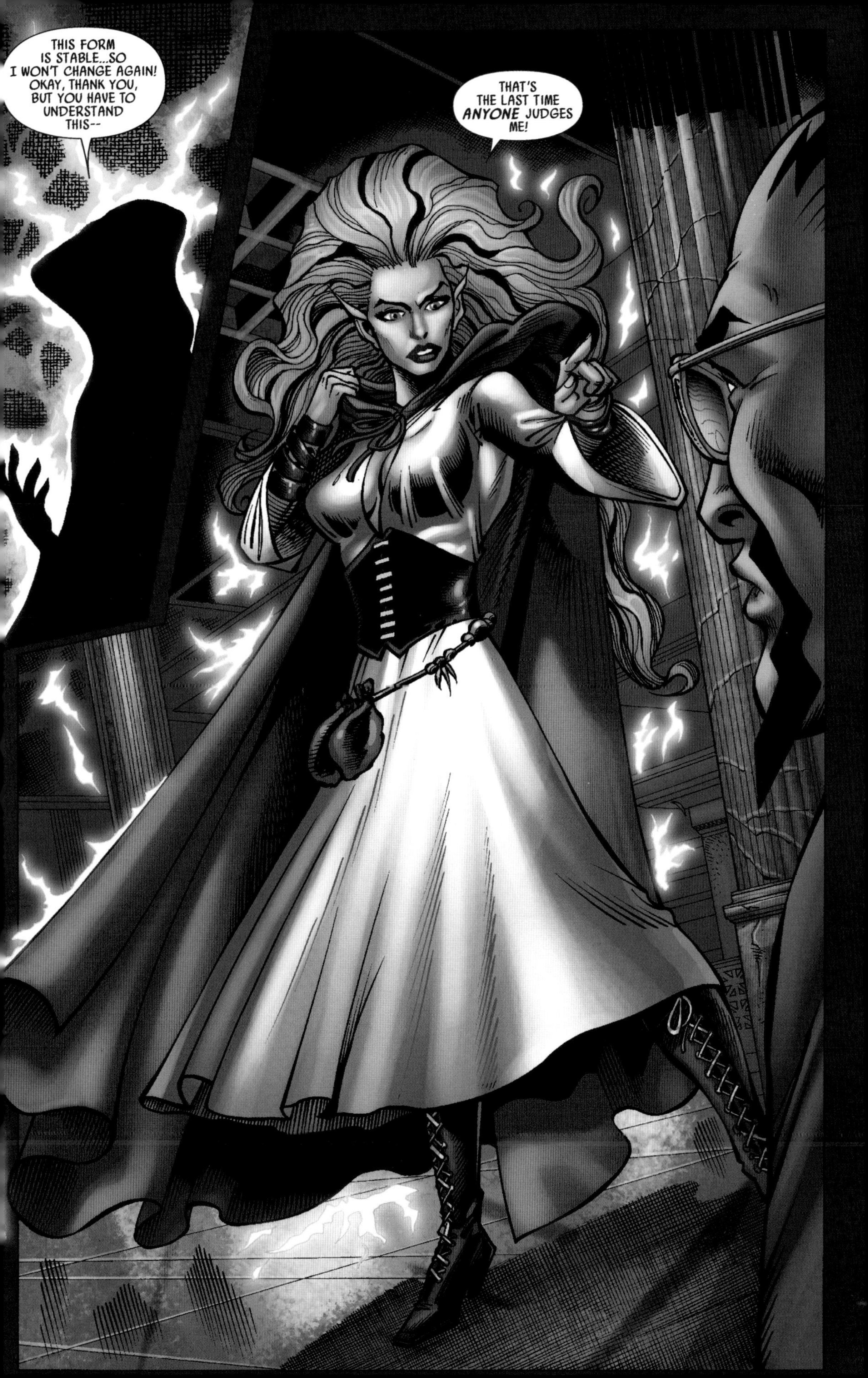
THIS FORM IS STABLE...SO I WON'T CHANGE AGAIN! OKAY, THANK YOU, BUT YOU HAVE TO UNDERSTAND THIS--
THAT'S THE LAST TIME ANYONE JUDGES ME!

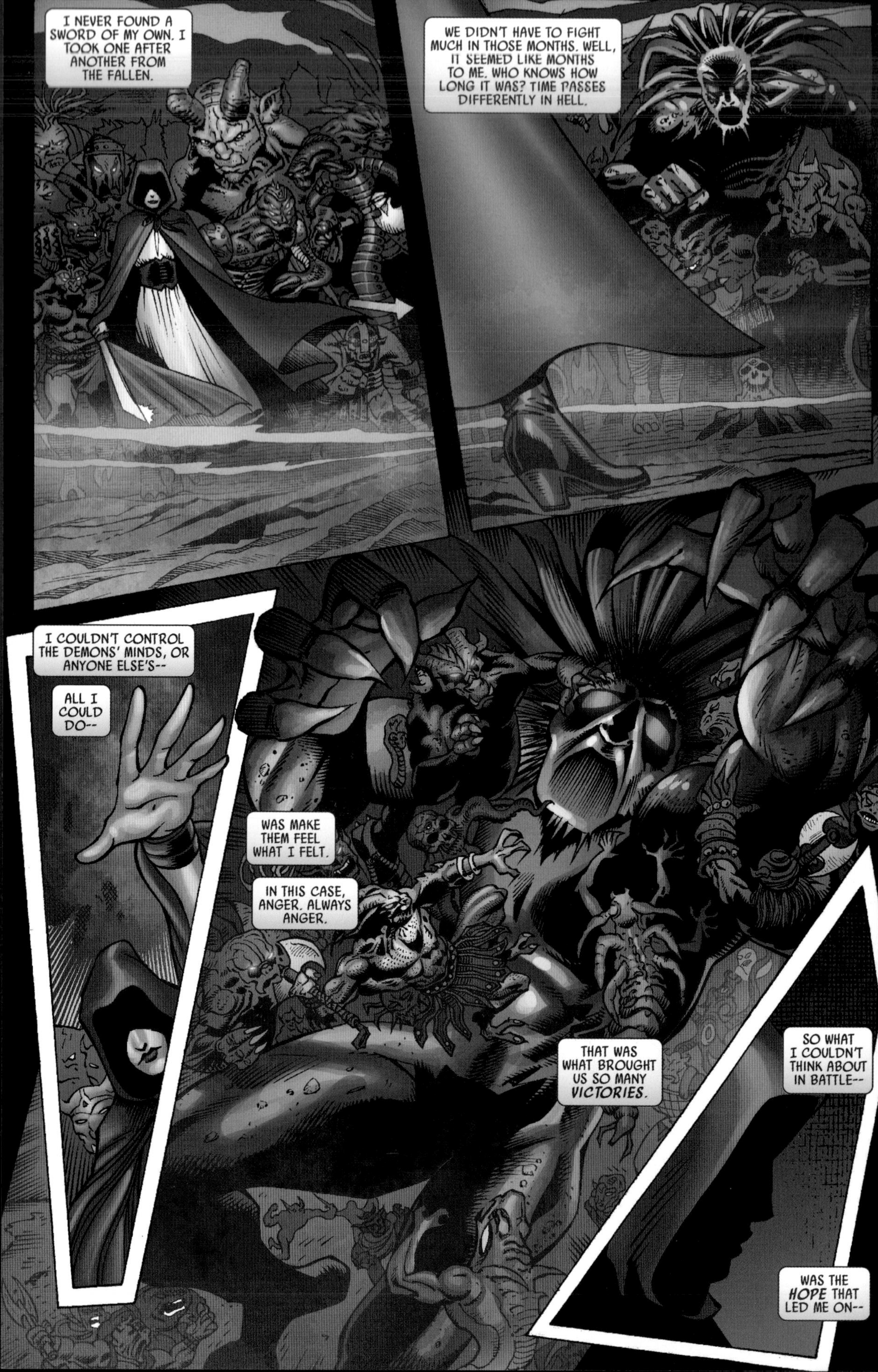
I NEVER FOUND A SWORD OF MY OWN. I TOOK ONE AFTER ANOTHER FROM THE FALLEN.
WE DIDN'T HAVE TO FIGHT MUCH IN THOSE MONTHS. WELL, IT SEEMED LIKE MONTHS TO ME. WHO KNOWS HOW LONG IT WAS? TIME PASSES DIFFERENTLY IN HELL.
I COULDN'T CONTROL THE DEMONS' MINDS, OR ANYONE ELSE'S--
ALL I COULD DO--
WAS MAKE THEM FEEL WHAT I FELT.
IN THIS CASE, ANGER. ALWAYS ANGER.
THAT WAS WHAT BROUGHT US SO MANY VICTORIES.
SO WHAT I COULDN'T THINK ABOUT IN BATTLE--
WAS THE HOPE THAT LED ME ON--

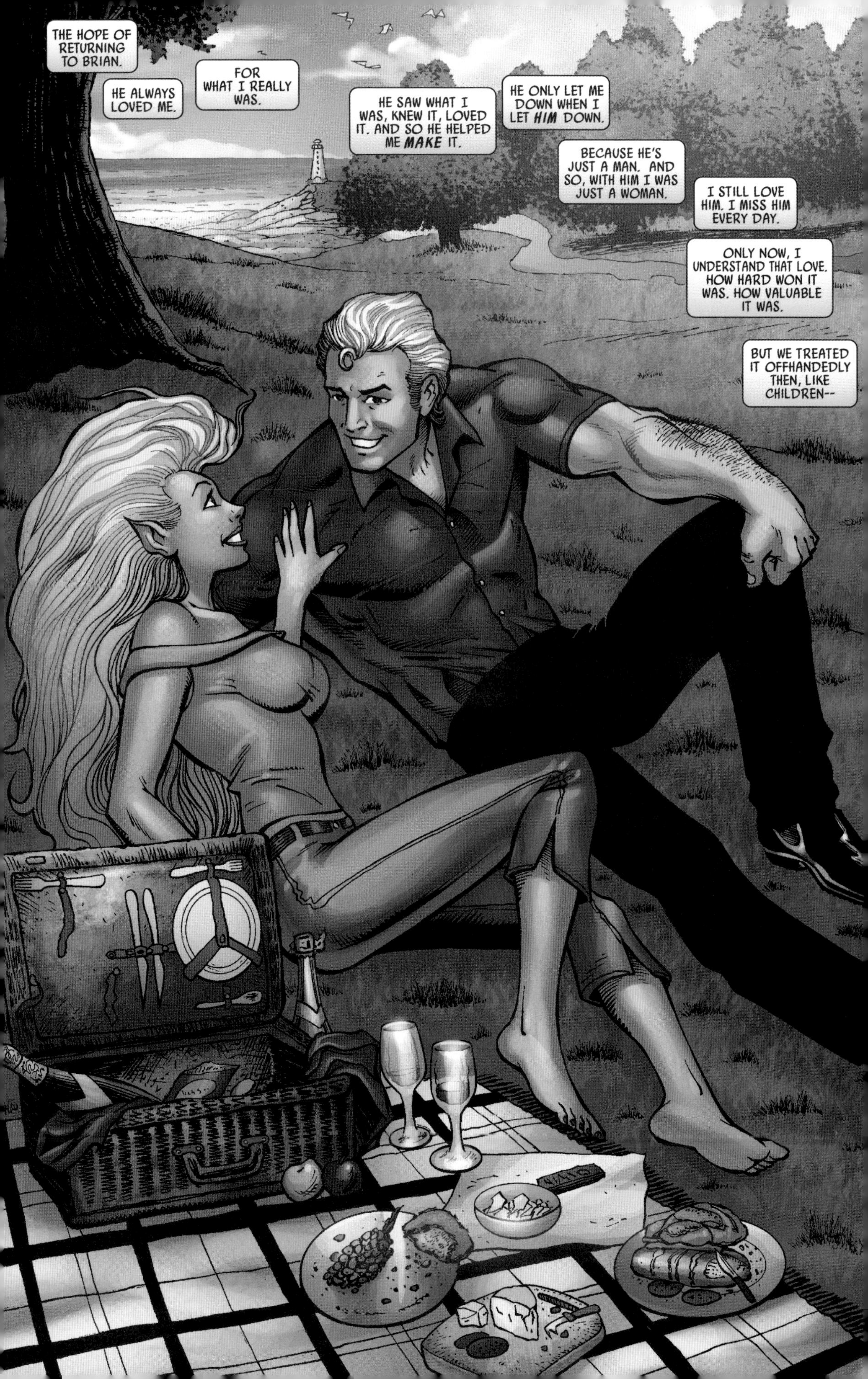
THE HOPE OF RETURNING TO BRIAN.
HE ALWAYS LOVED ME.
FOR WHAT I REALLY WAS.
HE SAW WHAT I WAS, KNEW IT, LOVED IT. AND SO HE HELPED ME *MAKE* IT.
HE ONLY LET ME DOWN WHEN I LET *HIM* DOWN.
BECAUSE HE'S JUST A MAN. AND SO, WITH HIM I WAS JUST A WOMAN.
I STILL LOVE HIM. I MISS HIM EVERY DAY.
ONLY NOW, I UNDERSTAND THAT LOVE. HOW HARD WON IT WAS. HOW VALUABLE IT WAS.
BUT WE TREATED IT OFFHANDEDLY THEN, LIKE CHILDREN--

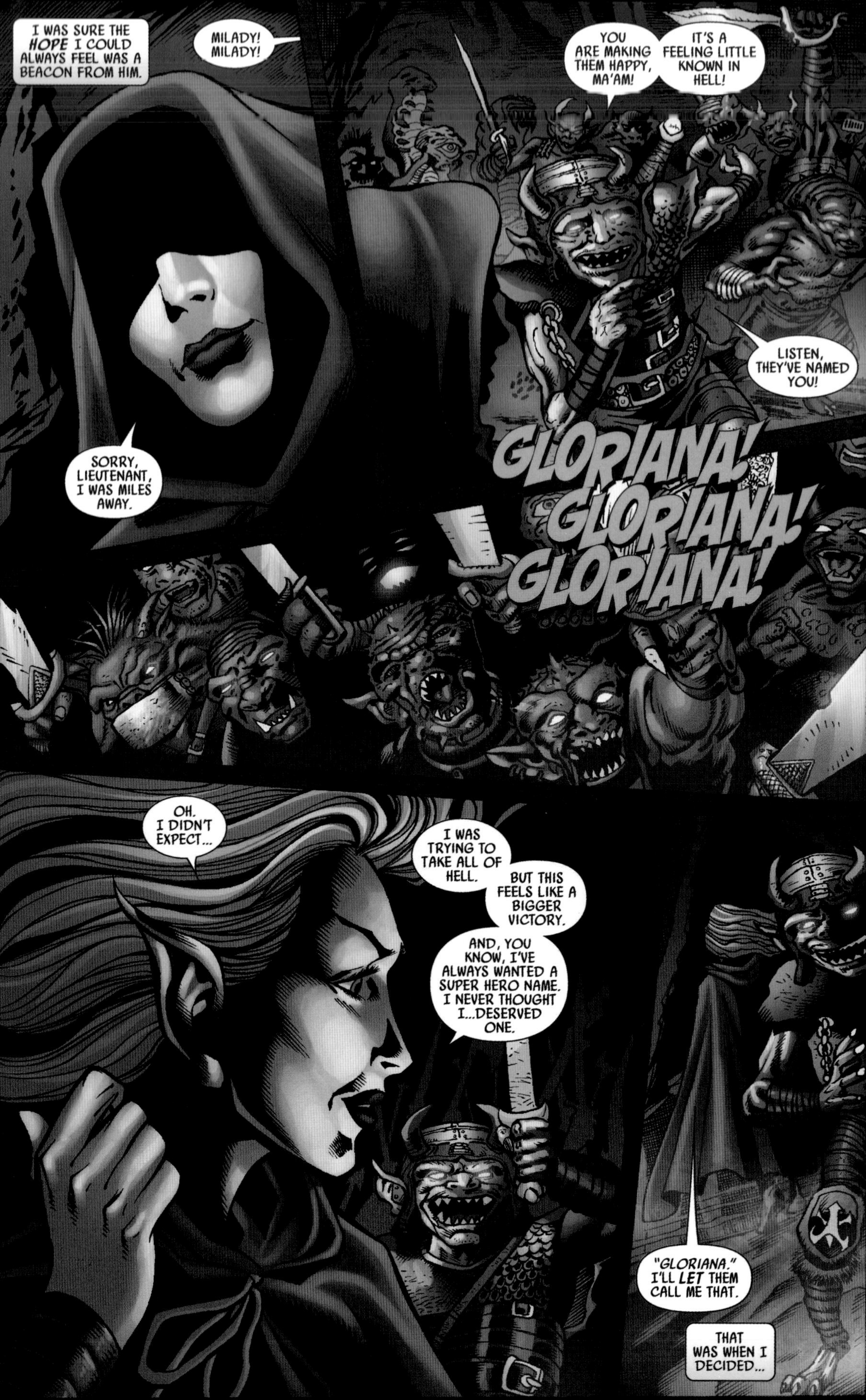
I WAS SURE THE HOPE I COULD ALWAYS FEEL WAS A BEACON FROM HIM.
MILADY! MILADY!
YOU ARE MAKING THEM HAPPY, MA'AM!
IT'S A FEELING LITTLE KNOWN IN HELL!
LISTEN, THEY'VE NAMED YOU!
SORRY, LIEUTENANT, I WAS MILES AWAY.
GLORIANA! GLORIANA! GLORIANA!
OH. I DIDN'T EXPECT...
I WAS TRYING TO TAKE ALL OF HELL.
BUT THIS FEELS LIKE A BIGGER VICTORY.
AND, YOU KNOW, I'VE ALWAYS WANTED A SUPER HERO NAME. I NEVER THOUGHT I...DESERVED ONE.
"GLORIANA." I'LL LET THEM CALL ME THAT.
THAT WAS WHEN I DECIDED...

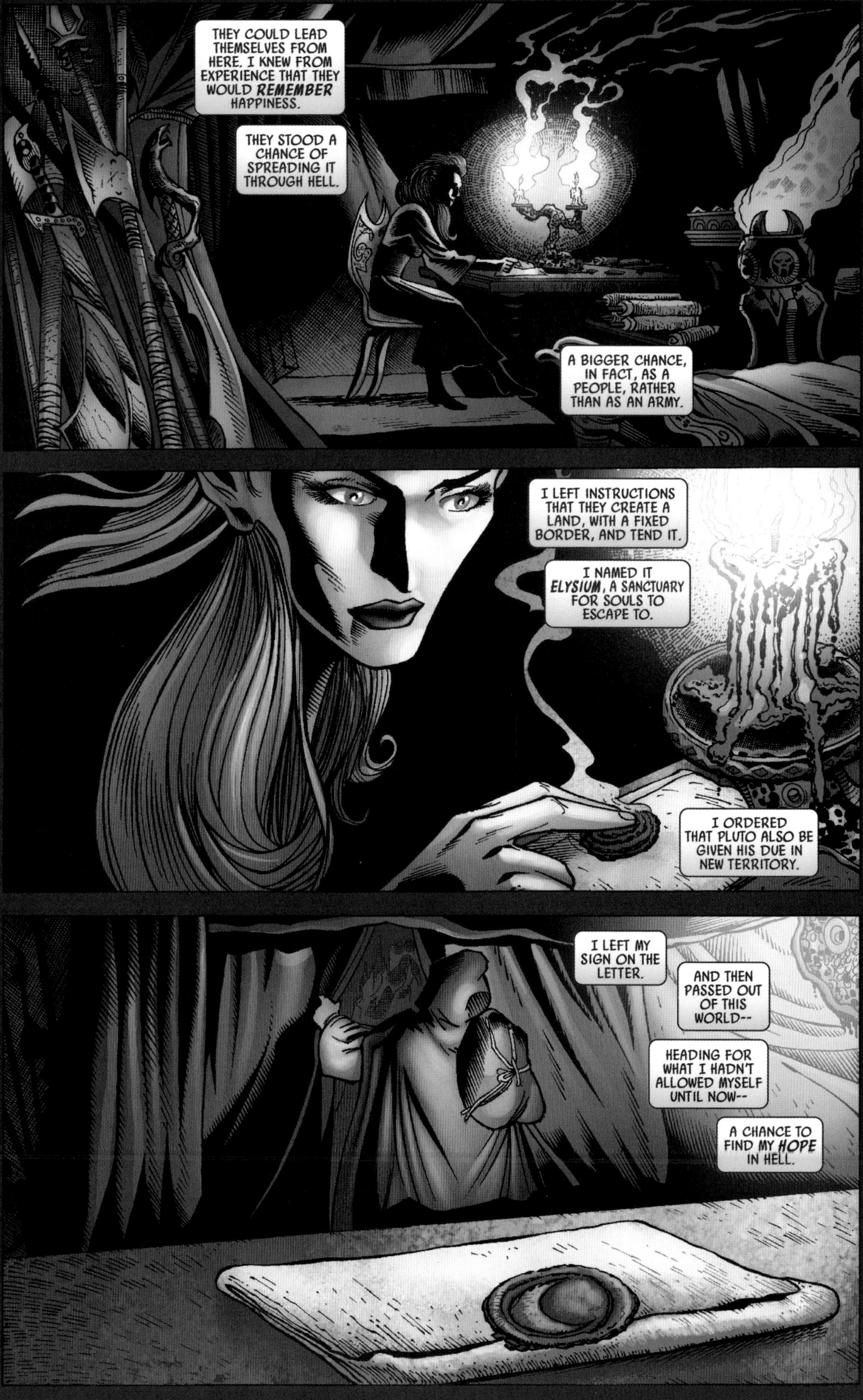
THEY COULD LEAD THEMSELVES FROM HERE. I KNEW FROM EXPERIENCE THAT THEY WOULD REMEMBER HAPPINESS.
THEY STOOD A CHANCE OF SPREADING IT THROUGH HELL.
A BIGGER CHANCE, IN FACT, AS A PEOPLE, RATHER THAN AS AN ARMY.
I LEFT INSTRUCTIONS THAT THEY CREATE A LAND, WITH A FIXED BORDER, AND TEND IT.
I NAMED IT ELYSIUM, A SANCTUARY FOR SOULS TO ESCAPE TO.
I ORDERED THAT PLUTO ALSO BE GIVEN HIS DUE IN NEW TERRITORY.
I LEFT MY SIGN ON THE LETTER.
AND THEN PASSED OUT OF THIS WORLD--
HEADING FOR WHAT I HADN'T ALLOWED MYSELF UNTIL NOW--
A CHANCE TO FIND MY HOPE IN HELL.

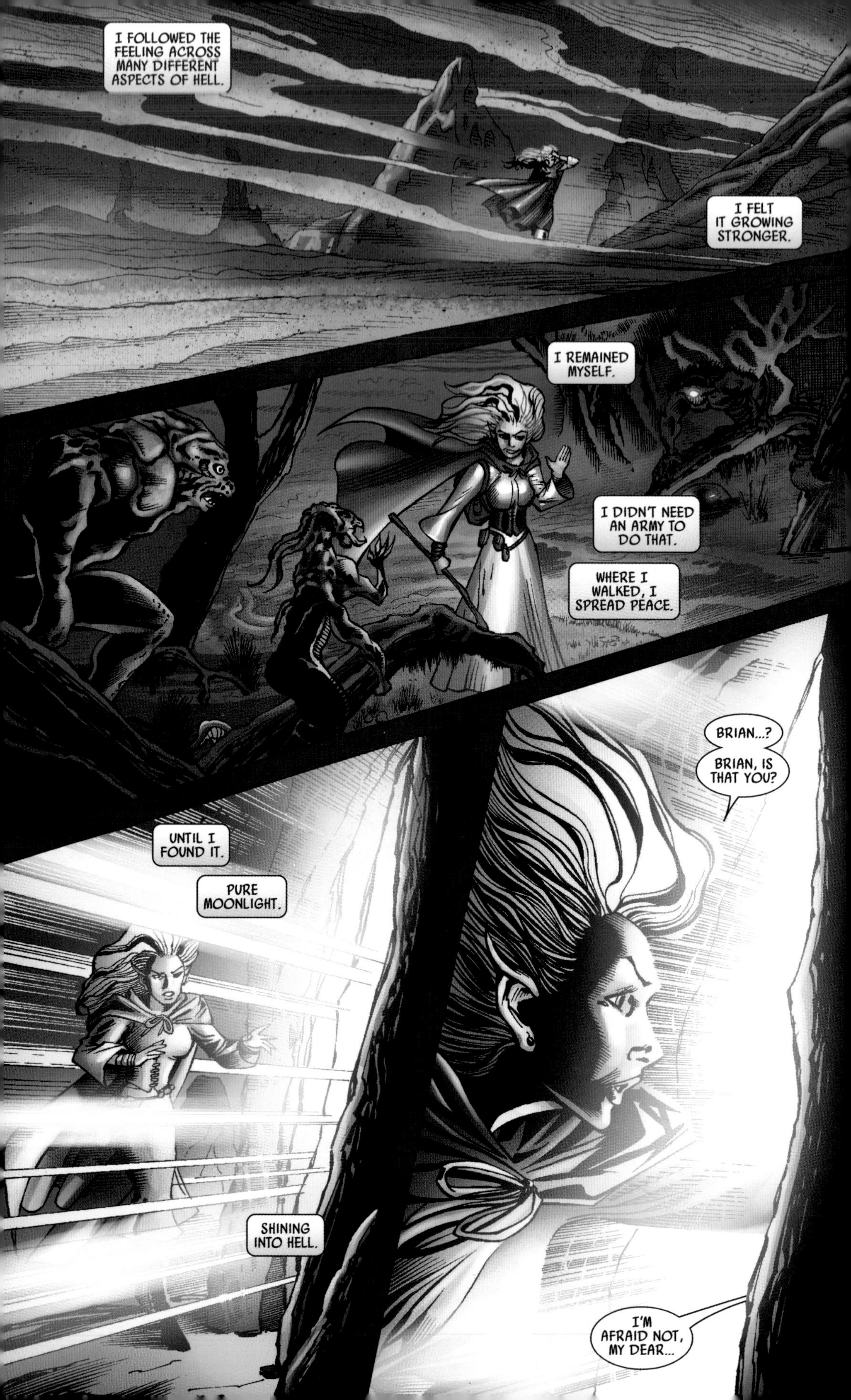
I FOLLOWED THE FEELING ACROSS MANY DIFFERENT ASPECTS OF HELL.
I FELT IT GROWING STRONGER.
I REMAINED MYSELF.
I DIDN'T NEED AN ARMY TO DO THAT.
WHERE I WALKED, I SPREAD PEACE.
UNTIL I FOUND IT.
PURE MOONLIGHT.
SHINING INTO HELL.
BRIAN...?
BRIAN, IS THAT YOU?
I'M AFRAID NOT, MY DEAR...

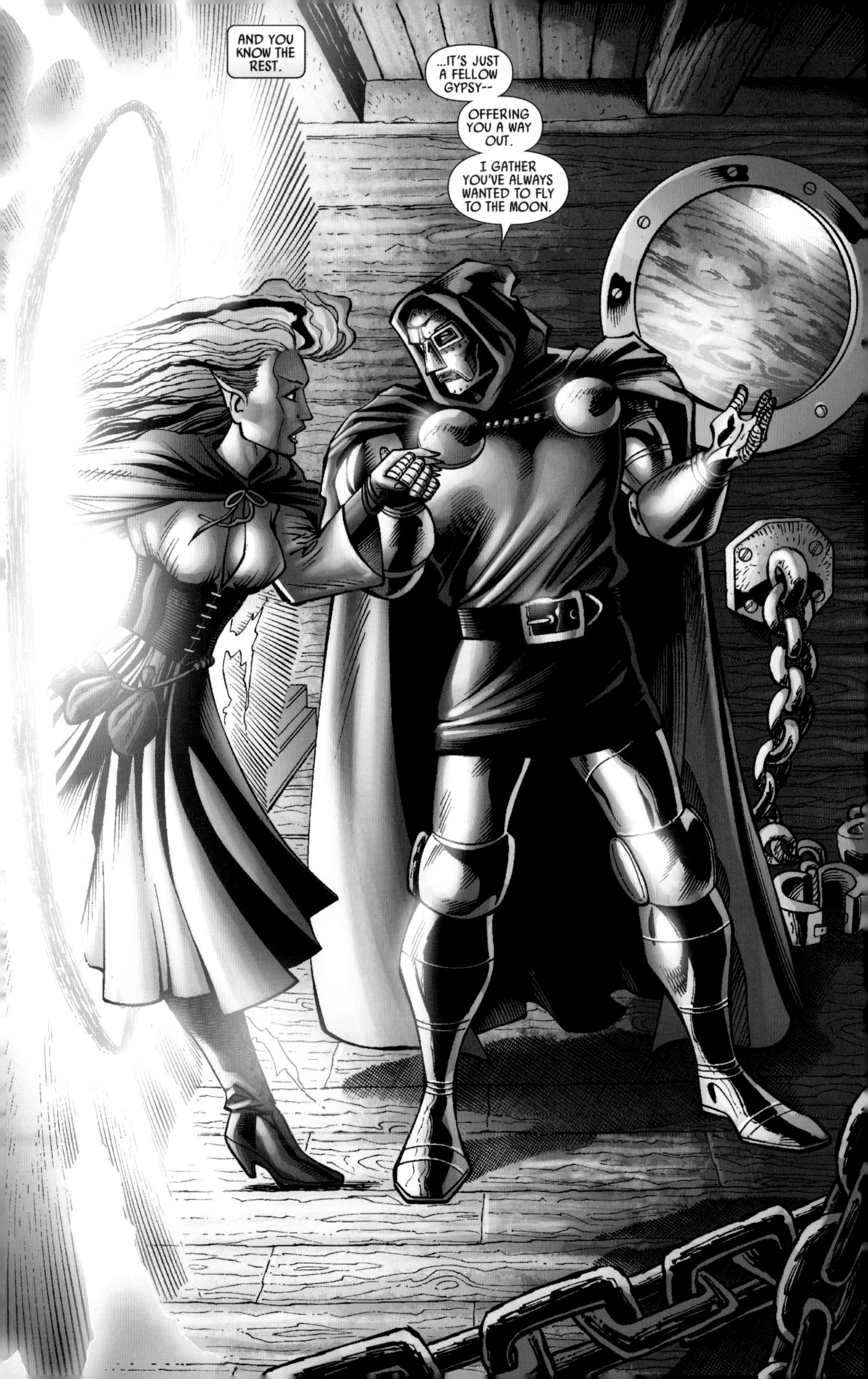
AND YOU KNOW THE REST.
...IT'S JUST A FELLOW GYPSY--
OFFERING YOU A WAY OUT.
I GATHER YOU'VE ALWAYS WANTED TO FLY TO THE MOON.

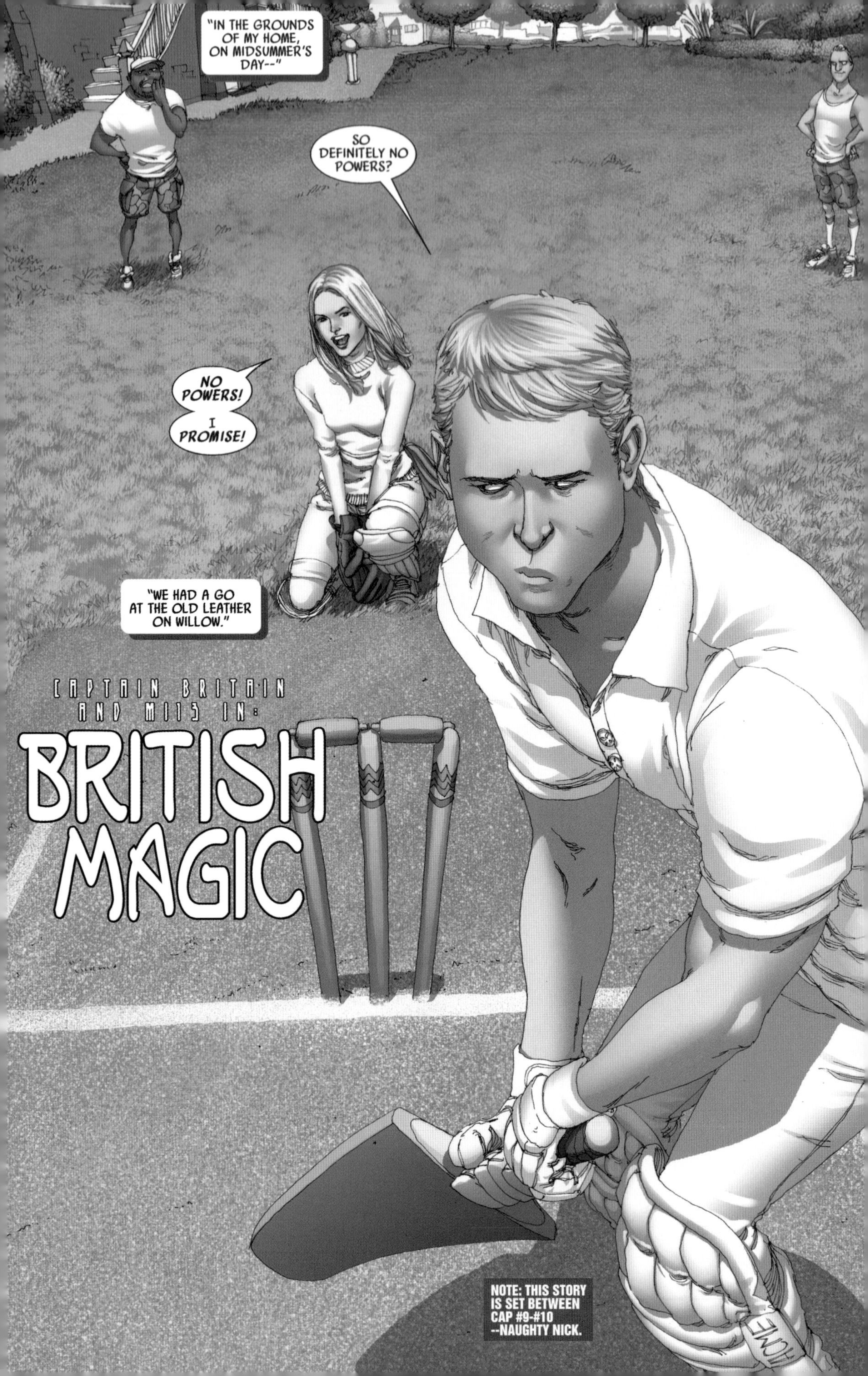
"IN THE GROUNDS OF MY HOME, ON MIDSUMMER'S DAY--"
SO DEFINITELY NO POWERS?
NO POWERS!
I PROMISE!
"WE HAD A GO AT THE OLD LEATHER ON WILLOW."
CAPTAIN BRITAIN AND MI13 IN:
BRITISH MAGIC
NOTE: THIS STORY IS SET BETWEEN CAP #9-#10 --NAUGHTY NICK.

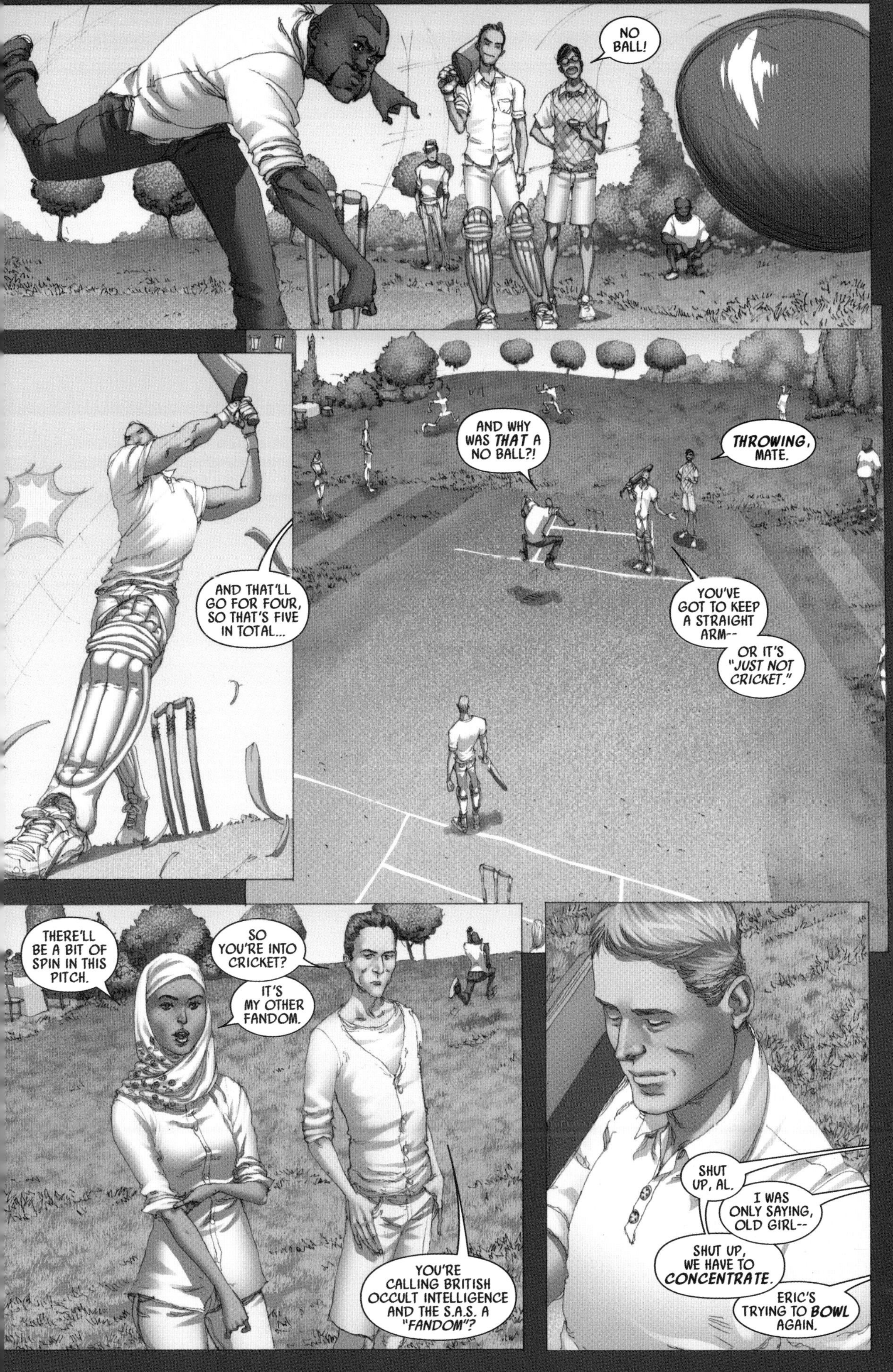
NO BALL!
AND WHY WAS THAT A NO BALL?!
THROWING, MATE.
YOU'VE GOT TO KEEP A STRAIGHT ARM--
OR IT'S "JUST NOT CRICKET."
AND THAT'LL GO FOR FOUR, SO THAT'S FIVE IN TOTAL...
THERE'LL BE A BIT OF SPIN IN THIS PITCH.
SO YOU'RE INTO CRICKET?
IT'S MY OTHER FANDOM.
YOU'RE CALLING BRITISH OCCULT INTELLIGENCE AND THE S.A.S. A "FANDOM"?
SHUT UP, AL.
I WAS ONLY SAYING, OLD GIRL--
SHUT UP, WE HAVE TO CONCENTRATE.
ERIC'S TRYING TO BOWL AGAIN.

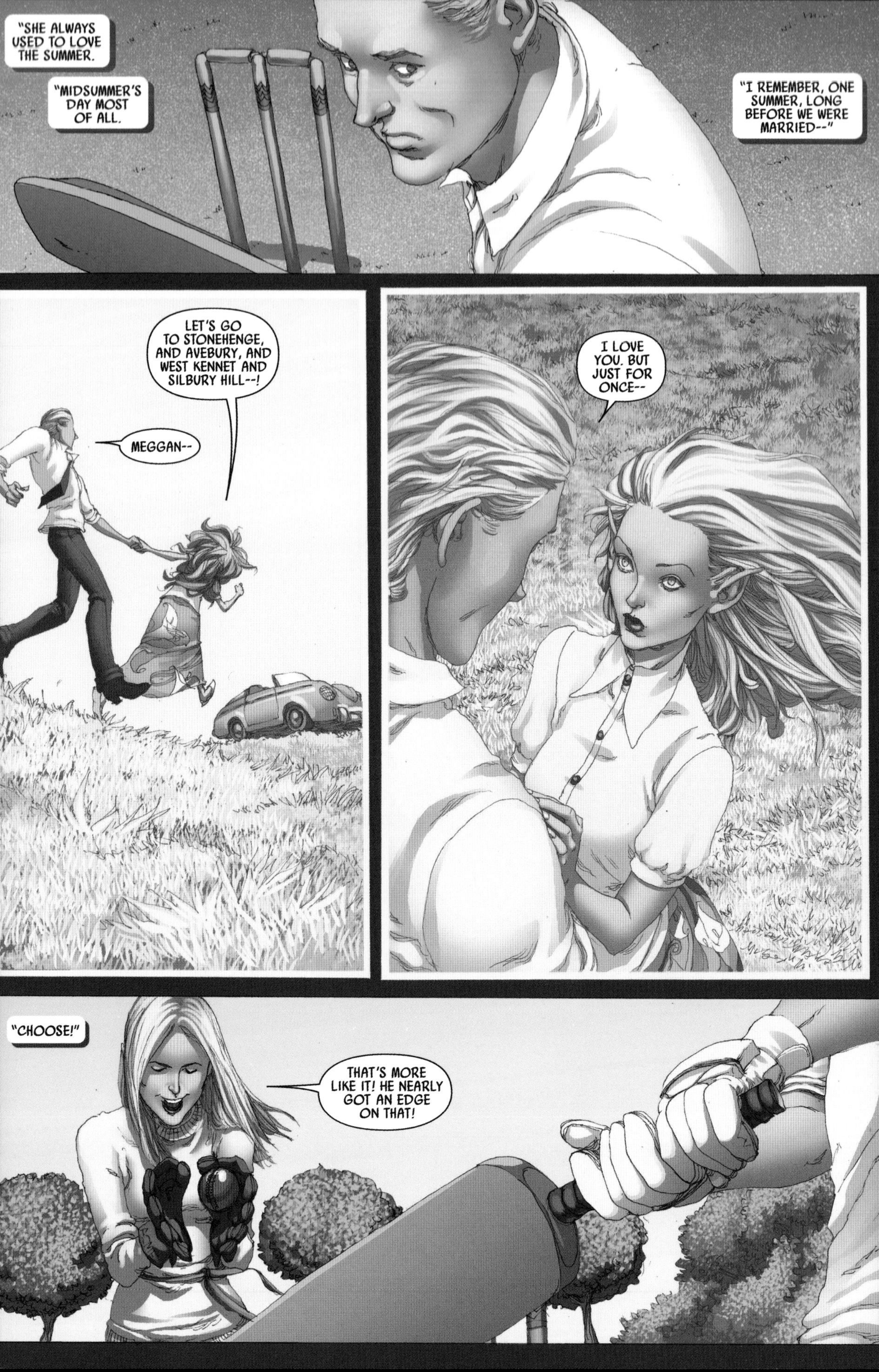
"SHE ALWAYS USED TO LOVE THE SUMMER.
"MIDSUMMER'S DAY MOST OF ALL.
"I REMEMBER, ONE SUMMER, LONG BEFORE WE WERE MARRIED--"
LET'S GO TO STONEHENGE, AND AVEBURY, AND WEST KENNET AND SILBURY HILL--!
MEGGAN--
I LOVE YOU. BUT JUST FOR ONCE--
"CHOOSE!"
THAT'S MORE LIKE IT! HE NEARLY GOT AN EDGE ON THAT!

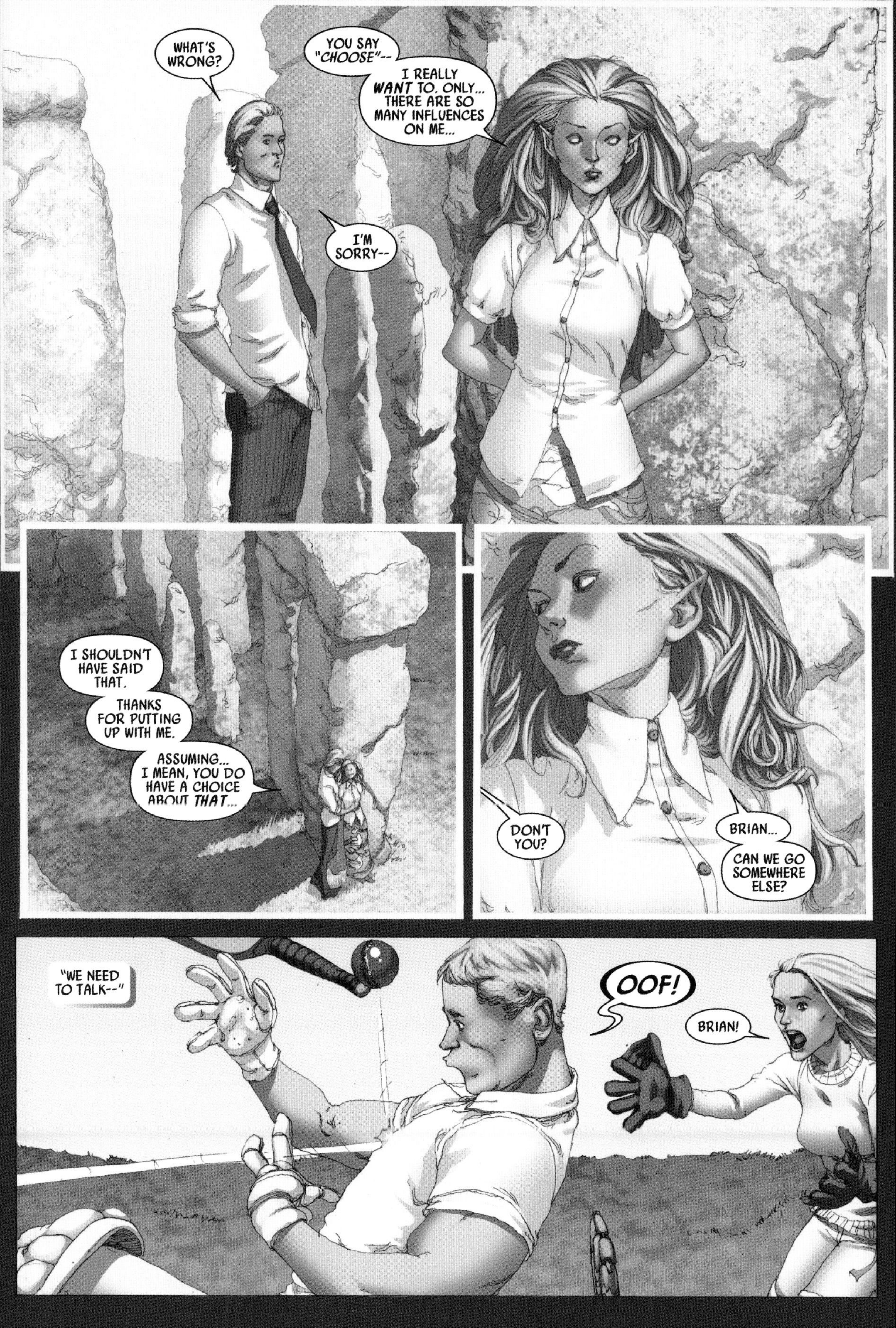
WHAT'S WRONG?
YOU SAY "CHOOSE"--
I REALLY WANT TO. ONLY... THERE ARE SO MANY INFLUENCES ON ME...
I'M SORRY--
I SHOULDN'T HAVE SAID THAT.
THANKS FOR PUTTING UP WITH ME.
ASSUMING... I MEAN, YOU DO HAVE A CHOICE ABOUT THAT...
DON'T YOU?
BRIAN...
CAN WE GO SOMEWHERE ELSE?
"WE NEED TO TALK--"
OOF!
BRIAN!

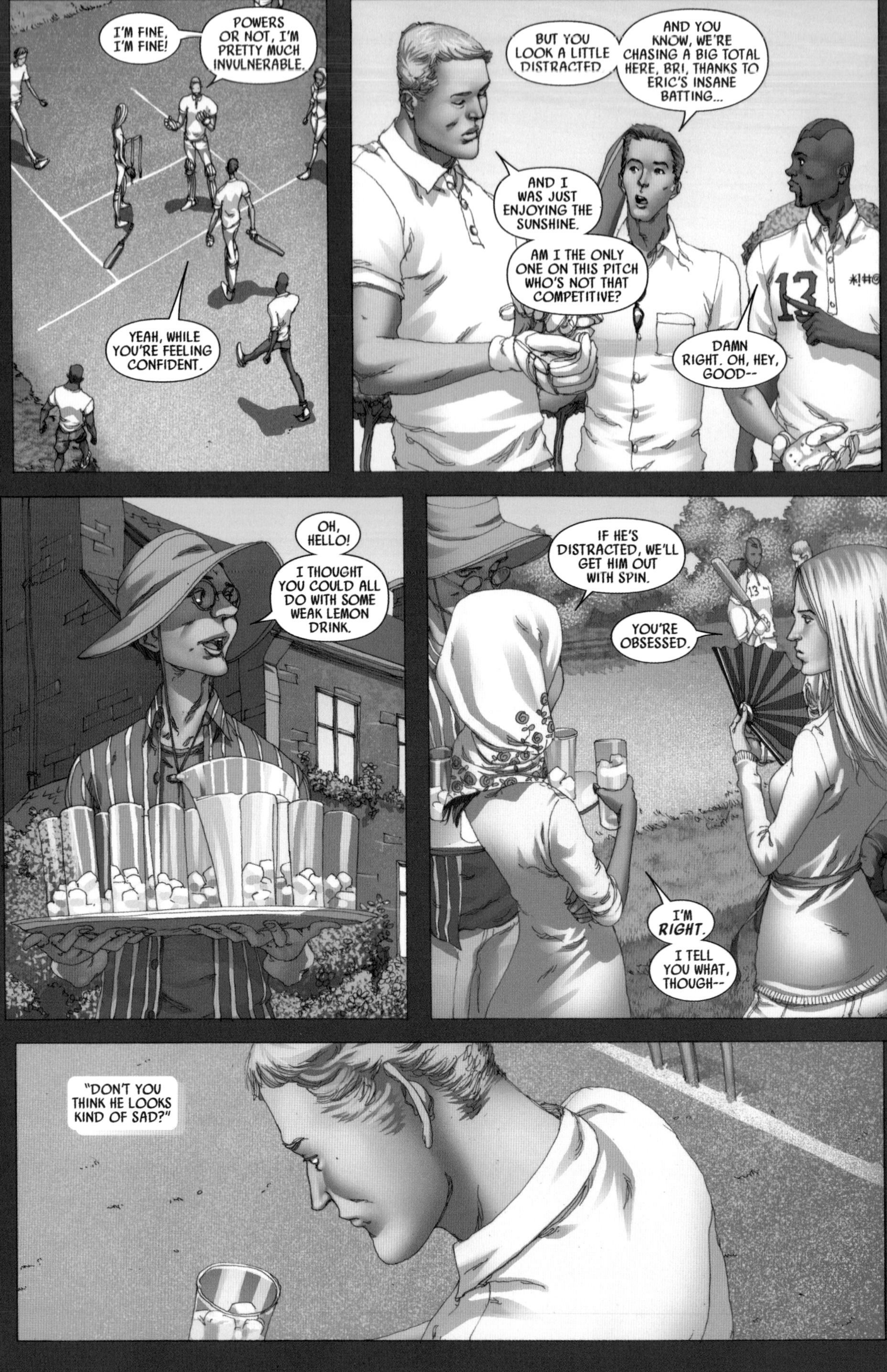

I'M FINE, I'M FINE!
POWERS OR NOT, I'M PRETTY MUCH INVULNERABLE.
YEAH, WHILE YOU'RE FEELING CONFIDENT.
BUT YOU LOOK A LITTLE DISTRACTED.
AND YOU KNOW, WE'RE CHASING A BIG TOTAL HERE, BRI, THANKS TO ERIC'S INSANE BATTING...
AND I WAS JUST ENJOYING THE SUNSHINE.
AM I THE ONLY ONE ON THIS PITCH WHO'S NOT THAT COMPETITIVE?
DAMN RIGHT. OH, HEY, GOOD--
13
OH, HELLO!
I THOUGHT YOU COULD ALL DO WITH SOME WEAK LEMON DRINK.
IF HE'S DISTRACTED, WE'LL GET HIM OUT WITH SPIN.
YOU'RE OBSESSED.
I'M *RIGHT*.
I TELL YOU WHAT, THOUGH--
"DON'T YOU THINK HE LOOKS KIND OF SAD?"

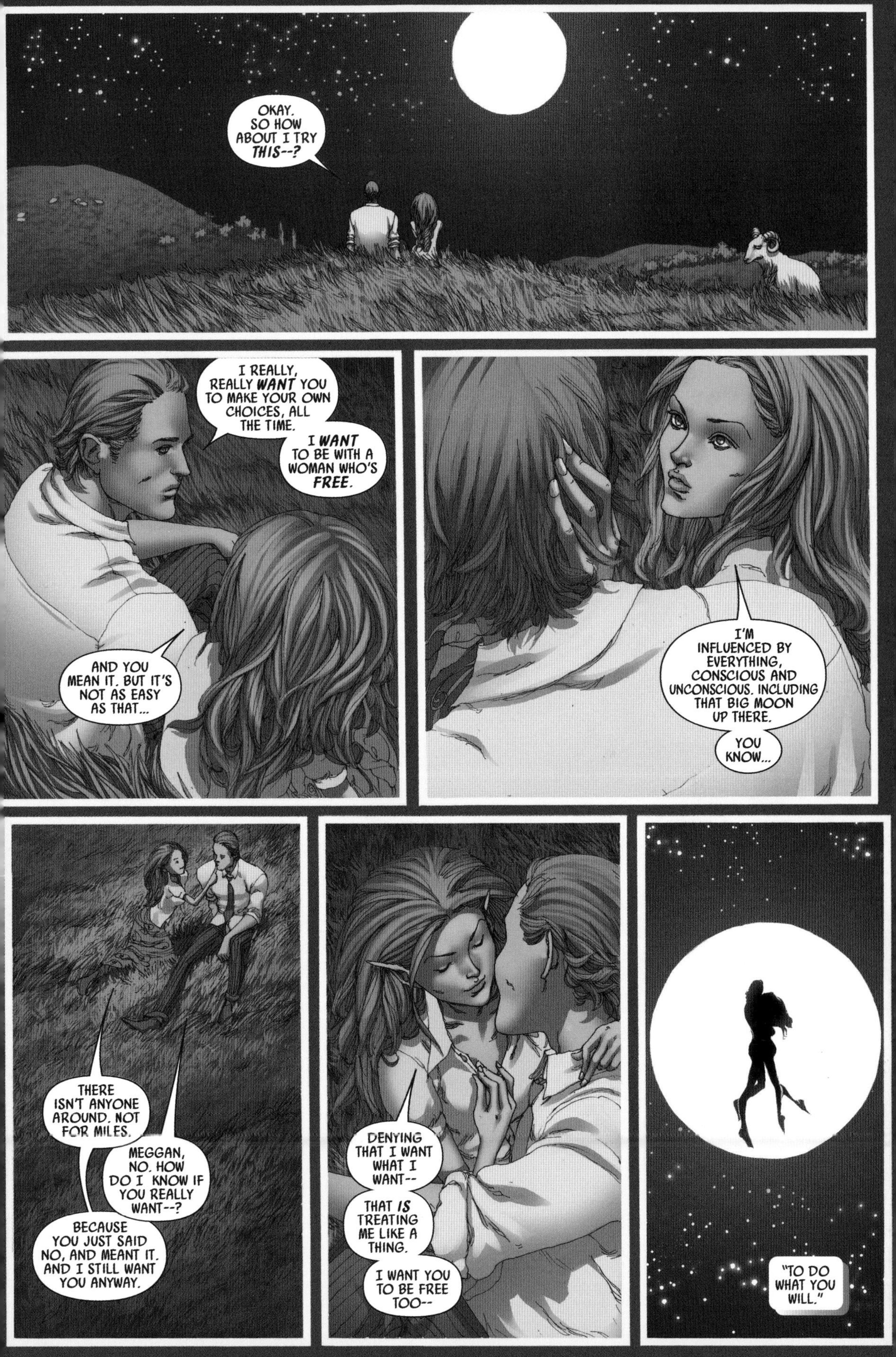
OKAY. SO HOW ABOUT I TRY *THIS--?*
I REALLY, REALLY *WANT* YOU TO MAKE YOUR OWN CHOICES, ALL THE TIME.
I *WANT* TO BE WITH A WOMAN WHO'S *FREE.*
AND YOU MEAN IT. BUT IT'S NOT AS EASY AS THAT...
I'M INFLUENCED BY EVERYTHING, CONSCIOUS AND UNCONSCIOUS. INCLUDING THAT BIG MOON UP THERE.
YOU KNOW...
THERE ISN'T ANYONE AROUND. NOT FOR MILES.
MEGGAN, NO. HOW DO I KNOW IF YOU REALLY WANT--?
BECAUSE YOU JUST SAID NO, AND MEANT IT. AND I STILL WANT YOU ANYWAY.
DENYING THAT I WANT WHAT I WANT--
THAT *IS* TREATING ME LIKE A THING.
I WANT YOU TO BE FREE TOO--
"TO DO WHAT YOU WILL."

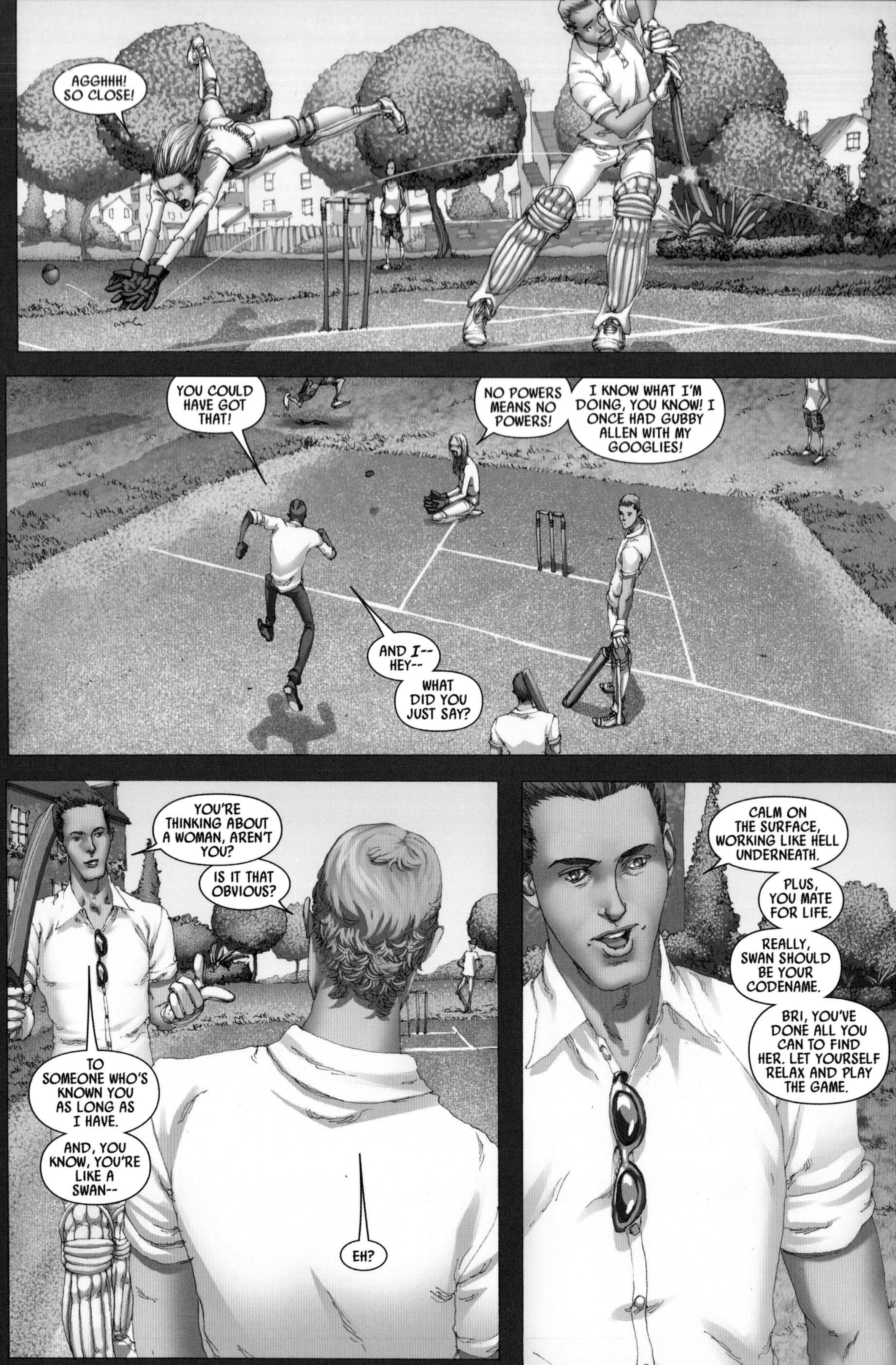
AGGHHH! SO CLOSE!
YOU COULD HAVE GOT THAT!
NO POWERS MEANS NO POWERS!
I KNOW WHAT I'M DOING, YOU KNOW! I ONCE HAD GUBBY ALLEN WITH MY GOOGLIES!
AND I-- HEY--
WHAT DID YOU JUST SAY?
YOU'RE THINKING ABOUT A WOMAN, AREN'T YOU?
IS IT THAT OBVIOUS?
TO SOMEONE WHO'S KNOWN YOU AS LONG AS I HAVE.
AND, YOU KNOW, YOU'RE LIKE A SWAN--
EH?
CALM ON THE SURFACE, WORKING LIKE HELL UNDERNEATH.
PLUS, YOU MATE FOR LIFE.
REALLY, SWAN SHOULD BE YOUR CODENAME.
BRI, YOU'VE DONE ALL YOU CAN TO FIND HER. LET YOURSELF RELAX AND PLAY THE GAME.

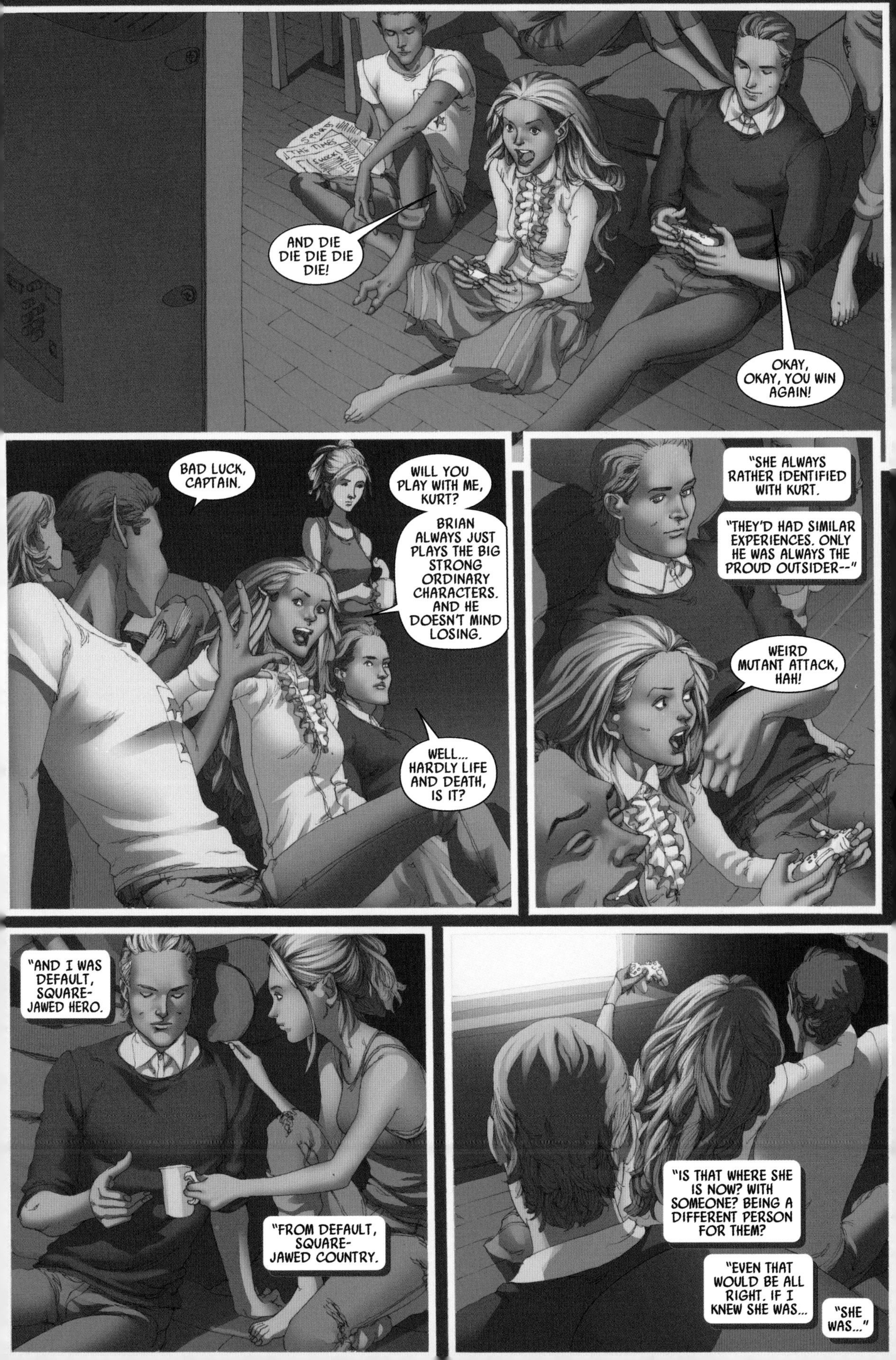
AND DIE DIE DIE DIE DIE!
OKAY, OKAY, YOU WIN AGAIN!
BAD LUCK, CAPTAIN.
WILL YOU PLAY WITH ME, KURT?
BRIAN ALWAYS JUST PLAYS THE BIG STRONG ORDINARY CHARACTERS. AND HE DOESN'T MIND LOSING.
WELL... HARDLY LIFE AND DEATH, IS IT?
"SHE ALWAYS RATHER IDENTIFIED WITH KURT.
"THEY'D HAD SIMILAR EXPERIENCES. ONLY HE WAS ALWAYS THE PROUD OUTSIDER--"
WEIRD MUTANT ATTACK, HAH!
"AND I WAS DEFAULT, SQUARE-JAWED HERO.
"FROM DEFAULT, SQUARE-JAWED COUNTRY.
"IS THAT WHERE SHE IS NOW? WITH SOMEONE? BEING A DIFFERENT PERSON FOR THEM?
"EVEN THAT WOULD BE ALL RIGHT. IF I KNEW SHE WAS...
"SHE WAS..."

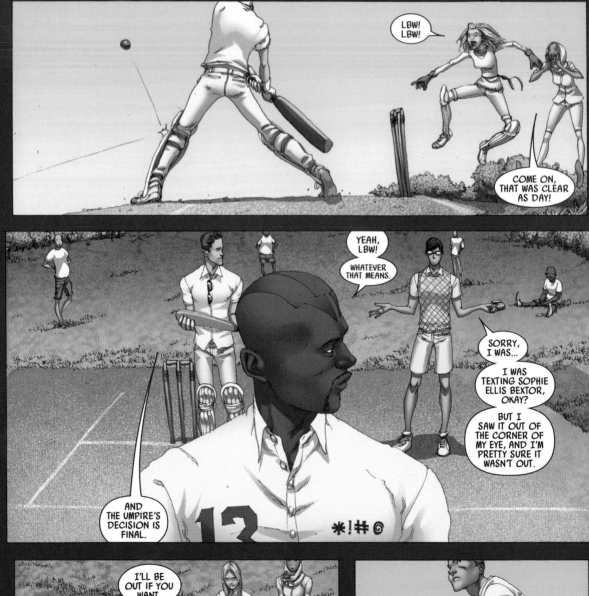

LBW! LBW!

COME ON, THAT WAS CLEAR AS DAY!

YEAH, LBW!

WHATEVER THAT MEANS.

SORRY, I WAS...

I WAS TEXTING SOPHIE ELLIS BEXTOR, OKAY?

BUT I SAW IT OUT OF THE CORNER OF MY EYE, AND I'M PRETTY SURE IT WASN'T OUT.

*!#☉

AND THE UMPIRE'S DECISION IS FINAL.

I'LL BE OUT IF YOU WANT.

NO, NO. LIBERTY HALL, BRIAN...

BESIDES, COLTON'S IN NEXT, AND HE MIGHT SCORE FASTER.

"RIGHT, IF YOU'RE GOING TO SLOG, SLOG HARD.

"HIT OUT OR GET OUT."

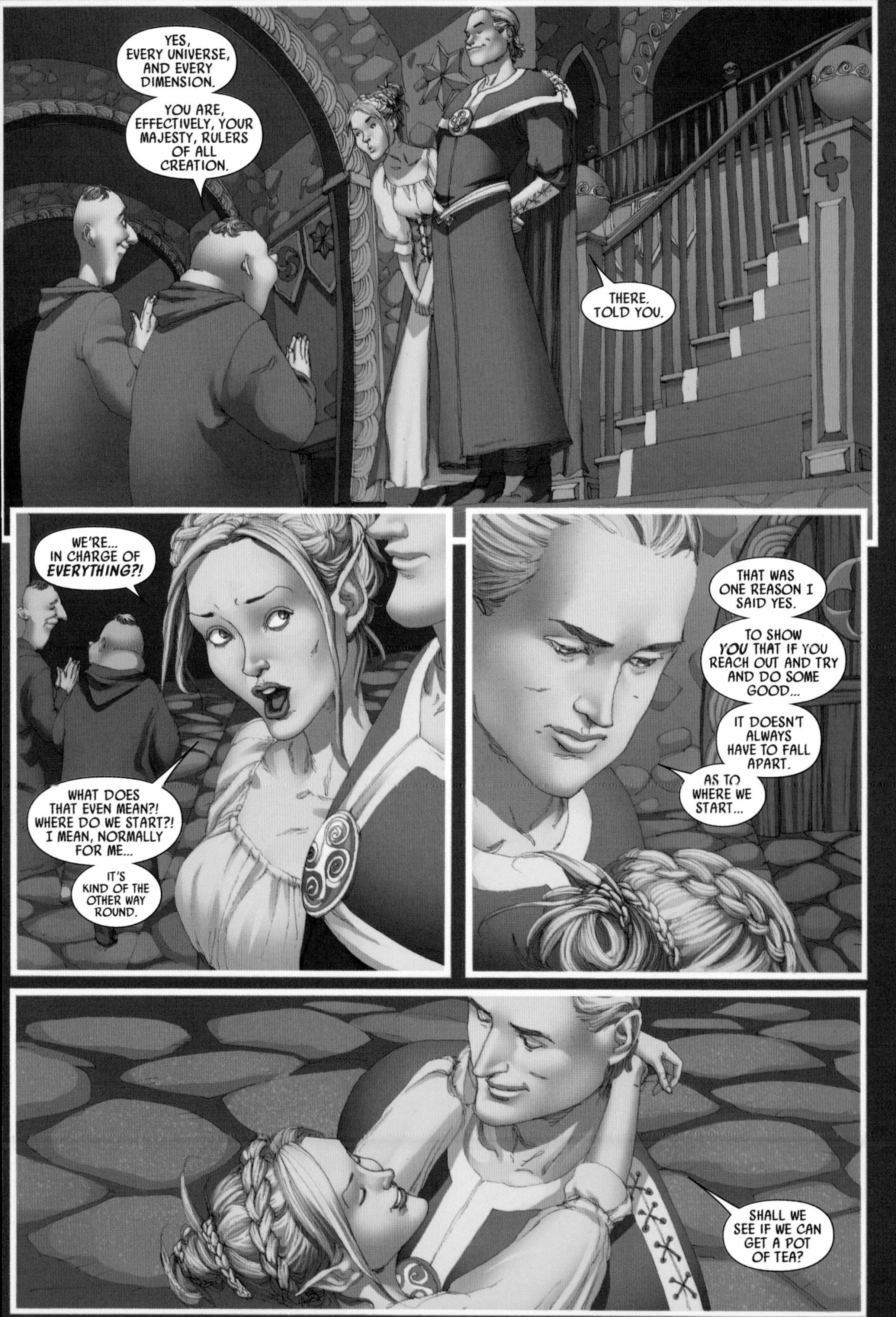
YES, EVERY UNIVERSE, AND EVERY DIMENSION.
YOU ARE, EFFECTIVELY, YOUR MAJESTY, RULERS OF ALL CREATION.
THERE. TOLD YOU.
WE'RE... IN CHARGE OF *EVERYTHING?!*
WHAT DOES THAT EVEN MEAN?! WHERE DO WE START?! I MEAN, NORMALLY FOR ME...
IT'S KIND OF THE OTHER WAY ROUND.
THAT WAS ONE REASON I SAID YES.
TO SHOW *YOU* THAT IF YOU REACH OUT AND TRY AND DO SOME GOOD...
IT DOESN'T ALWAYS HAVE TO FALL APART.
AS TO WHERE WE START...
SHALL WE SEE IF WE CAN GET A POT OF TEA?

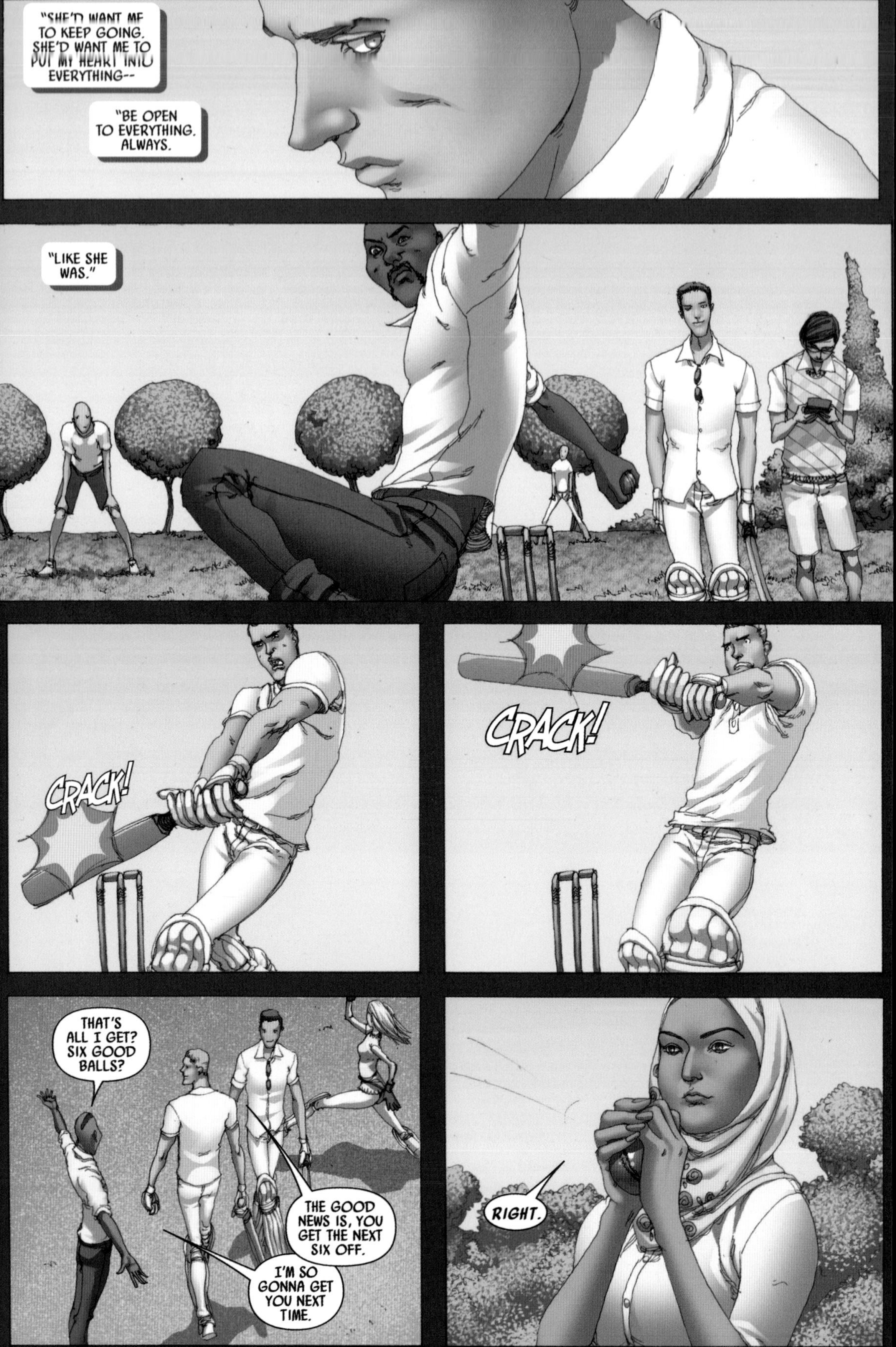
"SHE'D WANT ME TO KEEP GOING. SHE'D WANT ME TO PUT MY HEART INTO EVERYTHING--
"BE OPEN TO EVERYTHING. ALWAYS.
"LIKE SHE WAS."
CRACK!
CRACK!
THAT'S ALL I GET? SIX GOOD BALLS?
THE GOOD NEWS IS, YOU GET THE NEXT SIX OFF.
I'M SO GONNA GET YOU NEXT TIME.
RIGHT.

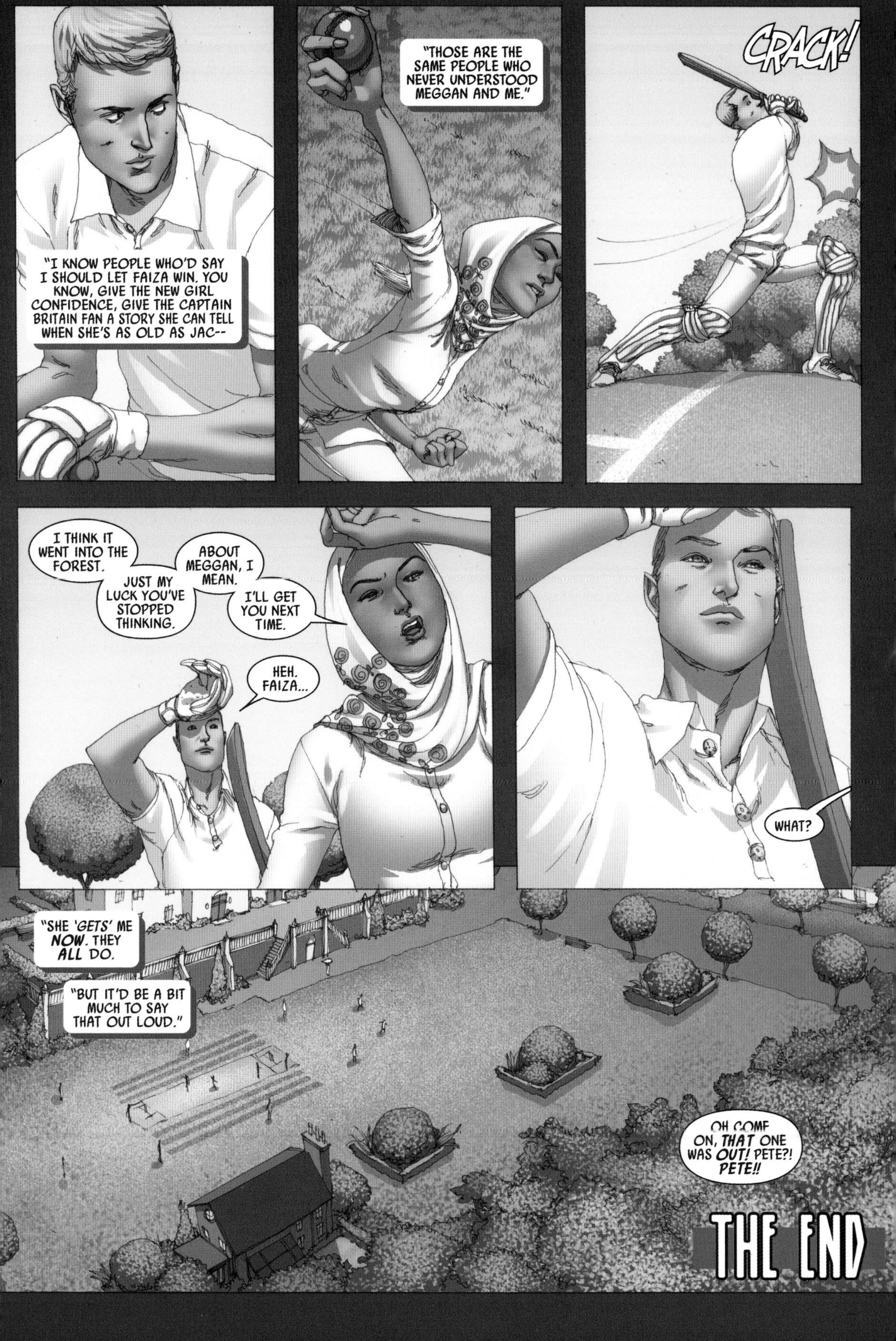
"I KNOW PEOPLE WHO'D SAY I SHOULD LET FAIZA WIN. YOU KNOW, GIVE THE NEW GIRL CONFIDENCE, GIVE THE CAPTAIN BRITAIN FAN A STORY SHE CAN TELL WHEN SHE'S AS OLD AS JAC--
"THOSE ARE THE SAME PEOPLE WHO NEVER UNDERSTOOD MEGGAN AND ME."
CRACK!
I THINK IT WENT INTO THE FOREST.
ABOUT MEGGAN, I MEAN.
JUST MY LUCK YOU'VE STOPPED THINKING.
I'LL GET YOU NEXT TIME.
HEH. FAIZA...
WHAT?
"SHE 'GETS' ME NOW. THEY ALL DO.
"BUT IT'D BE A BIT MUCH TO SAY THAT OUT LOUD."
OH COME ON, THAT ONE WAS OUT! PETE?! PETE!!
THE END

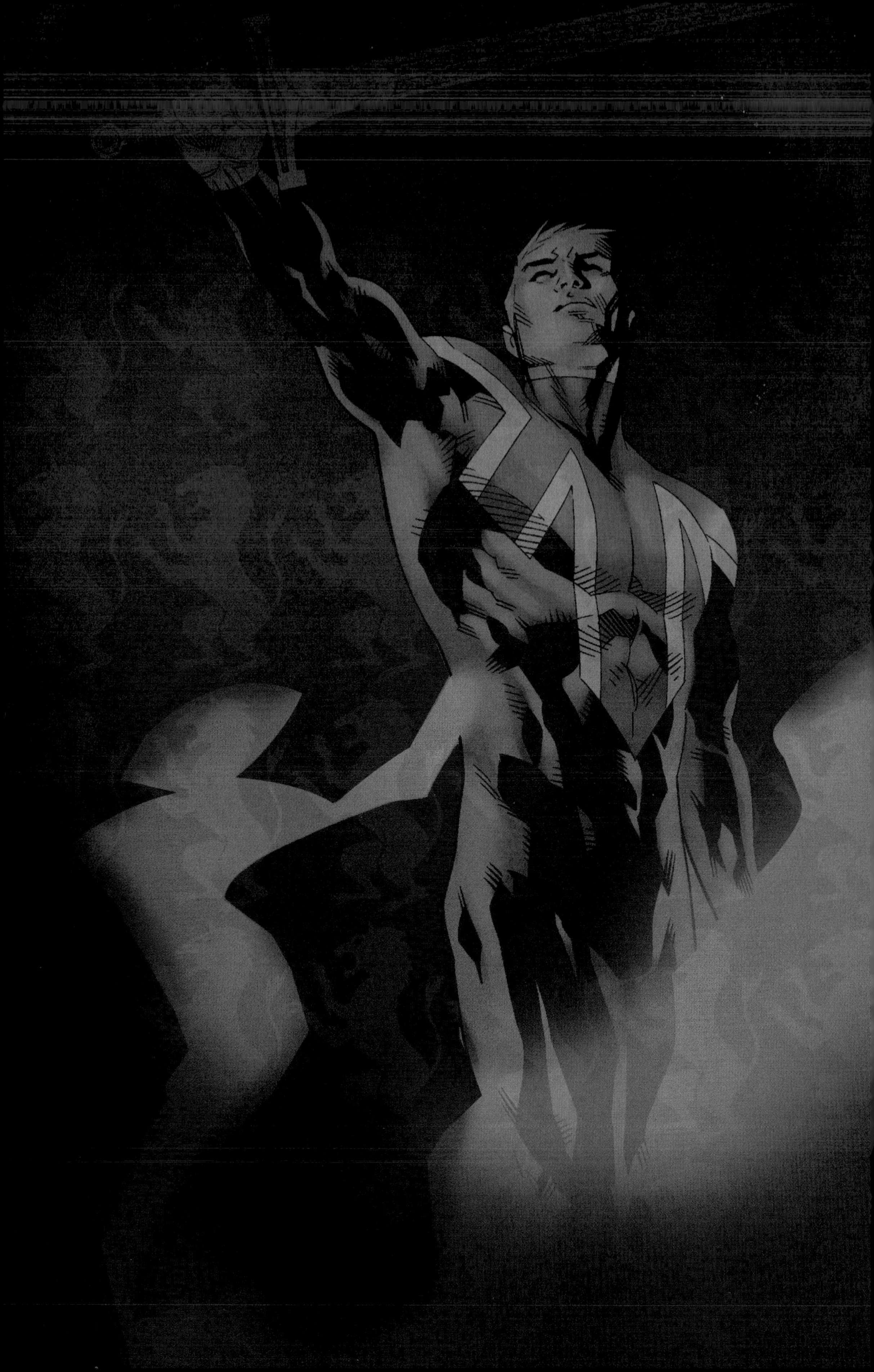

CAPTAIN BRITAIN AND MI13 #14
COVER ARTWORK

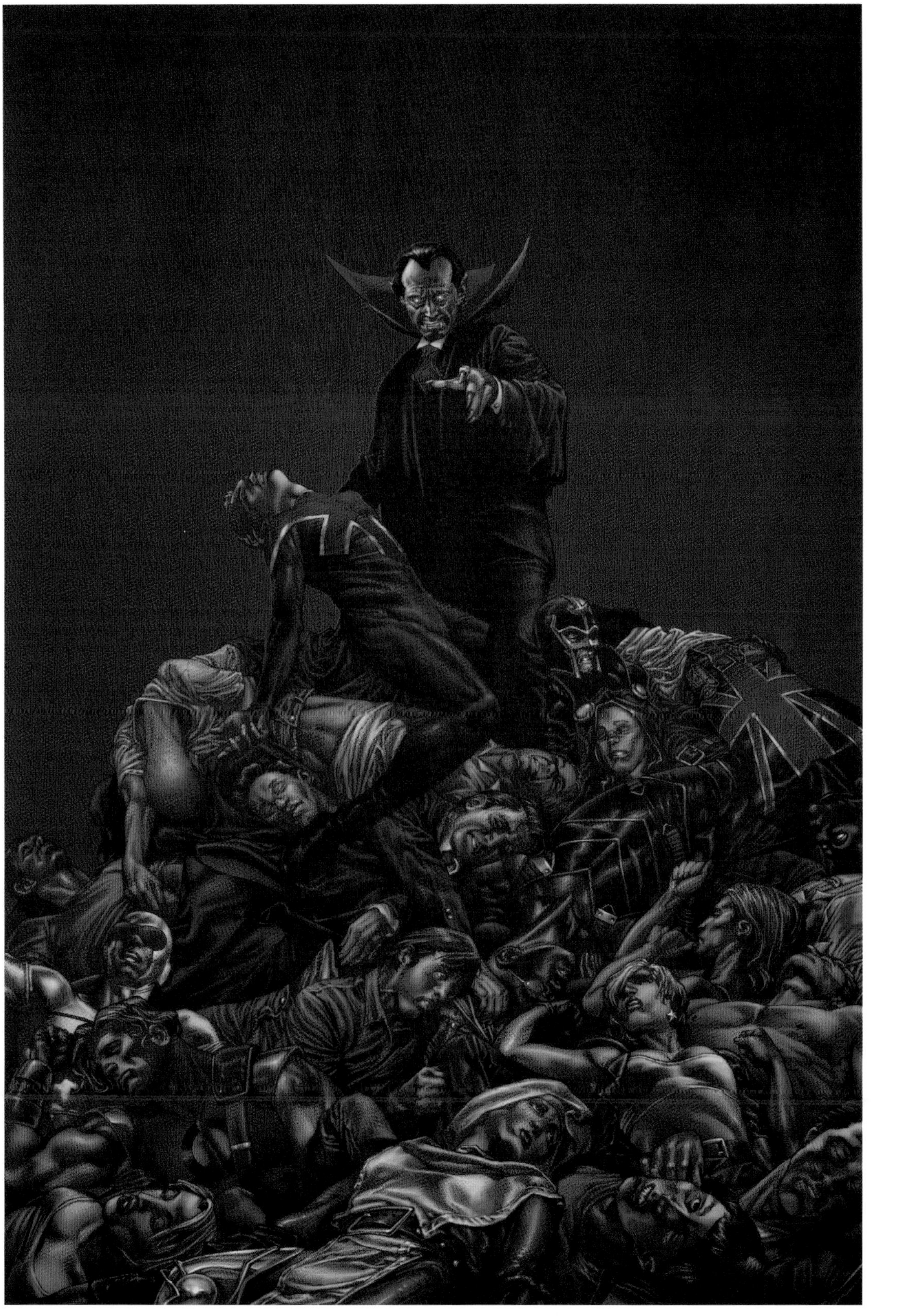

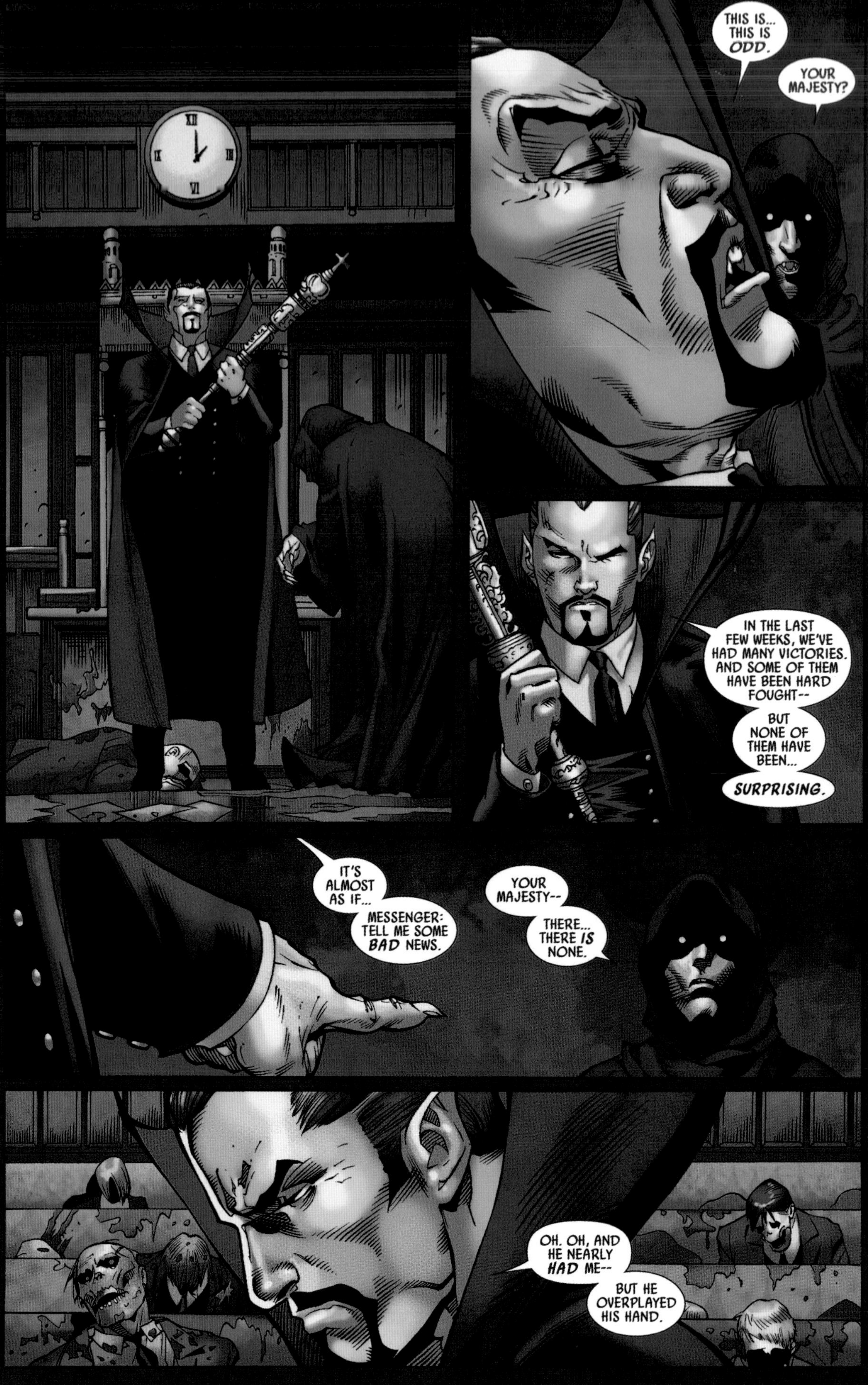
THIS IS... THIS IS ODD.
YOUR MAJESTY?
IN THE LAST FEW WEEKS, WE'VE HAD MANY VICTORIES. AND SOME OF THEM HAVE BEEN HARD FOUGHT--
BUT NONE OF THEM HAVE BEEN...
SURPRISING.
IT'S ALMOST AS IF...
MESSENGER: TELL ME SOME BAD NEWS.
YOUR MAJESTY--
THERE... THERE IS NONE.
OH. OH, AND HE NEARLY HAD ME--
BUT HE OVERPLAYED HIS HAND.

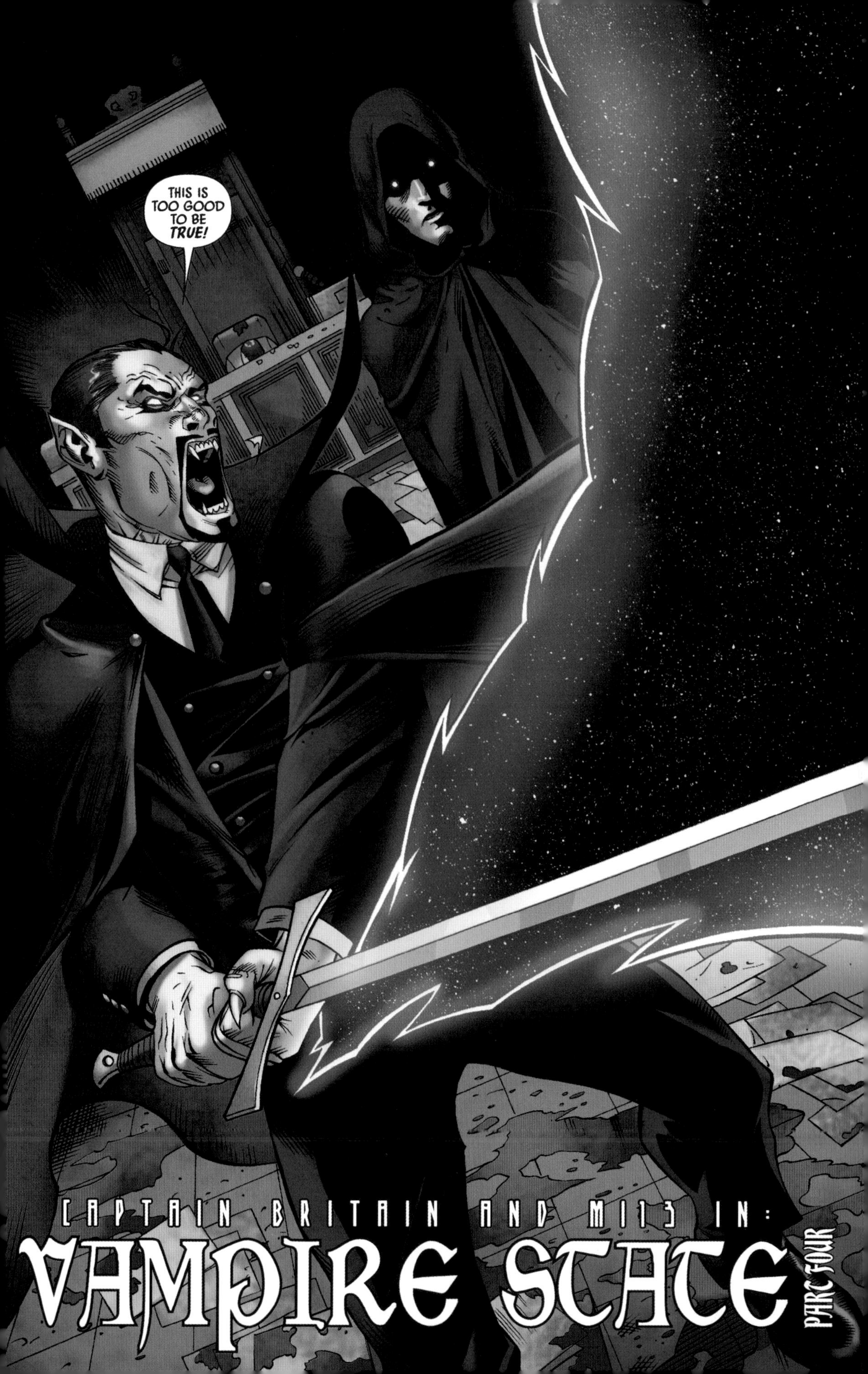
THIS IS TOO GOOD TO BE TRUE!
CAPTAIN BRITAIN AND MI13 IN:
VAMPIRE STATE
PART FOUR

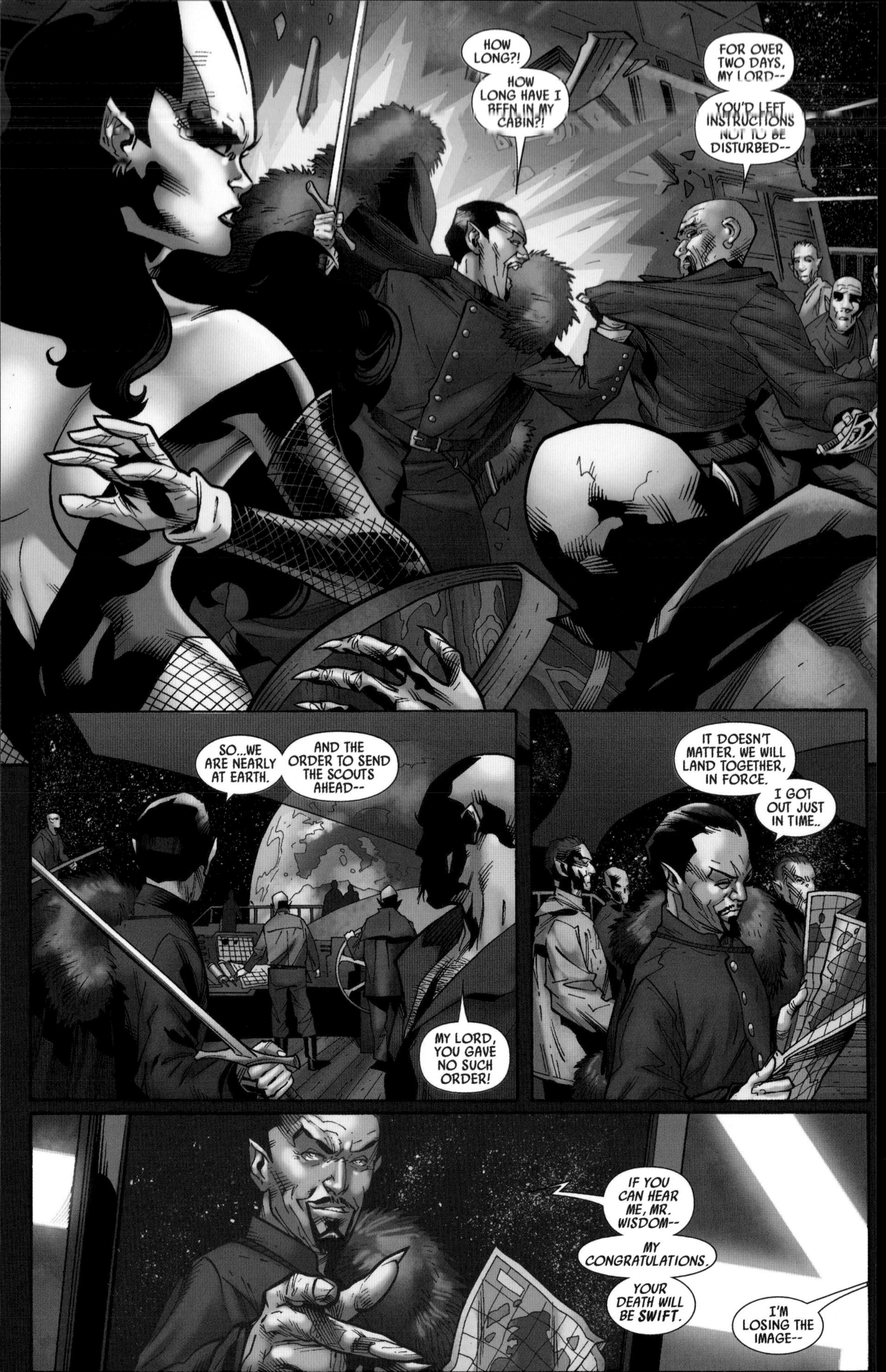

HOW LONG?!
HOW LONG HAVE I BEEN IN MY CABIN?!
FOR OVER TWO DAYS, MY LORD--
YOU'D LEFT INSTRUCTIONS NOT TO BE DISTURBED--
SO...WE ARE NEARLY AT EARTH.
AND THE ORDER TO SEND THE SCOUTS AHEAD--
MY LORD, YOU GAVE NO SUCH ORDER!
IT DOESN'T MATTER. WE WILL LAND TOGETHER, IN FORCE.
I GOT OUT JUST IN TIME..
IF YOU CAN HEAR ME, MR. WISDOM--
MY CONGRATULATIONS.
YOUR DEATH WILL BE SWIFT.
I'M LOSING THE IMAGE--

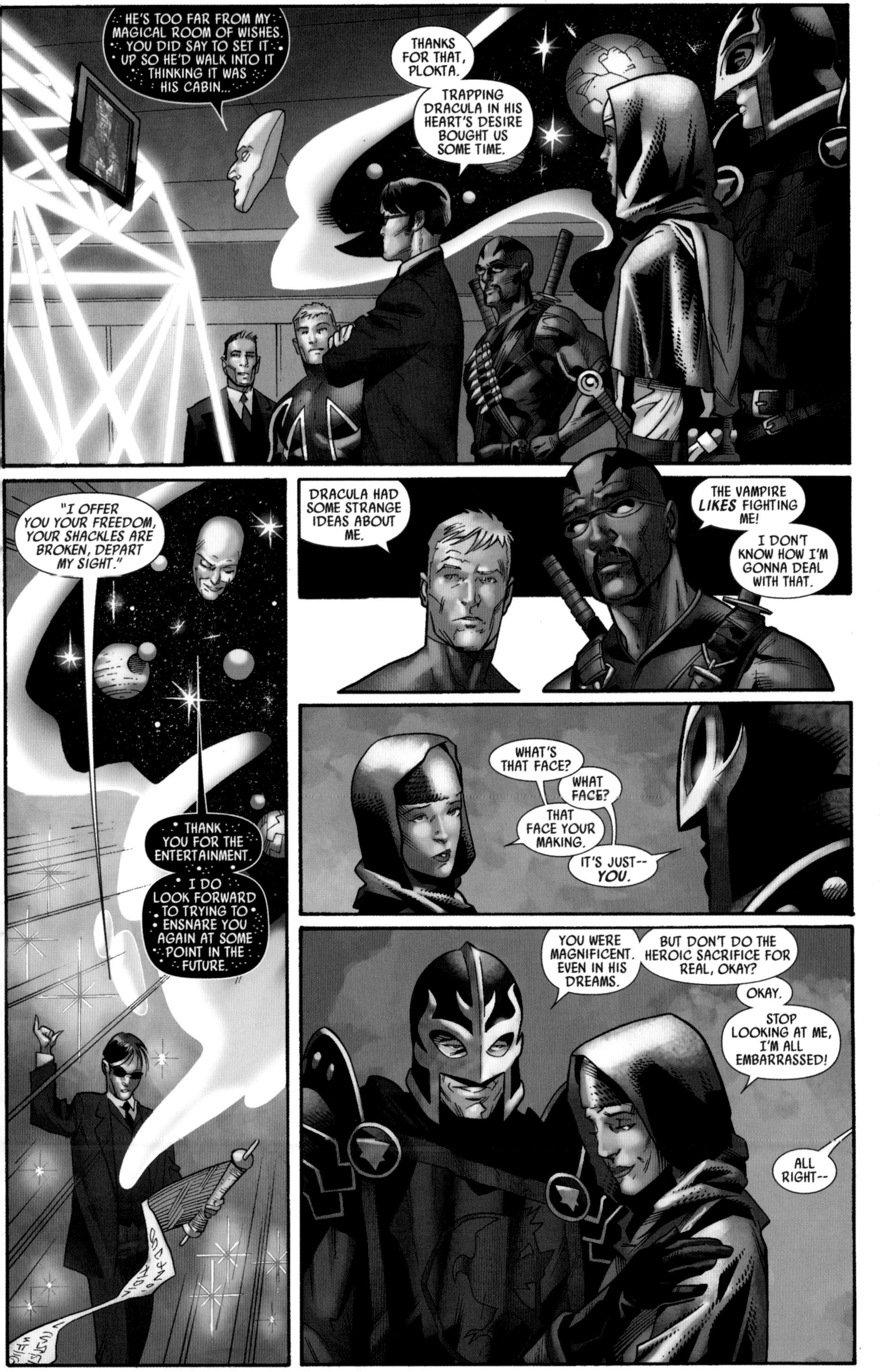
HE'S TOO FAR FROM MY MAGICAL ROOM OF WISHES. YOU DID SAY TO SET IT UP SO HE'D WALK INTO IT THINKING IT WAS HIS CABIN...
THANKS FOR THAT, PLOKTA.
TRAPPING DRACULA IN HIS HEART'S DESIRE BOUGHT US SOME TIME.
"I OFFER YOU YOUR FREEDOM, YOUR SHACKLES ARE BROKEN, DEPART MY SIGHT."
THANK YOU FOR THE ENTERTAINMENT.
I DO LOOK FORWARD TO TRYING TO ENSNARE YOU AGAIN AT SOME POINT IN THE FUTURE.
DRACULA HAD SOME STRANGE IDEAS ABOUT ME.
THE VAMPIRE LIKES FIGHTING ME!
I DON'T KNOW HOW I'M GONNA DEAL WITH THAT.
WHAT'S THAT FACE?
WHAT FACE?
THAT FACE YOUR MAKING.
IT'S JUST-- YOU.
YOU WERE MAGNIFICENT. EVEN IN HIS DREAMS.
BUT DON'T DO THE HEROIC SACRIFICE FOR REAL, OKAY?
OKAY.
STOP LOOKING AT ME, I'M ALL EMBARRASSED!
ALL RIGHT--

DRACULA WON'T HAVE SPITFIRE CALL US NOW. HE KNOWS WHAT WE'VE SEEN.

HE'S CLEARLY INFORMED ABOUT THE INTERNATIONAL SITUATION, SO LET'S TAKE THAT AS HOW IT'D PLAY AND SAVE OUR ENERGY.

IN THESE TWO DAYS, WE'VE FORMED UP THE RESOURCES WE HAVE. AND, CRUCIALLY, THANKS TO PLOKTA'S DOWNLOAD OF DRACULA'S DREAMS INTO OUR SYSTEMS, AND OUR OTHER SOURCES...

WE NOW KNOW *EVERYTHING* ABOUT HIS FORCES.

KNIGHT, EXCALIBUR, TO THE TECH LAB.

BLADE, THERE'S A TAXI OUTSIDE TO MI16.

CAP--

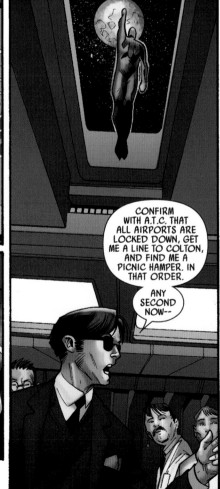

CONFIRM WITH A.T.C. THAT ALL AIRPORTS ARE LOCKED DOWN, GET ME A LINE TO COLTON, AND FIND ME A PICNIC HAMPER. IN THAT ORDER.

ANY SECOND NOW--

NAH, I DON'T NEED TO SAY A WORD TO YOU. YOU'RE CAPTAIN BRITAIN.

I BELIEVE WE'VE MET.

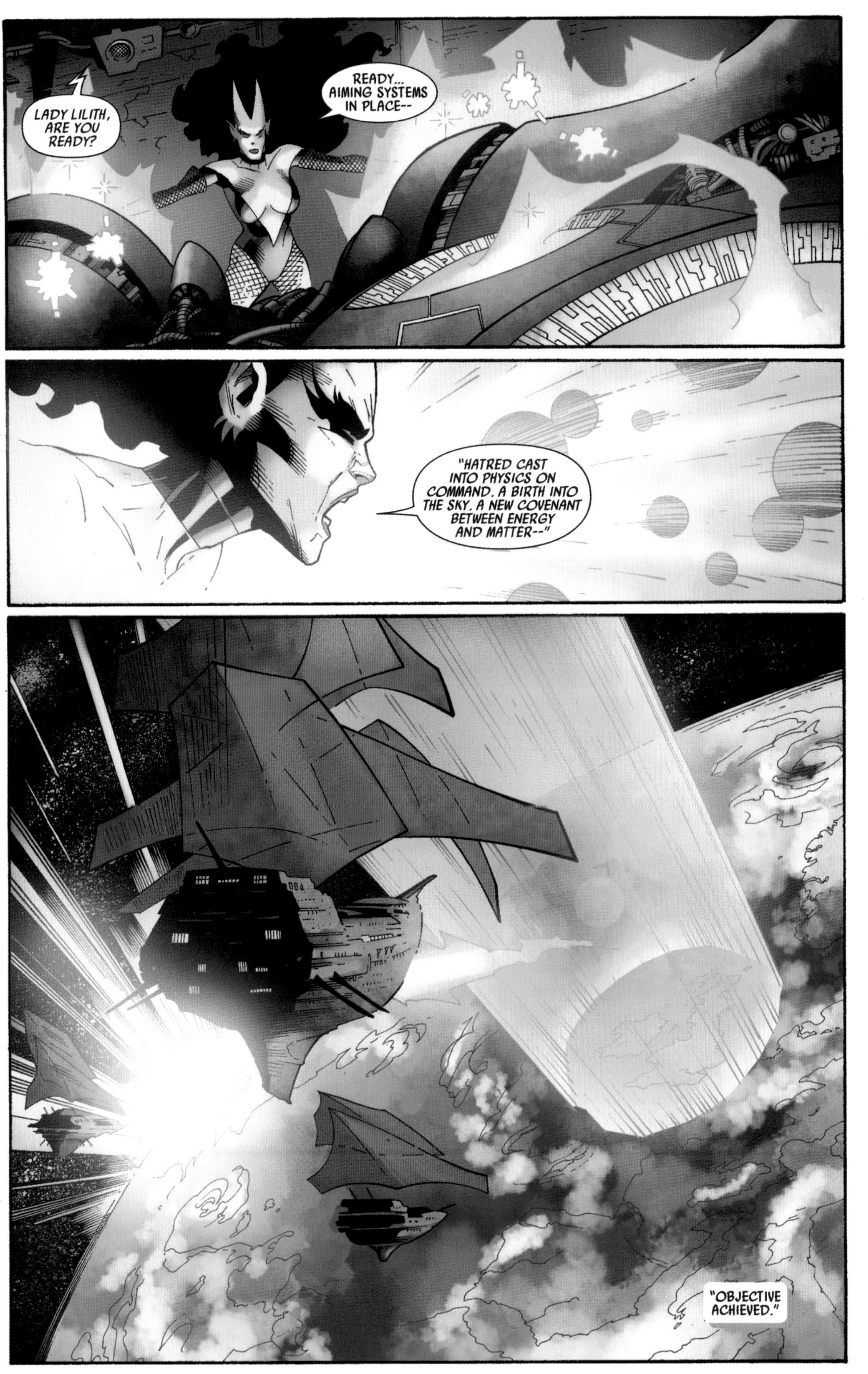
LADY LILITH, ARE YOU READY?
READY... AIMING SYSTEMS IN PLACE--
"HATRED CAST INTO PHYSICS ON COMMAND. A BIRTH INTO THE SKY. A NEW COVENANT BETWEEN ENERGY AND MATTER--"
"OBJECTIVE ACHIEVED."

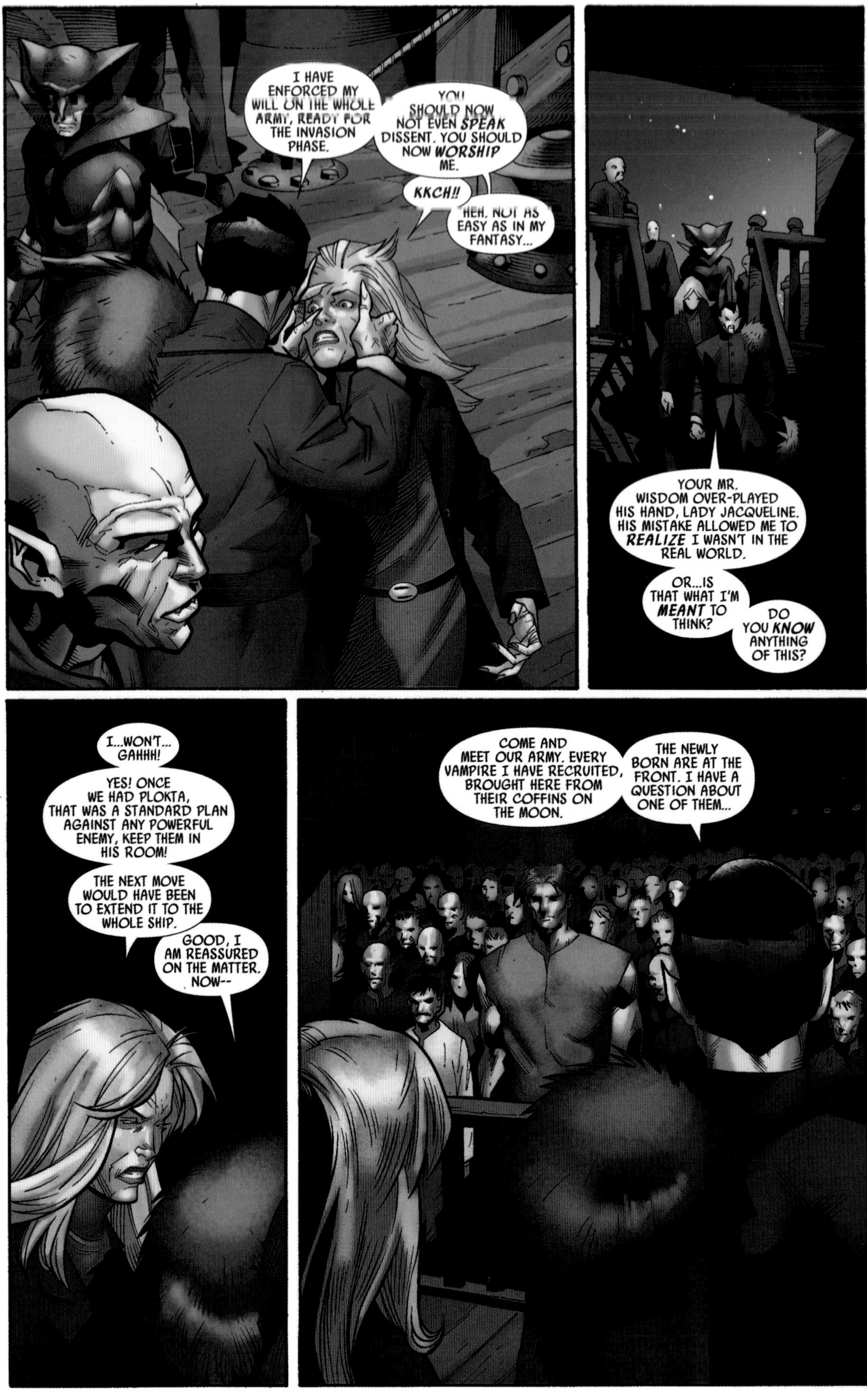
I HAVE ENFORCED MY WILL ON THE WHOLE ARMY, READY FOR THE INVASION PHASE.
YOU SHOULD NOW NOT EVEN SPEAK DISSENT. YOU SHOULD NOW WORSHIP ME.
KKCH!!
HEH. NOT AS EASY AS IN MY FANTASY...
YOUR MR. WISDOM OVER-PLAYED HIS HAND, LADY JACQUELINE. HIS MISTAKE ALLOWED ME TO REALIZE I WASN'T IN THE REAL WORLD.
OR...IS THAT WHAT I'M MEANT TO THINK?
DO YOU KNOW ANYTHING OF THIS?
I...WON'T... GAHHH!
YES! ONCE WE HAD PLOKTA, THAT WAS A STANDARD PLAN AGAINST ANY POWERFUL ENEMY, KEEP THEM IN HIS ROOM!
THE NEXT MOVE WOULD HAVE BEEN TO EXTEND IT TO THE WHOLE SHIP.
GOOD, I AM REASSURED ON THE MATTER. NOW--
COME AND MEET OUR ARMY. EVERY VAMPIRE I HAVE RECRUITED, BROUGHT HERE FROM THEIR COFFINS ON THE MOON.
THE NEWLY BORN ARE AT THE FRONT. I HAVE A QUESTION ABOUT ONE OF THEM...

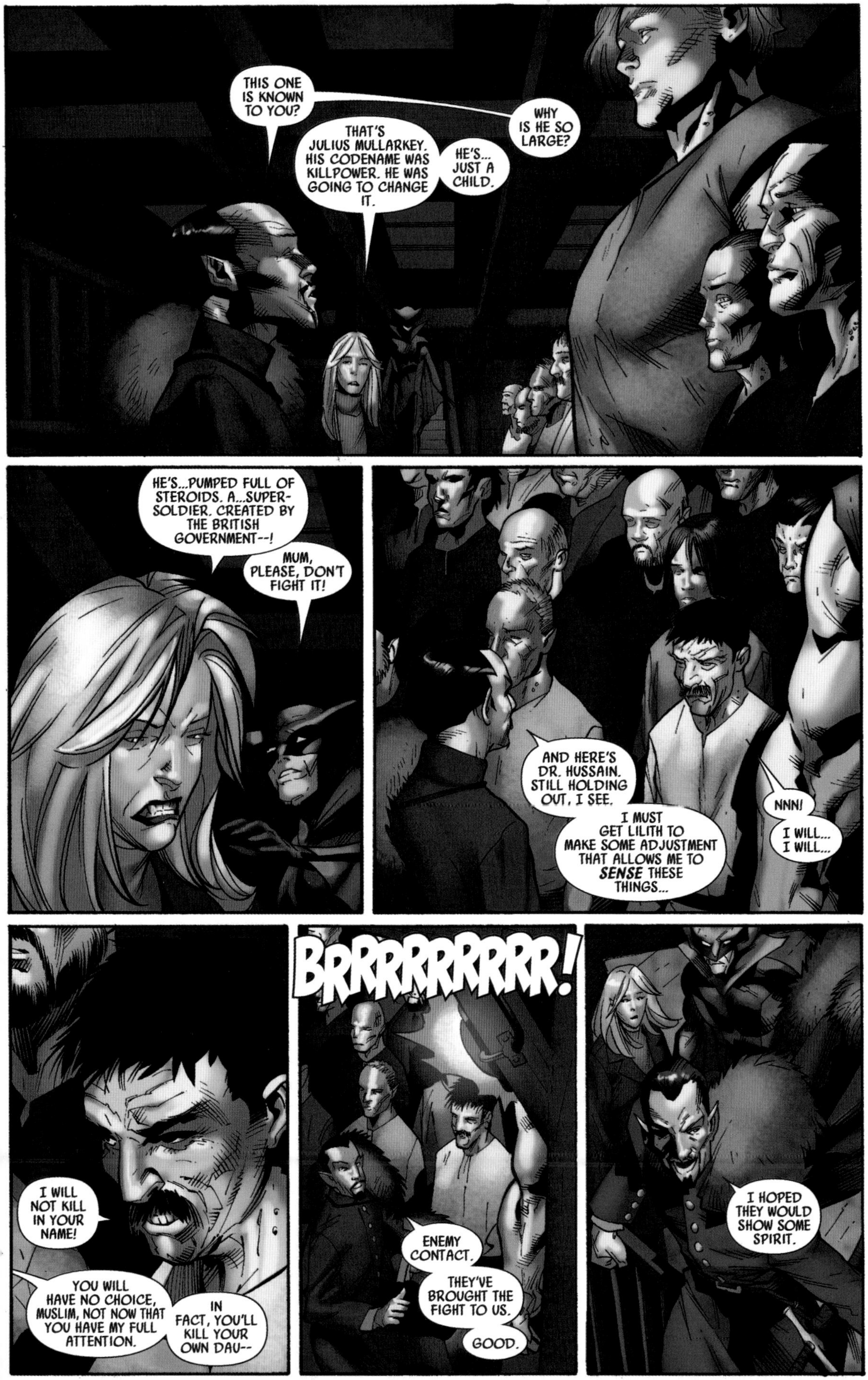
THIS ONE IS KNOWN TO YOU?
THAT'S JULIUS MULLARKEY. HIS CODENAME WAS KILLPOWER. HE WAS GOING TO CHANGE IT.
HE'S... JUST A CHILD.
WHY IS HE SO LARGE?
HE'S...PUMPED FULL OF STEROIDS. A...SUPER-SOLDIER. CREATED BY THE BRITISH GOVERNMENT--!
MUM, PLEASE, DON'T FIGHT IT!
AND HERE'S DR. HUSSAIN. STILL HOLDING OUT, I SEE.
I MUST GET LILITH TO MAKE SOME ADJUSTMENT THAT ALLOWS ME TO SENSE THESE THINGS...
NNN!
I WILL... I WILL...
I WILL NOT KILL IN YOUR NAME!
YOU WILL HAVE NO CHOICE, MUSLIM, NOT NOW THAT YOU HAVE MY FULL ATTENTION.
IN FACT, YOU'LL KILL YOUR OWN DAU--
BRRRRRRRRR!
ENEMY CONTACT.
THEY'VE BROUGHT THE FIGHT TO US.
GOOD.
I HOPED THEY WOULD SHOW SOME SPIRIT.

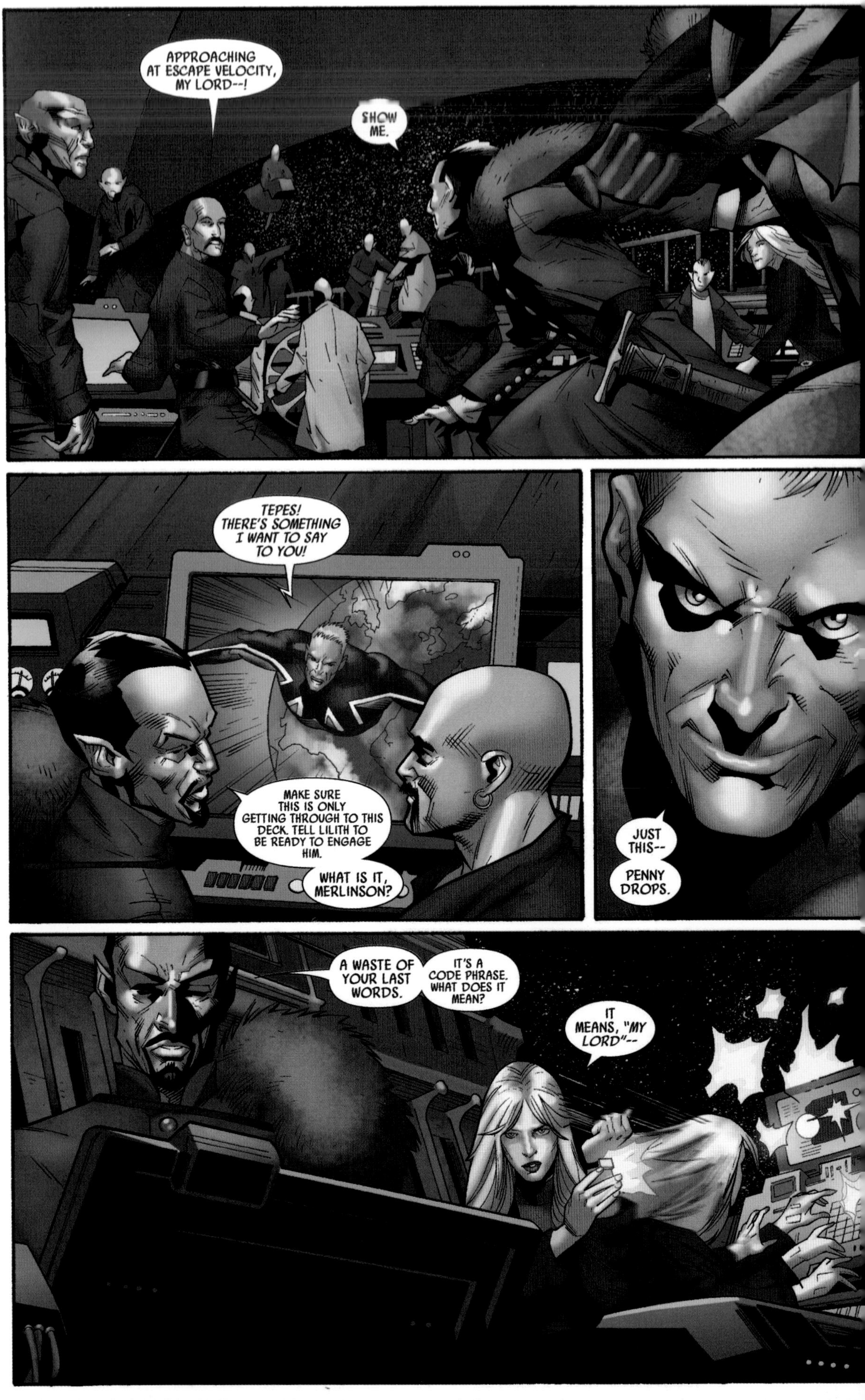
APPROACHING AT ESCAPE VELOCITY, MY LORD--!
SHOW ME.
TEPES! THERE'S SOMETHING I WANT TO SAY TO YOU!
MAKE SURE THIS IS ONLY GETTING THROUGH TO THIS DECK. TELL LILITH TO BE READY TO ENGAGE HIM.
WHAT IS IT, MERLINSON?
JUST THIS--
PENNY DROPS.
A WASTE OF YOUR LAST WORDS.
IT'S A CODE PHRASE. WHAT DOES IT MEAN?
IT MEANS, "MY LORD"--

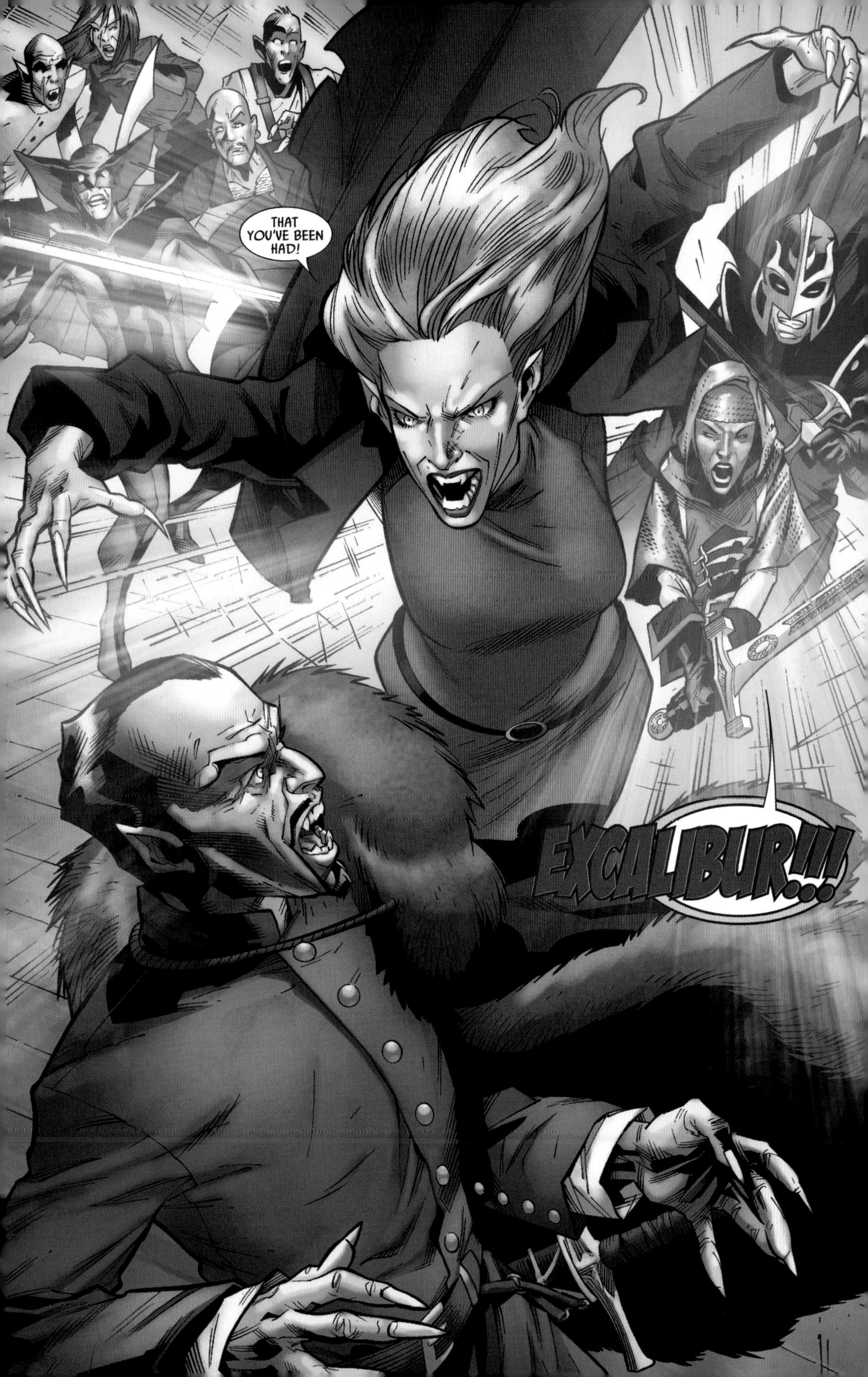
THAT YOU'VE BEEN HAD!
EXCALIBUR!!!

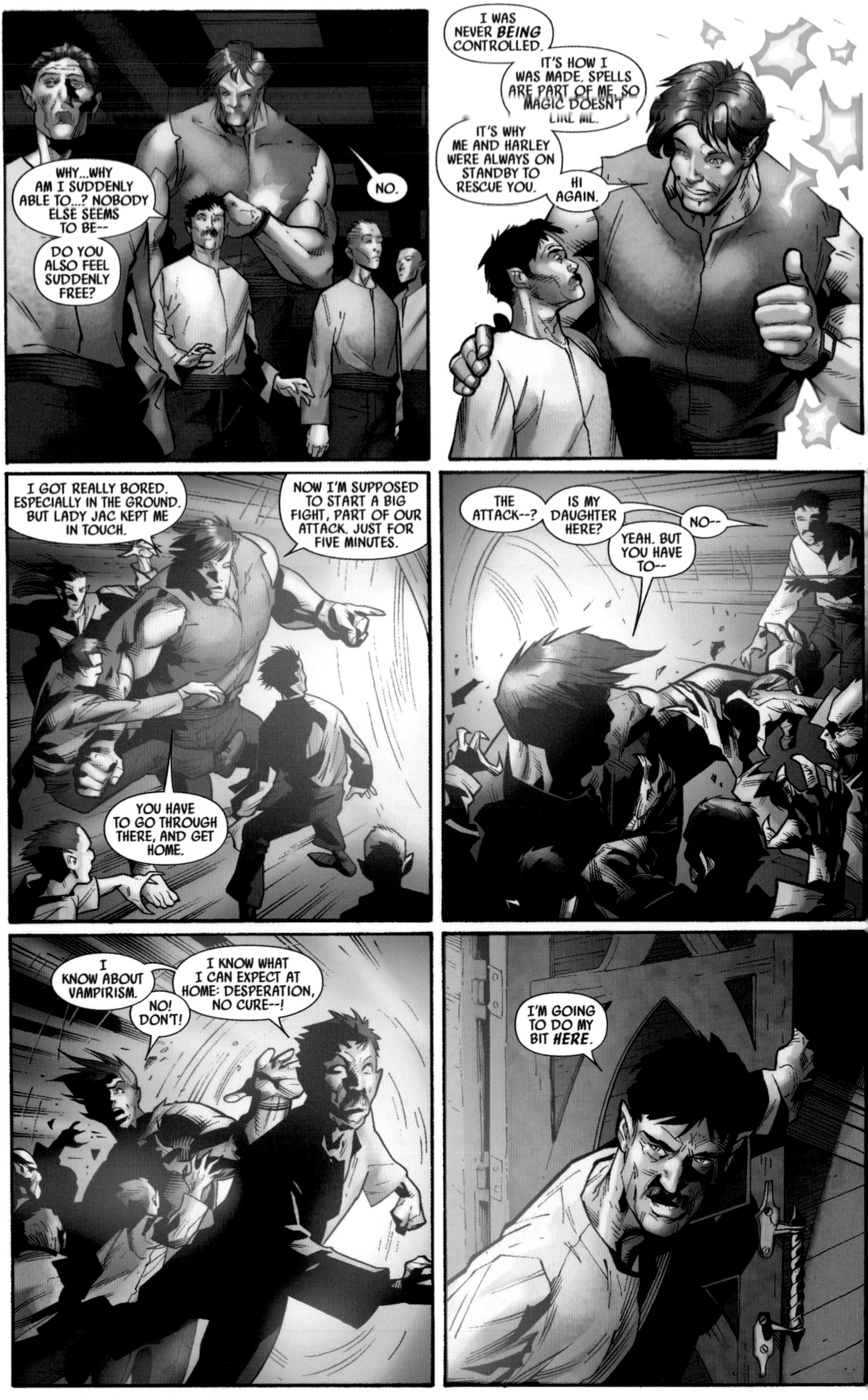
WHY...WHY AM I SUDDENLY ABLE TO...? NOBODY ELSE SEEMS TO BE--
DO YOU ALSO FEEL SUDDENLY FREE?
NO.
I WAS NEVER BEING CONTROLLED.
IT'S HOW I WAS MADE. SPELLS ARE PART OF ME, SO MAGIC DOESN'T LIKE ME.
IT'S WHY ME AND HARLEY WERE ALWAYS ON STANDBY TO RESCUE YOU.
HI AGAIN.
I GOT REALLY BORED. ESPECIALLY IN THE GROUND. BUT LADY JAC KEPT ME IN TOUCH.
NOW I'M SUPPOSED TO START A BIG FIGHT, PART OF OUR ATTACK. JUST FOR FIVE MINUTES.
YOU HAVE TO GO THROUGH THERE, AND GET HOME.
THE ATTACK--?
IS MY DAUGHTER HERE?
NO--
YEAH. BUT YOU HAVE TO--
I KNOW ABOUT VAMPIRISM.
I KNOW WHAT I CAN EXPECT AT HOME: DESPERATION, NO CURE--!
NO! DON'T!
I'M GOING TO DO MY BIT HERE.

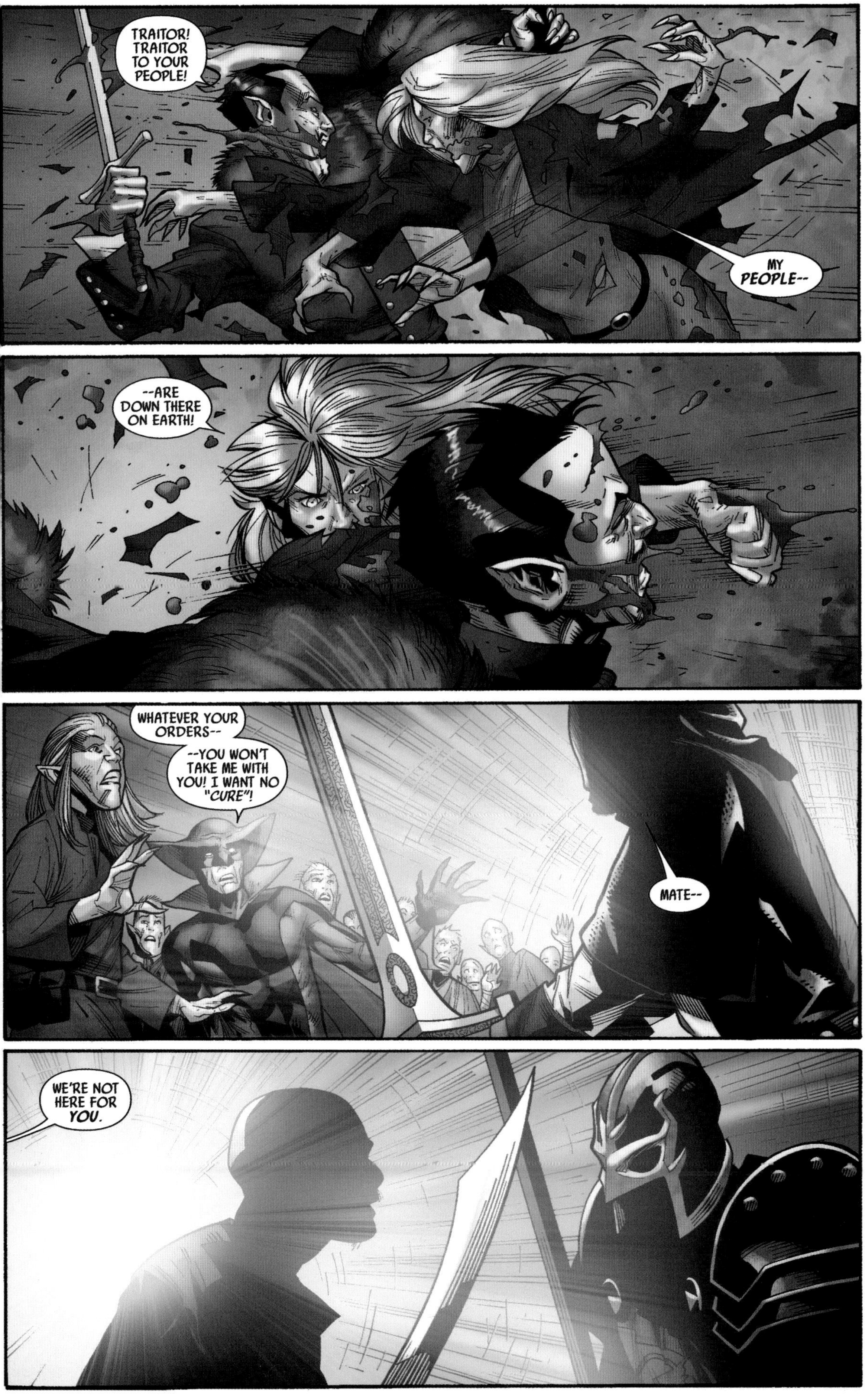
TRAITOR! TRAITOR TO YOUR PEOPLE!
MY PEOPLE--
--ARE DOWN THERE ON EARTH!
WHATEVER YOUR ORDERS--
--YOU WON'T TAKE ME WITH YOU! I WANT NO "CURE"!
MATE--
WE'RE NOT HERE FOR YOU.

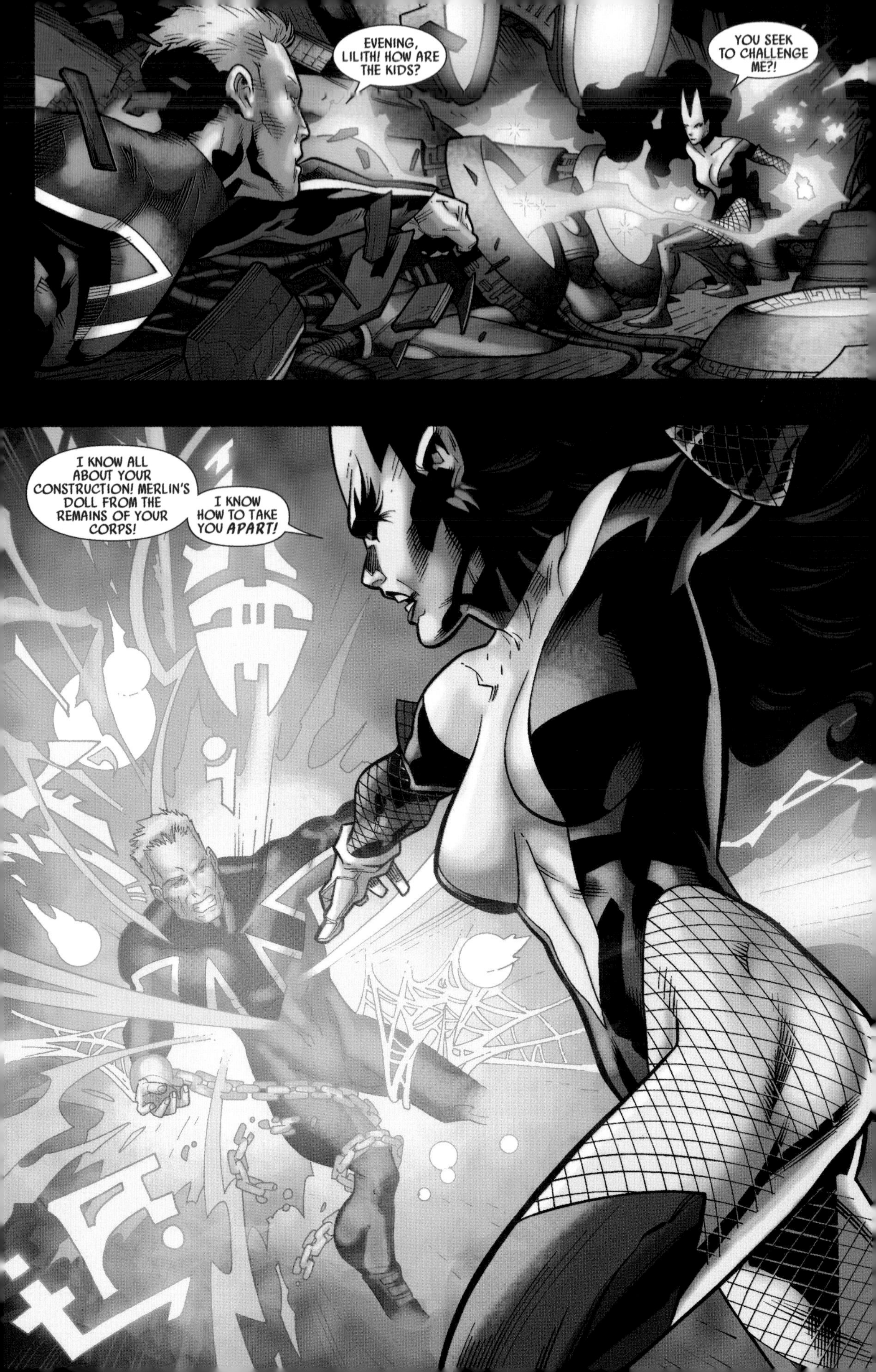
EVENING, LILITH! HOW ARE THE KIDS?
YOU SEEK TO CHALLENGE ME?!
I KNOW ALL ABOUT YOUR CONSTRUCTION! MERLIN'S DOLL FROM THE REMAINS OF YOUR CORPS!
I KNOW HOW TO TAKE YOU APART!

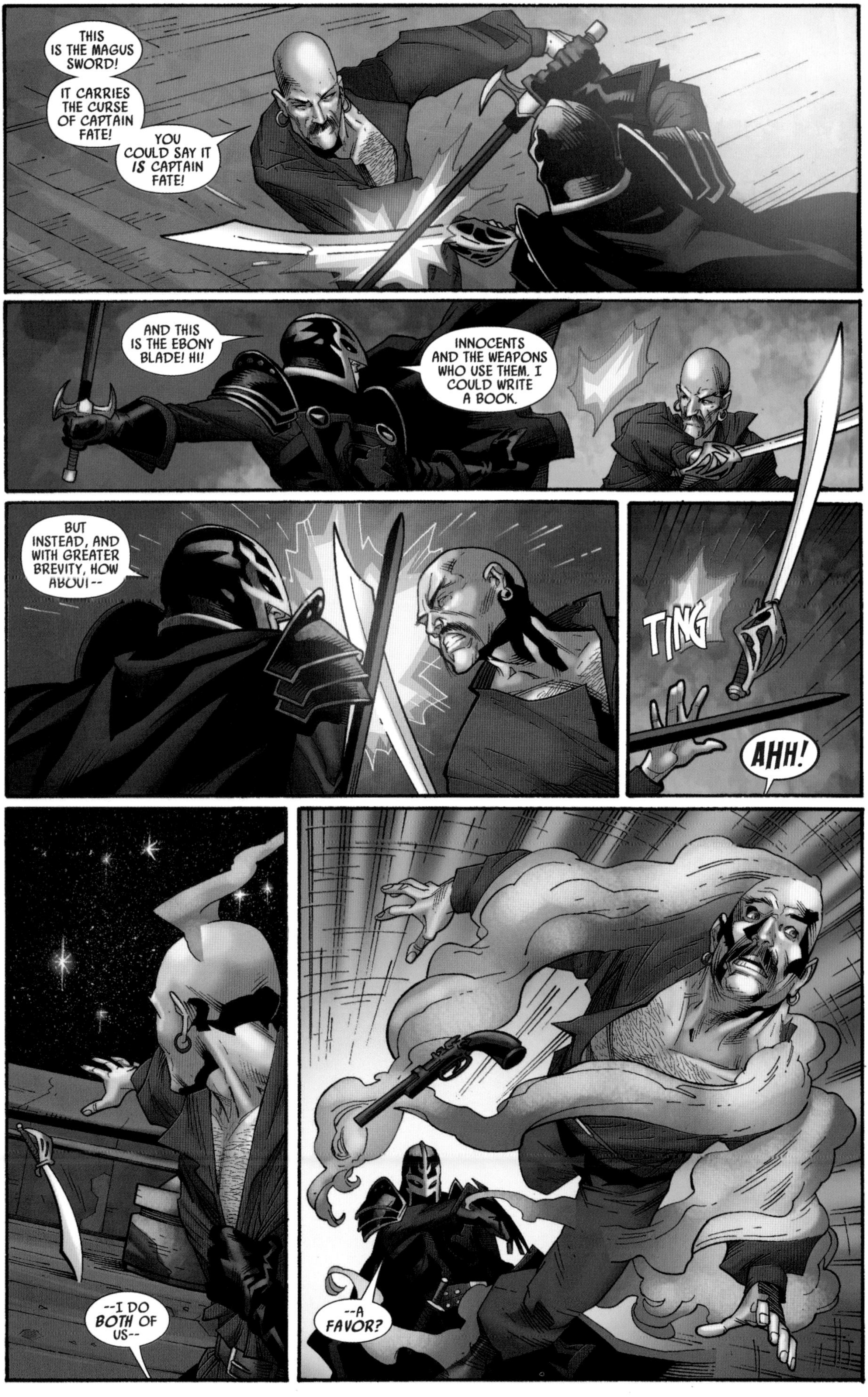
THIS IS THE MAGUS SWORD!
IT CARRIES THE CURSE OF CAPTAIN FATE!
YOU COULD SAY IT IS CAPTAIN FATE!
AND THIS IS THE EBONY BLADE! HI!
INNOCENTS AND THE WEAPONS WHO USE THEM. I COULD WRITE A BOOK.
BUT INSTEAD, AND WITH GREATER BREVITY, HOW ABOUT--
TING
AHH!
--I DO BOTH OF US--
--A FAVOR?

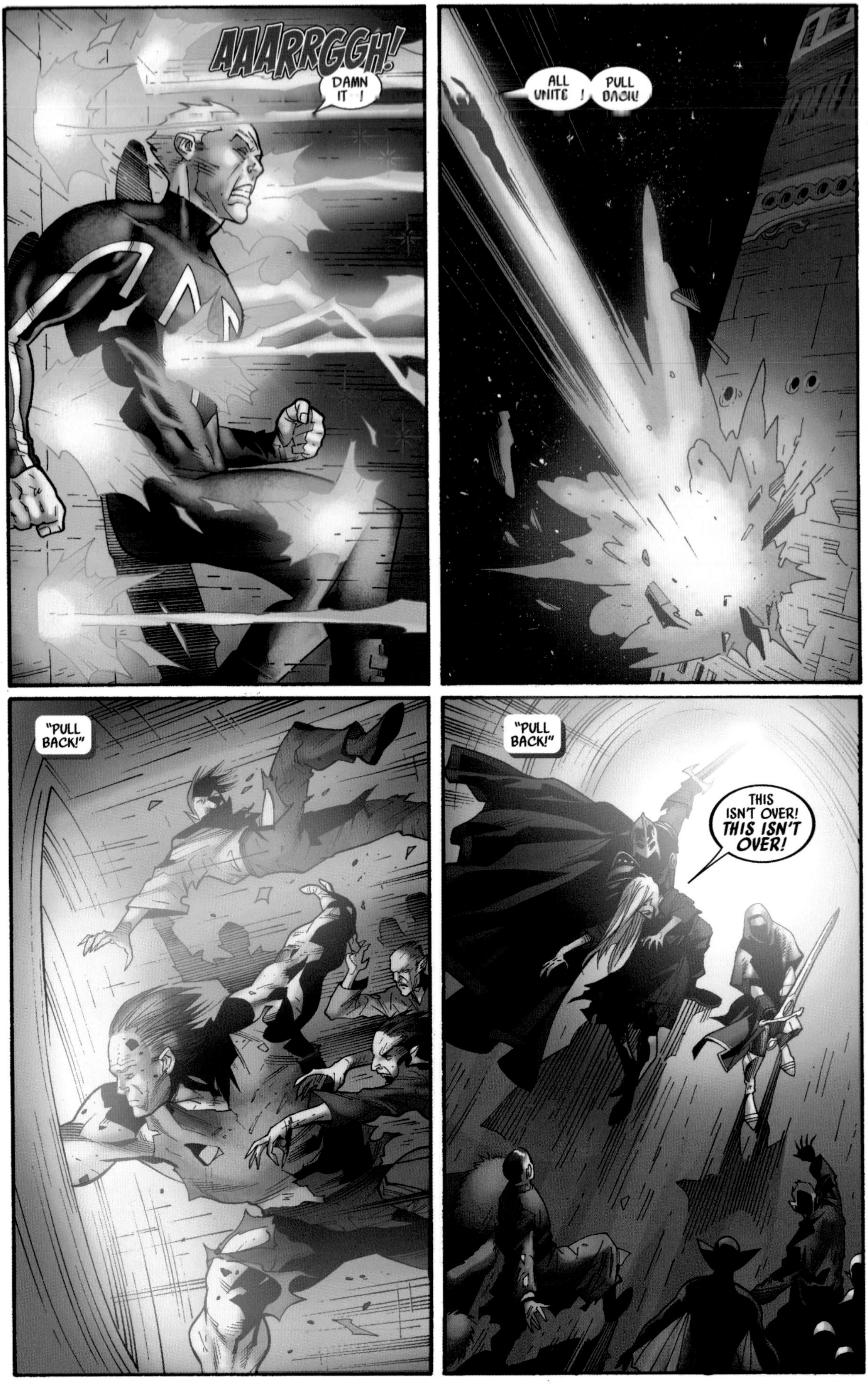
AAARRGGH!
DAMN IT !
ALL UNITE !
PULL BACK!
"PULL BACK!"
"PULL BACK!"
THIS ISN'T OVER! THIS ISN'T OVER!

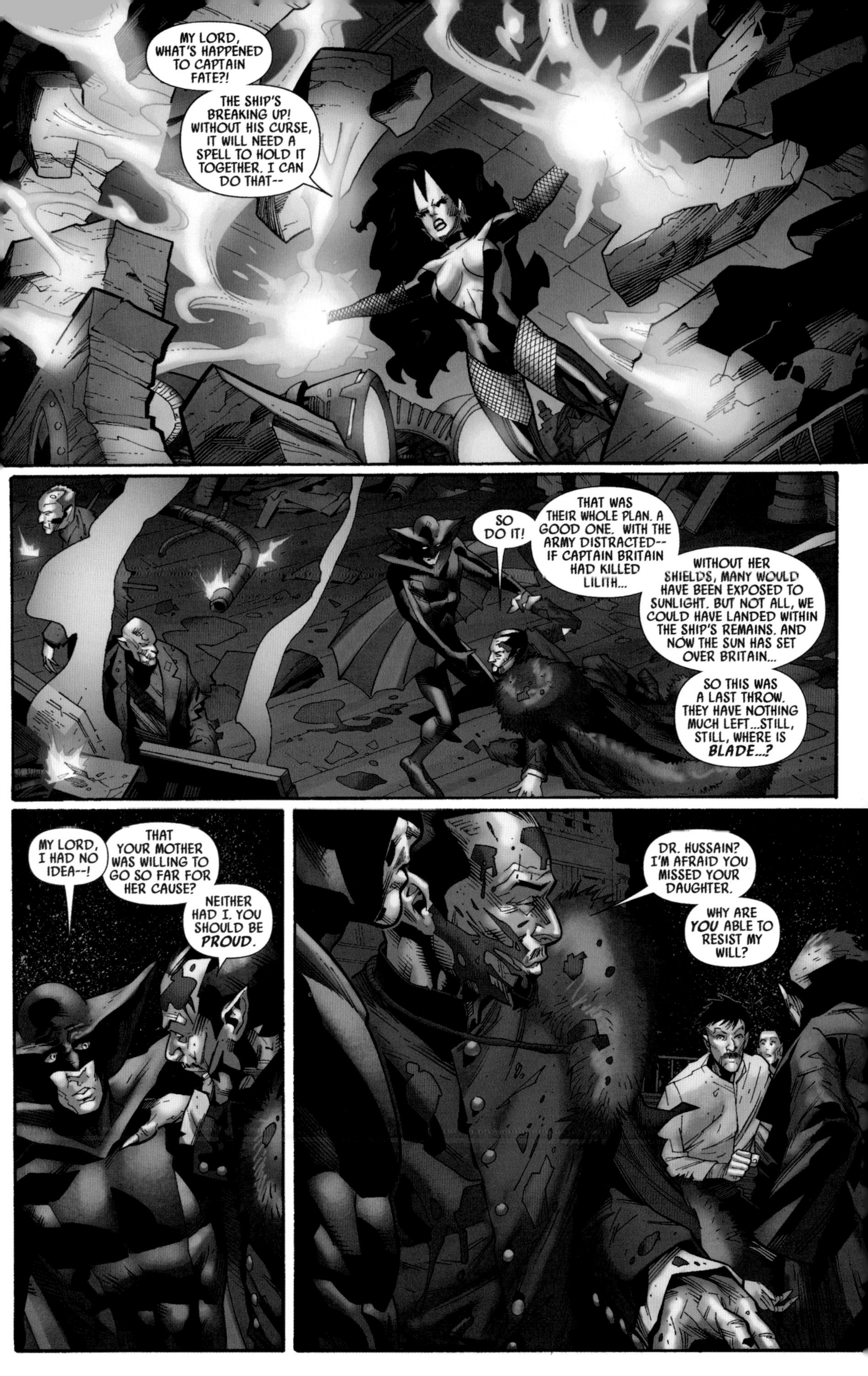
MY LORD, WHAT'S HAPPENED TO CAPTAIN FATE?!
THE SHIP'S BREAKING UP! WITHOUT HIS CURSE, IT WILL NEED A SPELL TO HOLD IT TOGETHER. I CAN DO THAT--
SO DO IT!
THAT WAS THEIR WHOLE PLAN. A GOOD ONE. WITH THE ARMY DISTRACTED-- IF CAPTAIN BRITAIN HAD KILLED LILITH...
WITHOUT HER SHIELDS, MANY WOULD HAVE BEEN EXPOSED TO SUNLIGHT. BUT NOT ALL, WE COULD HAVE LANDED WITHIN THE SHIP'S REMAINS. AND NOW THE SUN HAS SET OVER BRITAIN...
SO THIS WAS A LAST THROW. THEY HAVE NOTHING MUCH LEFT...STILL, STILL, WHERE IS BLADE...?
MY LORD, I HAD NO IDEA--!
THAT YOUR MOTHER WAS WILLING TO GO SO FAR FOR HER CAUSE?
NEITHER HAD I. YOU SHOULD BE PROUD.
DR. HUSSAIN? I'M AFRAID YOU MISSED YOUR DAUGHTER.
WHY ARE YOU ABLE TO RESIST MY WILL?

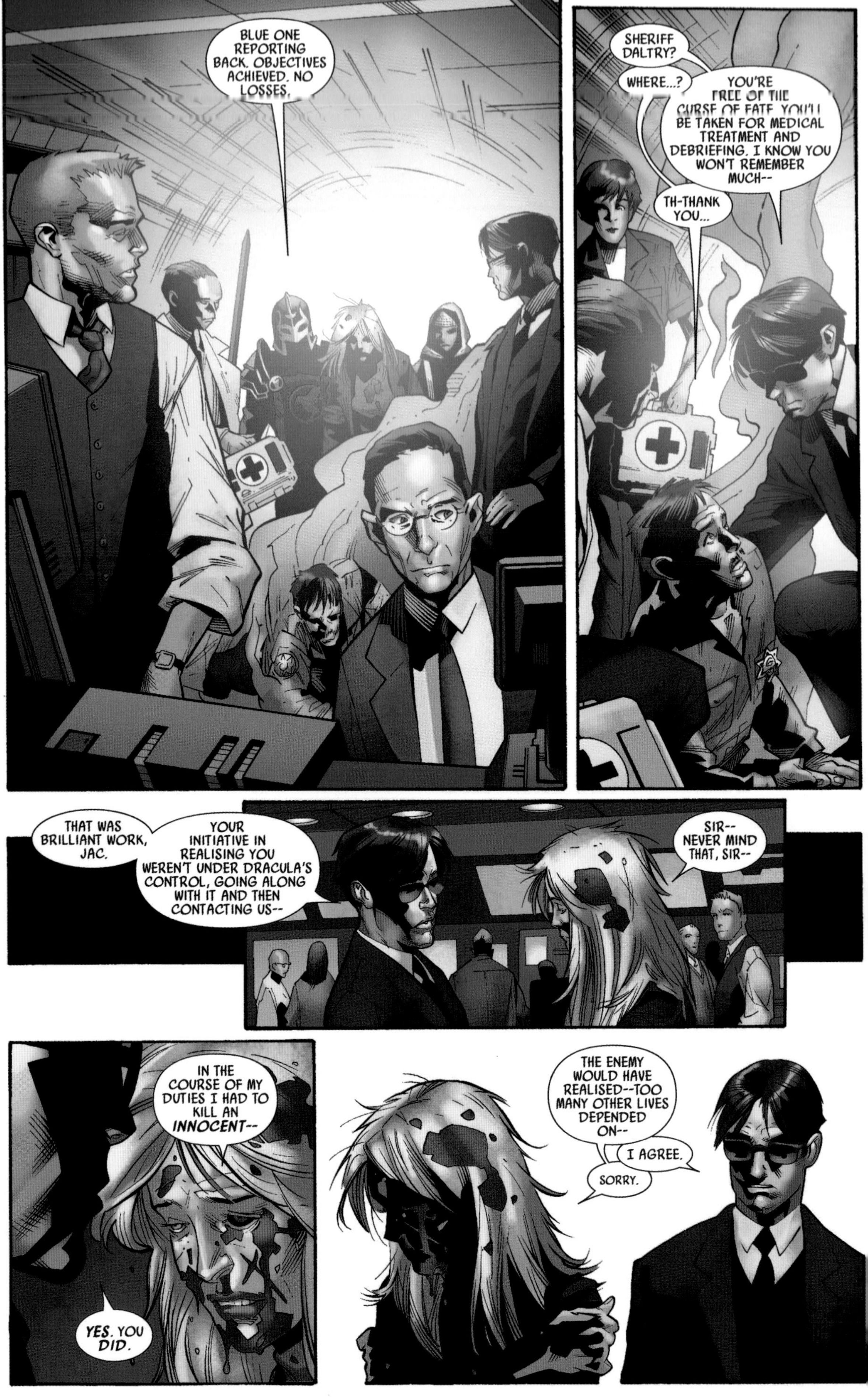

BLUE ONE REPORTING BACK. OBJECTIVES ACHIEVED. NO LOSSES.
SHERIFF DALTRY?
WHERE...?
YOU'RE FREE OF THE CURSE OF FATE. YOU'LL BE TAKEN FOR MEDICAL TREATMENT AND DEBRIEFING. I KNOW YOU WON'T REMEMBER MUCH--
TH-THANK YOU...
THAT WAS BRILLIANT WORK, JAC.
YOUR INITIATIVE IN REALISING YOU WEREN'T UNDER DRACULA'S CONTROL, GOING ALONG WITH IT AND THEN CONTACTING US--
SIR-- NEVER MIND THAT, SIR--
IN THE COURSE OF MY DUTIES I HAD TO KILL AN INNOCENT--
YES. YOU DID.
THE ENEMY WOULD HAVE REALISED--TOO MANY OTHER LIVES DEPENDED ON--
I AGREE.
SORRY.

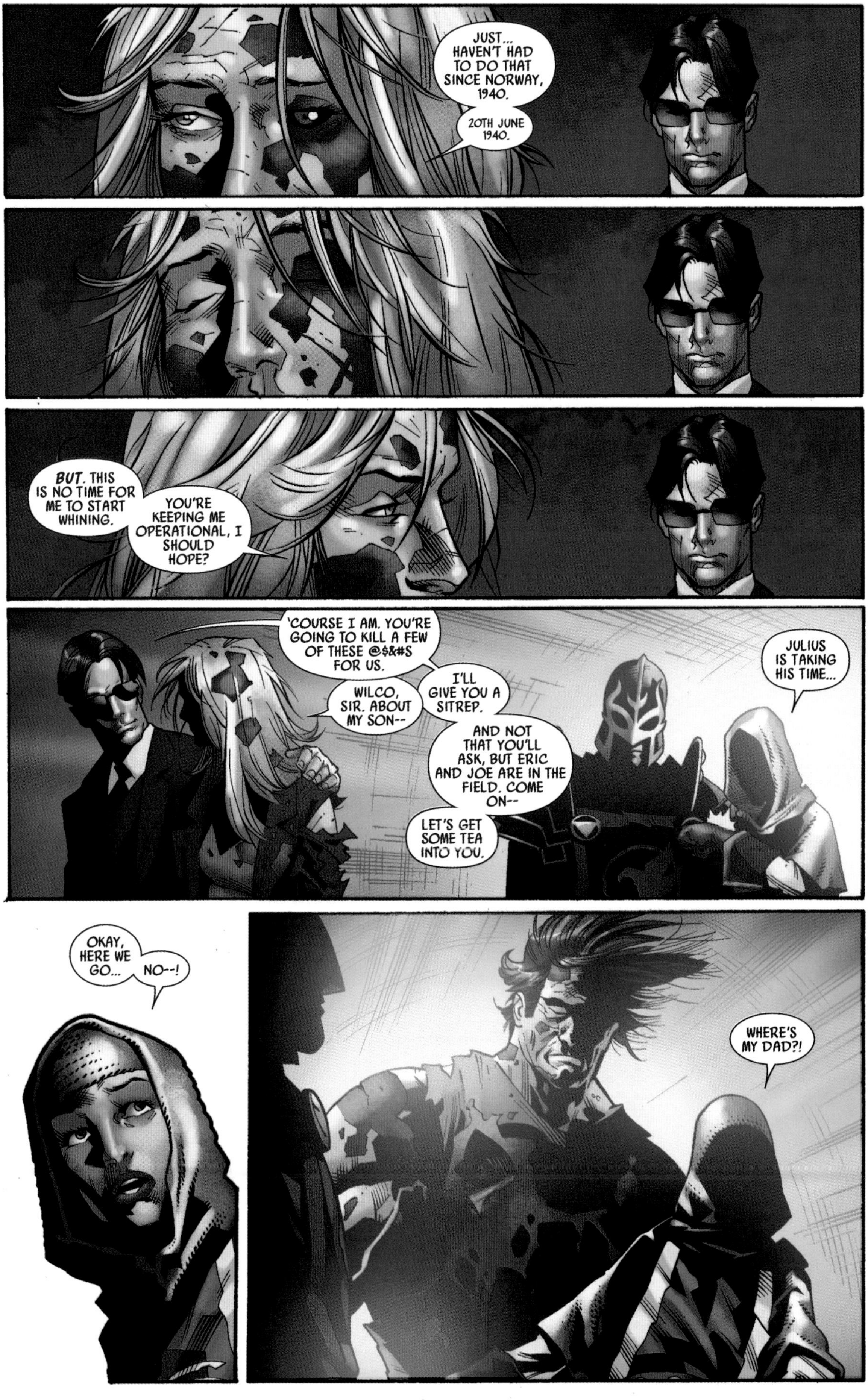
JUST... HAVEN'T HAD TO DO THAT SINCE NORWAY, 1940.
20TH JUNE 1940.
BUT. THIS IS NO TIME FOR ME TO START WHINING.
YOU'RE KEEPING ME OPERATIONAL, I SHOULD HOPE?
'COURSE I AM. YOU'RE GOING TO KILL A FEW OF THESE @$&#S FOR US.
WILCO, SIR. ABOUT MY SON--
I'LL GIVE YOU A SITREP.
AND NOT THAT YOU'LL ASK, BUT ERIC AND JOE ARE IN THE FIELD. COME ON--
LET'S GET SOME TEA INTO YOU.
JULIUS IS TAKING HIS TIME...
OKAY, HERE WE GO...
NO--!
WHERE'S MY DAD?!

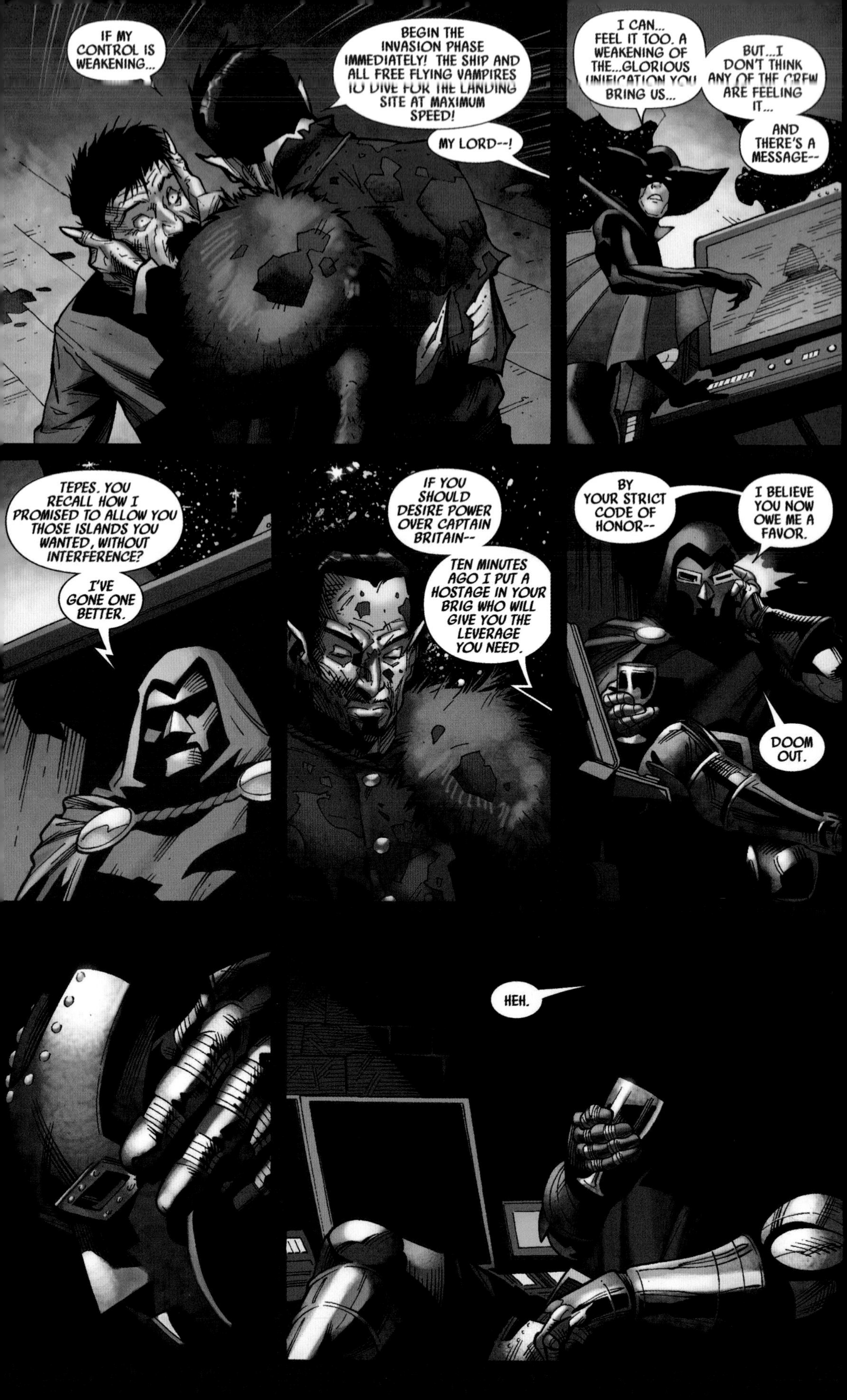
IF MY CONTROL IS WEAKENING...
BEGIN THE INVASION PHASE IMMEDIATELY! THE SHIP AND ALL FREE FLYING VAMPIRES TO DIVE FOR THE LANDING SITE AT MAXIMUM SPEED!
MY LORD--!
I CAN... FEEL IT TOO. A WEAKENING OF THE...GLORIOUS UNIFICATION YOU BRING US...
BUT...I DON'T THINK ANY OF THE CREW ARE FEELING IT...
AND THERE'S A MESSAGE--
TEPES. YOU RECALL HOW I PROMISED TO ALLOW YOU THOSE ISLANDS YOU WANTED, WITHOUT INTERFERENCE?
I'VE GONE ONE BETTER.
IF YOU SHOULD DESIRE POWER OVER CAPTAIN BRITAIN--
TEN MINUTES AGO I PUT A HOSTAGE IN YOUR BRIG WHO WILL GIVE YOU THE LEVERAGE YOU NEED.
BY YOUR STRICT CODE OF HONOR--
I BELIEVE YOU NOW OWE ME A FAVOR.
DOOM OUT.
HEH.

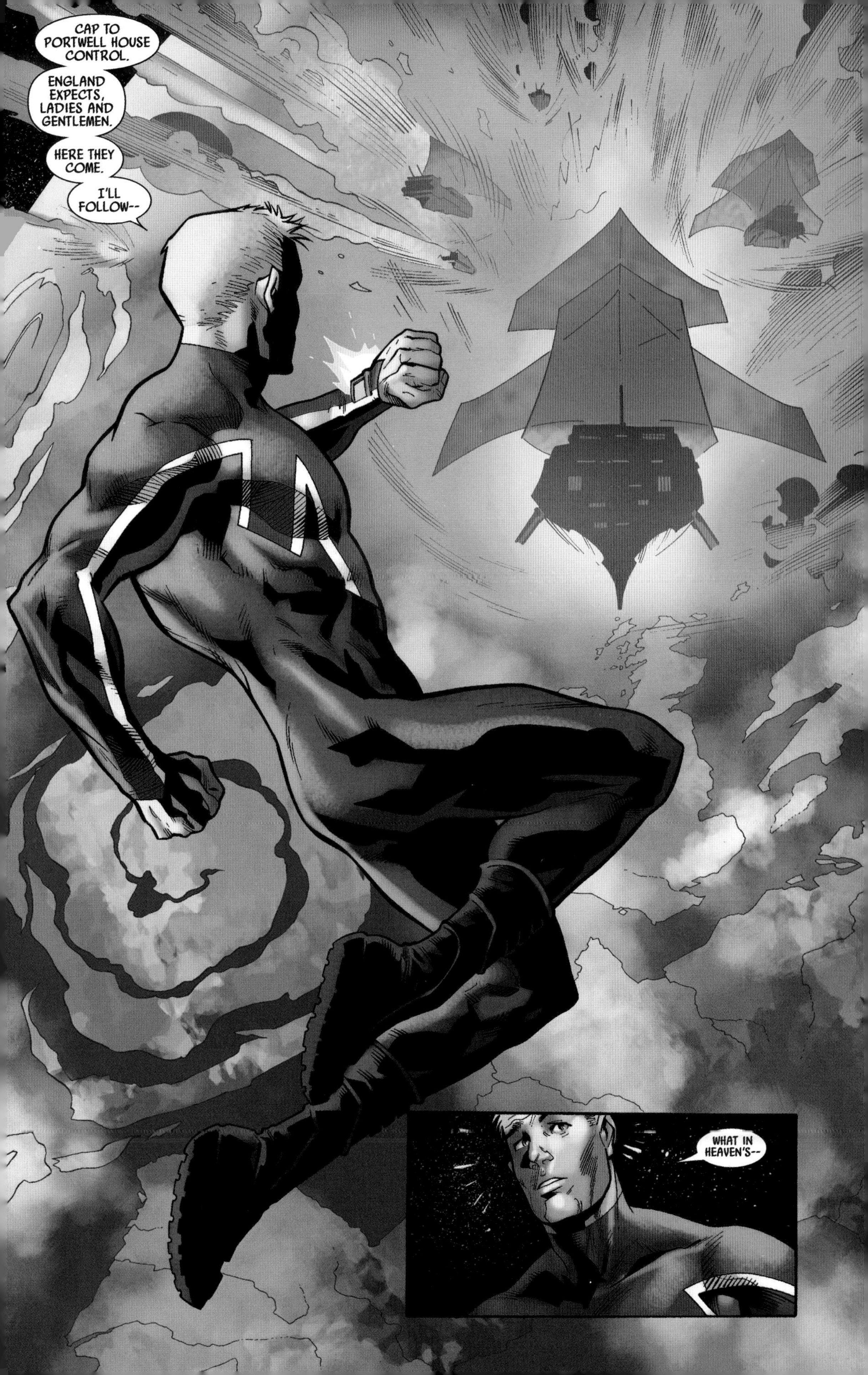
CAP TO PORTWELL HOUSE CONTROL.
ENGLAND EXPECTS, LADIES AND GENTLEMEN.
HERE THEY COME.
I'LL FOLLOW--
WHAT IN HEAVEN'S--

WE HAVE FIFTEEN MINUTES BEFORE WE ENTER BRITISH AIR
SURELY, MY LORD, NOTHING CAN GO WRONG NOW?! THE ARMY IS STILL LOYAL--
BE SILENT!
YOU WILL NOT MAKE ASSUMPTIONS ABOUT THIS CAMPAIGN!
THIS IS EVERYTHING FOR US! EVERYTHING!
AND THIS IS DOOM.
DOOM, WHO STUDIED UNDER CAGLIOSTRO.
DOOM, WHO DISSECTED VAMPIRES IN LATVERIA.
A GIFT FROM HIM IS A SWORD--
A SWORD WITHOUT A HILT!
WE HAVEN'T EVEN MET, BUT ALREADY--

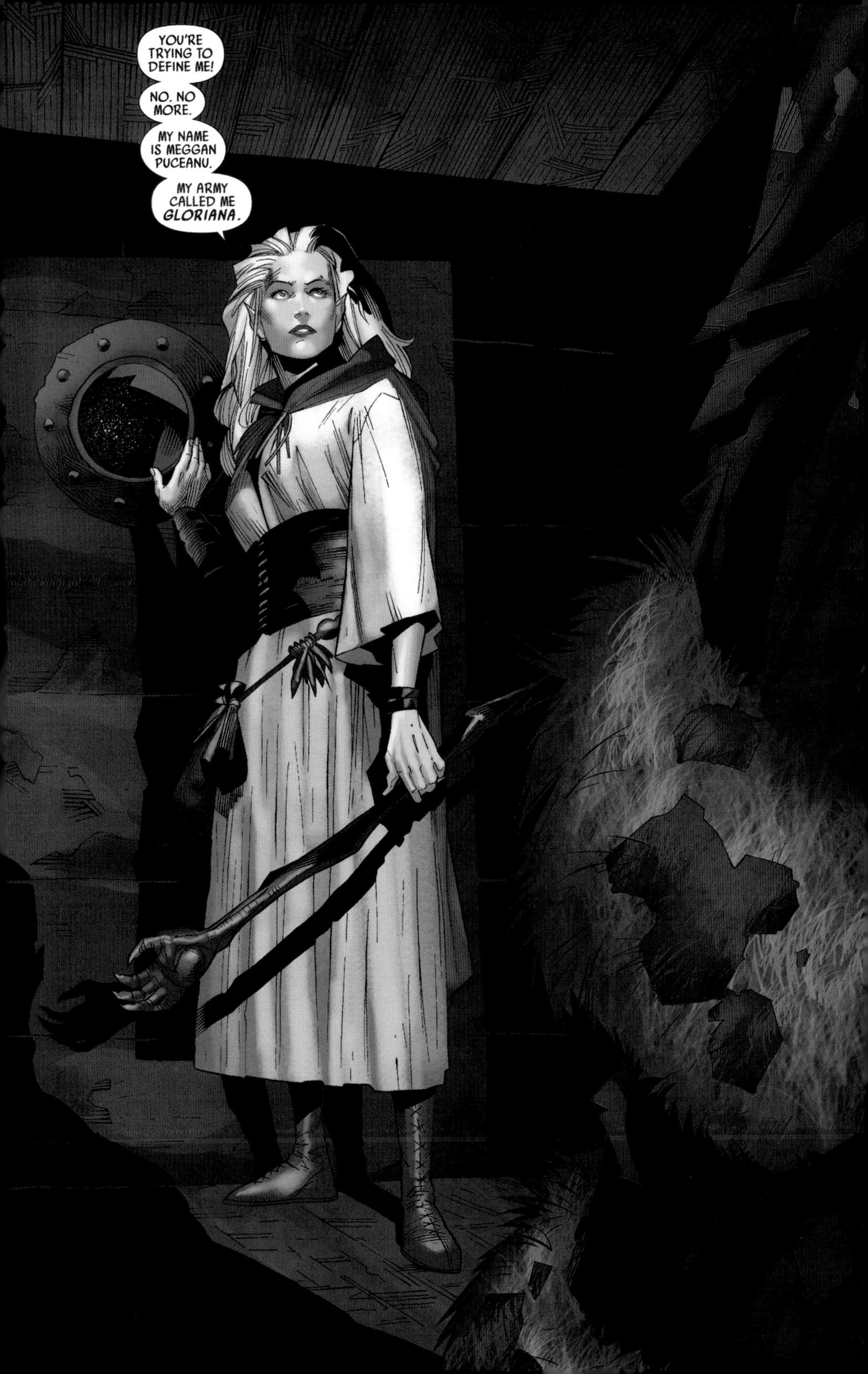
YOU'RE TRYING TO DEFINE ME!
NO. NO MORE.
MY NAME IS MEGGAN PUCEANU.
MY ARMY CALLED ME GLORIANA.

Captain Britain and MI13 #15
Cover Artwork

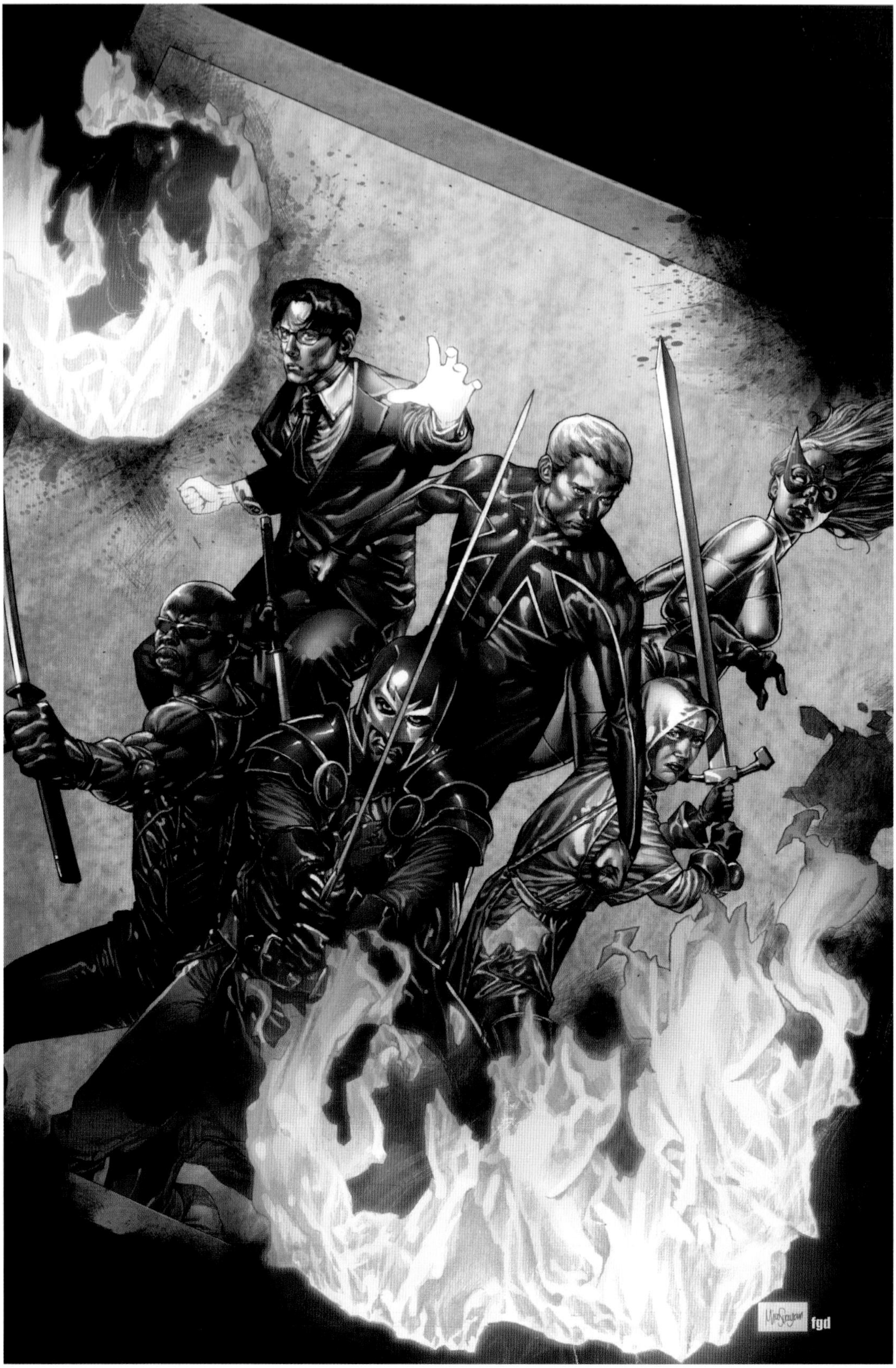

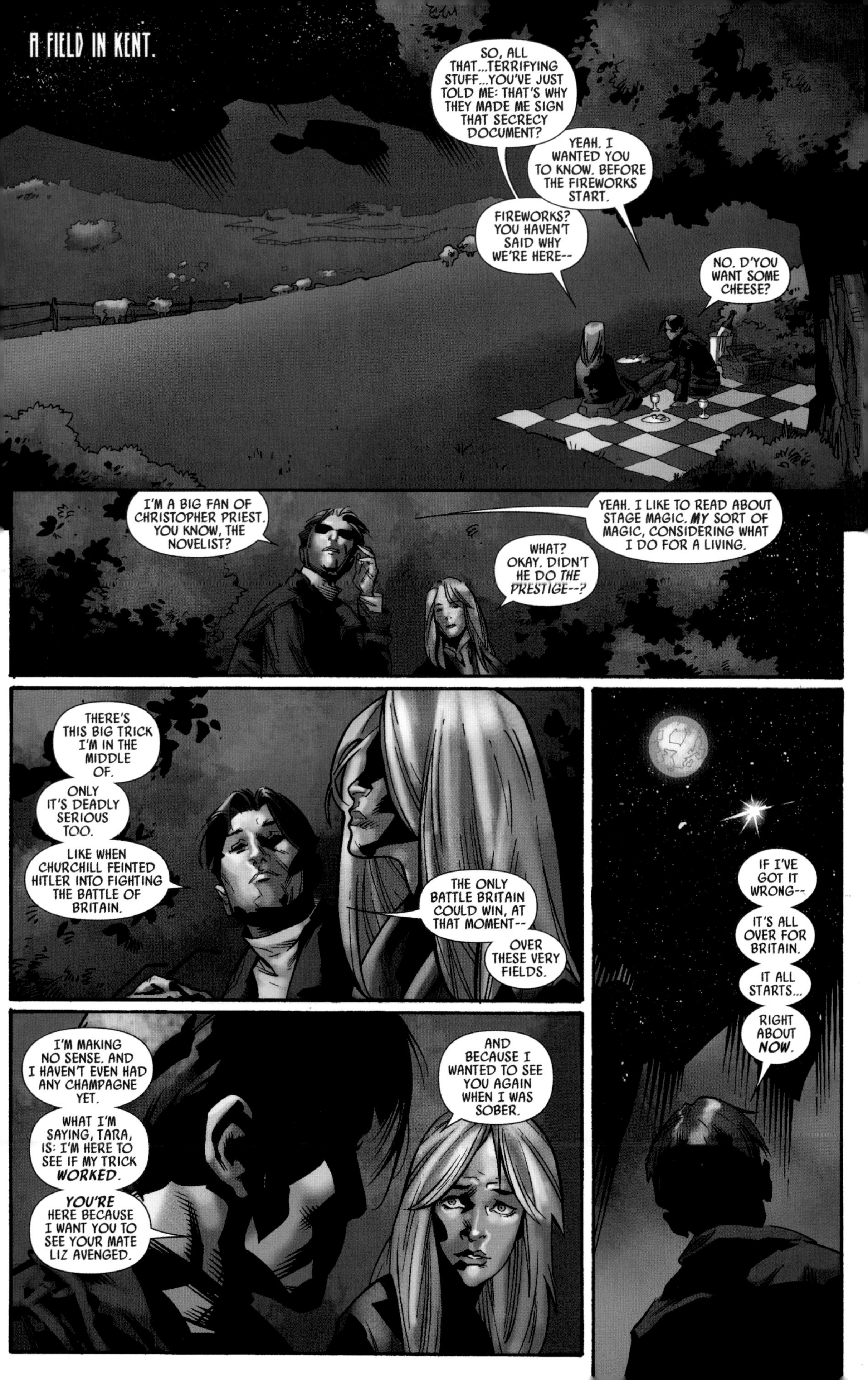
A FIELD IN KENT.
SO, ALL THAT...TERRIFYING STUFF...YOU'VE JUST TOLD ME: THAT'S WHY THEY MADE ME SIGN THAT SECRECY DOCUMENT?
YEAH. I WANTED YOU TO KNOW. BEFORE THE FIREWORKS START.
FIREWORKS? YOU HAVEN'T SAID WHY WE'RE HERE--
NO. D'YOU WANT SOME CHEESE?
I'M A BIG FAN OF CHRISTOPHER PRIEST. YOU KNOW, THE NOVELIST?
WHAT? OKAY. DIDN'T HE DO *THE PRESTIGE*--?
YEAH. I LIKE TO READ ABOUT STAGE MAGIC. ***MY*** SORT OF MAGIC, CONSIDERING WHAT I DO FOR A LIVING.
THERE'S THIS BIG TRICK I'M IN THE MIDDLE OF.
ONLY IT'S DEADLY SERIOUS TOO.
LIKE WHEN CHURCHILL FEINTED HITLER INTO FIGHTING THE BATTLE OF BRITAIN.
THE ONLY BATTLE BRITAIN COULD WIN, AT THAT MOMENT--
OVER THESE VERY FIELDS.
IF I'VE GOT IT WRONG--
IT'S ALL OVER FOR BRITAIN.
IT ALL STARTS...
RIGHT ABOUT ***NOW***.
I'M MAKING NO SENSE. AND I HAVEN'T EVEN HAD ANY CHAMPAGNE YET.
WHAT I'M SAYING, TARA, IS: I'M HERE TO SEE IF MY TRICK ***WORKED***.
YOU'RE HERE BECAUSE I WANT YOU TO SEE YOUR MATE LIZ AVENGED.
AND BECAUSE I WANTED TO SEE YOU AGAIN WHEN I WAS SOBER.

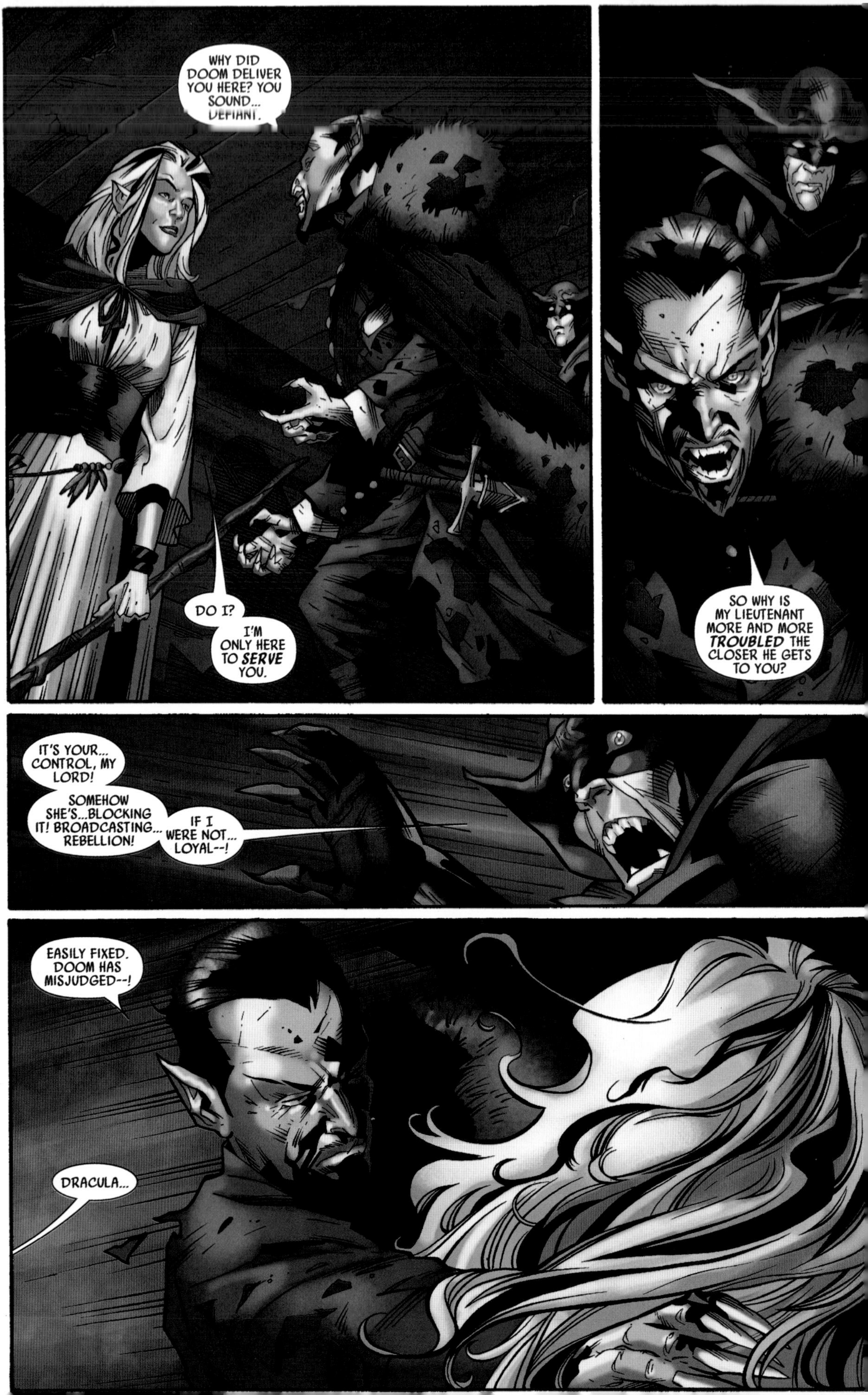
WHY DID DOOM DELIVER YOU HERE? YOU SOUND... DEFIANT.
DO I?
I'M ONLY HERE TO SERVE YOU.
SO WHY IS MY LIEUTENANT MORE AND MORE TROUBLED THE CLOSER HE GETS TO YOU?
IT'S YOUR... CONTROL, MY LORD!
SOMEHOW SHE'S...BLOCKING IT! BROADCASTING... REBELLION!
IF I WERE NOT... LOYAL--!
EASILY FIXED. DOOM HAS MISJUDGED--!
DRACULA...

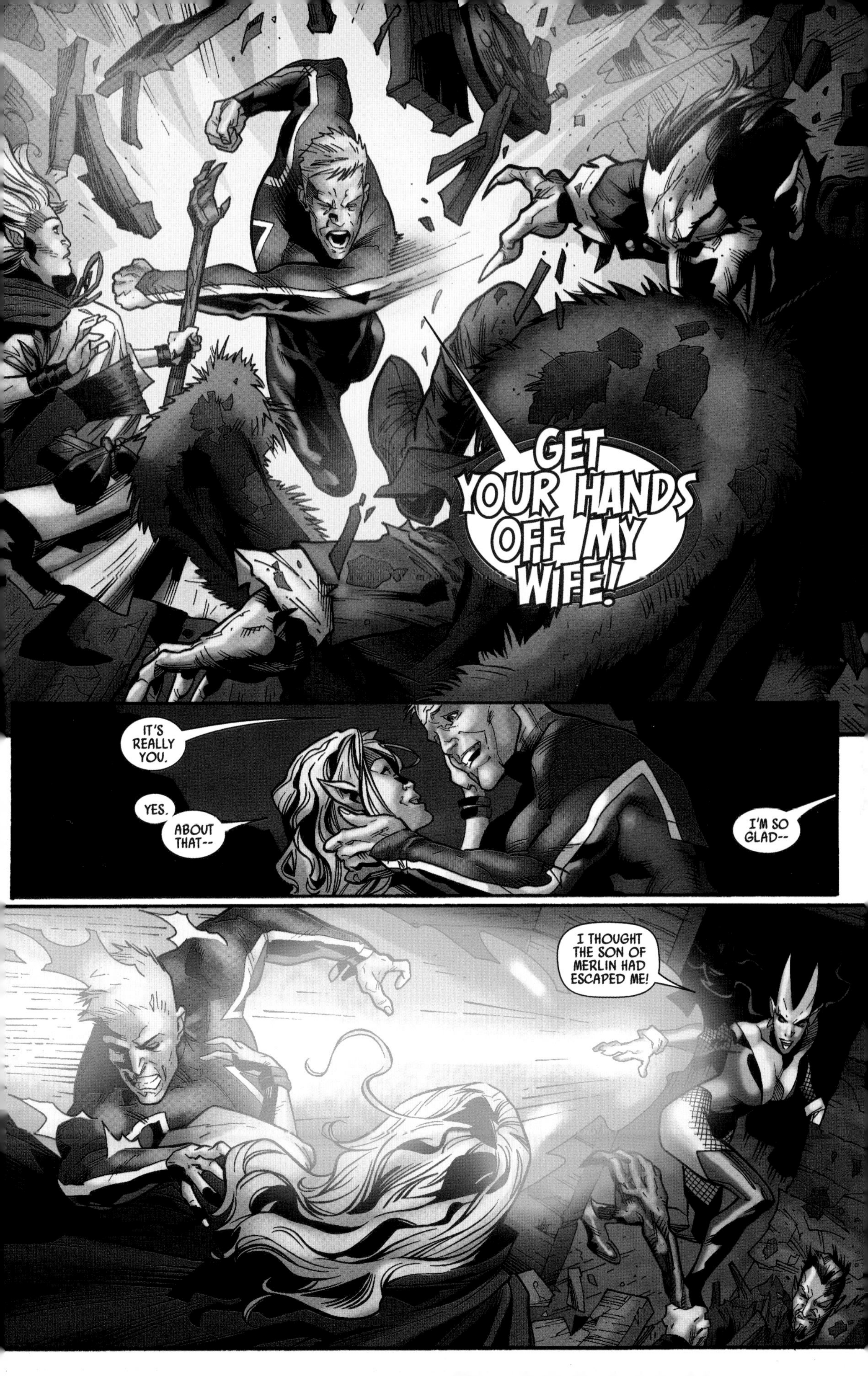
GET YOUR HANDS OFF MY WIFE!
IT'S REALLY YOU.
YES. ABOUT THAT--
I'M SO GLAD--
I THOUGHT THE SON OF MERLIN HAD ESCAPED ME!

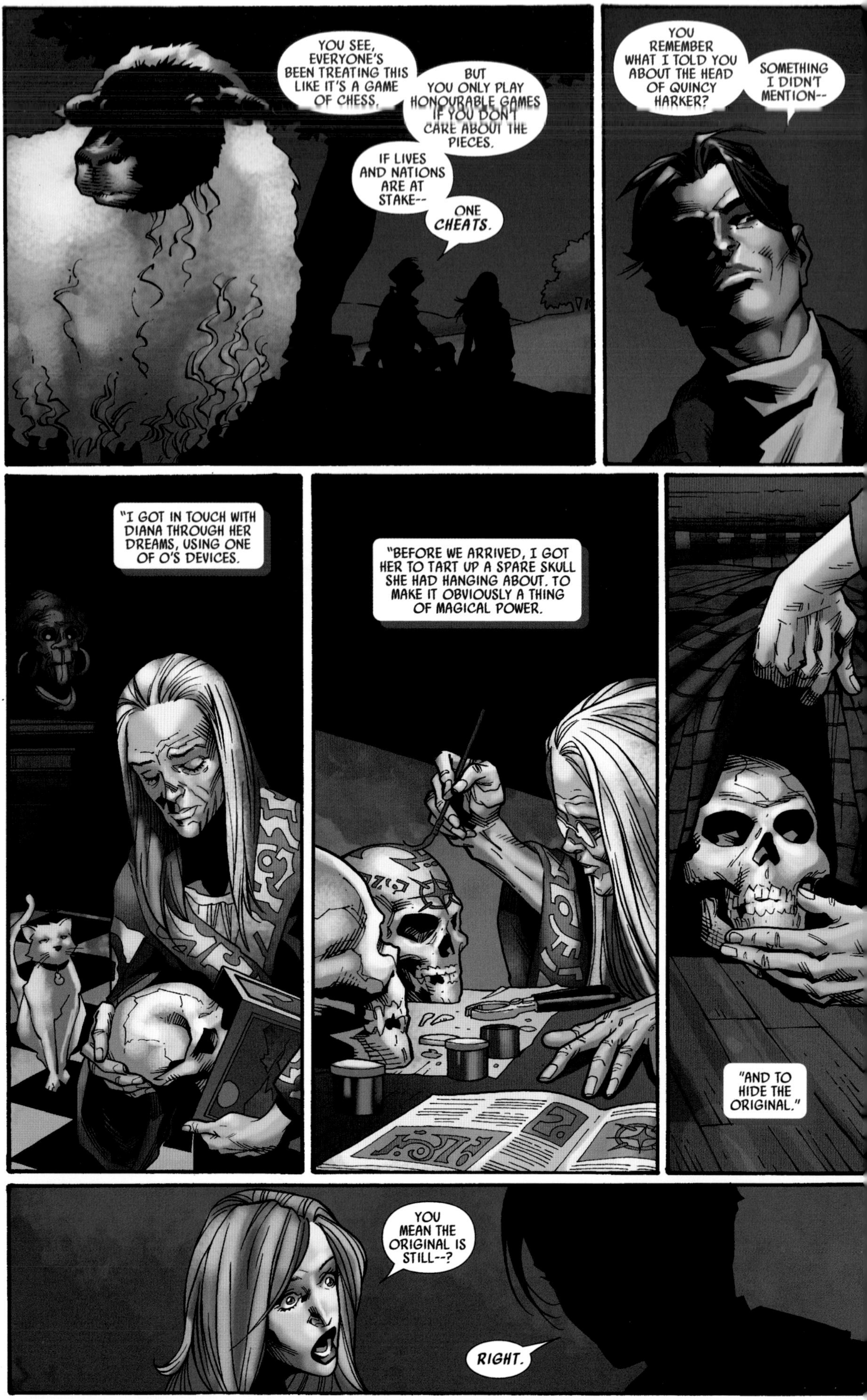
YOU SEE, EVERYONE'S BEEN TREATING THIS LIKE IT'S A GAME OF CHESS.
BUT YOU ONLY PLAY HONOURABLE GAMES IF YOU DON'T CARE ABOUT THE PIECES.
IF LIVES AND NATIONS ARE AT STAKE--
ONE CHEATS.
YOU REMEMBER WHAT I TOLD YOU ABOUT THE HEAD OF QUINCY HARKER?
SOMETHING I DIDN'T MENTION--
"I GOT IN TOUCH WITH DIANA THROUGH HER DREAMS, USING ONE OF O'S DEVICES.
"BEFORE WE ARRIVED, I GOT HER TO TART UP A SPARE SKULL SHE HAD HANGING ABOUT. TO MAKE IT OBVIOUSLY A THING OF MAGICAL POWER.
"AND TO HIDE THE ORIGINAL."
YOU MEAN THE ORIGINAL IS STILL--?
RIGHT.

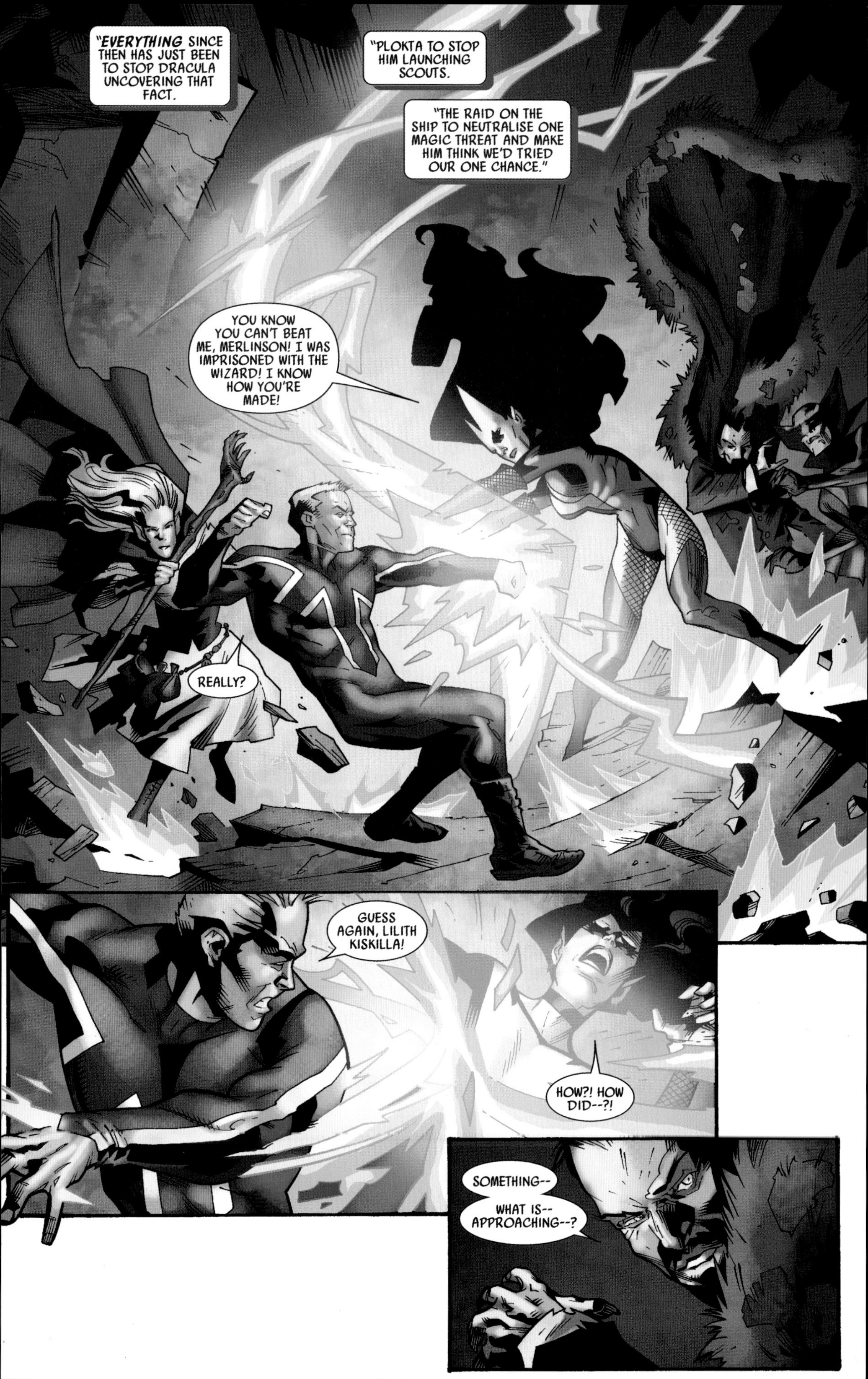
"EVERYTHING SINCE THEN HAS JUST BEEN TO STOP DRACULA UNCOVERING THAT FACT.
"PLOKTA TO STOP HIM LAUNCHING SCOUTS.
"THE RAID ON THE SHIP TO NEUTRALISE ONE MAGIC THREAT AND MAKE HIM THINK WE'D TRIED OUR ONE CHANCE."
YOU KNOW YOU CAN'T BEAT ME, MERLINSON! I WAS IMPRISONED WITH THE WIZARD! I KNOW HOW YOU'RE MADE!
REALLY?
GUESS AGAIN, LILITH KISKILLA!
HOW?! HOW DID--?!
SOMETHING--
WHAT IS-- APPROACHING--?

"SEE THOSE LIGHTS JUST THERE?
"THOSE ARE THE FIRST VAMPIRES, ARRIVING AT ORBITAL VELOCITY--
"AND REALIZING THAT, UNLIKE DR. YUSUF HUSSAIN, WHO I NOW DECLARE IS WELCOME TO COME HOME--
"THEY HAVEN'T BEEN *INVITED*.

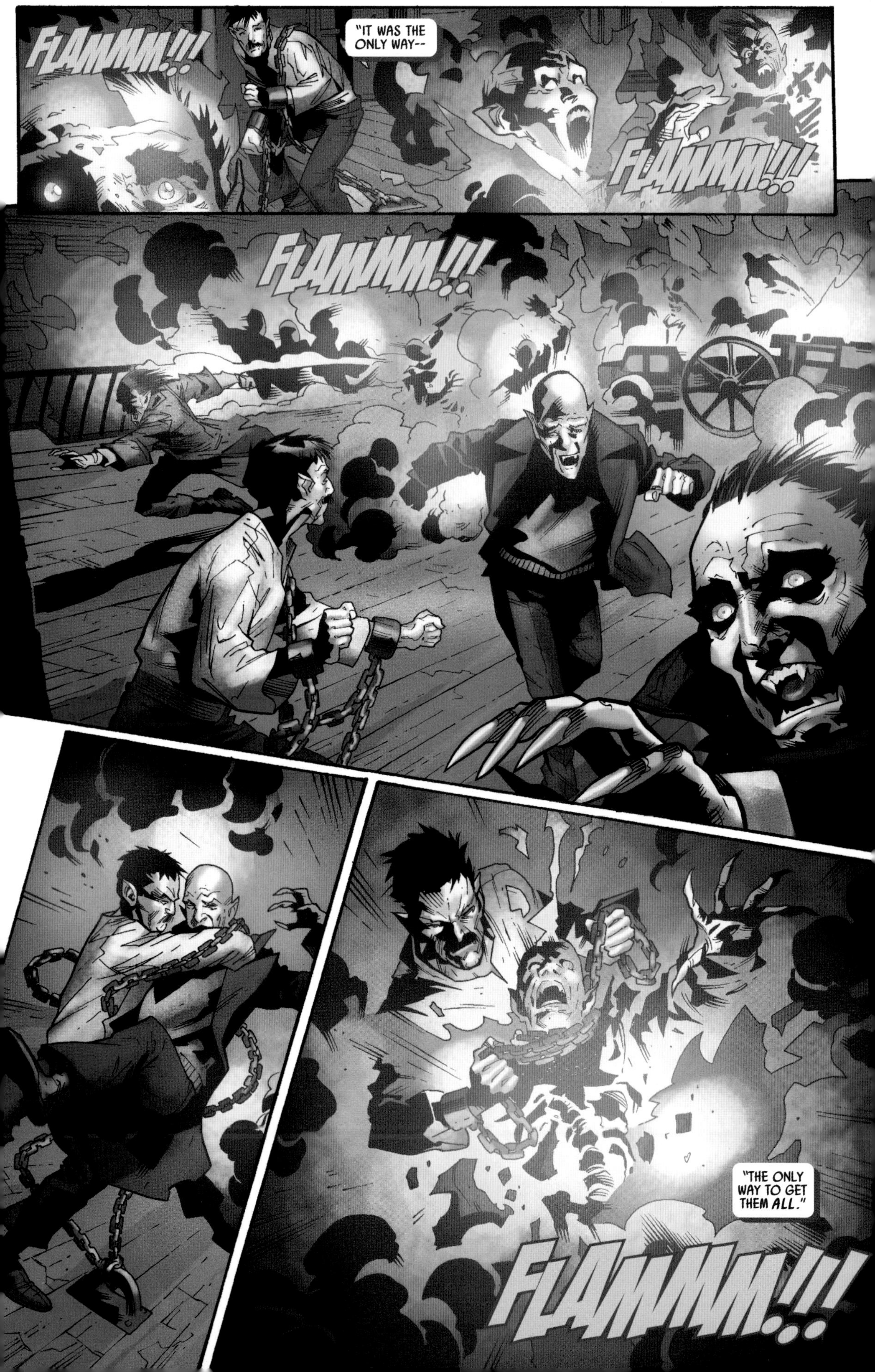
FLAMMM!!!
"IT WAS THE ONLY WAY--
FLAMMM!!!
FLAMMM!!!
"THE ONLY WAY TO GET THEM ALL."
FLAMMM!!!

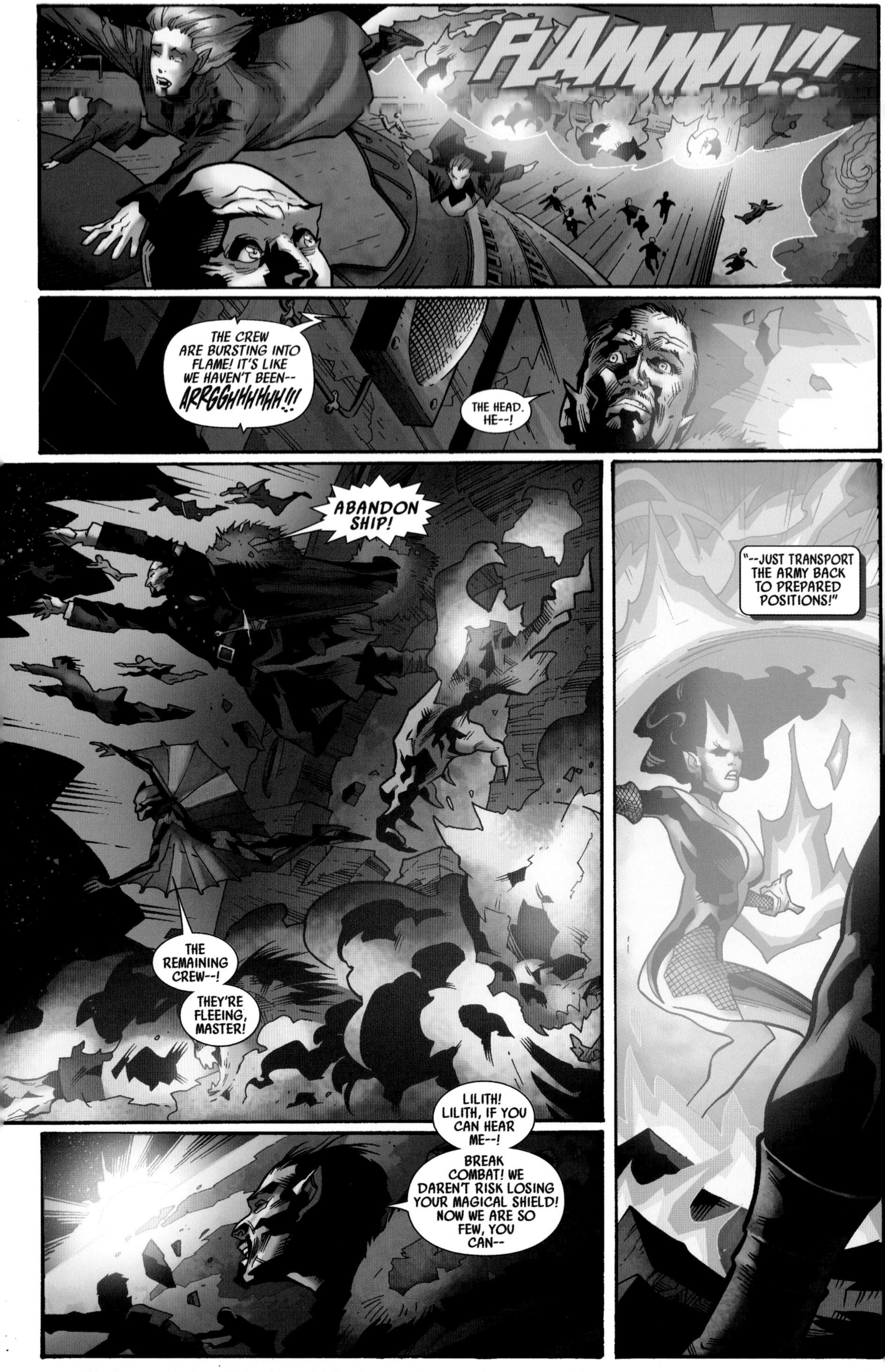
FLAMMM!!!
THE CREW ARE BURSTING INTO FLAME! IT'S LIKE WE HAVEN'T BEEN-- ARRGGHHHHHH!!!
THE HEAD. HE--!
ABANDON SHIP!
THE REMAINING CREW--!
THEY'RE FLEEING, MASTER!
"--JUST TRANSPORT THE ARMY BACK TO PREPARED POSITIONS!"
LILITH! LILITH, IF YOU CAN HEAR ME--!
BREAK COMBAT! WE DAREN'T RISK LOSING YOUR MAGICAL SHIELD! NOW WE ARE SO FEW, YOU CAN--

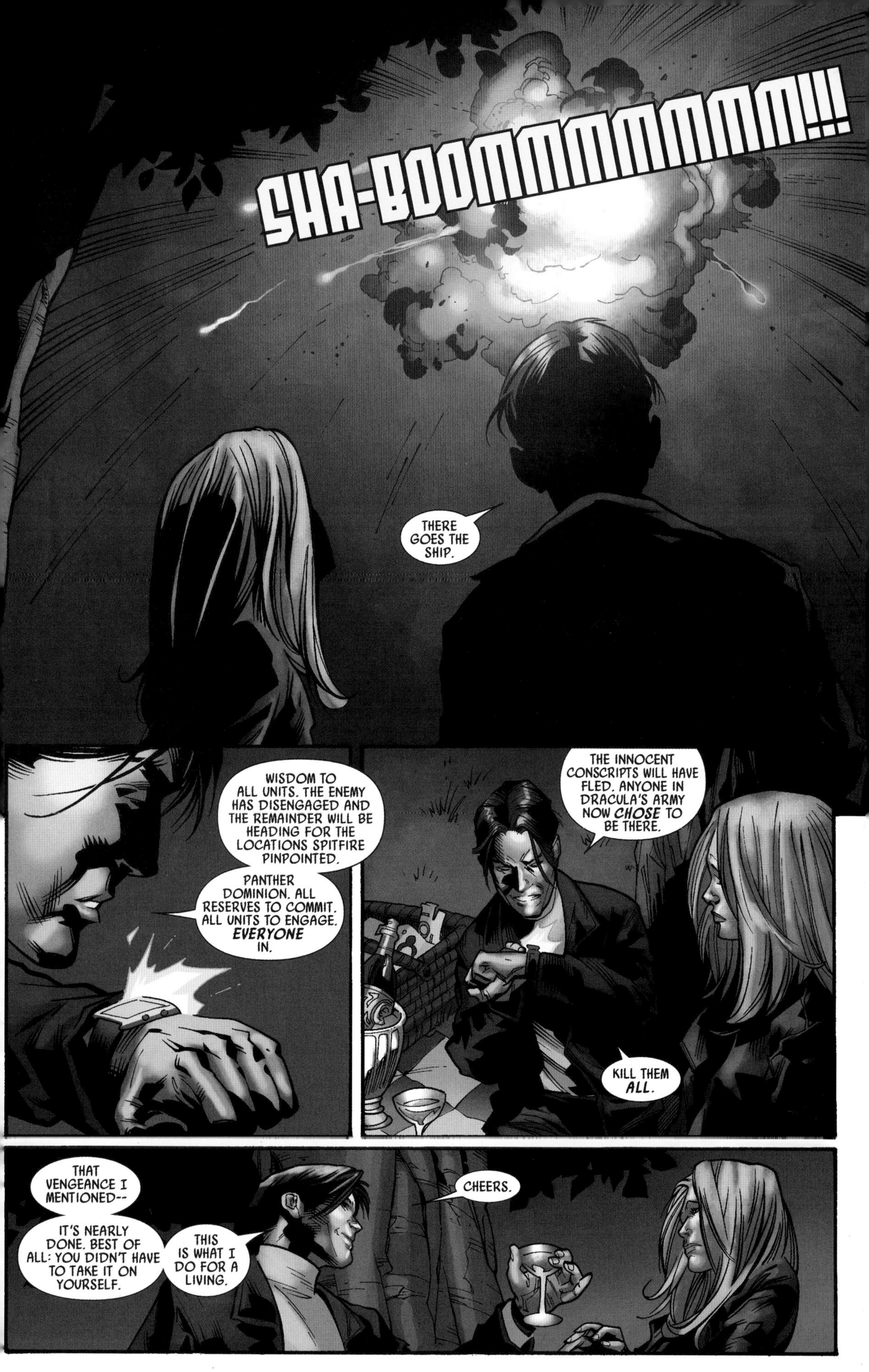
SHA-BOOMMMMMMMM!!!
THERE GOES THE SHIP.
WISDOM TO ALL UNITS. THE ENEMY HAS DISENGAGED AND THE REMAINDER WILL BE HEADING FOR THE LOCATIONS SPITFIRE PINPOINTED.
PANTHER DOMINION. ALL RESERVES TO COMMIT. ALL UNITS TO ENGAGE. EVERYONE IN.
THE INNOCENT CONSCRIPTS WILL HAVE FLED. ANYONE IN DRACULA'S ARMY NOW CHOSE TO BE THERE.
KILL THEM ALL.
THAT VENGEANCE I MENTIONED--
IT'S NEARLY DONE. BEST OF ALL: YOU DIDN'T HAVE TO TAKE IT ON YOURSELF.
THIS IS WHAT I DO FOR A LIVING.
CHEERS.

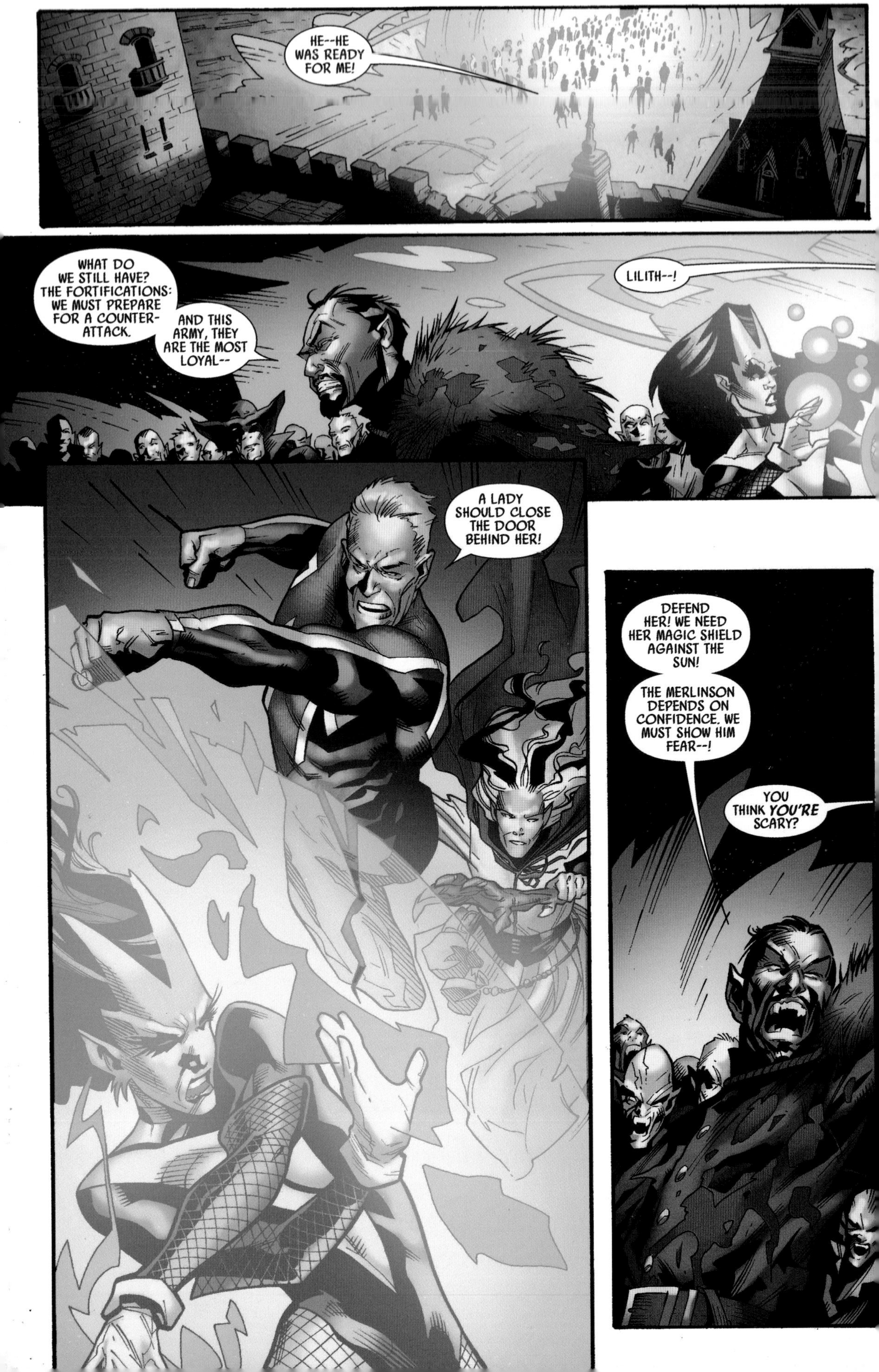
HE--HE WAS READY FOR ME!
WHAT DO WE STILL HAVE? THE FORTIFICATIONS: WE MUST PREPARE FOR A COUNTER-ATTACK.
AND THIS ARMY, THEY ARE THE MOST LOYAL--
LILITH--!
A LADY SHOULD CLOSE THE DOOR BEHIND HER!
DEFEND HER! WE NEED HER MAGIC SHIELD AGAINST THE SUN!
THE MERLINSON DEPENDS ON CONFIDENCE. WE MUST SHOW HIM FEAR--!
YOU THINK *YOU'RE* SCARY?

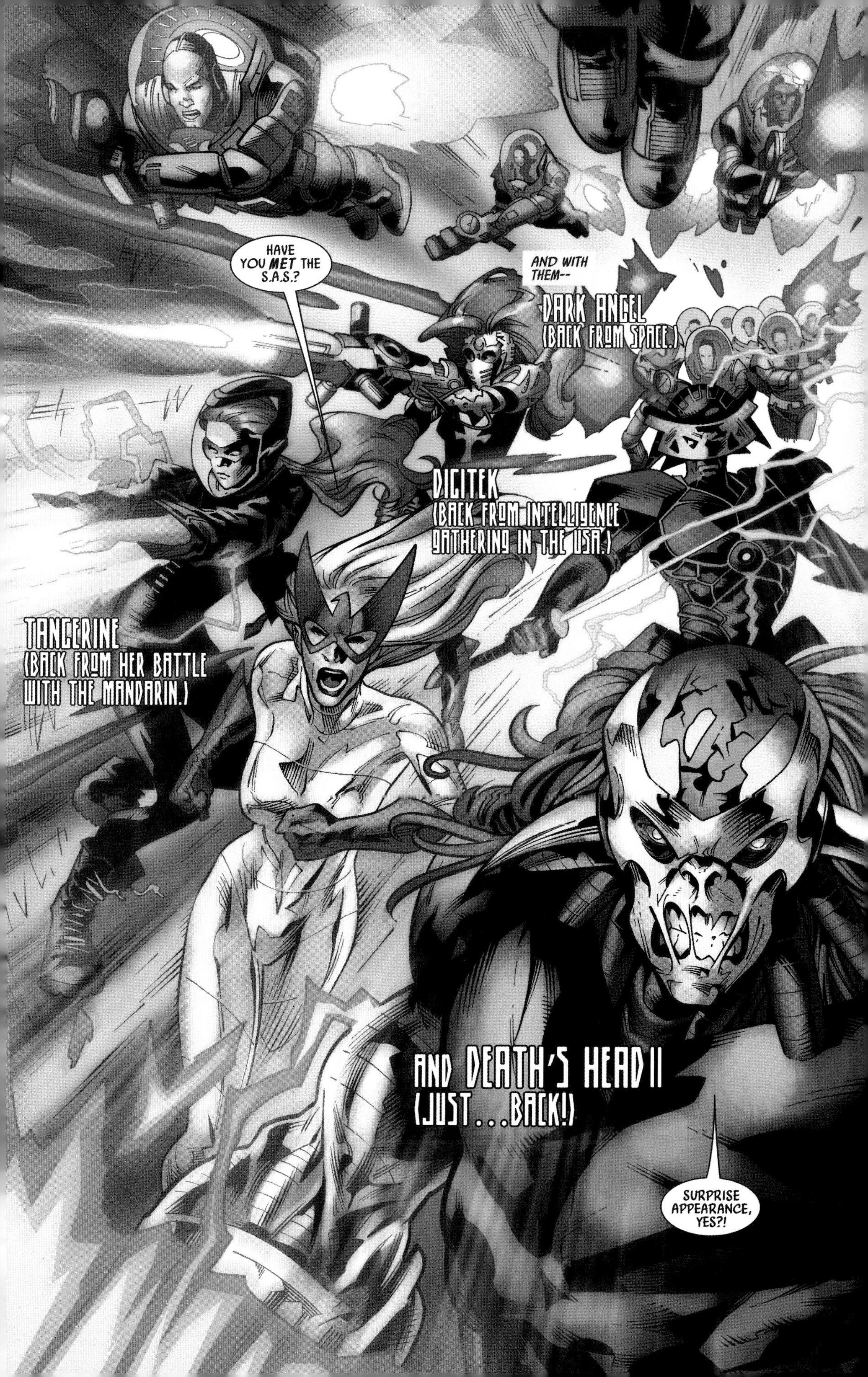

HAVE YOU MET THE S.A.S.?
AND WITH THEM--
DARK ANGEL (BACK FROM SPACE.)
DIGITEK (BACK FROM INTELLIGENCE GATHERING IN THE USA.)
TANGERINE (BACK FROM HER BATTLE WITH THE MANDARIN.)
AND DEATH'S HEAD II (JUST...BACK!)
SURPRISE APPEARANCE, YES?!

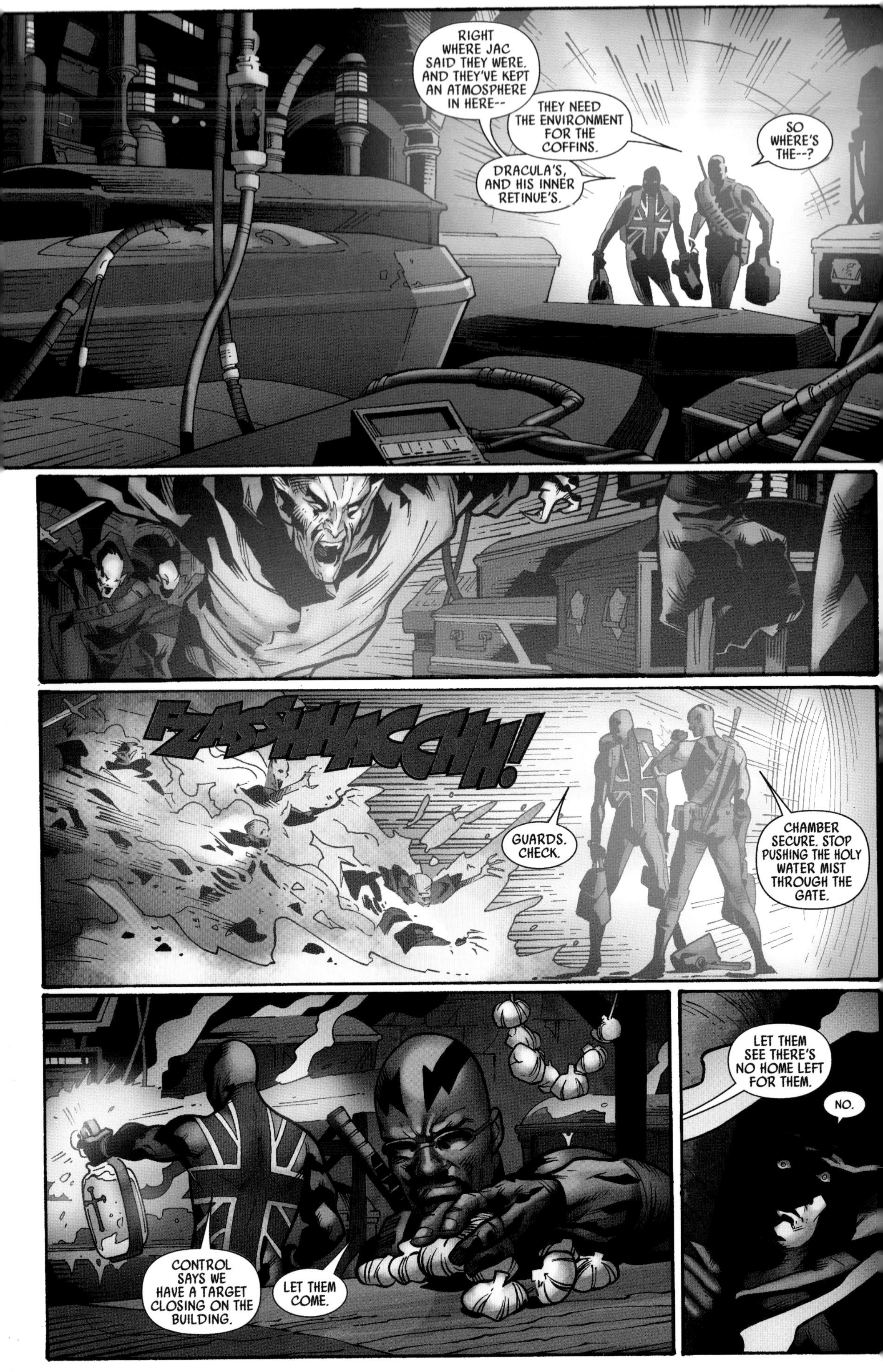
RIGHT WHERE JAC SAID THEY WERE. AND THEY'VE KEPT AN ATMOSPHERE IN HERE--
THEY NEED THE ENVIRONMENT FOR THE COFFINS.
DRACULA'S, AND HIS INNER RETINUE'S.
SO WHERE'S THE--?
FZASHHACCHH!
GUARDS. CHECK.
CHAMBER SECURE. STOP PUSHING THE HOLY WATER MIST THROUGH THE GATE.
CONTROL SAYS WE HAVE A TARGET CLOSING ON THE BUILDING.
LET THEM COME.
LET THEM SEE THERE'S NO HOME LEFT FOR THEM.
NO.

JOE? JOE, THAT'S YOU, ISN'T IT?

IT'S ME, KEN!

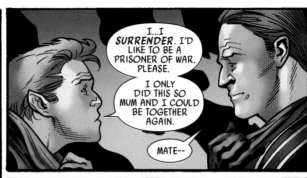

I...I *SURRENDER*. I'D LIKE TO BE A PRISONER OF WAR. PLEASE.

I ONLY DID THIS SO MUM AND I COULD BE TOGETHER AGAIN.

MATE--

IT'S ALL RIGHT. YOU COME WITH US. IT'S WHAT JAC WOULD WANT.

EVEN IF THERE'S NO CURE NOW, MAYBE ONE DAY--

AGRHHHHHHHH!!!

NO!

BLADE! HE'S HER SON!

BLADE TO SPITFIRE.

IT'S DONE.

EXACTLY LIKE YOU ASKED.

YOU KNOW, I THINK I WAS WRONG ABOUT YOU AND JAC.

YOU'RE BLOODY MADE FOR EACH OTHER.

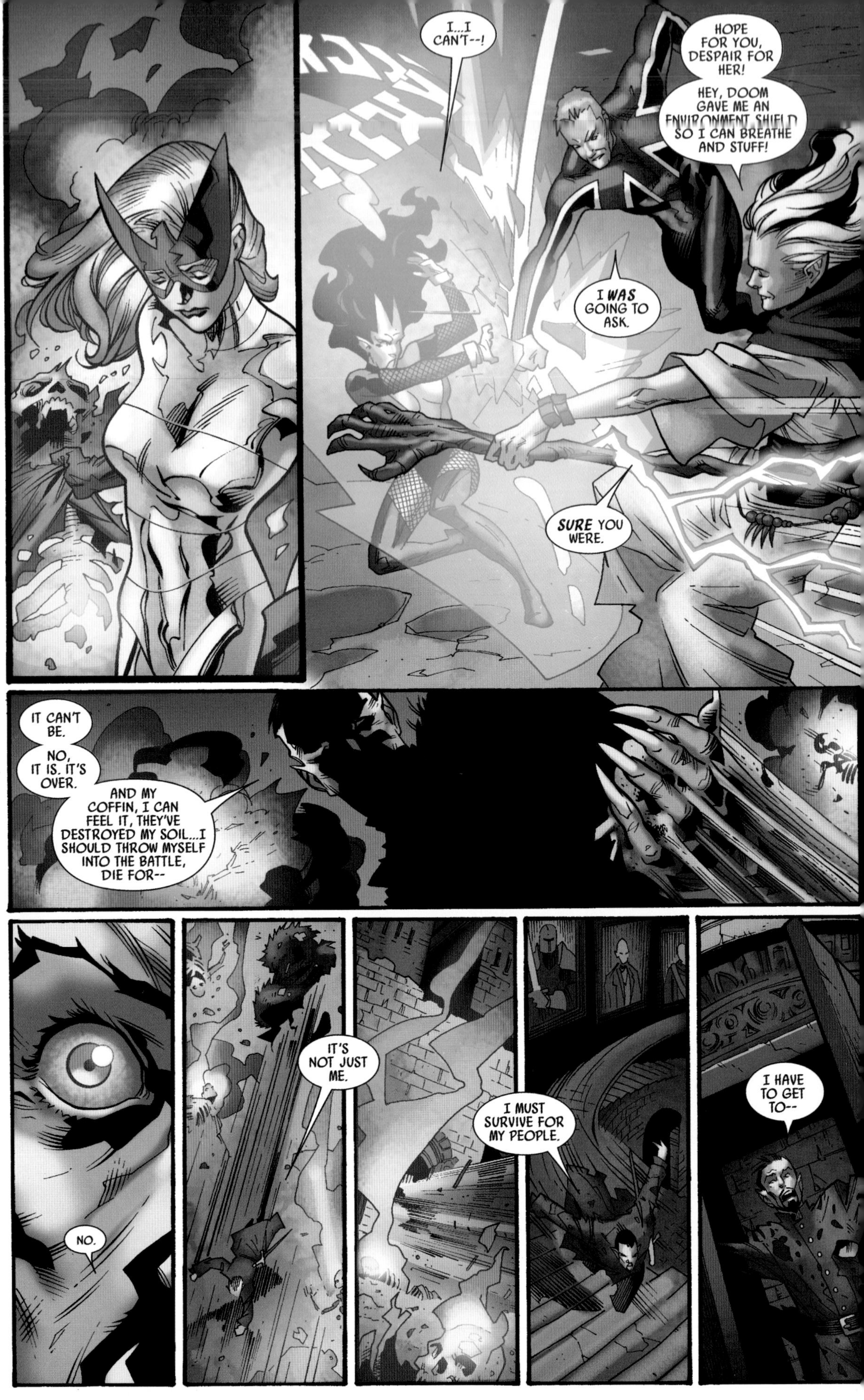
I...I CAN'T--!
HOPE FOR YOU, DESPAIR FOR HER!
HEY, DOOM GAVE ME AN ENVIRONMENT SHIELD SO I CAN BREATHE AND STUFF!
I *WAS* GOING TO ASK.
SURE YOU WERE.
IT CAN'T BE.
NO, IT IS. IT'S OVER.
AND MY COFFIN, I CAN FEEL IT, THEY'VE DESTROYED MY SOIL...I SHOULD THROW MYSELF INTO THE BATTLE, DIE FOR--
NO.
IT'S NOT JUST ME.
I MUST SURVIVE FOR MY PEOPLE.
I HAVE TO GET TO--

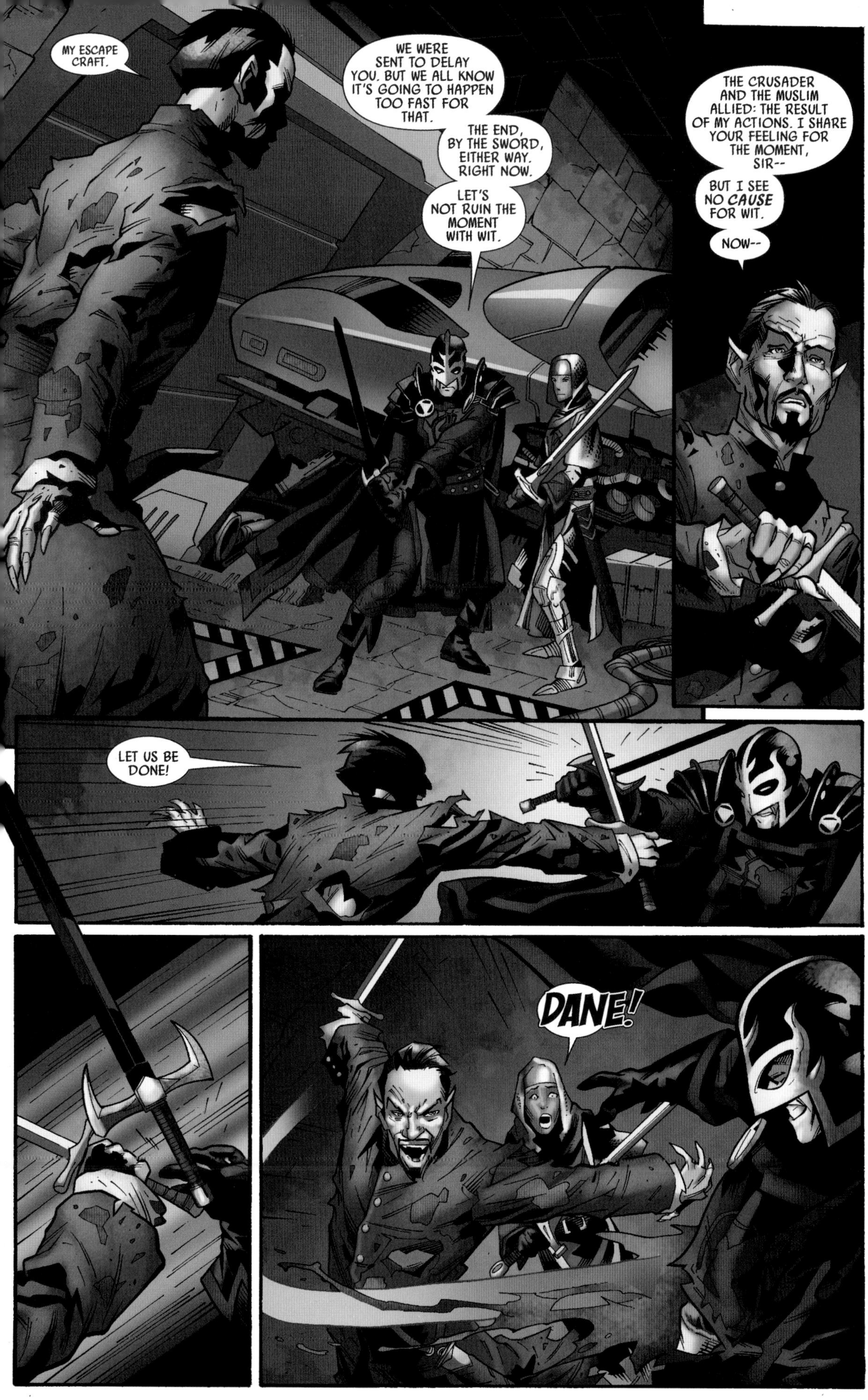
MY ESCAPE CRAFT.
WE WERE SENT TO DELAY YOU. BUT WE ALL KNOW IT'S GOING TO HAPPEN TOO FAST FOR THAT.
THE END, BY THE SWORD, EITHER WAY. RIGHT NOW.
LET'S NOT RUIN THE MOMENT WITH WIT.
THE CRUSADER AND THE MUSLIM ALLIED: THE RESULT OF MY ACTIONS. I SHARE YOUR FEELING FOR THE MOMENT, SIR--
BUT I SEE NO CAUSE FOR WIT.
NOW--
LET US BE DONE!
DANE!

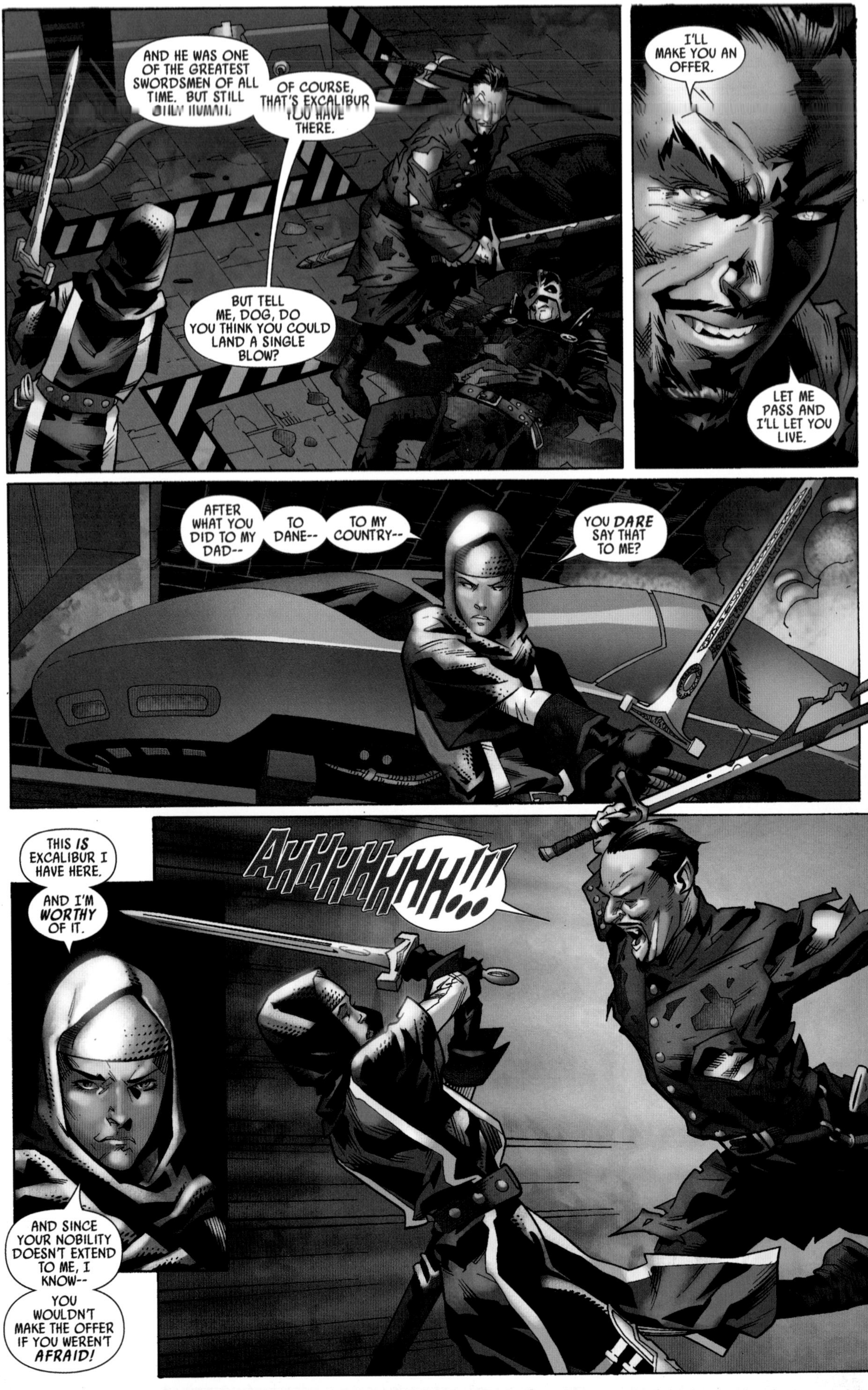
AND HE WAS ONE OF THE GREATEST SWORDSMEN OF ALL TIME. BUT STILL
OF COURSE, THAT'S EXCALIBUR YOU HAVE THERE.
BUT TELL ME, DOG, DO YOU THINK YOU COULD LAND A SINGLE BLOW?
I'LL MAKE YOU AN OFFER.
LET ME PASS AND I'LL LET YOU LIVE.
AFTER WHAT YOU DID TO MY DAD--
TO DANE--
TO MY COUNTRY--
YOU DARE SAY THAT TO ME?
THIS IS EXCALIBUR I HAVE HERE.
AND I'M WORTHY OF IT.
AHHHHHHHH!!!
AND SINCE YOUR NOBILITY DOESN'T EXTEND TO ME, I KNOW--
YOU WOULDN'T MAKE THE OFFER IF YOU WEREN'T AFRAID!

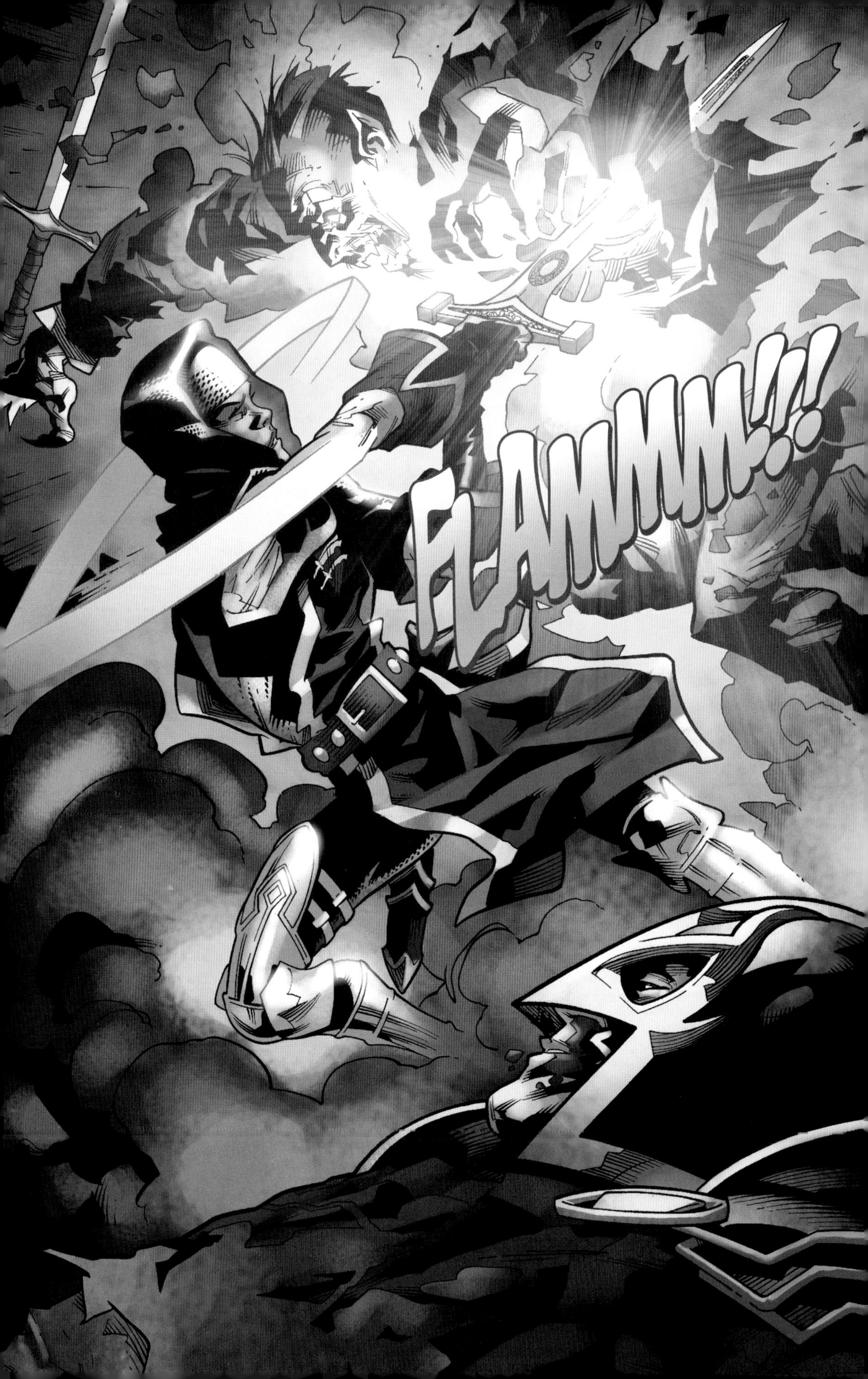
FLAMMM!!!

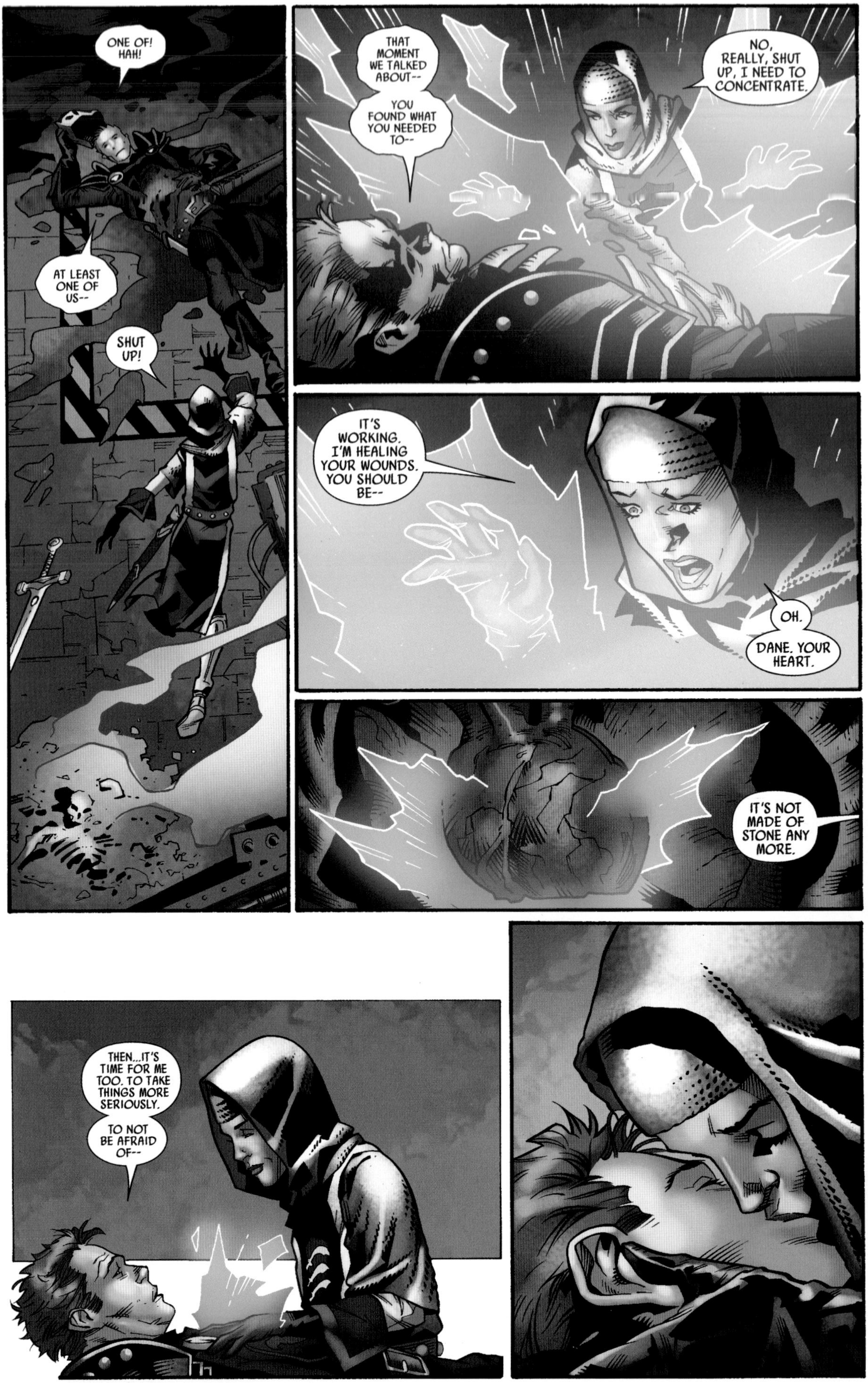
ONE OF! HAH!
AT LEAST ONE OF US--
SHUT UP!
THAT MOMENT WE TALKED ABOUT--
YOU FOUND WHAT YOU NEEDED TO--
NO, REALLY, SHUT UP, I NEED TO CONCENTRATE.
IT'S WORKING. I'M HEALING YOUR WOUNDS. YOU SHOULD BE--
OH.
DANE. YOUR HEART.
IT'S NOT MADE OF STONE ANY MORE.
THEN...IT'S TIME FOR ME TOO. TO TAKE THINGS MORE SERIOUSLY.
TO NOT BE AFRAID OF--

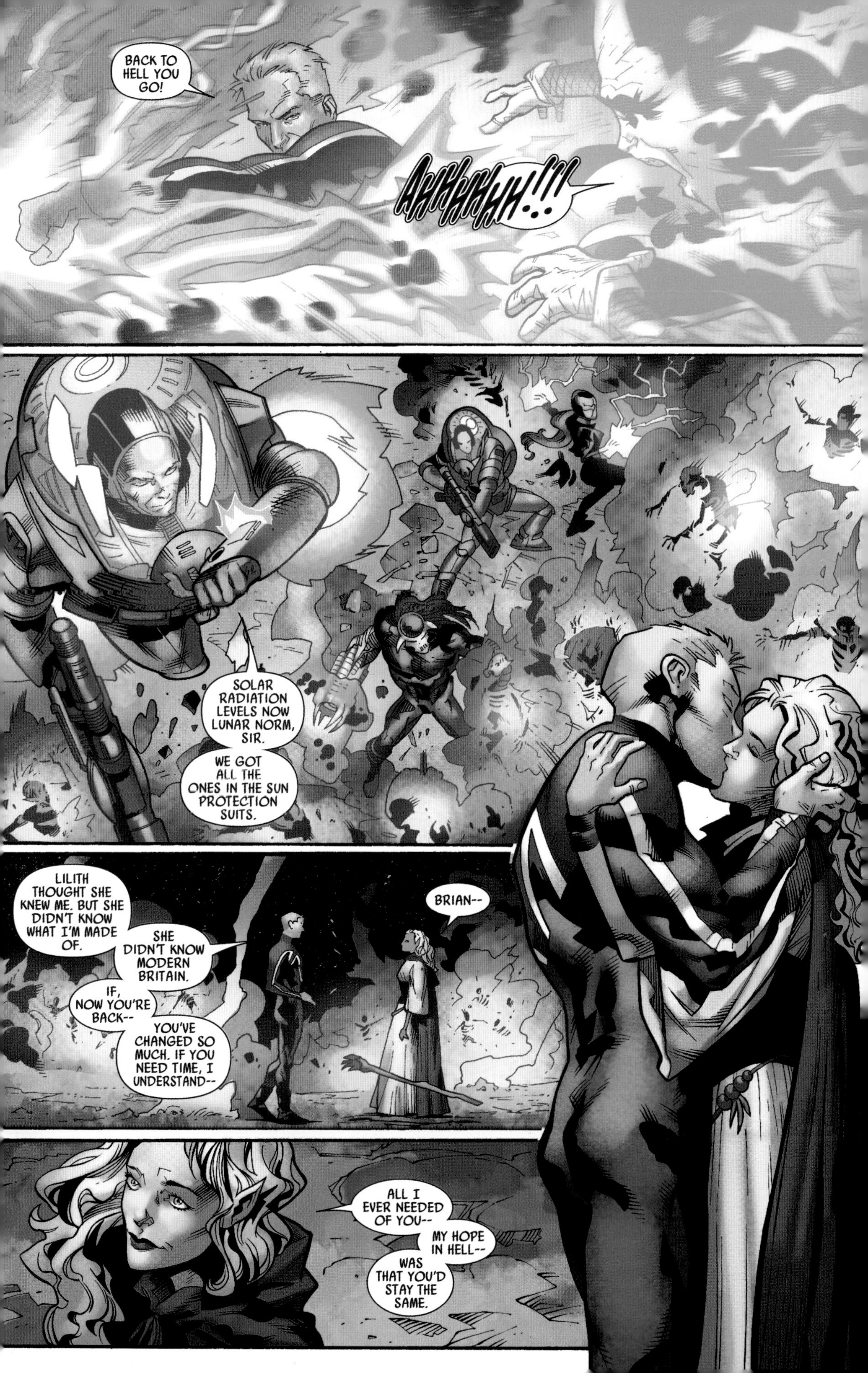
BACK TO HELL YOU GO!
AHHHHHH!!!
SOLAR RADIATION LEVELS NOW LUNAR NORM, SIR.
WE GOT ALL THE ONES IN THE SUN PROTECTION SUITS.
LILITH THOUGHT SHE KNEW ME. BUT SHE DIDN'T KNOW WHAT I'M MADE OF.
SHE DIDN'T KNOW MODERN BRITAIN.
BRIAN--
IF, NOW YOU'RE BACK--
YOU'VE CHANGED SO MUCH. IF YOU NEED TIME, I UNDERSTAND--
ALL I EVER NEEDED OF YOU--
MY HOPE IN HELL--
WAS THAT YOU'D STAY THE SAME.

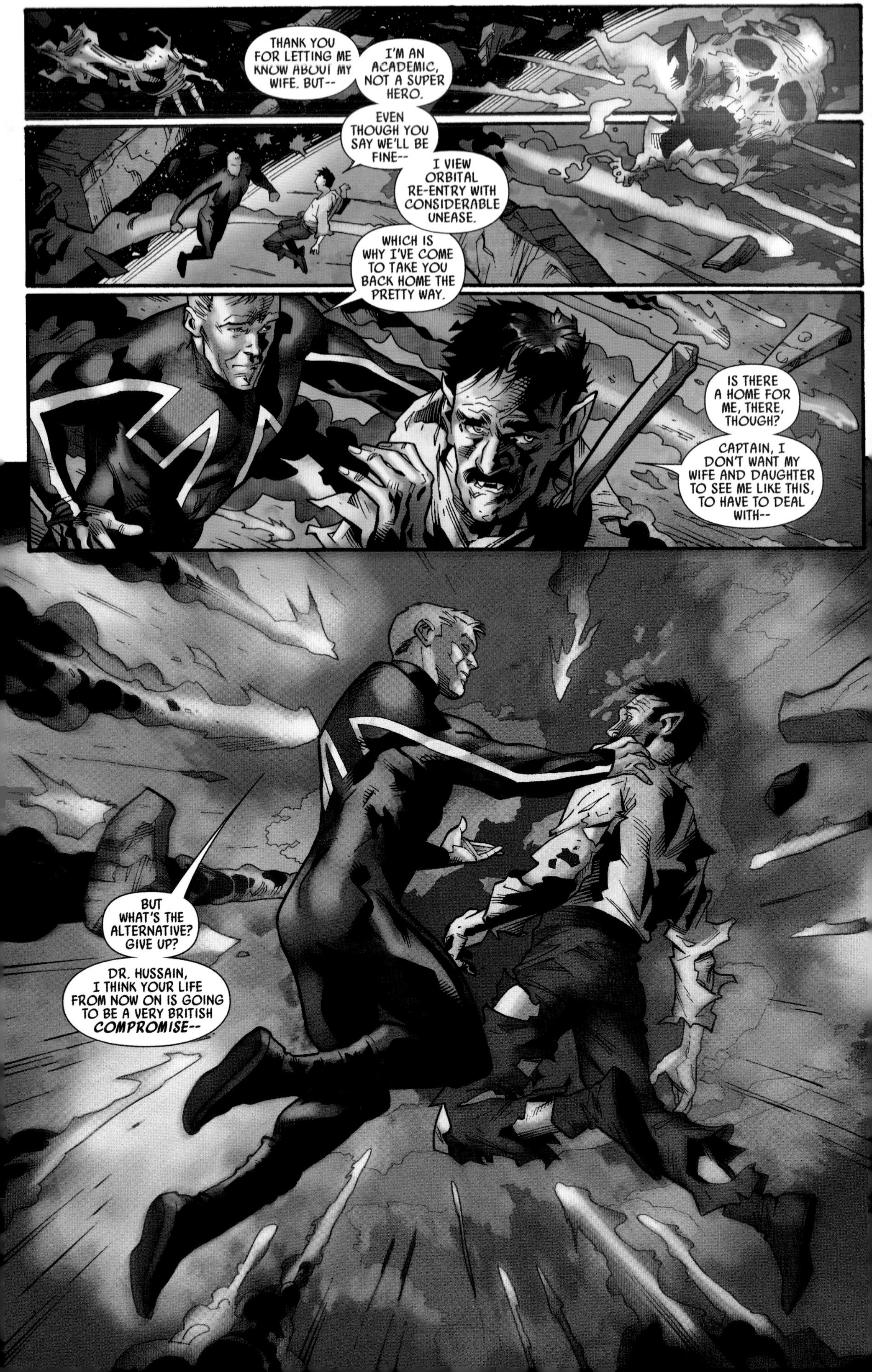
THANK YOU FOR LETTING ME KNOW ABOUT MY WIFE. BUT--
I'M AN ACADEMIC, NOT A SUPER HERO.
EVEN THOUGH YOU SAY WE'LL BE FINE--
I VIEW ORBITAL RE-ENTRY WITH CONSIDERABLE UNEASE.
WHICH IS WHY I'VE COME TO TAKE YOU BACK HOME THE PRETTY WAY.
IS THERE A HOME FOR ME, THERE, THOUGH?
CAPTAIN, I DON'T WANT MY WIFE AND DAUGHTER TO SEE ME LIKE THIS, TO HAVE TO DEAL WITH--
BUT WHAT'S THE ALTERNATIVE? GIVE UP?
DR. HUSSAIN, I THINK YOUR LIFE FROM NOW ON IS GOING TO BE A VERY BRITISH COMPROMISE--

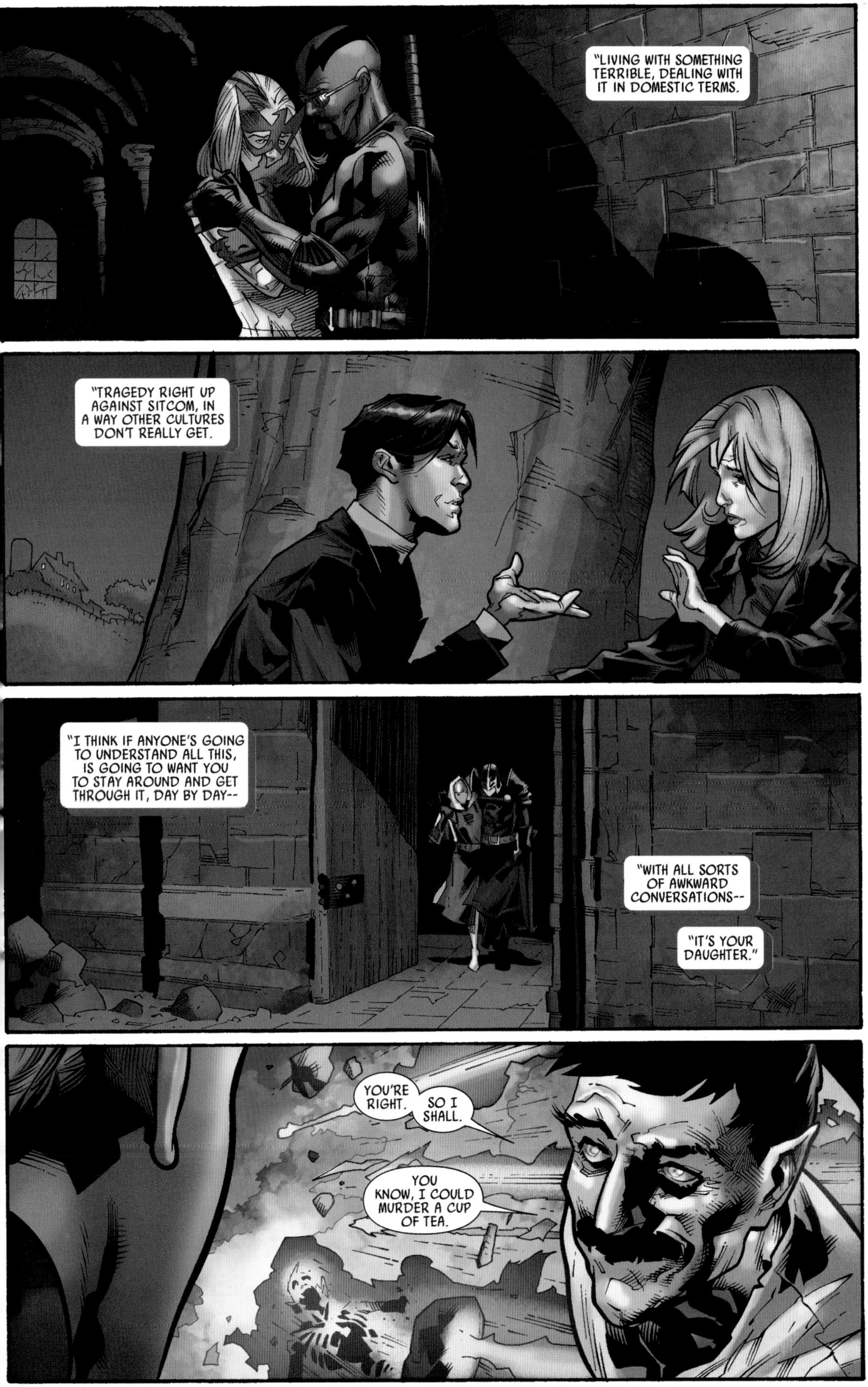
"LIVING WITH SOMETHING TERRIBLE, DEALING WITH IT IN DOMESTIC TERMS.
"TRAGEDY RIGHT UP AGAINST SITCOM, IN A WAY OTHER CULTURES DON'T REALLY GET.
"I THINK IF ANYONE'S GOING TO UNDERSTAND ALL THIS, IS GOING TO WANT YOU TO STAY AROUND AND GET THROUGH IT, DAY BY DAY--
"WITH ALL SORTS OF AWKWARD CONVERSATIONS--
"IT'S YOUR DAUGHTER."
YOU'RE RIGHT.
SO I SHALL.
YOU KNOW, I COULD MURDER A CUP OF TEA.

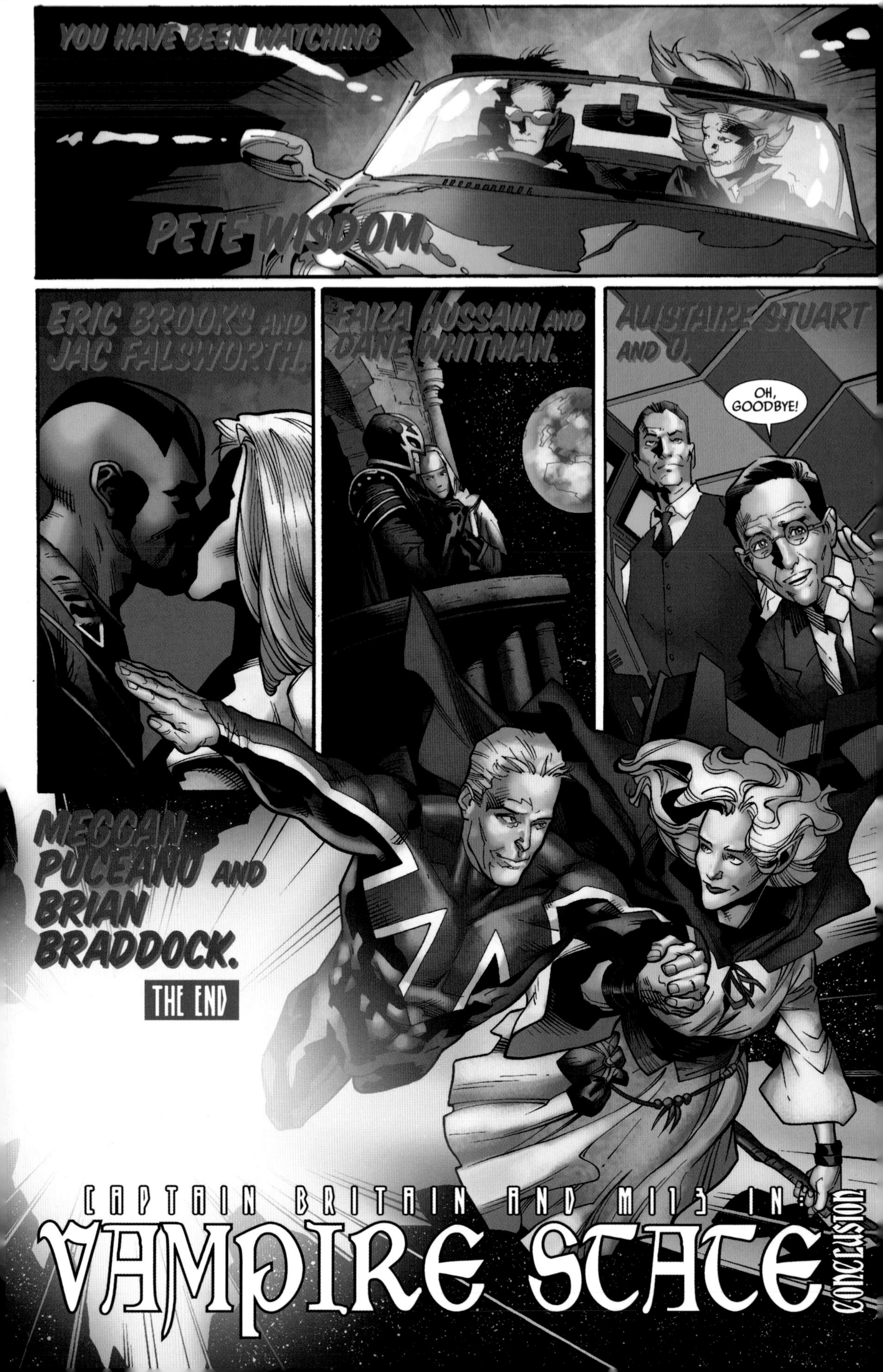

YOU HAVE BEEN WATCHING
PETE WISDOM.
ERIC BROOKS AND JAC FALSWORTH.
FAIZA HUSSAIN AND DANE WHITMAN.
ALISTAIRE STUART AND O.
OH, GOODBYE!
MEGGAN PUCEANU AND BRIAN BRADDOCK.
THE END
CAPTAIN BRITAIN AND MI13 IN:
VAMPIRE STATE
CONCLUSION

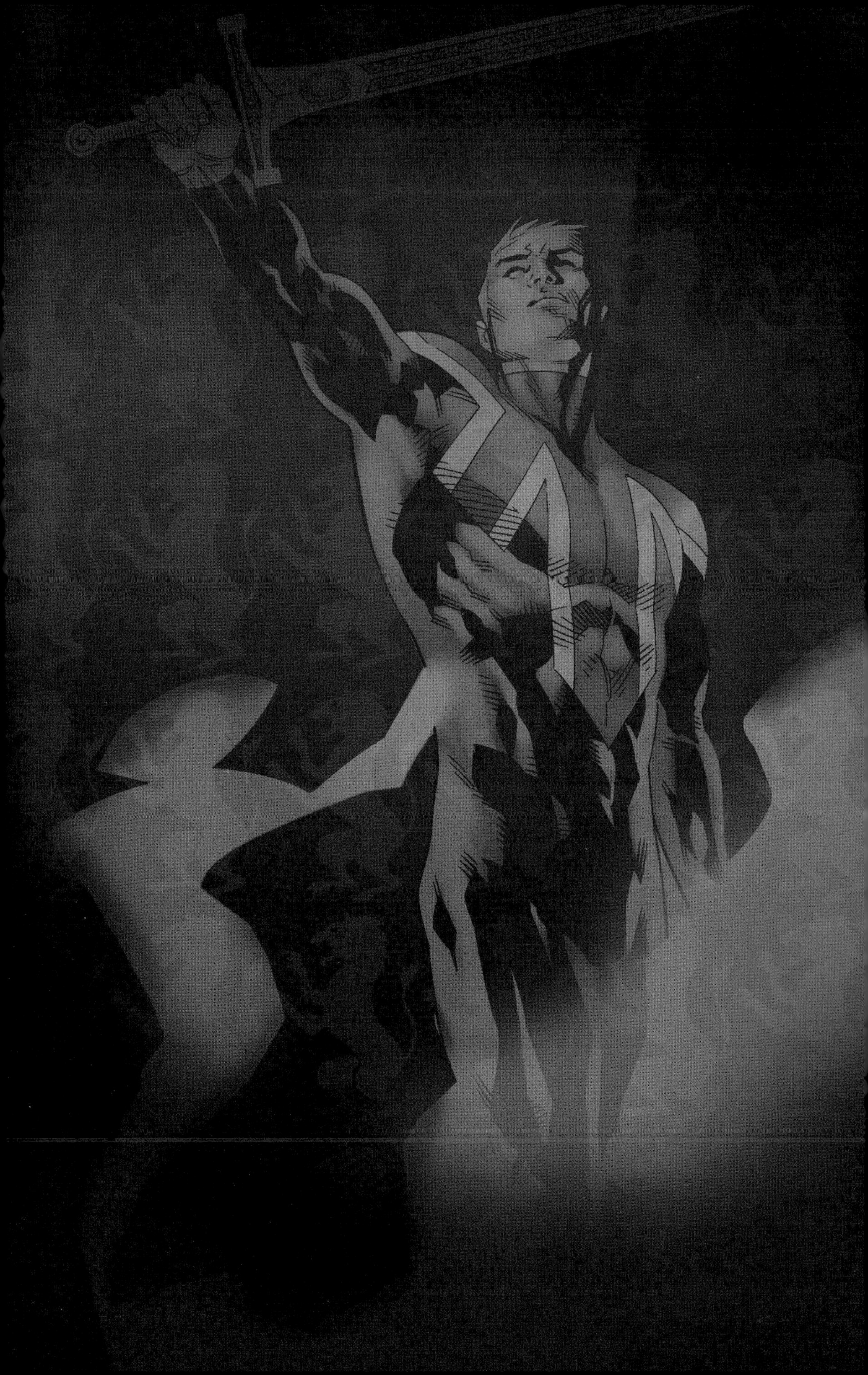

COSTUMES GALLERY
Captain Britain

Depending on the tone of the title, the artist responsible, the style of the period or even just the situation the hero finds themself in, almost every Marvel hero has experienced some level of visual diversity since their inception. Through the work of **Herb Trimpe**, **Alan Davis** and **Leonard Kirk** (and a whole host of others along the way), **Captain Britain**'s costume has always succeeded in displaying a distinctly *British* aesthetic. Read on to discover **Brian Braddock**'s different looks over his three decades in the spotlight...

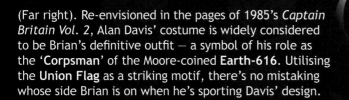

(Right). One of the key influences of penciller **Herb Trimpe**'s original 1976 version of **Captain Britain** was the **Beefeater**, the sworn 'Yeoman Warder', protector of the **Tower of London**. Brandishing a sceptre (an ornate symbol of British heritage) and emblazoned with the *Lion Rampant*, a popular facet of both allegiance and family crests, Brian's costume is a bona fide classic.

(Far right). Re-envisioned in the pages of 1985's *Captain Britain Vol. 2*, Alan Davis' costume is widely considered to be Brian's definitive outfit — a symbol of his role as the '**Corpsman**' of the Moore-coined **Earth-616**. Utilising the **Union Flag** as a striking motif, there's no mistaking whose side Brian is on when he's sporting Davis' design.

(Left). Brian in the traditional regal garb of **The Otherworld**, designed by **Pablo Raimondi**, from *Excalibur Vol. 2 #4.*

(Right). **Chuck Austen** and **Olivier Coipel** introduced the character **Lionheart,** the female equivalent of Captain Britain (right) in the pages of *Avengers Vol. 3 #77*. **Kelsey Leigh**'s costume is a clear homage/amalgamation of aspects of all three generations of Brian's design; the *Lion Rampant* crest of Trimpe's original, the mask of Davis' reboot, and the muted blue of the Otherworld design all feature.

(Left). Braddock's portrayal in the Ultimate universe, appearing on Bryan Hitch's clean, stylish cover of *Ultimates 2 #4*. In Mark Millar and Hitch's gritty re-imagining of the Avengers, the artist seems to pay homage to Davis' redesign. In the grounded world of the Ultimate universe, it's at its most aerodynamic, evocative of Olympian sportswear, right down to the streamlined helmet. Rather than a member of the **Corps**, Millar envisioned Braddock as a member of the **European Defense Initiative** (alongside **Captains Italy**, **France** and **Spain**), whose powers are the product of **Professor James Braddock**'s high-tech exo-suits.

(Below). Even when Davis returned to Cap B in 2005's *Uncanny X-Men #463*, some 20 years after he originally redesigned the character, he still wasn't afraid to tweak it; perhaps a nod to the evolution that had occurred in his hiatus.

(Left). In recent years, Brian's costume has evolved to reflect modern military garb, similar to **Captain America**'s overt, practical update. Pictured left is his Michael Ryan-designed costume from *New Excalibur*.

(Right). In the pages of *Vampire State*, (shown here on **Mico Suayan**'s cover for *Captain Britain and MI13 #13*), his outfit is a lot more utilitarian — reminiscent of the hero **Union Jack**. Brian forgoes his helmet as his powers are redefined to be self-generated, rather than relying on his suit's technology.

THE WRITER

Paul Cornell

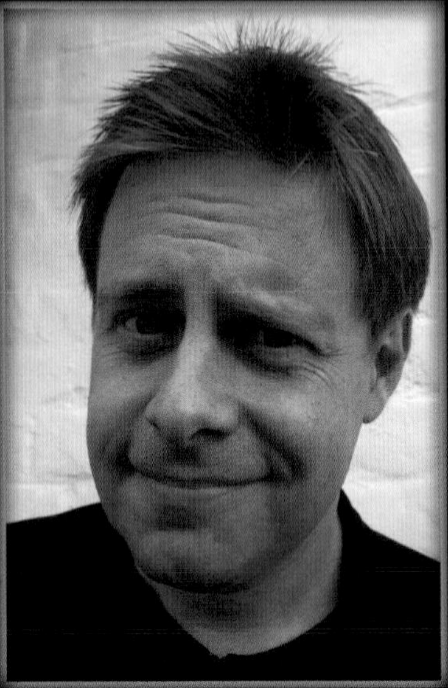

INSPIRED BY AN ICON

Like many prominent British writers, **Paul Cornell** owes a lot to **Doctor Who**. Television's longest-running science fiction hero has inspired generations. It was the good doctor's adventures in the **T.A.R.D.I.S.** that encouraged the young Cornell to first pick up a pen and start contributing to '**Whovian**' fanzines.

His professional career kicked off in 1990, when he won a young writers' competition; his entry was eventually given life, and aired fully formed on **BBC Two**. More television work followed, but Cornell had already moved onto the job of his dreams, writing Doctor Who novels, as well as audio dramas and comic strips – the first of which was published by **Marvel U.K.** in *Doctor Who Magazine #156* [1990].

Born July 18th, 1967, the writer spoke of his early love for the British sci-fi institution, "I really did grow up in Doctor Who fandom. I was a fan from about the age of ten. It was my first large-scale social interaction; it was my escape; it was how I got out of a very small town; it gave me my career and everything." He continued, "Doctor Who runs like a thread through my life – I think culture has caught up with subculture. I distrust ghettos, now. People who think that as fans they are persecuted and special – I think outside the ghetto walls there are lots and lots of people enjoying exactly the same things that people enjoy inside. This wasn't the case when I was a kid."

SUBTLETIES OF THE MEDIUM

After more contributions to *DWM*, in 1993, he also began writing for *Judge Dredd: The Megazine*, alongside a burgeoning television career. The writer eventually saw his professional work on Doctor Who make it to television, as his episodes broadcast between 2005 and 2007. "I think TV and comics have a lot more in common than either do with prose; comics are kind of like frozen TV," he beamed. "I've started to use the past tense in my comic scripts ('he's

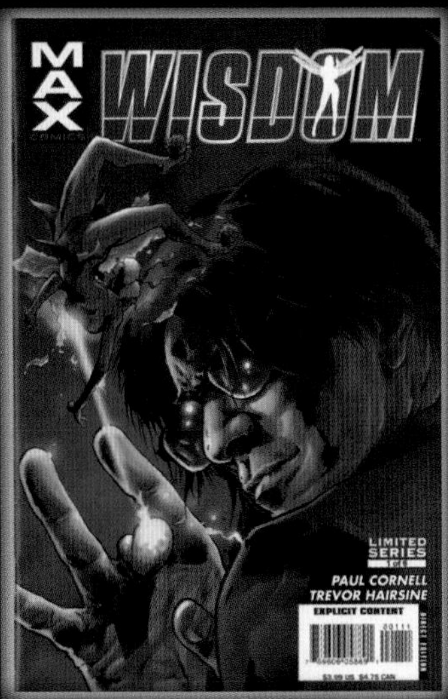
MAX
WISDOM
LIMITED SERIES
PAUL CORNELL
TREVOR HAIRSINE
EXPLICIT CONTENT

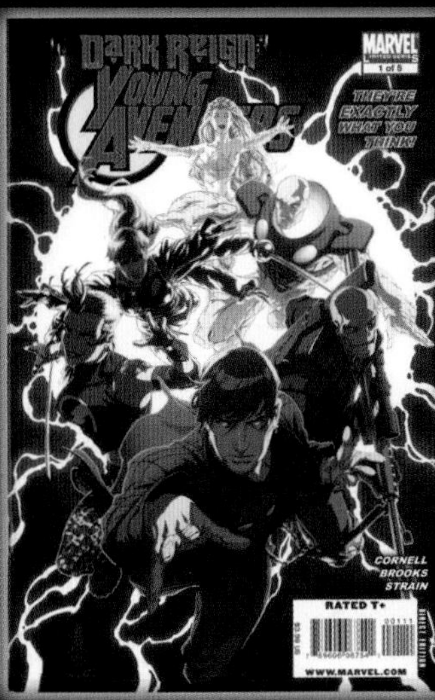
DARK REIGN
YOUNG AVENGERS
MARVEL
THEY'RE EXACTLY WHAT YOU THINK!
CORNELL
BROOKS
STRAIN
RATED T+
WWW.MARVEL.COM

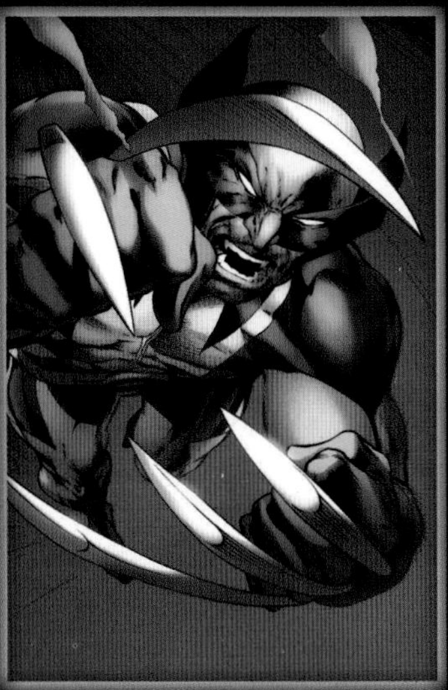

closed the door'), because it's always about completed actions. And TV is all about continuing actions. I find it hard to write any two in the same day, because it can really mess you up if you move from one to the other too quickly. It sounds a little precious, but it's true!"

"What stays the same? There's often a need for the prosaic in comic scripts," he added, talking about the disparity between the two mediums. "When writing stage directions, the artist will appreciate it if you put in emotional content – if you actually wax lyrical. The audience will never see those words, but they will see the artist's reaction to the words.

"When I first started writing comics I made the mistake of following the template of a **2000 AD** script I was shown by [writer and co-creator of Judge Dredd, amongst others] **John Wagner**," he revealed. "And, of course, he knows his artists so well, and has been doing this for such a long time, that his script literally read: 'Dredd points,' 'Dredd with bike.' I was swiftly told they really needed a bit more than that! That's where prose works in comics."

THAT'S AN INTERESTING REQUEST, TEPES. A NON-AGGRESSION TREATY.
WHAT DO I STAND TO GAIN?

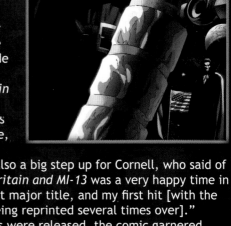

WORDS OF WISDOM

As for his comics output, the British writer stopped working for *DWM* in 2003, and *The Megazine* in 2004. Three years later he resurfaced at **Marvel** where he scripted a six-part *Wisdom* miniseries and a *Dark Reign: Young Avengers* five-parter before being assigned to the imaginative world of *Captain Britain and MI-13* alongside artist **Leonard Kirk**.

The coupling was an inspired choice, and *Captain Britain and MI-13* enjoyed modest success, viewing Britain through the uncanny, mystical prism it typically benefits from in Marvel cannon. Notwithstanding the shared title, the comic was a major profile boost for the eponymous **Brian Braddock**, and also a big step up for Cornell, who said of the series, "*Captain Britain and MI-13* was a very happy time in my comics life, my first major title, and my first hit [with the first three issues all being reprinted several times over]."

Although only 15 issues were released, the comic garnered many accolades, but it was the final story arc of the title's tenure (issues #10-15) that truly put Cornell's name on the map. "*Vampire State* was the last in the series, and perhaps, judging by how well it was received, it should have been our first!"

Discussing what had driven the story, Cornell, who had pushed MI-13 to the forefront of his 2006 **Marvel MAX** series, *Wisdom* said, "I wanted to return **Dracula** to being a major threat in the Marvel Universe, and I wanted to tweak his character a little to give him a modern edge. I wanted to have more Marvel UK heroes appear, such as the obscure **Motormouth** and the rather better-known [erstwhile fan favourite] **Death's Head**."

"Putting **Blade** on the team was an excellent decision by my wonderful editor, **Nick Lowe**, who remembered that the vampire slayer was actually British."

Although former Prime Minister **Gordon Brown** had turned up in the pages of *Captain Britain and MI13* issue #1, Cornell had in fact planned another real world politician to make an

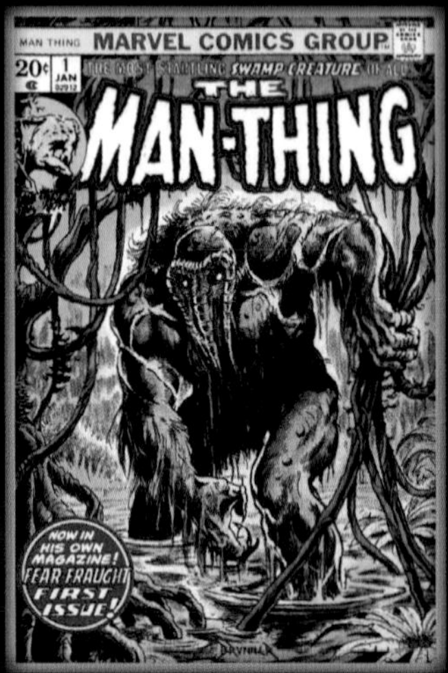
MAN THING
MARVEL COMICS GROUP
20¢
1 JAN
THE MAN-THING
NOW IN HIS OWN MAGAZINE! FEAR-FRAUGHT FIRST ISSUE!

appearance; the idea, unfortunately didn't make it past the discerning eyes of Marvel's legal team: "The scene between **Dr. Doom** and Dracula on the moon was initially written as having **David Cameron** meeting the vampire, pretending to go along with his plans, then calling MI13 when he got home... but Marvel's lawyers ruled *that* out!"

Offering another revelation, the writer said, "I also do a bit of continuity exploration, bringing back the **Sheriff** who'd been corrupted by a phantom pirate ship in **Chris Claremont**'s decades-old run on **Man-Thing** [1980's #4-8 and #10-11], only because, his story having been left hanging, I felt sorry for him and wanted to save him, and I thought the character was interesting."

"It was also important to me," Cornell shared, "to reunite Brian with his wife. We continued our portrayal of him as not being 'an alcoholic' as some writers have made him, nor a buffoon, but a capable man who has a normal relationship with alcohol."

Concluding, Cornell added, "Our big fake-out concerning Dracula's seeming destruction of Britain was only possible because we were the only title set there. If we'd been more mainstream, in the Marvel Universe, people wouldn't have bought into it as much as they did."

IN CONCLUSION

Finally, when asked about whether he felt he had acheived what he'd set out to do, depite the series' abrupt ending, Cornell had this to say, "As to the story itself: I like twists and reversals and proper endings. And I wanted to show, again, how hard Pete Wisdom can be in a good cause. I wanted to kill the nice girl and leave the flirty one alive. I wanted to at least show a few of the characters from Marvel UK that I'd have featured in more depth if we'd stayed around. I wanted Faiza and Dane to have their moment. I also wanted that final chat between Brian and Dr. Hussain, which I think sums up the book.

I still find myself thinking of plots for the next arc. We'd talked about Rachel and The Fury, and maybe tying-in to Secret Warriors, but that was just one hopeful lunch in New York. I miss this title terribly. If I can ever bring it back, I will. Thanks to Marvel's patience, I got to do a proper ending, and I'll always be grateful for that."

CORNELL ON CRICKET

Feeling that it was appropriate to maintain the distictly British sensibilities of *Captain Britain and MI-13*, it seems fitting that Cornell would elect for Brian and his teammates to indulge in a spot of cricket in their downtime. To many living outside the British isles, the sport is considered as curious as Pete Wisdom's supernatural foes, yet, as he shares below, Cornell took inspiration from a fragment of Marvel history close to his heart...

"The Annual gave me space to give Brian himself a bit more of a central role (being the nice guy pivot around which the group turns can leave a character out of the action), and to do another thing on my list. I always used to love those Chris Claremont baseball games the X-Men played, and doing a cricket match seemed obvious. I should mention the enormous efforts Adrian Alphona and Christina Strain put into getting the details of the game right. Adrian re-drew several panels, and Christina actually asked for pictures of a Lord's wicket so she could get the colouring of the pitch correct. I think they did a wonderful job. It was also excellent to welcome my old friend Mike Collins back to US comics on the lead."

COVER GALLERY

Captain Britain and MI13

For the first issue of *Captain Britain and MI13*, Marvel superstar artist Bryan Hitch was commissioned to create this iconic cover featuring Captain Britain and his new team of British heroes.

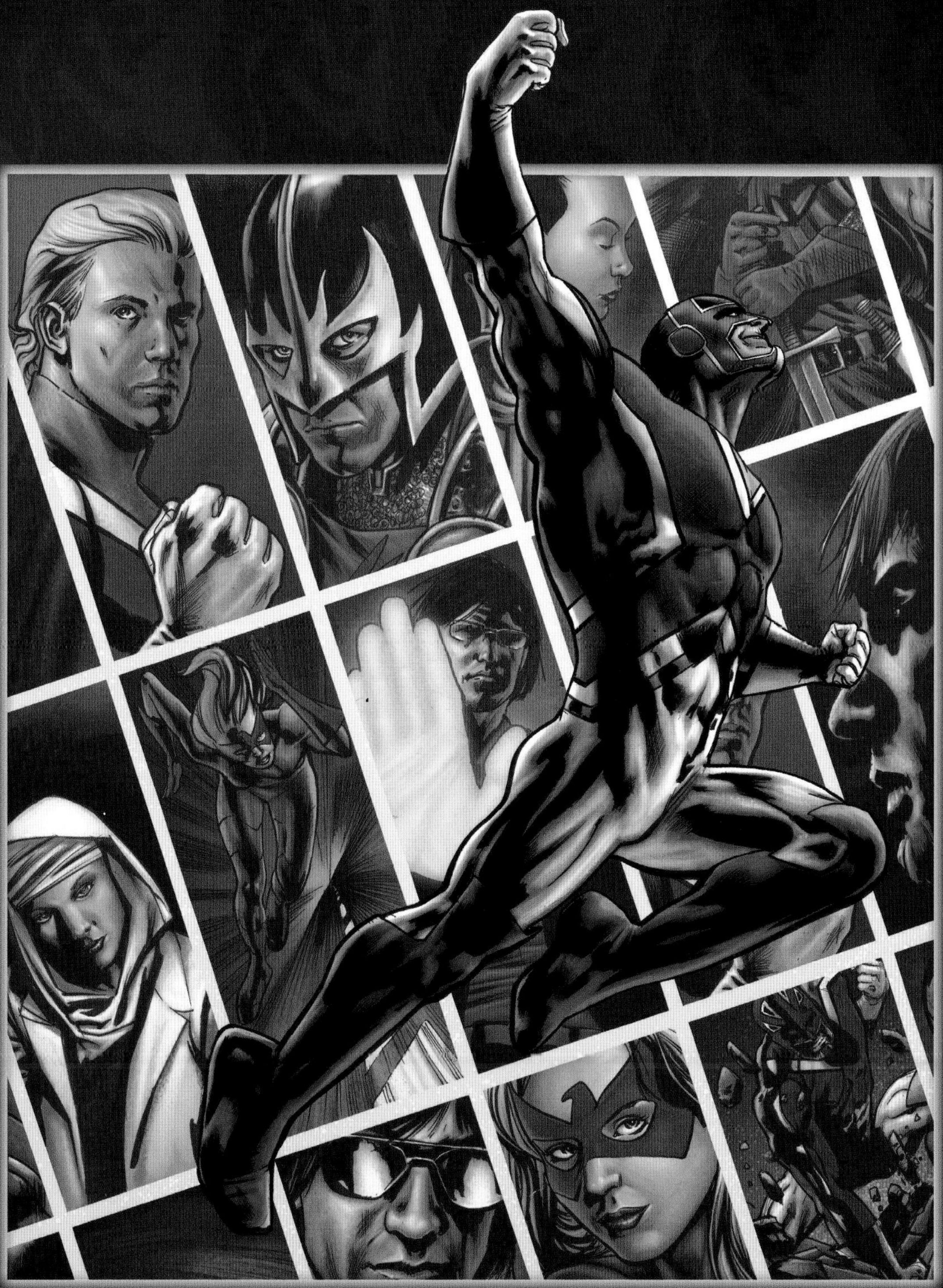

THE ARTIST

Leonard Kirk

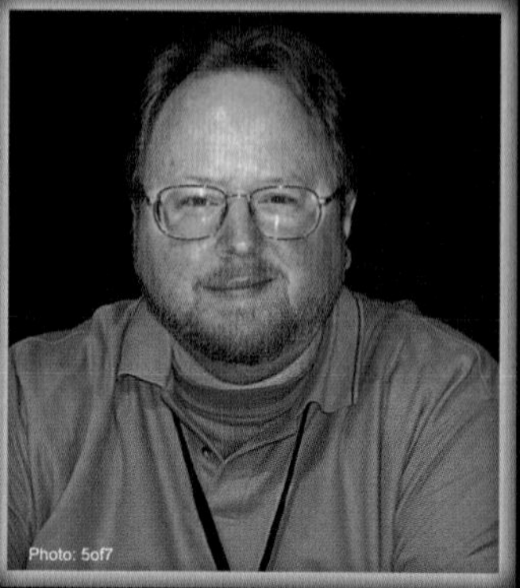

Photo: 5of7

THE COMICS scene in the US in the early '90s was flourishing with a seemingly unending stream of new publishers entering the arena on a regular basis. It was the time of what came to be called the black and white boom, with the vast majority of the newcomers eschewing colour in favour of the cost-saving advantages of monochromatic printing.

Among their number was **Eternity.** It was there **Leonard Kirk** made his debut, although as a writer rather than an artist. Co-writing the 1991 first issue of *Eliminator* was to be his only foray into comicbook scripting for many years, as he chose to focus on his art.

Eternity was allied with **Aircel**, **Adventure** and **Malibu**, which eventually absorbed the others as its imprints. It was among these companies that Kirk first found work as an artist. He drew such four-parters as *Galaxina, Alien Nation: The Skin Trade* and *Planet of the Apes: The Forbidden Zone* for them, as well as *Baseball Superstars Comics Annual* #1 for **Revolutionary** between 1991 and 1993, with a seven-issue run on Malibu's *Dinosaurs for Hire* following in 1993-94.

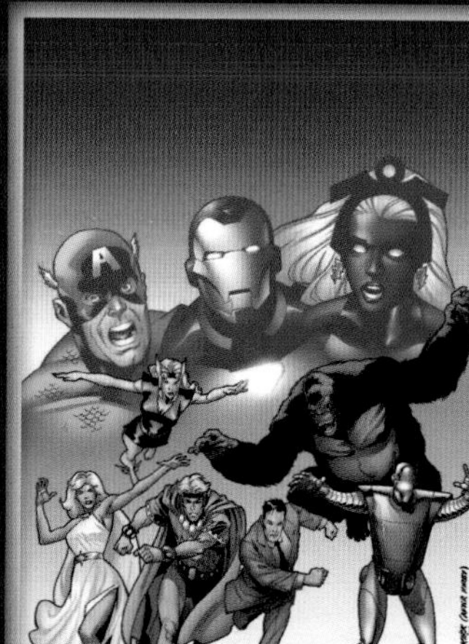

From the first two issues of **Semple**'s *Captain Canuck Reborn* and a single issue (#7) of Malibu's **Ultraverse** title *Prototype,* he segued into his first high profile assignment. An American living in Canada, he illustrated multiple issues of Malibu's *Star Trek: Deep Space Nine* comic and its spin-offs, which took him up to the end of 1995, by which time Malibu, and its Ultraverse imprint had been acquired by **Marvel**.

After a handful of one-offs for various publishers, Kirk was handed his first Marvel assignment, drawing the three issues of 1996's *Ultragirl,* before bounding over to DC to work on the similarly-titled *Supergirl*. This was to be the move that kickstarted Kirk's career. He stayed on the title until 2002, pencilling all but nine issues between #10 and #74. He also dabbled with the occasional side project, such as the two issues of **Silverline**'s *Switchblade* [1997], three issues of *Deadman: Dead Again* for **DC Comics** in 2001, 1999's *Captain Marvel* #26 for Marvel, but further enhanced his profile when he moved over to *JSA* as he was winding up his tenure on Supergirl.

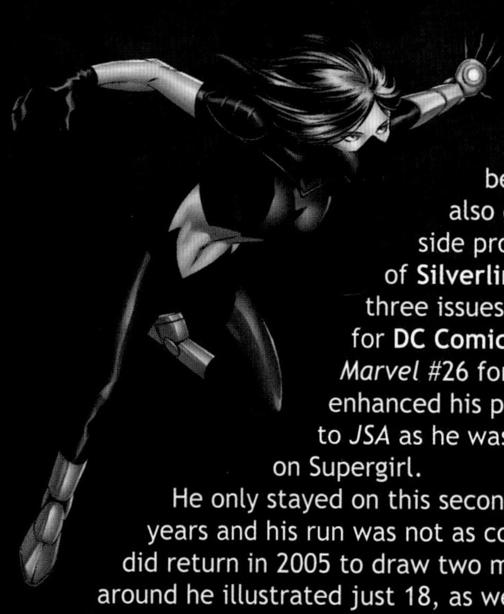

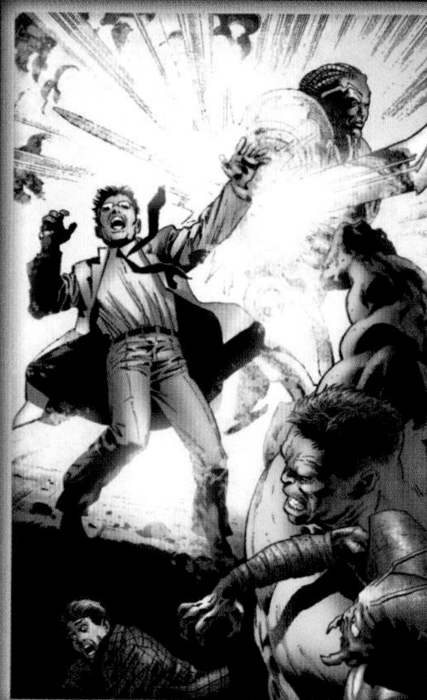

He only stayed on this second DC series for two years and his run was not as consistent. Although he did return in 2005 to draw two more issues, this time around he illustrated just 18, as well as single issues of *Solus* (**Crossgeneration Comics**) and *Witchblade* (**Image/Top Cow**). With his *JSA* work coming to an end, he pencilled three 2004

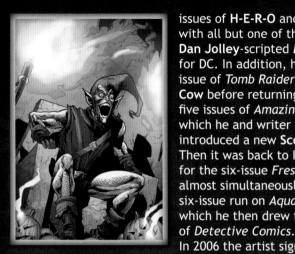

issues of **H-E-R-O** and followed those with all but one of the 10 of 2004's **Dan Jolley**-scripted *Bloodhound* for DC. In addition, he fitted in an issue of *Tomb Raider* for **Image/Top Cow** before returning to Marvel for five issues of *Amazing Fantasy*, for which he and writer **Fred Van Lente** introduced a new **Scorpion**.

Then it was back to Image/Top Cow for the six-issue *Freshmen* while almost simultaneously pencilling a six-issue run on *Aquaman* for DC, for which he then drew four 2006 issues of *Detective Comics*.

In 2006 the artist signed exclusively to Marvel. His first assignment under his new contract was an *Agents of Atlas* six-parter after which he illustrated odd issues of such titles as *Marvel Adventures: The Avengers*, *Heroes for Hire* and *Incredible Hulk*, before moving on to 2008's *World War Hulk: Aftersmash!* five-parter.

Next he teamed up with writer **Paul Cornell** to launch *Captain Britain and MI-13*. It was a collaboration that was to last until late 2009 with Kirk drawing all but one of the 15 issues before migrating to three issues of the Cornell-penned *Dark X-Men: The Beginning*.

Late in 2010, Kirk began a seven-issue run on *New Mutants* having contributed single issues to *Savage She-Hulk*, *Nation X*, *Avengers vs. Atlas*, *Age of Heroes*, *Marvel Zombies* and *Uncanny X-Men* along the way. After that he drew Marvel's four-issue resurrection of **CrossGen**'s *Sigil* before moving on to the renowned X-title, *X-Factor* in 2011. Titles he worked on concurrently with X-Factor included *Gambit*, *Marvel Adventures Super Heroes* and *Ultimate Comics: Ultimates*.

He has also embarked on his first non-Marvel project since 2006. With the writer having regained the rights to *Bloodhound* from DC, Jolley and Kirk have recently resurrected the character in a series of new stories in **Dark Horse**'s flagship anthology *Dark Horse Presents*.

Leonard Kirk has forged an unlikely path throughout his career, seeking out an incredibly varied array of comicbook titles that have benefited from his clean, punchy images — qualities most noticeable in the book you now hold in your hands, *Vampire State*. Praised for his talents by fans and collaborators alike, Kirk continues to dazzle an impressive four decades into his career.

FURTHER READING

If you've enjoyed the style and art in this graphic novel, you may be interested in exploring some of these books too.

Marvels
Volume 13 of the Ultimate Marvel Graphic Novels Collection

At the book shop:
ISBN: 9780785142867

MARVEL
ALL-NEW X-MEN
Here Comes Yesterday
BRIAN MICHAEL BENDIS • STUART IMMONEN

All-New X-Men Vol. 1: Here Comes Yesterday

At the book shop:
ISBN: 9781846535321

Captain Britain: A Crooked World
Volume 3 of the Ultimate Marvel Graphic Novels Collection
At the book shop:
ISBN: 9781905239108

Captain Britain and MI-13 Vol. 2: Hell Comes to Birmingham

At the book shop:
ISBN: 9781846534232

THE ULTIMATES
Mark Millar • Bryan Hitch • Andrew Currie

The Ultimates Vol. 1: Super-Human
Volume 28 of the Ultimate Marvel Graphic Novels Collection
At the book shop:
ISBN: 9780785109600

ALAN GRANT • ALAN DAVIS • WARREN ELLIS
PAUL JENKINS • PETER MILLIGAN • NEIL GAIMAN
MARK MILLAR • GARTH ENNIS
MARVEL GRAPHIC NOVEL
MARVEL MASTERS
THE BRITISH INVASION
VOLUME 1

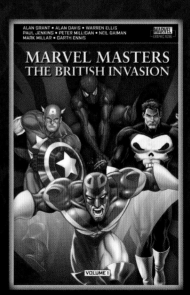

Marvel Masters: The British Invasion Vol. 1

At the book shop:
ISBN: 9781905239634

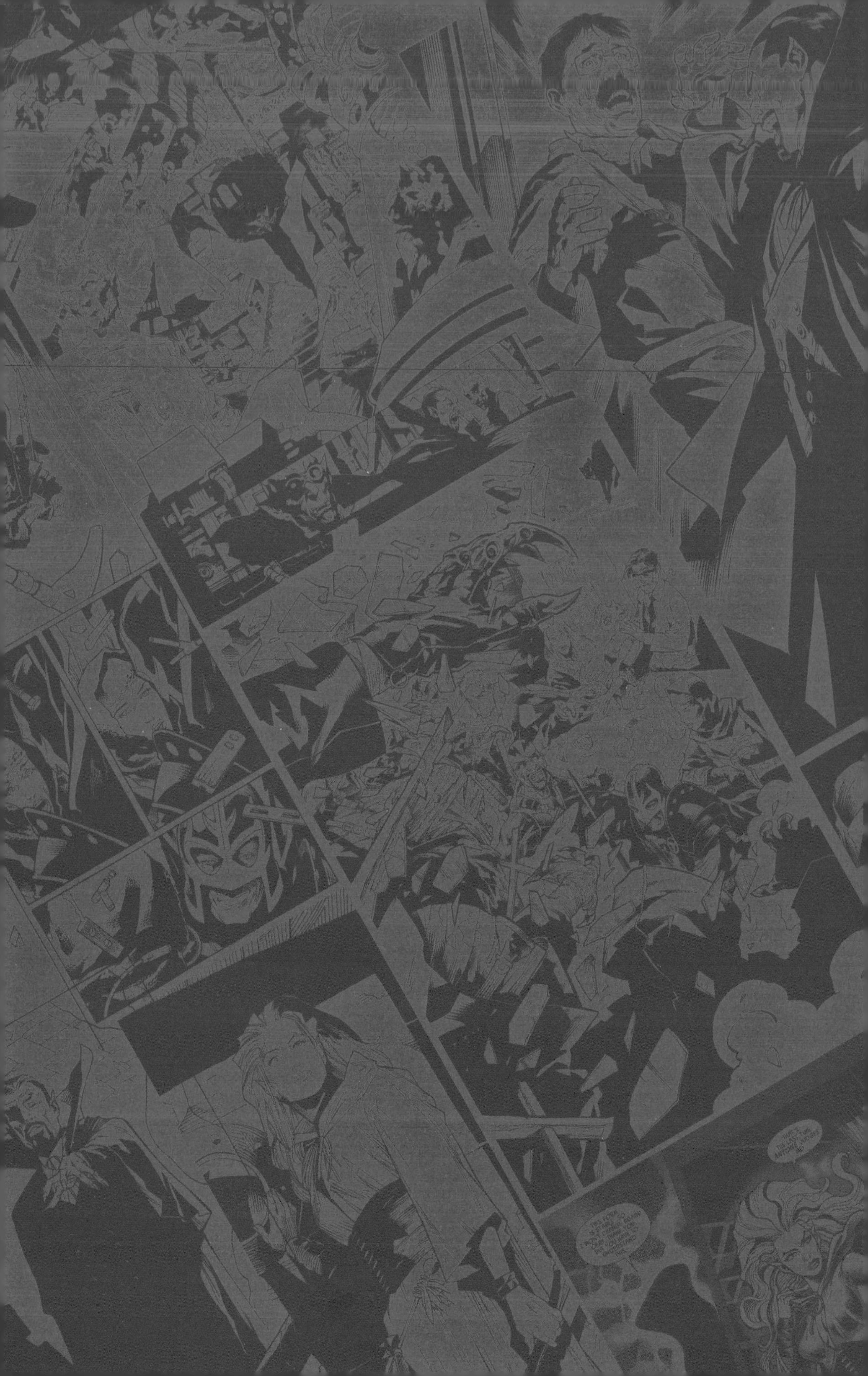

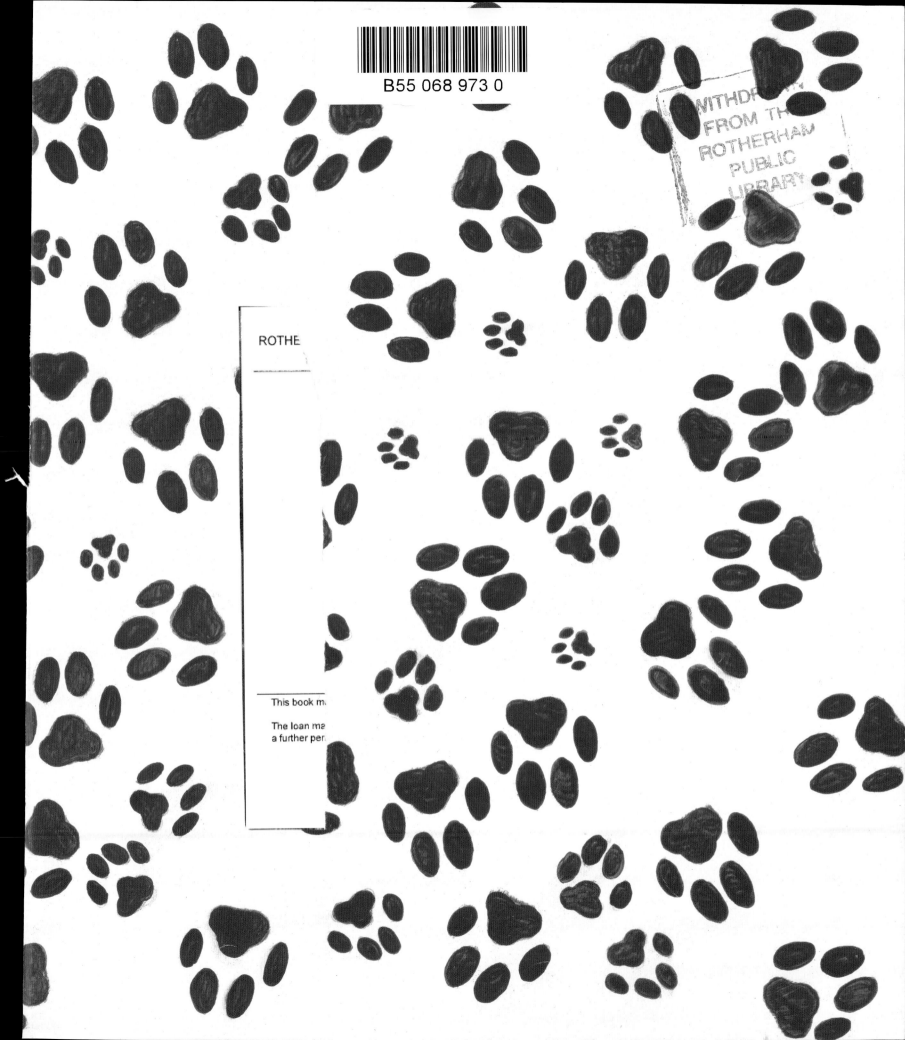

For Hogan and Tamara

A book to share from

Scallywag Press

First published in Great Britain in 2021
by Scallywag Press Ltd, 10 Sutherland Row, London SW1V 4JT

Text and illustration copyright © Ruth Brown, 2021
The rights of Ruth Brown to be identified as the author and illustrator
of this work have been asserted by her in accordance with the
Copyright, Designs and Patents Act, 1988

Printed on FSC paper in China by Toppan Leefung

001

British Library Cataloguing in Publication Data available
ISBN 978–1–912650–53–8